France and 1848

1848 was a year of revolution throughout Europe. In France, the monarchy of King Louis-Philippe was overthrown, the Second Republic was proclaimed, and manhood suffrage was introduced. In the subsequent national and local elections, contrary to previous expectations, conservative candidates generally triumphed. In this comprehensive and authoritative study, which provides an analysis of original sources, William Fortescue considers recent research and offers new interpretations of events.

Examining the economic, social and political crises, *France and 1848* evaluates the political history of France during the revolution of 1848 and the French political culture of the time. This title will be of interest to all students of nineteenth-century European history, political scientists and all those with an interest in the historical development of French political culture.

William Fortescue was formerly Senior Lecturer in History at the University of Kent at Canterbury. He is the author of *The Third Republic in France, 1870–1940: conflicts and continuities* (2000).

France and 1848

The end of monarchy

William Fortescue

Routledge
Taylor & Francis Group

LONDON AND NEW YORK

First published 2005
by Routledge
2 Park Square, Milton Park, Abingdon, Oxon OX14 4RN

Simultaneously published in the USA and Canada
by Taylor & Francis
270 Madison Ave, New York, NY 10016

Routledge is an imprint of the Taylor & Francis Group

© 2005 William Fortescue

Typeset in Goudy by The Running Head Limited, Cambridge
Printed and bound in Great Britain by Antony Rowe Ltd, Chippenham, Wiltshire

British Library Cataloguing in Publication Data
A catalogue record for this book is available from the British Library

Library of Congress Cataloging in Publication Data
Fortescue, William, 1945–
France and 1848: the end of monarchy/William Fortescue
1. France–History–February Revolution, 1848. 2. France–History–
Second Republic, 1848–1852 3. France–Politics and government–
19th century. 4. Conservatism–France–History–19th century.
5. Political culture–France–History–19th century. I. Title.
DC270.F67 2005
944.06'3—dc22   2004021437

ISBN 0–415–31461–5 (hbk)
ISBN 0–415–31462–3 (pbk)

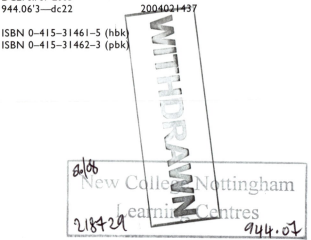

Contents

Acknowledgements

This book could not have been written without the help of the archivists and librarians of the Archives Nationales, the Bibliothèque Nationale de France, the former annexe of the Bibliothèque Nationale at Versailles, the British Library and the British Newspaper Library at Colindale. The Templeman Library at the University of Kent, particularly its Inter-Library Loan Department, also provided invaluable assistance.

I am grateful to the British Academy for a grant that financed two research trips to Paris. I am also grateful to Professor William Doyle and Professor Roger Price for their support of my grant application. In Paris I was privileged to enjoy the hospitality of Mme Marie-Renée Morin. Trish Hatton rescued my footnotes and helped enormously with the final presentation of the typescript. My wife Clare tried once again to improve my literary style.

Introduction

Throughout the nineteenth century, some form of monarchy was the constitutional norm for European states of any significance. Switzerland was an obvious exception to this generalisation, but Switzerland clearly constituted a special case. The other important exception was France, ruled by republican regimes from 1792 to 1804, from 1848 to 1852 and from 1870. France's experience of revolution and republicanism gave it a unique political culture that helps to explain the character of the French Revolution of 1848. The year 1848 witnessed an explosion of revolutionary and nationalist movements in many European states, with similar causes and with largely similar outcomes. Harvest failures, economic recession, high urban unemployment and a collapse of financial confidence were European-wide phenomena in the years 1846 to 1849. Similarly, the capitulation of illiberal regimes to popular urban revolts, the introduction of liberal and democratic reforms, and the eventual triumph of reaction and re-assertion of traditional authorities through military force characterised the fundamental pattern of events in the European states affected by the revolutionary and nationalist upheavals of 1848–9. Again the exception was France and again the explanation, it is argued, lay in France's revolutionary and republican tradition and in her unique political culture. This book therefore attempts to situate the 1848 revolution in France in the context of France's revolutionary and republican tradition and to relate the events of 1848 in France to France's political culture. The themes of monarchy, revolution and republicanism in France before 1848 are explored, while, for the events of 1848, extensive use is made of published writings by contemporaries and of the contemporary newspaper press, both Parisian and provincial. It is argued that the institution of monarchy became fatally undermined in France, arguably to a much greater degree than in any other nineteenth-century European state. At the same time, as a result of the experience of the 1790s, revolution and republicanism came to be associated with popular violence, anti-clericalism, foreign wars, high inflation and taxation, centralised dictatorship and State terror. Another important consequence of the revolution of 1789 was, through the extensive sales of confiscated property, the consolidation of a large land-owning peasant class, which, at least in 1848, tended to be politically conservative. In addition, the Napoleonic period bequeathed France with a legacy of glorious military victories,

French domination of most of Continental Europe, and sustained conflict with Britain and with the conservative European powers. The French could also cherish the memory of efficient, centralised and meritocratic administration and the legend of a charismatic leader and of his extraordinary achievements. Whereas revolution and republicanism continued to have unpleasant associations for many French people, the less attractive features and consequences of Napoleonic rule became largely forgotten so that Bonapartism could exercise a widespread emotional and irrational attraction. All this encouraged political instability in France and militated against the achievement of a national political consensus. In February 1848 the permanent overthrow of the July monarchy arguably owed as much to France's unique political culture as to any other factor. Once the Second Republic had been proclaimed, France's revolutionary and republican tradition provided inspiration for some but provoked fear among others. The reality and threat of popular violence, evidence of dictatorial government tendencies, and continuing economic difficulties and uncertainties exacerbated those fears. In this situation, a new political conservatism and a new political consensus emerged. Divorced from monarchy, this new conservatism found political expression in what contemporaries often referred to as the Party of Order. By claiming to defend 'order', peace, property, religion and the family, the Party of Order could pose as the upholder of a national and moral consensus which could embrace all but left-wing republicans and socialists. The popular appeal of this new conservatism was not surprising, given the extreme rhetoric of some elements of the French Left, the apparent radicalism of some government policies, the explosions of popular violence, particularly in Paris, and the massive increase in the property tax. When, in the autumn of 1848, the Party of Order largely aligned itself with Bonapartism and with the presidential candidature of Louis Napoleon Bonaparte, the outcome was one of the most decisive electoral victories in French history.

Chapter 1

The French revolutionary tradition from 1789 to the July monarchy

The revolutionary legacy

Classic interpretations of the overthrow of Louis-Philippe all view the 1848 revolution in France as a phase in a long-term revolutionary process which began in 1789. Daniel Stern[1] claimed that February 1848 was not the result of an accident or a surprise, but rather the natural consequence of the legacy of the eighteenth century which had given the educated classes freedom of political thought and the working classes freedom of political action. This set in motion forces for democracy, rationalism and social inclusion which undermined monarchical, Catholic and aristocratic society. Alfred Delvau[2] maintained that the great work of the revolution, which the overthrow of Robespierre had effectively interrupted in July 1794, had been briefly renewed in July 1830, only to be interrupted again by the bourgeoisie's betrayal of the brave and heroic people of Paris through the establishment of the July monarchy. However, the revolutionary tradition was revived in February 1848 with the abdication of Louis-Philippe and the proclamation of the Second Republic. For Alexis de Tocqueville,[3] the period from 1789 to 1830 had witnessed a struggle to the death between the *Ancien Régime* and the New France of the bourgeoisie, a struggle which the bourgeoisie had won through the revolution of 1830. However, the bourgeoisie and bourgeois values had thereafter so dominated the July monarchy of Louis-Philippe as to provoke a reaction in the form of a new struggle, this time between those who owned property and those who did not. Karl Marx[4] similarly interpreted the revolution of 1789 as a class struggle between the feudal aristocracy and its allies on the one hand and the capitalist bourgeoisie on the other. The revolution of 1830 for Marx, though, witnessed the triumph of just one section of the bourgeoisie, the financial aristocracy of bankers, capitalists, railway barons and wealthy landowners. After 1830 this class pursued its self-enrichment with such greed, ruthlessness and success that the economic crisis which began in 1845 eventually provoked the explosion of February 1848 in which all of France's other social classes united to overthrow the rule of the financial aristocracy. Once the revolution had begun, the traditions of past revolutions weighed 'like a nightmare on the minds of the living'. The revolutionaries of 1848, however, ended up just parodying the revolutionaries of 1789–99, 'For it was only the ghost of the old revolution which walked in the years from 1848 to 1851'.[5] Thus the great events and characters of the revolutionary decade 1789–99 were re-enacted during the Second Republic not as tragedy, but as farce. While intending ridicule, Marx was also indicating the crucial role of historical memory and of political culture.

Recent studies have tended to confirm these classic interpretations. François Furet, Robert Gildea, Pierre Rosanvallon and Robert Tombs[6] also emphasise the importance of placing the 1848 revolution in France in the context of France's revolutionary tradition. Furet quotes at the beginning of his book the following observation by Ernest Renan, which appeared in the *Revue des Deux Mondes* in 1869:

> The French Revolution is such an extraordinary event that it must serve as the starting-point for any systematic consideration of the affairs of our own times. Everything of importance which takes place in France is a direct consequence of this fundamental event, which has profoundly altered the conditions of life in our country.[7]

Furet interprets French history between 1789 and the end of the 1870s as a successively renewed confrontation between the *Ancien Régime* and the revolution, a confrontation which did not end until 1876–7, when republicans and republican values finally gained an ascendancy in the Third Republic. Gildea has similarly studied the importance of a long-standing political culture, defined by him as 'the culture elaborated by communities competing for political power', with particular emphasis on 'the relationship between political culture and collective memory'.[8] He argues that the importance of France's revolutionary and counterrevolutionary cultures, and the enduring appeal and legacy of Bonapartism, contrasted with the fragility of France's liberal political culture. This helps to explain the failures of the July monarchy and the fate of the February 1848 revolution. Moreover, within French revolutionary political culture, liberal republicanism conflicted with Jacobin republicanism, as was violently demonstrated during the June Days of 1848. Further left still was the anarchist revolutionary tradition represented by the followers of Auguste Blanqui. Rosanvallon stresses two aspects of the French revolutionary legacy, the concept of popular sovereignty and the fundamental illiberalism of French political culture. The former was antimonarchical and militated against the role of the monarch as a neutral arbiter, while the latter discouraged problem resolution through compromise and concession.[9] Further, the institution of monarchy became saddled with an accumulation of negative associations – fiscal exemptions, social privileges, legal inequalities, electoral property franchises and an inequitable distribution of wealth.[10]

'The Revolution and the State are what modern French history is about', Tombs declares.[11] The two were linked because the revolution had given the French State greater powers than in other western societies and because 'the Revolution had left a nagging problem of legitimacy: who should rule and by what right?'[12] The revolution had also generated hatreds, engrained fears, manufactured myths, aligned Catholicism with conservatism and anti-clericalism with republicanism, consolidated a system of small-scale peasant agriculture and bequeathed France a tradition of aggressive nationalism and war. So many people had suffered so much during the revolutionary decade that revenge featured on many political agendas, as did fear. 'What the Holocaust and the Gulag are for us,' Tombs observes, 'the violence of the French revolution was for the nineteenth century.'[13] For historical explanation and political justification, French people often turned to myths which were illustrated and elaborated in every conceivable medium throughout the nineteenth century. Thus conservatives might blame the outbreak and continuation of the revolution on a conspiracy of Freemasons, Protestants and Jews, and dwell on images such as those of the *tricoteuses* knitting at the foot of the guillotine, while the left had their own conspiracy theories, such as that of the Congregation and the Jesuits secretly plotting reaction, and their own images of heroic popular revolt, such as the storming of the Bastille. The astonishing durability of Jesuit conspiracies in the left-wing French mentality illustrates the enduring division between the Roman Catholic Church and its opponents created by the revolution's assault on the Church and many of its priesthood. On the other hand, the consolidation through the revolutionary land settlement of a system of small-scale peasant agriculture tended to promote conservatism, at least in social and economic matters. Also, memories of military victories, foreign conquests and martial glory derived from both the revolutionary and Napoleonic eras could appeal to both left and right, thus providing some sort of national consensus. Nevertheless France, despite being one of the wealthiest countries in the world, had developed 'a uniquely revolution-prone political culture'.[14] Politically, the French people were divided on fundamental issues, while regimes and governments could not tolerate political opposition and constantly sought to exclude their political opponents permanently from power.[15]

It is clear that the revolutionary decade from 1789 to 1799 fundamentally and permanently changed the political and social landscapes of France. The key institutions of the monarchy and Catholic Church were subjected to an unprecedented assault. The *Ancien Régime* system of privilege was abolished forever. The nobility suffered a traumatic eclipse with the abolition of its titles and privileges, the confiscation of much of its wealth, and the ordeals of emigration, imprisonment and execution suffered by many of its members. The royal army of Louis XVI was transformed into an agent of social mobility and an instrument of mass patriotic mobilisation. New traditions were established, of legal equality, uniform administration, professional service to the State, and parliamentary government, as well as of popular militancy and political republicanism. Despite the formal replacement of the Republic in 1804 by the Napoleonic Empire, the increasing conservatism of Napoleonic rule, and the restorations of the Bourbon monarchy in 1814 and 1815, the impact of the revolution lived on. The revolutionary changes were too profound to be obliterated and the collective memories of the revolutionary decade were retained and transmitted from one generation to another, so that the whole political culture of France became steeped in the experience of the revolutionary decade of the 1790s.

The restored Bourbon monarchy

The overthrow of the monarchy in February 1848 occurred within the context of an anti-monarchical French political culture. Even before 1789, the institution of the monarchy had been undermined by a barrage of scurrilous publications directed particularly at Queen Marie Antoinette. The policies of the Crown were continuously frustrated by court intrigue and the obstructive opposition of powerful institutions and interest groups within the French elite. Louis XVI's inability to cope with the challenges of the revolution, his forced removal from Versailles to Paris by a revolutionary crowd in October 1789, his ignominious flight to Varennes in June 1791, his treasonous correspondence with the Habsburg Court after the outbreak of war in April 1792, his desperate escape from the Tuileries Palace on 10 August 1792, and finally his trial and execution (21 January 1793), brought the French monarchy to its nadir. While Napoleon eventually established in France a new kind of monarchy from 1804, it was a monarchy that was anti-Bourbon, 'meritocratic' and associated with exceptional military achievements. Moreover, Napoleon's monarchy was finally overthrown and the Senate's declaration of 3 April 1814, declaring Napoleon to have lost his throne and releasing the French people from their oath of allegiance to Napoleon, clearly stated the principle that in a constitutional monarchy the monarch existed only by virtue of the constitution and of the social contract, and that a monarch who failed to observe the constitution and the social contract forfeited his right to rule. Louis XVI's brothers (unlike his sons) survived the revolution and Napoleon, but their prolonged residence in exile on enemy territory and their identification with émigré armies and counter-revolution associated the Bourbons with France's enemies.

The association of France's monarchs with France's enemies was reinforced by the restorations of 1814 and 1815. On both occasions the Bourbons were restored following French military defeats and with the support of France's national enemies. The constitution of the Restoration monarchy, with its Chamber of Peers and Chamber of Deputies allegedly replicating the British House of Lords and House of Commons, was judged by many to be a foreign 'English' implant, in contrast to the 'French' constitutions of the revolutionary and Napoleonic periods. Further, despite the liberal promises made by Louis XVIII in the Proclamation of St Ouen (2 May 1814), the attempt to create a fusion between the elites of the Ancien Régime and the Napoleonic regime, and the establishment of a parliamentary constitution, Louis XVIII was rapidly identified by many of his subjects with royal absolutism, aristocratic privilege, seigneurial rights, clerical reaction and with at least a potential threat to all those who had acquired land confiscated during the revolution. The return of Napoleon to France in March

1815, and the whole Hundred-Day episode, made the situation very much worse. While almost the entire French army rallied to Napoleon, active resistance was confined to outbreaks of lawlessness in the Vendée region. Louis XVIII himself was forced to make a rapid and humiliating flight from Paris to Belgium, to witness many of his appointees accept office under Napoleon and to await salvation in the form of an Allied military victory over Napoleon. Yet Waterloo, although it permitted Louis XVIII's second Restoration, was a millstone for the Bourbon monarchy which became inescapably associated with one of the most decisive military defeats in the history of France.

Equally crippling for the Bourbon monarchy was the aftermath of the Hundred Days. News of the French defeat at Waterloo provoked explosions of popular violence, fuelled by frustrated nationalism and fears of political reaction, which in turn helped to encourage a 'white terror' in which the victims of popular violence were those identified as the enemies of Catholic royalism (Bonapartists, Jacobins and Protestants). The 'white terror' had its official counterpart. A handful of army commanders (notably Marshal Ney), who had betrayed Louis XVIII during the Hundred Days, was executed. Other traitors to the Bourbon cause, as well as those considered responsible for the execution of Louis XVI and all members of the Bonaparte family, were exiled. There was a massive purge of office-holders, in which some 50,000 to 80,000 people, together with approximately 15,000 army officers, representing between a quarter and a third of all those in official posts, lost their jobs. Finally, the new peace treaty further reduced France's frontiers, subjected sixty-one French departments to military occupation by over a million Allied troops, imposed an indemnity of 700 million francs, and forced France to return many of the works of art looted during the revolutionary and Napoleonic wars to their former owners.

Despite the unfavourable circumstances of the Bourbon restorations of 1814 and 1815, the Bourbon monarchy still enjoyed a number of advantages. Centuries of rule by Bourbon kings meant that the restored Bourbon kings could count on at least some popular acceptance and personal loyalty based on tradition and custom. Whereas the pre-1789 monarchy had been weakened by noble and aristocratic revolts, and by an occasionally unco-operative Roman Catholic Church, the shared experience of suffering and displacement under the revolution and Napoleon helped to renew traditional alliances between the old monarchy and the old nobility and aristocracy, and between throne and altar. Ironically, the creation after 1789 of legal and institutional structures which were uniform and efficient ensured that the kingdom was far easier to administer than it had been before 1789. Similarly, the Restoration monarchy inherited a system of taxation and tax collection which freed it from the financial problems which has so plagued its *Ancien Régime* predecessor. Moreover, by establishing an imperial system with monarchical institutions and symbols, Napoleon had made monarchy and hierarchy familiar once more in France, and Napoleon had greatly extended the scope and scale of official patronage. Abroad, the Allied sovereigns were generally supportive and there were no serious diplomatic difficulties.

Within France, after the upheavals and traumas of the revolutionary and Napoleonic periods, the majority of the population wanted peace and stability. Republicanism for many in France was associated with the Terror and the guillotine, and had been effectively suppressed by Napoleon. A revival of republicanism did occur during the Hundred Days, to the extent that manifestations of revolutionary Bonapartism involved anti-Bourbon, anti-Allied, anti-aristocratic and anti-clerical sentiments. However, Waterloo, the 'white terror' and the political reaction of 1815–16 prevented any significant republican movement from developing. Bonapartism suffered a similar fate, and was further handicapped by Napoleon's exile in St Helena and early death (5 May 1821). Some form of monarchy was the constitutional norm for nearly all European states during the first half of the nineteenth century, and among the French elite there was a considerable degree of consensus over acceptance of the principles of 1789 – a constitutional monarchy with a parliamentary system representing the propertied classes, civil equality, religious toleration, the inviolability of private property, and limited freedom of the press.

Louis XVIII, and to a lesser extent his successor Charles X, enjoyed some measure of success in building on these advantages. The charters of 1814 and 1815 established a reasonably satisfactory constitutional system for France. An attempt was made to reconcile the often conflicting legacies of the Ancien Régime, the revolution and Napoleon and to achieve some sort of fusion between France's pre-1789 and post-1789 elites. The regime survived the economic recession caused by the poor cereal harvests of 1816 and 1817. The indemnities imposed by the Allies were paid off by 1818, enabling the withdrawal of all foreign troops from France two years ahead of schedule. Saint-Cyr's army reforms of 1818 helped to create a more professional army. On the whole, Louis XVIII chose wisely when making ministerial and official appointments, and even Charles X could select the sensible Martignac to head a ministry in January 1828. Above all, the Restoration monarchy could claim successes in the field of foreign affairs – the intervention in Spain from 1823, participation in the battle of Navarino (20 October 1827) and in the Greek war of independence against the Turks, and the beginning of the conquest of Algeria (June 1830).

The Restoration monarchy, nevertheless, suffered from many important weaknesses. As with any royal dynasty, the competence and behaviour of its members were crucial. Louis XVIII was quite intelligent, had considerable charm, and was willing to salute crowds and common people. At the same time, though, he was indolent, physically overweight, forty-nine years old in 1814, and had lived in exile for twenty-three years. He has been described as 'a twilight monarch', lacking the energy and the imagination for a dynamic policy of national reconciliation.[16] He was also guilty of avoidable acts of political provocation. The tricolour could have been retained as France's national flag, with the Bourbon flag becoming the monarch's personal standard. The insistence on being styled Louis XVIII (thereby assuming that Louis XVI's son had actually reigned between 1793 and 1795), the re-adoption of the pre-1789 royal title 'King of France and

Navarre' (implying dynastic rule over inherited territories) instead of 'King of the French' (the title bestowed on Louis XVI by the 1791 constitution, implying ruler of the French people), the assertion that 1814 was the nineteenth year of his reign, the refusal to wear the Legion of Honour, the restoration of the etiquette of the Versailles court, the excessive deference paid to the British and, particularly, to the Duke of Wellington, the holding of religious services to commemorate royal victims of the revolution and even would-be assassins of Napoleon, were all unnecessary and provocative acts. Yet they were principally symbolic in nature and, though damaging, were far from being fatal to the monarchy.

Charles X, sixty-seven when he succeeded to the throne in September 1824, even more obviously than his brother was too old to be an effective monarch. He had been one of the most prominent figures in the counter-revolution and he had become a devout Catholic, so that Catholic and ultra-royalist extremism dominated his political outlook. Moreover, he invariably interpreted political opposition as disloyalty to the Crown, instead of accepting the principle that the king should reign but not govern. Like his brother Louis XVIII, Charles X was attracted to unnecessary and provocative symbolic acts, such as his *Ancien-Régime* style coronation at Reims (29 May 1825) and his personal participation in the elaborate public celebrations of a Papal jubilee in Paris (3 May 1826).

To compound the situation, the Bourbon monarchy suffered from an overall lack of adequate support. Between 1814 and 1830 the Roman Catholic Church probably provided the staunchest support for the Bourbon monarchy. However, the Church had lost most of its wealth and much of its influence, and, because of the strength of anti-clericalism, this resurrection of the traditional alliance between throne and altar may have done more to weaken rather than to strengthen both institutions. In contrast, the army had dramatically and comprehensively demonstrated its disloyalty to the Bourbons and its Bonapartist sympathies by rallying to Napoleon during the Hundred Days. Thereafter the military reforms of 1818 helped to produce a more professional army which remained relatively immune to subversion, plots and conspiracies, and which performed competently in Spain, Greece and Algeria. However, the army had been generally dismayed by the abandonment of the blue, white and red tricolour for the royal Bourbon standard (gold fleurs-de-lis on a white background) and by the re-establishment of an aristocratic royal bodyguard and of five Swiss regiments (which wore their *Ancien Régime* uniforms). At the same time, the overall size of the army had been drastically reduced and this, combined with low rates of pay and poor prospects of promotion, contributed to the continuing unreliability of the army in any serious crisis.[17] The nobility and aristocracy were another obvious pillar of support for the Bourbon monarchy. Despite their loss of rights, privileges, offices and property during the revolution, they remained an important element in the French elite throughout the nineteenth century, particularly as they dominated the ranks of major landowners. Yet politically they were divided into Bonapartists, liberals, moderate royalists and ultra-royalists. The misfortunes which many noble and aristocratic families had suffered during the revolution encouraged many of the survivors to form a closed, backward-looking caste, hostile to the new elites which had emerged during the revolutionary and Napoleonic periods, and suspicious of the new economic opportunities which came with the development of a capitalist economy. Above all, the nobility and aristocracy were too few in number, and too cut off from the rest of the population, to provide a solid foundation for Bourbon rule after 1814.[18]

In social and political terms, the restored Bourbon monarchy was not of course just based on the Catholic Church and on the nobility and aristocracy. The charters of 1814 and 1815 established a constitutional monarchy with a two-chamber parliament, a Chamber of Peers and a Chamber of Deputies (known officially as 'the Chamber of the Deputies of the Departments', suggesting that it represented the departments of France, not the French people). Members of the Chamber of Peers, appointed by the king, were drawn from both the *Ancien Régime* and Napoleonic elites. The members (258 in 1814, 402 in 1815) of the Chamber of Deputies were elected by the eighty-four departments on a narrow franchise. Only male French citizens aged thirty or over who paid annually 300 francs in direct taxes were entitled to vote in parliamentary elections, and only male French citizens aged forty or over who paid annually 1,000 francs in direct taxes were eligible to be parliamentary candidates. In practical terms, this created an electorate of approximately 72,000 in 1814 and a pool of some 15,000 parliamentary candidates. For a country with a total population of some thirty million in 1814, and with the experience of the 1791 constitution, which had given the vote to approximately four and a half million adult male French citizens, this was not a generous franchise.

Clearly, middle-aged wealthy Frenchmen shared a common interest in supporting conservative economic and social policies. However, the majority of the electorate was, in political terms, normally liberal, except when special factors, such as Waterloo and Napoleon's second abdication, the assassination of the duc de Berry or the successful French military intervention in Spain (which liberals had opposed) led to a period of reaction. This might not have mattered if the restored Bourbons had been figurehead monarchs, presiding like natural arbiters over the political system. Instead, Louis XVIII and especially Charles X were partisan monarchs with their own royalist political agendas, and the charters of 1814 and 1815 entrusted the king alone with the power of appointing and dismissing government ministers. It was therefore difficult to distinguish between opposition to the government, and opposition to the king and even to the whole Restoration regime. Patronage could buy some support for the Crown, but financial constraints and the drastic reduction in the size of the military establishment dictated a modest programme of public works and a scarcity of official jobs. Prefects and other officials sought to manage elections through their influence and through various corrupt practices but, after 1824, divisions among royalists and a determination among liberals to control the electoral process made such efforts increasingly ineffective. Other attempts to curtail liberalism, through making parliament even less democratic and through imposing restrictions on the newspaper press, were inevitably unpopular and could be counter-productive. On the other hand, if liberalism remained unchecked, liberal newspapers attracted more and more readers, liberal opposition candidates won more and more parliamentary elections, liberal majorities defeated governments with increasing frequency in the Chamber of Deputies, and even a majority in the Chamber of Peers might vote against government legislation.

In a context already in many respects unfavourable to the Restoration monarchy, Charles X precipitated a political crisis by a well-known series of reactionary measures – laws introducing the death penalty for certain acts of sacrilege and providing indemnities for émigré aristocrats whose property had been confiscated during the revolution (April 1825), the unsuccessful attempt to re-introduce primogeniture (1826), the dissolution of the Paris National Guard (29 April 1827), the appointment of the reactionary Polignac government (8 August 1829), the decision (taken in April 1830 and acted on the following month) to dissolve a parliament with a liberal majority rather than to dismiss a deeply unpopular government, and finally the so-called Four Ordinances (signed on 25 July and published on 26 July 1830). These ordinances imposed strict government censorship on newspapers, journals and political pamphlets, dissolved the newly-elected Chamber of Deputies, reduced the total number of deputies, a fifth of whom were to be elected annually on a more restricted franchise, and ordered new elections for September. According to article 14 of the charter of 1814, the monarch did have the power to issue decrees vital for the maintenance of the rule of law and the security of the State. Charles X and Polignac claimed that this article, together with the general principle that any government had the right to provide for its own security, legally justified the Four Ordinances. If the Four Ordinances had been successfully enforced, however, they would have completely undermined the liberty of the press and restricted the parliamentary franchise to a tiny minority, composed almost entirely of the wealthiest landowners of France. Consequently, France would virtually have ceased to have been a constitutional monarchy. Hence the Four Ordinances almost immediately provoked violent resistance in Paris which rapidly led to the overthrow of the Bourbon monarchy.

The Four Ordinances surprised and shocked contemporaries, but they were arguably just the climax of a long-term failure on the part of the Bourbon monarchy to manage parliament and regulate the newspaper press effectively. Passionately partisan, the governments of Louis XVIII and Charles X attempted to use the prefects and sub-prefects to secure the return of government supporters in parliamentary elections. Prefects doctored the electoral lists so as to exclude, if possible, known opposition voters; they contributed to the travelling expenses of pro-government voters; they entertained actual and potential government supporters; and they financed the printing of campaign literature for pro-government candidates.[19] The Catholic Church was also enlisted as a pro-government electioneering agent, particularly in the parliamentary elections of 23 June and 3 July 1830, with bishops and priests instructing their congregations from the pulpit how to vote. Charles X himself on 13 June 1830 issued a personal appeal to his subjects not to allow themselves 'to be misled by the insidious words of enemies of public tranquillity' in the forthcoming elections.[20] The Restoration prefects and sub-prefects were successful in reducing the size of the electorate. Despite the slow increase in the population and wealth of France, the total number of registered voters fell steadily (110,000 in 1817, 96,525 in 1820, 79,138 in 1829).[21] On the other hand, Restoration governments, and ultimately the regime itself, through these dubious electoral practices became vulnerable to charges of fraud and corruption and, generally, of illegal and unconstitutional behaviour. Also, the liberal opposition, responding to blatant government manipulation of the electoral system, became much more professional in its approach to parliamentary elections. By 1827 two organisations, the *Société des Amis de la Liberté de la Presse* and *Aide-toi, le ciel t'aidera*, had been established to encourage liberals to register as voters, to select liberal candidates for parliamentary elections and to campaign for the election of those candidates. At a grass roots level, liberals organised political subscriptions, banquets and demonstrations. The political results were startling. In a Chamber of Deputies of 428 members, approximately seventeen liberals were elected in February/March 1824, 180 in November 1827 and 274 in June/July 1830, by which time they constituted a clear majority.[22]

The attempts by Restoration governments to regulate the newspaper press were similarly counter-productive. The charter of 1814 established freedom of the press within legal limits designed to repress the abuse of that freedom. Given the role of newspapers such as Marat's *L'Ami du peuple* and Hébert's *Le Père Duchesne* in the French Revolution, the political influence of radical newspapers and of their editors and contributors understandably concerned Restoration governments. A press law of October 1814 established preliminary official authorisation of newspapers and preliminary censorship for writings of less than twenty pages. In 1819 caution money was introduced – newspaper directors had to deposit a sum of money with the Treasury as a guarantee for the payment of fines. After the assassination of the duc de Berry, new press laws (March/April 1820) tightened up the regulations concerning authorisation and censorship prior to publication. A further press law in 1828 dispensed with juries in newspaper trials. On the basis of this legislation, newspaper editors were fined and imprisoned, the publication of newspapers was suspended, and some opposition newspapers suffered so much harassment that they were forced to close. Newspaper trials inevitably attracted a great deal of publicity, which was invariably damaging to successive Restoration governments. Successful government prosecutions were increasingly interpreted as evidence of a politically-biased judicial system, while acquittals increasingly became the focus of popular celebration and constituted a blow to the government's prestige. Restoration governments also founded newspapers such as *Le Conservateur* in 1818, and paid subsidies to existing newspapers – for instance, under Martignac *Le Journal des Débats* received a monthly subsidy of 12,000 francs.[23] In addition, from January 1824 the government spent some three million francs in buying up opposition newspapers. However, the scheme was discovered and publicly denounced; the newspapers purchased by the government soon lost readers and money; and new opposition newspapers were founded, including *Le Temps* (October 1829) and *Le National* (January 1830).[24]

Government attempts to regulate the newspaper press were thus as counter-productive as their policies of parliamentary management. By 1828 the most successful liberal opposition newspaper, *Le Constitutionnel*, had nearly 20,000 subscribers, over half of whom lived outside Paris. In contrast, the most important pro-ministerial royalist newspapers, *La Gazette de France* and *La Quotidienne*, had by 1828 only 10,000 and 6,000 subscribers respectively.[25] Altogether, it has been calculated that by July 1830 opposition newspapers had over 50,000 subscribers, while royalist newspapers had less than 20,000.[26] Opposition newspapers not only won the circulation war, they also won the political argument. Comparing the situation in France with that in England at the time of the Civil War and the revolution of 1688, they accustomed their readers to think that Charles X was acting in an illegal and unconstitutional manner, that some sort of royal *coup d'état* might be attempted, and that a change of royal dynasty might be both possible and desirable.

The revolution of July 1830

It has been suggested that the revolution of July 1830 'hinged far more on the collapse of existing authority than on the existence of a force for violent change', and that a revolutionary situation in Paris did not exist before the publication of the Four Ordinances.[27] This downplaying of 'the machinations of republicans, Bonapartists or liberals'[28] has been challenged.[29] Certainly, as argued previously, a vigorous opposition to the Bourbon monarchy existed for most of the period from 1814 to 1830. This opposition came from ultra-royalists on the right and from liberals, Bonapartists and republicans on the left. Ultra-royalists could be considered, and doubtless saw themselves, as supporters of the Bourbon monarchy. They were indeed royalists, and many of them identified themselves with the comte d'Artois, later Charles X. However, ultra-royalists tended to support an idealised memory of the pre-1789 Bourbon monarchy rather than the Bourbon monarchy as restored in 1814. Thus they seemed to want to restore the *Ancien Régime* and to oppose compromise with the legacy of the revolution and the Empire. A secret society known as the Chevaliers de la Foi brought together prominent ultra-royalists, partly directed the 'white terror' of 1815, and helped to secure the election of many ultra-royalists in the national parliamentary elections of August 1815. Although the 'white terror' of 1815 was never repeated, the Bourbon monarchy was embarrassed by the ultra-royalist parliaments elected in August 1815 and February/March 1824, by obscure ultra-royalist plots and conspiracies, and by ultra-royalist hostility towards central government and ultra-royalist defence of provincial liberties. Ultra-royalism, though, was too elitist and backward-looking to capture much of a popular following, unless exceptional circumstances favoured a violent political reaction, as at the end of the Hundred Days, after the duc de Berry's assassination[30] or following the successful French military intervention in Spain. Altogether, ultra-royalism associated the restored Bourbon monarchy with royalist extremism and reaction, and it exercised a fatal influence over the last Bourbon king, Charles X.

Much more serious for the Bourbon monarchy was the opposition on the left from liberals, Bonapartists and republicans. In a situation in which there were no organised political parties and liberals, Bonapartists and republicans shared much common political ground, it was a case of an 'opposition of the left' or a Liberal Opposition with liberal, Bonapartist and republican strands rather than three rigidly distinct left-wing traditions.[31] Politically, liberals claimed to stand for the principles of 1789 and the charters of 1814 and 1815. In practical terms, this meant support for a constitutional monarchy, for a parliament representing the propertied classes, for a reasonable degree of personal liberty (religious toleration, limited press censorship, limits on the role and influence of the Catholic Church, a judicial system relatively free of political bias), and for policies which generally maintained the conservative social and economic status quo. By the late 1820s the Liberal Opposition had shed its earlier association with conspiracy and revolt to assume the role of the defender of the charters of 1814 and 1815. Through effective political and parliamentary tactics, it had also developed strong local and national leadership which enjoyed widespread public support.

Liberals were convinced that, in retaining the Polignac ministry against the wishes of a majority in the Chamber of Deputies, Charles X was acting contrary to the spirit, if not the letter, of the charters of 1814 and 1815. On 17 March 1830 a liberal majority of 221 deputies voted an address, responding to Charles X's speech from the throne at the opening of the new parliamentary session. This so-called Address of the 221 implicitly affirmed the principle that the government had to have majority parliamentary support. Charles X immediately reacted by issuing a royal ordinance on 19 March suspending the Chamber of Deputies until 1 September. With parliament no longer in session, liberals organised a series of opposition banquets while liberal newspapers intensified their denunciations of Charles X and his ministers. On 16 May another royal ordinance arranged for new parliamentary elections to be held on 23 and 24 June and on 3 July in the hope that French military success in Algeria and all the influence that the royal administration and the Catholic Church could bring to bear on voters would result in a government election victory. Yet the Liberal Opposition won 274 seats and government supporters just 143 which led to the fatal decision to issue the Four Ordinances on 26 July. The same day forty-four journalists and directors of newspapers including *Le Constitutionnel*, *Le Courrier français*, *Le Globe*, *Le National* and *Le Temps*, signed a protest against the Four Ordinances, declaring that the government had violated the law and that they were going to publish their newspapers without authorisation. Even on the eve of the July revolution, most liberals were contemplating forms of non-violent resistance, such as the illegal printing and circulation of newspapers and a concerted refusal to pay taxes, rather than revolutionary violence. However, on

27 July the July revolution began, with the eruption of street violence in many parts of Paris.

Those who actually fought in Paris during the July Days (27, 28 and 29 July 1830) were, with few exceptions, not individuals who had been associated with the Liberal Opposition to the Bourbon monarchy. Instead, they were mostly skilled workers and artisans drawn particularly from the building trades and aged between twenty and thirty-five.[32] The willingness of such people to risk their lives in three days of street fighting in support of the Liberal Opposition against Charles X is, superficially, surprising. The charters of 1814 and 1815, in which most liberals believed, left workers without a vote so they were not directly affected by the constitutional crisis. Also, most liberals believed in maintaining the existing social and economic status quo, which meant that liberal ideas and policies had little to offer the working class. However, liberals and Paris workers had developed a common opposition front to Charles X and his reactionary policies. They shared an hostility towards policies favouring the Catholic Church, the imposition of restrictions on the parliamentary franchise and the newspaper press, and such measures as the disbandment of the Paris National Guard (April 1827). In the absence of any popular political leadership and organisation, whether Bonapartist or republican, Paris workers accepted liberal political leadership, fêted liberal political leaders such as Jacques-Antoine Manuel, and celebrated liberal triumphs such as the parliamentary election successes of November 1827. Moreover, liberal political campaigning and propaganda helped to encourage this popular support. The July Ordinances simultaneously provoked popular resistance and mobilised the liberal–worker united front. Both liberals and workers opposed what seemed to be a royal *coup d'état* leading to authoritarian monarchical rule. At the same time, jobs in the newspaper industry were directly threatened and on 27 July some liberal employees closed their workshops, thereby putting perhaps 60,000 workers on the streets. In fact, liberals and Paris workers had very different political, social and economic agendas, but during the July Days they seemed to be united in the same cause, the cause of 'liberty'.[33]

In addition to the political crisis, an essential ingredient in the revolution of July 1830 was an economic recession that lasted from approximately 1827 to 1832. A financial crisis in Britain in 1826 had repercussions in France, and government protectionist tariff policies could lead to high prices for key commodities such as iron ore which restricted economic growth. However, the main factor was a run of bad harvests affecting cereal crops and, in 1827 and 1828, potatoes as well. Again government policy, which generally allowed the free circulation of French grain while prohibiting the import of foreign grain, tended to make this situation worse, as did the inevitable hoarding and speculation. Between April 1827 and April 1829 the price of cereals in some parts of France increased by approximately seventy-five per cent, with significant price fluctuations from one market to the next.[34] Problems in other countries led to a fall in exports, and there was a general loss of economic confidence, with the building and textile industries going into decline from 1827. For the urban working class, food became scarce and expensive at a time when employers were reducing wages and laying off employees. Between 1825 and 1830 wage rates in the building trades of Paris declined by thirty per cent, in the metalwork industry by 35 per cent, and in the provincial textile industry by forty per cent.[35] Those out of work had to depend on charity. In 1828 the Prefect of the Nord reckoned that one-sixth of the population of his department and half the population of Lille were in this situation.[36] An exceptionally severe winter in 1829–30, when the river Seine at Paris froze so solidly that stalls could be erected on the ice,[37] brought the building industry to a standstill and generally meant extra hardship for the poor.

These difficult circumstances led to various forms of violent protest, particularly from the beginning of 1829 – threats and violence against bakers, the forcible prevention of the movement of cereals, the forced sale of cereals at below market prices, and attacks on the property of alleged grain hoarders and speculators. There were also demonstrations by unemployed workers, violent tax protests (taxes on wine being especially unpopular), an epidemic of arson attacks on buildings, woods and forests, and violent resistance to the new forest code of 20 May 1827, which regulated rights of pasturing animals and collecting wood in forests. In the Ariège peasants dressed as women repeatedly challenged the forest code which 1,200 troops were trying to enforce in the department by April 1830.[38] Between February and June 1830 the departments of Normandy and north-eastern France suffered particularly severely from a series of arson attacks.[39] Economic recession cannot explain why a revolution occurred in Paris in July 1830 rather than at any other time between 1827 and 1832. Yet by stoking up popular discontent, by accustoming the population to violent protest, and by focusing popular hatred on the government and on the Bourbon monarchy, the economic crisis and the accompanying popular unrest and law-breaking helped to create a political climate favourable to revolution. This in turn partly explains the explosion of violence triggered by the Four Ordinances and the subsequent extraordinarily rapid disappearance of the Bourbon regime in Paris and in the provinces.

The Four Ordinances had been drawn up in the greatest secrecy, so there had been no attempt to win over public opinion. This preoccupation with secrecy and Charles X's sublime over-confidence also meant that there had been no military preparations either. With a third of the French army (including many of the best troops) either in Algeria or in reserve in southern France, and with further troop deployments in Normandy (to deal with the arson attacks) and on the Belgian frontier (since a Belgian revolt against Dutch rule seemed imminent), the Paris military garrison plus units of the Royal Gendarmerie amounted to approximately 11,000 men, though only approximately 7,000 were available for combat duties at any one time.[40] The Four Ordinances became public when their texts appeared in the official government newspaper, *Le Moniteur*, in its morning issue for Monday 26 July. Since *Le Moniteur* had a relatively small circulation, it was only when later editions of Paris newspapers republished the texts of the Four Ordinances that many Parisians became aware of them. During the afternoon of 26 July, Adolphe Thiers in the editorial offices of Le National drew up a protest declaring that the Four Ordinances were a flagrant violation of the laws, that, according to the charter, parliament had to approve changes to the press and electoral laws and that journalists had a duty to resist the government's violation of the law by continuing to publish their newspapers. Forty-four journalists and editors representing eleven Paris newspapers signed this protest, which was published in Le National and three other opposition newspapers on 27 July, despite an edict issued by the Prefect of Police prohibiting the publication of any newspaper without prior authorisation. Individual copies of the protest were also printed in large numbers and distributed in Paris streets and cafés.

Workers' protests began on the evening of 26 July with demonstrations near the Bourse (the Paris Stock Exchange) and the Palais Royal (the Paris residence of the duc d'Orléans) and outside the Ministry of Finance. Throughout the following morning crowds of workers gathered in and around the Palais Royal and, encouraged by the condemnation of the Four Ordinances in opposition newspapers, began to throw stones at police and soldiers. This led to violent incidents in which several demonstrators were killed. Their corpses were placed on stretchers and paraded through the streets of Paris to the cries of 'Death to the ministers!' and 'Death to Polignac!' The Prefect of Police tried to silence opposition by issuing warrants for the arrest of the forty-four journalists and by dismantling the printing presses of the four newspapers which had printed their protest. Undaunted, opposition deputies and journalists continued to hold meetings on 27 July, although only legal resistance seems to have been contemplated. However, the initiative was seized by working-class Parisians, determined not just to oppose the Four Ordinances but also to overthrow the regime of Charles X by force.

Having been informed of the first popular protests against the Four Ordinances on the morning of 27 July, Charles X appointed Marshal Marmont, duc de Raguse, commander of all military forces in Paris. Although a competent soldier, Marmont was not an inspired choice – he had handed Paris over to the Allies in March 1814 and he believed that he had been passed over as a potential commander of the Algerian expedition and that the policies of the Polignac government were misguided. More important, he lacked any preparation for his command, had no tactical plan to put into operation and did not have adequate military forces at his disposal. Marmont ordered his troops to occupy the main strategic points in the capital, which was successfully accomplished. Yet crowds continued to roam the streets, tearing down representations of the royal coat of arms, raiding gunsmiths for weapons, constructing street barricades and everywhere attacking soldiers and gendarmes. During the night an uneasy calm descended, though demonstrators destroyed many of the street lights. Early in the morning of 28 July the crowds assembled again, more numerous and more threatening than before. Marmont issued orders for troop reinforcements from provincial garrisons while Charles X, at last aware of the gravity of his position, signed an ordinance proclaiming martial law in Paris. Troop reinforcements remained a distant prospect and the king's writ no longer ran in much of Paris. Marmont attempted to go on the offensive by launching three columns to subdue the principal centres of revolt, but the columns, trapped by street barricades and exposed to constant attack, had to withdraw. Soldiers, suffering from the hot weather and short of ammunition, as well as of supplies of food and drink, became increasingly ineffective and in some cases began to desert. In contrast, the demonstrators, ever more formidable in numbers, confidence and weaponry, managed to occupy important public buildings such as the Hôtel de Ville and the cathedral of Notre Dame, from which tricolour flags were triumphantly flown. During the night of 28–9 July nearly every street in the city was blocked by barricades, forcing Marmont to concentrate his troops in defensive positions around the Louvre and the Tuileries. Further troop desertions during the morning of 29 July, and an unauthorised withdrawal of Swiss Guards from the Louvre, rapidly resulted in the remnants of Marmont's forces having to retreat in disorder up the Champs Elysées. By the afternoon of 29 July the whole of Paris was in the hands of the insurgents.

Throughout the July Days, Charles X remained at the Palace of Saint-Cloud on the outskirts of Paris, where he was cut off from events in the capital and could not communicate easily with Polignac and his other ministers. Misled and misinformed by Polignac, he at first completely underestimated the force of the storm which he had provoked and refused to allow events to intrude into his daily routine of religious worship, hunting and card playing. On 28 July he ignored a parliamentary deputation representing the Liberal Opposition, which wanted to negotiate a cease-fire in return for the revocation of the Four Ordinances and the dismissal of the Polignac government. Only after he had learnt that the Tuileries Palace had fallen did he consent to making these concessions on 29 July. However, he at first failed to sign a document announcing the concessions and he had no printing press at his disposal, so could not communicate with his subjects. In any case, by 29 July the situation was fast slipping out of Charles X's control. The king's authority had been overthrown in Paris and others were seizing the political initiative.

The overthrow of the authority of Charles X in his capital after just three days' street-fighting surprised and alarmed members of the Liberal Opposition. To prevent popular violence going unchecked, a group of parliamentary deputies agreed during 29 July to establish at the Hôtel de Ville a municipal commission (which styled itself a Provisional Government the next day) and to reconstitute the Paris National Guard under the command of Lafayette. When the news of Charles X's proposed concessions eventually reached the municipal commissioners at the Hôtel de Ville, they did not respond. The same day two of the editors of Le National, Adolphe Thiers and François Mignet, met at the house of a wealthy banker, Jacques Laffitte, and there drafted a proclamation calling for the overthrow of Charles X and for his succession by his cousin the duc d'Orléans. Thousands of copies of this proclamation were printed and distributed throughout Paris. Thiers, Mignet and Laffitte had acted on their own initiative, without the consent of the duc d'Orléans or the support of other members of the opposition. However, members of the Orléans family and the duke himself cautiously welcomed the proclamation and, on 30 July, representatives of the Chamber of Peers and the Chamber of Deputies agreed to offer the duc d'Orléans the title of Lieutenant-General of the Kingdom.

On 30 July a document signed by Charles X, annulling the Four Ordinances and announcing a new government including the prominent liberal Casimir Périer, was at last brought to Paris, but the king's concessions were too late and were ignored by both newspapers and politicians. Instead, representatives of the Chamber of Peers and the Chamber of Deputies agreed almost unanimously that the duc d'Orléans should be invited to serve as Lieutenant-General of the Kingdom. In so doing they recognised that the people of Paris would not now accept Charles X and that unless the power vacuum was quickly filled there might be a popular takeover of Paris, leading possibly to a republic. Having been persuaded to come to Paris, the duc d'Orléans accepted the post of Lieutenant-General during the morning of 31 July, promising at the same time to adopt the tricolour, summon parliament and respect the charter ('La Charte sera désormais une vérité', he claimed). This acceptance was immediately repeated in a declaration, of which 10,000 copies were printed and distributed. After members of the Chamber of Deputies under the presidency of Laffitte had met to ratify the duke's acceptance, a huge procession accompanied the duke from the Palais Bourbon to the Hôtel de Ville, where Lafayette, as commander of the Paris National Guard, embraced the duke before an enthusiastic crowd.

Unable to rely on the effectiveness or loyalty of his army and at the age of seventy-two lacking the stomach for a civil war, Charles X capitulated. On 1 August he agreed to the proclamation of the duc d'Orléans as Lieutenant-General of the kingdom. The following day he abdicated in favour of his grandson, the duc de Bordeaux. The duc d'Orléans communicated the abdication to the Chamber of Deputies which, as he hoped and expected, ignored it. Far from proclaiming the duc de Bordeaux as Henri V, Orléans wanted Charles X and his family out of France. When persuasion failed, on 3 August Orléans and Lafayette encouraged a large crowd to set out for Rambouillet, the royal palace between Paris and Chartres to which Charles X had withdrawn. As his former ministers scattered, Charles X finally agreed to being escorted to Cherbourg, from which on 16 August he sailed with his entourage to spend the last six years of his life in exile.

With Charles X out of the way, what became known as the July monarchy could be established. On 3 August the duc d'Orléans opened the new session of parliament. Addressing a minority of peers and deputies (sixty-seven out of a total of 365 peers and 194 out of a total of 428 deputies), he offered his services as a defender of law and order, as a guardian of the constitution, and as a supporter of an immediate examination of the organisation of the National Guard, the use of juries in trials involving newspapers, the reform of local government, and the interpretation of article 14 of the charter. Against a background of popular unrest in Paris and in provincial cities such as Bordeaux, Lyons and Nantes, the Chamber of Peers and the Chamber of Deputies met daily to debate the institution of a new monarchy and the drafting of a new constitution. On 7 August the Chamber of Deputies reached agreement on several crucial issues. In view of the alleged violation of the charter inherent in the Four Ordinances, the resistance of the citizens of Paris during the July Days, and the departure of Charles X and his family from France, the throne was declared to be vacant. The charter itself was to be revised so that Roman Catholicism would be recognised as the religion professed by the majority of Frenchmen rather than the religion of the State and press censorship would be formally disallowed. The monarch's authority to issue ordinances in the interests of State security would be annulled, parliament would be able to initiate legislation, the tax and age qualifications required of parliamentary voters and candidates would be revised, and the tricolour would be adopted as France's national flag. Finally, the duc d'Orléans would be invited to accept these reforms and, having sworn before parliament to observe the revised charter, to assume the title of King of the French. These resolutions were approved by large majorities in both the Chamber of Deputies (219 to thirty-three) and the Chamber of Peers (eighty-nine to ten with fourteen abstentions), though over a third of the deputies and over two-thirds of the peers did not attend to vote. Unsurprisingly, the duc d'Orléans enthusiastically welcomed the resolutions and, in a civil ceremony at the Palais Bourbon on 9 August, he was formally proclaimed Louis-Philippe, King of the French.

It was Paris which witnessed the determined resistance to the Four Ordinances, the violent overthrow of the authority of Charles X and the enthronement of Louis-Philippe. Yet deputies representing provincial departments composed the majority of the liberal readership which decisively influenced the course of events, and provincial reactions to developments in the capital were crucial for a swift and successful transfer of power. Stagecoaches often first brought news of the revolution to provincial towns. They carried letters, newspapers and travellers with tales to tell, and they proclaimed the success of the revolution with their fleurs-de-lis escutcheons removed and with tricolour flags flying from their upper decks.[41] Provincial towns and cities, though, did not always wait on events in Paris. As early as 27 July 1830, several provincial newspaper editors decided to continue to publish their newspapers in defiance of the Four Ordinances and, in Lyons, liberal opposition leaders demanded the immediate mobilisation of the National Guard, a demand that began to be implemented the following day.[42] By 31 July 1830, in towns such as Rouen, Evreux and Caen, local liberal opposition leaders had formed municipal committees which took over the local administrations, reorganised the National Guard, and ordered the display of the tricolour on public buildings – a painful sight for those accompanying Charles X into exile.[43]

Thereafter, throughout France, self-appointed committees representing the local liberal opposition composed mainly of merchants, lawyers, bankers and members of the liberal professions, took over the department and municipal administrations from prefects and mayors. Acting on their own initiative and without orders from Paris, these committees reorganised the National Guard units, purged the local administration of royalists, proclaimed the Orleanist regime, and collected donations for the victims of the July Days. The Rouen municipal committee even sent two battalions of its National Guard to Paris. The French army in the provinces and in Algeria transferred its allegiance to Louis-Philippe rapidly and relatively smoothly, with just a small mutiny in the Besançon garrison on 5 August and the voluntary departure of Legitimist officers. While senior officers tended to adopt a wait-and-see attitude, junior officers and non-commissioned officers generally welcomed the revolution. Thousands of desertions occurred by soldiers who made for Paris, eager to defend the revolution and to enrol in the supposedly well-paid National Guard.[44] Prefects and mayors, unprepared for the Four Ordinances, overtaken by the rapidity of events and, in the case of a number of prefects, not even at their posts because they were on holiday or had not returned from voting in the recent elections, tendered their resignations without a struggle.

Violent resistance to the July 1830 revolution in the provinces was extremely rare. A clash between demonstrators and soldiers in Nantes on 30 July resulted in thirteen dead and fifty-two seriously injured, but the problem here was that crowd control had been left to the army rather than to the National Guard.[45] In Nîmes, following a ceremony on 15 August to proclaim the Orleanist regime, violent rioting broke out which caused three deaths. More riots and seven more deaths occurred in Nîmes at the end of August after the departure of a Swiss regiment from the city.[46] Again, though, special circumstances explained the violence – the long-standing political conflict between the Catholic and Protestant communities in Nîmes and in the department of the Gard. Non-violent opposition to the July 1830 revolution was not uncommon but remained largely confined to those aristocrats and clergy who retained their loyalty to Charles X – office-holders resigned their posts and army officers their commissions, while Catholic clergy refused to participate in Orleanist celebrations or to fly the tricolour from their parish church tower. Such opposition had little impact. On the other hand, popular violence in the provinces did target those associated with the Bourbon regime, symbols of the Bourbon monarchy and of the counter-revolution, such as the statue of General Pichegru at Besançon,[47] and some of the buildings and missionary crosses of the Catholic Church. The most significant incident of anti-clerical violence was probably the attack on the cathedral and seminary of Nancy on 30 June to 1 July 1830. However, no lives were lost and nothing resembling a revolutionary terror developed.

Although the July 1830 revolution was itself relatively non-violent, the establishment of the Orleanist regime began rather than ended a period of political violence and popular revolt in France. The novelist George Sand, writing from

Paris in a private letter of 6 March 1831, observed that the revolution, like parliament, was in permanent session, and that Parisians lived as happily amidst bayonets, riots and ruins, as they would have done in completely peaceful conditions.[48] Generally, the overthrow of Charles X was a welcome event in France. It meant the removal of an unpopular king and government and of any threat to re-establish the *Ancien Régime*, and it seemed to represent a blow to the 1815 Settlement and a palliative to the shame of Waterloo. Of course Legitimists, those still loyal to Charles X and his heir, opposed the July revolution and the Orleanist regime. This Legitimist opposition led to one serious outbreak of violence during April and May 1832, when the duchesse de Berry attempted to lead a revolt in the traditionally royalist region of the Vendée, south of Brittany. The whole affair at once became a complete fiasco – the government learnt of her plans, the prospect of armed revolt attracted neither aristocrats nor peasants, and the duchess herself was eventually captured and found to be pregnant, although she had been a widow since 1820. Yet over a hundred lives were lost in several clashes between royalist bands and government troops, and the duchess, imprisoned in the fortress of Blaye, could pose as a martyr to the royalist cause. Despite this disaster, Legitimism retained the loyalty of many aristocrats (especially victims of the official purges) and some Catholics (especially those living in areas with significant Protestant communities, and it lingered on in the Vendée and, to a lesser extent, in parts of southern France, particularly the regions around Toulouse, Avignon, Aix-en-Provence and Marseilles. Yet Legitimist opposition to the Orleanist regime constituted an embarrassment rather than a threat. Charles X and, after his death in 1836, the duc de Bordeaux, made no serious attempt to regain the throne. After July 1830 the purges of the civil service, the judicial system and the armed forces were so thorough that few Legitimists were left in positions of power and influence. Popular hatred of the Bourbons and their supporters continued after the overthrow of Charles X. Moreover, Legitimists featured prominently among the wealthy land-owning elite. They did not want to endanger their social and economic status by embarking upon dangerous adventures, nor did they want to undermine a regime which had rapidly assumed the role of the defender of the social and economic status quo at a time of widespread popular unrest.[49] Rather than in conspiracy, violence and revolt, Legitimism under the July monarchy found expression in parliamentary politics, journalism, the Catholic Church, masonic lodges, and charitable activities and organisations.[50]

A more serious threat to the Orleanist regime seemed to be presented by popular protest. The economic recession which had begun in 1827 continued until at least 1832. Poor cereal harvests in 1830 and 1831, a disastrous grape harvest in 1830, political uncertainties at home and revolts and international tension abroad, meant high food prices and high levels of unemployment. Consequently, economic factors helped to fuel popular protest and popular violence. In Paris and other urban centres after the July Days, workers demonstrated for higher wages, a shorter working day, the provision of more jobs and the expulsion of foreign workers. In the provinces there were demonstrations against taxes and the high price of bread, as well as widespread attacks on machines such as power looms which were blamed for having caused unemployment. In addition to harvest failures and a decline in the volume of trade, structural changes in the economy and the introduction of new technology threatened, or seemed to threaten, many workers. Following the 1830 revolution, the most important outbreak of popular violence with a predominantly economic character occurred in Lyons during November 1831 when its long-established silk industry was staging a slow recovery. A strike in protest at the failure of silk merchants to accept a fixed minimum rate for finished cloth turned violent, resulting in hundreds of casualties and the temporary withdrawal of an unprepared military garrison from the city (22 November to 2 December 1831). The crucial factors in this revolt seem to have been the concentration of nearly half of the city's labour force in the silk industry, the unusual degree of organisation among the silk workers, and the solidarity between master weavers and journeymen, rather than just despair over poverty, unemployment and high food prices.[51]

Popular protest was not just caused by the economic recession and developments within the labour force, but also by political factors. Patriotic, republican, anti-clerical and Bonapartist sentiments had played a role in the July 1830 revolution and could not suddenly be switched off. In fact republicanism, in particular, developed into a political movement of some significance. Two republican societies were founded in Paris, the *Amis du Peuple* and the *Société des Droits de l'homme*, as well as other republican clubs, societies and associations in Paris and the provinces; the republican and left-wing newspaper press expanded in Paris and gained a foothold in the provinces, despite much government harassment; and a republican leadership began to emerge around such figures as Godefroy Cavaignac, François Raspail and Ulysse Trélat (all members of the *Amis du Peuple*), Armand Marrast and Armand Carrel (both newspaper editors) and Louis-Antoine Garnier-Pagès (a deputy). This emerging republican movement made radical demands. For instance, the programme of the *Amis du Peuple* included salaries for deputies, the reorganisation of the magistrature, the abolition of taxes on wine, a general reform of indirect taxation, free education, the cancellation of State financial subsidies to the Catholic Church, the reform of the banking system and the granting of political rights to workers.[52] In contrast to the radicalism of such programmes, the Orleanist regime introduced a conservative constitution, refused to intervene in the economy so as to help workers and failed to assist foreign revolutionaries in Belgium, the Italian states or Russian Poland. Hopes among many workers after the July revolution for radical change which would benefit them were therefore dashed and the belief gained ground that the workers, and the July revolution, had been betrayed.

With this political climate, and the continuing economic crisis, it is not surprising that a series of outbreaks of popular violence occurred. Demands for the death penalty for Polignac and his government colleagues led to violent demonstrations in Paris on 17, 18 and 19 October 1830 and, during the trial of the ministers in December 1830, a massive deployment of troops was necessary to maintain order in Paris. Violence again erupted in Paris on 14 February 1831, following a religious service in the church of Saint-Germain-l'Auxerrois to commemorate the assassination of the duc de Berry. The gathering of a fashionable crowd for such a purpose at a church in central Paris beside the Louvre was regarded as Legitimist and clerical provocation, and an angry crowd sacked both the church and the residence of the Archbishop of Paris. In 1832 a cholera epidemic reached France, hitting urban populations particularly hard, with over 18,000 victims in Paris alone. One of the victims of the cholera epidemic was General Lamarque, a Napoleonic veteran who had rallied to Napoleon during the Hundred Days and who had subsequently become a liberal opposition deputy and an impassioned opponent of the treaties of 1815. Thus for Bonapartists, radicals and frustrated nationalists, Lamarque could serve as a symbolic figure; the elaborate official funeral on 19 May 1832 for Casimir Périer, head of a repressive government since 13 March 1831 and another victim of the cholera epidemic, could serve as both a provocation and an inspiration. Consequently, Lamarque's funeral in Paris on 5 June 1832 was turned into a demonstration of political opposition to the government and the regime. Clashes with the police provoked a riot and the erection of street barricades. Order was quickly restored, though it took the next day and artillery to dislodge about a hundred republicans who had barricaded themselves in and around a church near the Hôtel de Ville. Altogether, approximately 800 were killed or wounded. The violence did not attract much popular support; potential republican leaders such as Lafayette and Armand Carrel (editor of *Le National*) did not back the rioters and police, soldiers and National Guardsmen were generally loyal and effective. Nevertheless, a panicked government placed Paris under martial law, closed the Ecole polytechnique, and dissolved the artillery corps of the Paris National Guard.

The Orleanist regime responded to political violence and popular revolt with reaction and repression. As early as December 1830, a shift towards the right could be detected with the resignations of Dupont de l'Eure from the government and of Lafayette from command of the Paris National Guard. Following the Paris riots of 14 February 1831, a more conservative government was formed on 13 March under Casimir Périer. In April republicans, allegedly responsible for the riots associated with the fate of the former ministers of Charles X, were put on trial, and a law of 10 April 1831 introduced restrictions on the right of assembly. Meanwhile, the first governments of Louis-Philippe had begun prosecuting opposition newspapers with spectacular vigour. Between July 1830 and February 1832 there were four hundred government-initiated prosecutions against newspapers, with one Paris republican newspaper, *La Tribune des départements*, undergoing 114 trials.[53] To a lesser extent, Legitimist newspapers also suffered government repression, so that republican and Legitimist newspaper editors found themselves incarcerated together in the Paris prison of Sainte-Pelagie, where a sense of republican–Legitimist solidarity developed.[54]

A general improvement in the economic situation after 1832 might have

ushered in a period of relative calm, but the Lyons silk industry began to experience a serious recession. The silk workers had already experienced the heady
power of violence in 1831, when they had temporarily expelled Lyons' military
garrison. Once again, the position of well-organised workers protecting their arti-
sanal trade in an economic recession was to be a catalyst for a major protest
which, born out of economic circumstances, was to have important political
repercussions. The cholera epidemic in Paris, revolutions in Latin America, a
banking crisis in the United States and the growth of foreign competition, all
contributed to a fall in orders for silk. Silk merchants responded by reducing
prices and orders, and workers in turn responded by going on strike. The adult
male Lyons silk workers, in comparison with most French workers at that time,
tended to be literate, well organised and politically conscious; master weavers
and their journeymen assistants presented a united front; the silk industry dominated the economy of Lyons, the third most populous city of France (after Paris
and Marseilles), with a population in 1834 of approximately 135,000. These
exceptional circumstances made possible an exceptional act of defiance by
workers – the organisation of a general strike – which paralysed the Lyons silk
industry from 14 to 22 February 1834. The government, claiming that the
general strike was the product of a political conspiracy, arrested six alleged strike
leaders and put them on trial on 5 April. The government also introduced a new
law on associations (10 April 1834). Official authorisation was now required for
all associations, even for those with sections of fewer than twenty members. Any
member of an illegal association could be fined up to 1,000 francs and imprisoned for up to a year. Owners of property used for illegal meetings could be
regarded as accomplices to a crime. Finally, the Chamber of Peers sitting as a
High Court was to try cases which, in the government's opinion, involved the
security of the State.

By the beginning of April 1834 the government had filled Lyons with troops
in expectation of trouble. Violent clashes between soldiers and demonstrating
silk workers began on 9 April, and there followed six days of street-fighting
which left over three hundred dead. The insurgents fought tenaciously, and the
last centres of revolt had to be bombarded into submission by artillery. In Paris an
inaccurate report that Lyons had fallen to the insurgents, and the government's
suspension of La Tribune des départements and arrest of about 150 leading
members of the Society of the Rights of Man led, on 13 and 14 April, to twenty-
four hours of violence and some twenty-five deaths, including innocent civilians
killed by soldiers in the so-called massacre of the Rue Transnonain. Less significant outbreaks of violence occurred at the same time in several provincial
cities. When it came to the trials of those accused of the Lyons insurrection
(May–August 1835), the Orleanist regime found itself in the dock as much as the
accused. Defending many of the accused, a republican lawyer, Jules Favre, argued
that the July monarchy had betrayed the principles of the 1830 revolution. He
argued that workers had a right to resort to violence against a government which
had illegally deprived them of their rights, that the government with its troop

concentrations had deliberately provoked the confrontation in Lyons, and that the army had behaved with unnecessary brutality against the insurgents. These arguments were widely publicised in press reporting of the trials and contributed to the alienation of the working class and of the left generally from the Orleanist regime.[55]

The Lyons silk-workers' insurrection of April 1834 was the last major popular revolt to confront the July monarchy until the revolution of February 1848. Yet various forms of violent opposition continued to challenge the Orleanist regime. During a review of the Paris National Guard on 28 July 1835, the anniversary of the revolution of 1830, an 'infernal machine' consisting of twenty-four muskets bound together discharged a murderous volley from an upper storey window into the royal procession. The king escaped. Nevertheless, eighteen were killed, including Marshal Mortier, the Minister of War, and a further twenty-three were seriously wounded. The perpetrators of this act of terrorism were a handful of republicans led by a Corsican adventurer called Joseph Fieschi, acting entirely on their own initiative. News of the outrage provoked a wave of sympathy and support for the royal family. Louis-Philippe and his government nevertheless chose to blame the incident, at least partly, on irresponsible newspapers which frequently seemed only too willing to incite and condone political violence. Parliament was hastily recalled and in a near-panic atmosphere passed severe measures against the newspaper press. What became known as the September 1835 Press Laws were designed virtually to silence Legitimist and republican newspapers by extending the definition of criminal libel, by introducing jury judgments by a simple majority verdict, by increasing the financial penalties for press offences, and by controlling the publication of political caricatures. Some republican newspapers, such as *La Tribune des départements*, had already been forced to cease publication because of official harassment, and approximately thirty more republican newspapers were closed down by the September 1835 Press Laws. However, what had become the main republican newspaper, *Le National*, continued to appear and, from 1839, a veritable renaissance of the French left-wing press occurred. Moreover, the government's attempts to censor and silence the opposition newspaper press earned it the hostility and contempt of many journalists and of much of the newspaper-reading public.

The year 1835 seemed to close the chapter of the 1830 revolution in France. From then, and until the beginning of 1848, the Orleanist regime seemed to be relatively secure and to be relatively free from the threat of popular revolt, though not entirely free from republican plots, Bonapartist *coups*, or assassination attempts directed against the king. Between 1830 and 1835 the July revolution had almost come full circle. The revolution had begun with resistance against what were widely perceived to have been illegal and unconstitutional acts by Charles X and his ministers. Liberty was the rallying cry, opposition newspapers and their editors were in the forefront of the struggle, and three days of street-fighting in Paris were the means whereby Charles X and the Bourbon monarchy were overthrown. Yet the July Days almost immediately led to the proclamation of another monarchy; the newly-installed Orleanist regime soon became identified with the maintenance of order rather than with the defence of liberty; the opposition newspaper press was harried with as much rigour as it had been before July 1830; and renewed street-fighting, particularly in Lyons in April 1834, was crushed with the utmost severity. Thus by 1835 Louis-Philippe, no longer 'King of the Barricades', was associated with bourgeois rule, political reaction and vigorous repression of all opposition – repression that could be both brutal and of questionable legality.

The July monarchy

Traditionally, the July 1830 revolution has been interpreted as a bourgeois revolution and the July monarchy as a bourgeois regime, though recently this interpretation has been questioned and qualified. Perhaps the most convincing interpretation is that advanced by Robert Tombs: 'The 1830 revolution was not the triumph of one socio-economic class over another, but of one socio-political faction over another, that of the majority of *notables* who had accepted and gained from the changes of 1789, over the ultra-royalist minority that had rejected them and lost.'[56] The ultra-royalists were a minority even within the French elite, while the majority of the *notables*, or members of the French elite, had triumphed in 1830. This support by the majority of the French elite should have helped to endow the July monarchy with a reasonable degree of stability and security. Yet quite apart from the various explosions of violence after 1830 and the eight assassination attempts directed at Louis-Philippe during his reign, the July monarchy suffered from a range of fundamental weaknesses, an examination of which is necessary for an understanding of the revolution of February 1848.

Louis-Philippe personified in himself a host of ambiguities and contradictions. He was a Bourbon and a descendant of Louis XIII, but he was also the son of a regicide who had inherited and maintained a family tradition of hostile relations with the reigning monarch. His father had espoused the revolution by calling himself Philippe-Egalité and by securing his election in Paris to the Convention parliament, but then, accused of plotting against the revolution, had fallen victim to the Terror. Similarly, Louis-Philippe had fought in the armies of the Republic only to desert to the enemy and join the emigration. By accepting the French throne in August 1830, Louis-Philippe confirmed the overthrow of Charles X, consolidated the revolution and undermined the monarchical principle of legitimacy, but simultaneously he scotched the possibility of a republic and, since no election or plebiscite was held, ignored the principle of popular sovereignty. Louis-Philippe owed his throne to a popular revolution in Paris, he was the 'King of the Barricades', yet he went on to preside over a regime which rapidly gained notoriety for political repression of the left, class oppression of the poor and rule in the interests of the rich. His 'bourgeois' manners and the relative modesty of his lifestyle and court helped to earn Louis-Philippe the title

'Citizen-King', but at the same time his fabulous personal wealth set him firmly apart from all his subjects. He might claim to be a bourgeois monarch and his regime might claim to embrace the principle of meritocracy. Yet he alienated the bourgeoisie by his excessive concern to provide for his large family. The dynastic principle which he partially represented conflicted with the concept of meritocracy; and proposals that merit and achievement (capacités), as demonstrated in intellectual distinction, career success or distinguished public service, would be rewarded with political rights, were effectively limited to municipal elections. Ultimately, to many French people, the July monarchy seemed to have repudiated its revolutionary origins, to have assumed many of the trappings of the Ancien Régime, and to have come to embody little more than greed, self-interest, exploitation, corruption, and rule by the representatives of the very wealthy.[57]

The symbolism associated with Louis-Philippe and the July monarchy reflected these ambiguities and contradictions. While the tricolour was readopted as France's national flag, signifying a continuity with France's revolutionary and Napoleonic past, a rather bulbous crown became the official symbol of the regime, emphasising its monarchical character. Louis-Philippe became king as Louis-Philippe I, not as 'Philippe VII', signalling the beginning of a new dynastic line, and he styled himself King of the French rather than King of France and Navarre, as Louis XVIII and Charles X had been styled. Louis XVI had become King of the French in 1791 and Napoleon Emperor of the French in 1804, so Louis-Philippe's title simultaneously recalled revolutionary and Napoleonic precedents and rejected the precedents of the Ancien Régime and the Restoration. Whereas Louis XVIII had granted the charter of 1814 and Charles X had even staged a coronation for himself at Reims, a simple ceremony in the Chamber of Deputies inaugurated the reign of Louis-Philippe on 9 August 1830, when the new king swore to observe a revised charter.

Lacking a Bourbon or an Orleanist political heritage which he could exploit to his advantage, Louis-Philippe turned to Napoleon and to the Napoleonic legend. In 1833 he decided that the Palace of Versailles should become a national museum, dedicated 'to all the glories of France', including those of the Napoleonic era. Leading artists were commissioned to paint large canvases depicting Napoleonic battle scenes, which were presented as glorious national achievements. In Paris a statue of Napoleon was restored to the top of the Vendôme column in July 1833 and the Arc de Triomphe – the huge monumental arch at the top of the Champs Elysées commemorating Napoleon's victories – was inaugurated in July 1836 (also on the anniversary of the July 1830 revolution). One of Louis-Philippe's sons, the duc de Joinville, brought back from St Helena the remains of Napoleon which were reburied in Paris with elaborate ceremony in the chapel of the Invalides (15 December 1840).[58] This attempt to exploit the prestige of Napoleon was not entirely inappropriate since Bonapartists had generally opposed Charles X and former members of the Napoleonic elite were well represented in the ranks of public office-holders after July 1830. However, Louis-Philippe was a decidedly unmartial figure and his foreign policies were resolutely pacific, except in Algeria, to the despair of those who hankered after the glories of Napoleon's military victories and domination of Europe. Perversely, perhaps, the French military campaigns in Algeria, in which four of Louis-Philippe's sons participated with distinction, signally failed to capture the French imagination or to arouse a unifying sense of nationalist fervour.

While no Napoleon, Louis-Philippe was by no means a figurehead monarch. According to the charter of 1830, he was the supreme head of State and the commander of the army and navy. He possessed the right to declare war and to make peace, and to negotiate alliances and commercial treaties. He was able to appoint and dismiss ministers and to approve all public administrative appointments. He could issue regulations and decrees necessary for the execution of legislation, though he could never suspend existing laws or refuse to enforce them. In practice, his powers were virtually identical to those of Charles X, except that he could not issue emergency decrees which he considered to be necessary for State security. It followed almost inevitably that Louis-Philippe, like Louis XVIII and Charles X, was actively involved in politics in a partisan manner rather than as a neutral arbiter. In fact Louis-Philippe often presided over meetings of his ministers and generally acted very much as the head of the executive, so he could not embrace the concept, inside or outside parliament, of a loyal opposition. Since the Crown was not politically neutral, it was difficult for the judicial system to be politically neutral either. Opposition to the government therefore usually also meant opposition to the Crown, and even to the July monarchy as a regime, which gave politics a dangerous edge. Hence Thiers could observe of Louis-Philippe in November 1852: 'The great error of his life was that he never would submit to be a constitutional King.'[59]

A further problem lay in the legitimacy of Louis-Philippe's title and rule. The parliamentary opponents of Charles X had seen themselves as defenders of the constitution, not as revolutionaries and few, if any, wanted to overthrow the king. Charles X's removal had been primarily the achievement of the artisans and workers who fought during the July Days. However, the enthronement of Louis-Philippe was the achievement of a small group of elite political figures representing the liberal opposition to Charles X, acting speedily to fill a political vacuum and to forestall a republican or Bonapartist resolution of the crisis. This achievement received parliamentary approval, but only from the last parliament of Charles X, less a significant number of absentees. Louis-Philippe himself was, of course, a Bourbon, but Charles X had abdicated in favour of his grandson, the duc de Bordeaux, whom Legitimists recognised as Henri V. Thus Louis-Philippe arguably enjoyed only a quasi-legitimate status as King of the French. This helps to explain the lack of respect in which he was held right from the outset of his reign. Whereas Charles X had received a civil list of forty million francs per year, the Chamber of Deputies in January 1832 accorded Louis-Philippe a mere twelve million; and subsequent attempts by Louis-Philippe to secure additional parliamentary grants for himself and his family invariably encountered stiff parliamentary resistance.[60] Similarly, the famous cartoon by Charles Philipon, in which the face of Louis-Philippe is transformed into a pear in four stages, first appeared in a satirical publication, *La Caricature*, as early as 24 November 1831.

The rhetoric of the July revolution of 1830 might describe the July monarchy as 'the best of republics' and as 'a popular throne surrounded by republican institutions', but in fact the revised charter of 1830 simply made parliament a slightly more liberal and democratic institution, while preserving political power at a national level in the hands of a small and wealthy male elite, most of whom were landowners and more than a third of whom were nobles and aristocrats.[61] The liberal intellectuals known as the *doctrinaires*, who had opposed Charles X and now supported Louis-Philippe, envisaged, however, not so much the rule of the rich, as the creation of a political class including both men of property and men distinguished by their abilities and achievements (*capacités*). This attempt to create a 'natural' political class never really succeeded, though, partly because membership of the political class seemed to depend almost exclusively on wealth rather than on merit. The more significant changes affected the Chamber of Peers. After the July Days the abolition of the hereditary peerage was a popular demand, and the left, led by Odilon Barrot, wanted an elected Chamber of Peers. The latter proposal was rejected, but Catholic archbishops and bishops, and peers created by Charles X, were excluded from the new Chamber of Peers, and a law of 29 December 1831 abolished the hereditary peerage. New peers, in effect life-peers, were to be created by the king, whose choice was restricted to certain categories of individuals, including parliamentary deputies, senior office-holders, members of the French Academy and high tax-payers.[62]

The Chamber of Deputies was made slightly more democratic and representative by lowering the tax and age qualifications for those eligible to stand as parliamentary candidates and to vote in parliamentary elections. According to a law of 19 April 1831, parliamentary candidates had to pay annually at least 500 rather than 1,000 francs in direct taxes and be aged at least thirty rather than forty, while parliamentary voters had to pay annually at least 200 rather than 300 francs in direct taxes and be aged at least twenty-five rather than thirty. In addition, members and corresponding members of the French Academy, and retired army and naval officers receiving pensions of at least 1,200 francs a year, could vote if they paid a minimum of 100 francs annually in direct taxes (the government had originally proposed more categories of *capacités*). The number of parliamentary constituencies was increased from 430 to 459. Departments were divided up into electoral *arrondissements*, which were not necessarily the same as the administrative *arrondissements*, and each electoral *arrondissement* returned one deputy to parliament.

The parliamentary system of the July monarchy suffered from a number of disadvantages. The Chamber of Peers had several distinguished members (de Broglie, Victor Cousin, Victor Hugo and Montalembert), but it never played a very significant role in the political life of the July monarchy. Its members were generally too conservative (apart from the odd radical such as the comte d'Alton-Shée) and too old (two-thirds were aged over sixty in 1840).[63] The

Chamber of Deputies was elected on too narrow a franchise, was too unrepresentative of the nation as a whole, and was too open to corruption and government influence. The number of electors rose from 166,583 in 1831 to 240,983 in 1846, which represented only 0.5 per cent of the total French population in 1831 and scarcely 0.7 per cent in 1846. Only about 50,000 voters were eligible for election to the Chamber of Deputies.[64] Also, the ratio of deputies to voters varied considerably and there were many constituencies with relatively small numbers of voters. In the department of the Seine, fourteen deputies represented over 18,000 voters, whereas in the department of the Creuse four deputies represented scarcely 900 voters. Between 1841 and 1842, out of 459 parliamentary constituencies, only 143 had more than 500 registered voters.[65] Thus urban voters were under-represented in comparison with rural voters, who were likely to be more conservative and, in the 316 constituencies with no more than 500 voters, personal or government influence could be particularly powerful.

At first there were official declarations of government non-intervention in parliamentary elections. François Guizot, Minister of the Interior from August to the beginning of November 1830, issued a circular to the prefects in September 1830 declaring that the government should remain entirely apart from the by-elections which were about to take place. His successor, the comte de Montalivet, stated in the Chamber of Deputies on 30 December 1830 that free elections meant non-intervention by the government and the removal of administrative influence. However, as early as the general parliamentary elections of July 1831, Casimir Périer, the Prime Minister, made it clear that his government had no intention of being neutral. The prefects were instructed to use all their influence to secure the return of suitable candidates. In addition to attempting to influence the choice and success of parliamentary candidates, the government could hope to influence members of parliament through patronage, particularly paid State employment, especially since, unlike their Napoleonic predecessors, peers and deputies received no parliamentary salaries. The issue of salaried officials becoming deputies was hotly debated. A small majority rejected attempts to ban office-holders from becoming deputies, and the number of office-holders sitting in the Chamber of Deputies steadily grew: there were 142 in 1832, 167 in 1842, 184 in 1846, and 193 in 1847. Particularly prominent among these *députés fonctionnaires* were magistrates, local government officials, army and naval officers, and members of the Conseil d'Etat. Similarly, in the Chamber of Peers in 1840, 140 peers (forty-four per cent of the total membership) held important positions in the civil or military services of the State.[66] These officials could normally be expected to vote for the government, but the general trend in the long term helped to undermine respect for the government and for parliament.

Whereas national parliamentary politics were restricted to a wealthy elite, local politics were much more democratic. A law of 21 March 1831 established an elected council in each commune and municipality. On the basis of tax returns, the wealthiest ten per cent of male citizens aged twenty-one or over in the commune or town could vote in the council elections, fourteen per cent if the population were over 1,000, and nineteen per cent if over 15,000. In addition, the vote in these council elections was extended to certain categories of *capacités* – justices of the peace, members of local hospital, school and charity boards, members of certain academies and learned societies, doctors of medicine, science and letters, lawyers, teachers, graduates of the Ecole polytechnique, and retired army and naval officers drawing pensions above a certain level. In 1834 the total number of voters in commune or municipal elections was 2,872,089, of whom 2,791,191 qualified through tax payments and 80,898 through *capacités*;[67] and by 1841 there were 2,880,131 local voters, or 8.1 per cent of the total population of France.[68] The mayor of each commune or town was chosen by the king from a list of elected councillors recommended by the prefect (the prefect chose the mayor in communes with up to 3,000 inhabitants). Each department had a general council (*conseil général*) and there were also councils for each district (*arrondissement*) in the department. According to a law of 22 June 1833, the fifty most important taxpayers in each canton (approximately one in forty of the adult male population) elected one member for these councils. Members of the general councils elected their own chairman. The councils of rural communes had few powers and tended to be conservative. In contrast, municipal councils were important and control of them could pass to opponents of the July monarchy. Similarly, the prefect could lose control of the general council of his department, particularly if the chairman of the general council were an opponent of the regime.

Potentially, the most democratic institution of the July monarchy was the National Guard, but the National Guard was yet another source of potential weakness for the regime. The Paris National Guard had been dissolved by Charles X, on the prompting of his prime minister Villèle, after some guardsmen had shouted subversive slogans during a royal review on 29 April 1827. The guardsmen, though, were not disarmed, and some participated in the street-fighting during the July Days. The Paris National Guard was then hastily reconstituted under the command of Lafayette. On 28 August 1830 Louis-Philippe reviewed nearly 50,000 members of the new National Guard, and approximately 80,000 guardsmen from Paris and its suburbs participated in a second royal review on 31 October 1830.[69] The new National Guard was regulated by a law of 22 March 1831, according to which all male French citizens aged between twenty and sixty were eligible to serve in the National Guard, and all officers and non-commissioned officers were elected by their fellow-guardsmen in their legion, except for legion commanders and lieutenant-colonels who were appointed by the king from a list of candidates presented by the legion. The National Guard might have provided the July monarchy with the support of a broadly-based paramilitary force, though National Guardsmen did have to pay for their own uniforms and weapons, thereby excluding the poor. However, there was too much apathy and too little money for the organisation of National Guard legions to be established throughout France. Also, in the various disturbances in Paris and Lyons between 1830 and 1834 the National Guard proved to be somewhat unreliable. At the same time, republicans gained control of several National Guard units, which led to their dissolution in Lyons, Grenoble, Marseilles and Strasbourg during 1834 and 1835. After 1835 morale declined as the National Guard became a popular target for ridicule, and fears of an attempt to assassinate Louis-Philippe ended all royal reviews. Consequently, the wealthy bourgeoisie of Paris tended to avoid service in the National Guard, which became more political and radical in character. Thus, members of the Paris National Guard drew up political petitions – for instance, in 1838 and 1840, for electoral reform and in 1840 and 1845, against the construction of fortifications around Paris.

The July 1830 revolution changed, not just institutions, but also to some extent the character of the French elite, as the official elite was vigorously purged. Ninety-nine deputies excluded themselves from parliament by refusing to swear an oath of allegiance to Louis-Philippe, as did one hundred and seventy-five of the three hundred and sixty-five members of the Chamber of Peers. Also excluded were ecclesiastical peers and all peers created by Charles X. Similarly, in the months following 1830, twenty of the thirty-eight members of the Conseil d'Etat were dismissed, as were seventy-nine of the eighty-six prefects, 196 of the 226 sub-prefects, forty-seven mayors of the fifty largest cities, the commanding officers in each of the nineteen military districts, 426 magistrates, and nearly all senior diplomats. The extent to which this represented a social as well as a political purge is a matter of some dispute. On the one hand, it has been argued that 'the social composition of the new group of office-holders was little different from that of the old.'[70] On the other hand, the revolution of July 1830 is seen as having ushered in an era of bourgeois class dominance, whereas the nobility and aristocracy had previously constituted the dominant class.[71] As far as service to the State was concerned, the Restoration was the Indian summer of the French nobility. For instance, nearly three-quarters of the prefects nominated between 1814 and 1830 were nobles.[72] Similarly, the political supporters of Charles X were often noble or aristocratic, whereas his political opponents tended to be bourgeois. Seventy-nine per cent of the 221 deputies who voted, on 18 March 1830, in favour of the address critical of Charles X's speech from the throne at the opening of parliament were bourgeois (including sixty bankers and businessmen and thirty lawyers), while sixty-three per cent of the 181 deputies who voted against the address were nobles.[73] When it came to the crisis of July and August 1830, bourgeois leadership predominated in the opposition to Charles X, but there was also a strong aristocratic element. David Pinkney has identified the Orleanist solution to the crisis as having been 'the work of a handful of men', namely two bankers (Laffitte and Périer), two lawyers (Dupin and Bérard), one professor (Guizot), two writers and journalists (Constant and Thiers) and five aristocrats (Broglie, Lafayette, Sébastiani, Laborde and Delessert).[74] In other words, those responsible for engineering the accession of Louis-Philippe belonged to three different social categories – the upper bourgeoisie, the professional middle class and the aristocracy. In social terms, they all belonged to the

French elite, but it was their opposition to Charles X and Polignac which united them, a political unity which proved fragile. Many of them moved into official posts after July 1830 but were soon disagreeing so fundamentally among themselves that Broglie and Guizot resigned from the government at the beginning of November 1830 and Lafayette from the command of the Paris National Guard at the end of the year. Thus they should be seen, not so much as political leaders of the bourgeoisie, but rather as a temporary coalition of the opponents of Charles X and Polignac whose members belonged to different sections of the French elite, including the aristocracy.

The character of the French elite during the July monarchy was complex and it is misleading to suggest that it was simply 'bourgeois'. In political terms, one of the consequences of the revolution of July 1830 was that royalist supporters of Charles X were often replaced by men who had held public office under Napoleon and whose careers had generally been blighted for the fifteen years of the Restoration monarchy. The 430 members of the Chamber of Deputies at the beginning of 1831 included eighty-two former officials of the Empire, sixty Napoleonic army veterans and sixty-six deputies with Napoleonic titles of nobility. At the same time, 112 of the 191 members of the Chamber of Peers had been public office-holders under Napoleon and eighty-eight bore imperial titles of nobility. All of the senior army commanders appointed in 1830 had served Napoleon, as had over a third of the new prefects and *procureurs-généraux*.[75] All this suggests that July 1830 'was more a Bonapartist than a bourgeois revolution.'[76] Yet since *Ancien Régime* nobles and aristocrats had tended to support Charles X, and since those who had served Napoleon often belonged to a newer elite, the political purges and changes of 1830 did have a social dimension. It is possible, though, to exaggerate the significance of the social change in the character of the French elite, at least in the longer term. In the short term, particularly, the character of the Chamber of Deputies did change. Noble landowners who had emigrated during the revolution became much less common, while the number of lawyers who were deputies increased significantly – from thirty-four in 1827 to ninety-eight in 1831. On the other hand, the proportion of titled nobles in the Chamber of Deputies had been falling since 1815 (though the number of Napoleonic nobles had increased), so 1830 simply accelerated an existing trend; there was no great influx of bankers, manufacturers and merchants into parliament after 1830; and the nobility staged a partial comeback during the July monarchy – more than a quarter of the deputies elected in 1841 belonged to *Ancien Régime* noble families.

Problems do, of course, arise over classification. It may often be misleading to classify a deputy simply as, for instance, a noble, landowner, banker or lawyer. A deputy could belong to more than one category, particularly during a long career; and the Orleanist elite, it has been suggested, was characterised by 'a constant osmosis between industry, finance, land and bureaucracy.'[77] Also, a lawyer-deputy might well represent the interests of bankers, manufacturers and businessmen, who lacked the time or inclination to become deputies themselves. Perhaps the main political development affecting the Chamber of Deputies after 1830 was as much regional as social: the large cities, and particularly the Paris region, increasingly tended to elect opposition deputies, whereas conservatives often retained power in rural constituencies, especially the poorest rural constituencies.[78]

One feature of the French elite during the July monarchy, which has so often been described as a 'bourgeois' regime, is the continuing importance of the nobility. The French diplomatic corps perhaps offers the best example of noble predominance. Of the nine ambassadors in 1840, only one was not noble (Guizot in London); of twenty-one ministers plenipotentiary, only two were not noble; and of thirty-one *secrétaires d'ambassade* or *secrétaires de légation*, only four were not noble. The noble presence within the hierarchy of the Roman Catholic Church also remained significant. A change of regime did not entail ecclesiastical resignations, and senior churchmen tended to be remarkably long-lived. Approximately forty of the eighty of the bishops and archbishops in 1840 came from noble families, and twenty-eight were former émigrés. More surprisingly, a generous sprinkling of nobles was to be found on the boards of directors of insurance, railway and coal-mining companies. Fifty-five of the two hundred members of the General Assembly of the Bank of France in 1840 were nobles. Most of the wealthier Frenchmen continued to be noble. Of the fifteen highest French tax-payers in 1840 (not necessarily the richest Frenchmen), ten belonged to the nobility; and of the fifty-eight most heavily taxed, thirty-nine were nobles. On the other hand, there were limits to the preponderance of the nobility. Just three of the eighty-five chairmen of the *conseils généraux* of the departments in 1840 came from the ranks of the pre-1789 nobility (including the duc de Broglie and the comte de La Rochefoucauld).[79]

As major landowners (owning perhaps ten per cent of all the land of France) and with their significant presence in parliament, the diplomatic corps, the Roman Catholic hierarchy, and in the boards of many commercial companies, the nobility remained a wealthy and influential class. However, the nobility tended to retreat into their own closed world defined by exclusive marriage alliances, codes of noble behaviour, and Legitimist politics and ideology; and the nobility constituted a static minority in a gradually expanding elite. In 1840, just 15,000 of the 200,000 adult male French citizens qualified to vote in parliamentary elections were noble, and just 2,000 of the 16,000 qualified to stand as parliamentary candidates were noble. By the end of the July monarchy over 240,000 had qualified to vote, but the number of nobles in this category had not significantly increased.[80]

The main characteristic, though, of the French elite during the July monarchy was the concentration of wealth in the hands of a small minority of the population. André-Jean Tudesq has defined this elite as those adult Frenchmen who paid annually one thousand francs or more in direct taxes.[81] The number of Frenchmen in this category during the July monarchy was around sixteen or seventeen thousand, out of a total French population of 32,569,000 in 1831 and 35,400,000 in 1846. The most important direct tax was a property tax, the *contribution foncière*, though there were three other direct taxes – the *contribution personnelle et mobilière* (a poll tax and a tax on rents), the *contribution des portes et fenêtres* (a tax on the doors and windows of the taxpayer's residence) and the *impôt des patentes* (a business tax). The importance of the property tax reflected the importance of landownership as a form of wealth and a source of income. This in turn reflected the fact that France remained overwhelmingly an agricultural society: the rural population of France in 1846 was approximately 27,330,000, over seventy-five per cent of the total.[82] Thus the typical member of the French elite during the July monarchy was a wealthy landowner. The uneven distribution of wealth is indicated by the declarations of property-ownership made to the tax authorities following the death of every property-owner. An examination of such declarations made for residents of Paris in 1847 suggests that one per cent of the population owned thirty per cent of the personal wealth and that three per cent of the population owned fifty per cent of the personal wealth.[83] At the other end of the scale, 9.6 per cent of Parisians who died in 1847 left estates valued at less than 100 francs.[84] A large proportion of this wealth took the form of property – at least forty-five per cent in 1847.[85] Similarly, in Lyons inheritance declarations suggest that about two per cent of the population owned forty per cent of the personal wealth.[86] In rural France, the situation was much the same. For instance, in Burgundy approximately three per cent of the population owned about fifty per cent of the land and of all industrial and commercial enterprises of any importance. Rural France did have a substantial class of peasant landowners and property-owning artisans. Nevertheless, nearly half of young couples in Burgundy at the time of their marriage had little or no property.[87] While landownership, usually inherited landownership, remained the key characteristic of elite status throughout the July monarchy, other forms of wealth, such as industrial and commercial investments, were gradually becoming more important, particularly for the urban elites. In Toulon, for instance, the composition of the electorate for the municipal council changed between 1831 and 1846, with fewer property-owners and more electors earning their living from industry, commerce and business.[88] By 1847–8, forty-one per cent of the wealthier notables of the textile town of Reims were woollen manufacturers.[89]

The July monarchy had been established to contain a revolution and to prevent a republic, after experiments in constitutional monarchy had twice failed in France. At its outset, the July monarchy could claim to have stood for compromise, the middle way, a judicious balance between order and liberty. However, it rapidly became identified with little more than the protection of the interests of a wealthy elite and with repression of political opposition, especially on the left. Unlike the Napoleonic regime, the July monarchy failed to develop a sense of mission or to promote an ethos of meritocracy, nor were the French people won over by a new ideology of Orleanism. The July monarchy could have become a flagship of liberalism in a largely conservative Europe, building on such measures as the law of June 1833 encouraging the spread of primary education in France. Instead, it retreated into a position of political immobilism and of almost unqualified support for *laissez-faire* capitalism, thereby allowing political power and wealth to remain concentrated in the hands of a very small elite. Louis-Philippe's quasi-legitimate status as King of the French, his widely-assumed personal greed and his alleged corruption of parliamentary politics eroded public respect for the monarch and for the regime. Even supporters of the July monarchy could not be relied upon, while government policies ensured that opponents, including Legitimists, liberals and republicans, remained unreconciled. Moreover, the Paris National Guard had been alienated. Thus Louis-Philippe and his regime were ill-equipped to face the challenges and crises which the 1840s were to bring.

Chapter 2

The economic, social and political crises

Population pressures

A fundamental factor behind the economic and social crisis which hit France in the mid-nineteenth century was the increase in the country's population. According to official figures, the population of France increased as follows:[1]

Year	Total
1801	27,349,631
1806	29,107,425
1821	30,461,875
1826	31,858,937
1831	32,509,223
1836	32,540,910
1841	34,230,178
1846	35,400,486

The annual rate of increase was not uniform, the highest level (approximately 6.7 per cent) being reached in the years 1816 to 1825 and 1841 to 1845.[2] Geographically, there were also significant variations. Departments with the highest population increases included those with large urban centres, notably the departments of the Seine (Paris), the Bouches-du-Rhône (Marseilles), the Rhône (Lyons), Loire-Inférieure (Nantes), the Nord (Lille), the Haute-Garonne (Toulouse) and the Bas-Rhin (Strasbourg). On the other hand, some departments without large population centres, such as the Ardèche, Corsica, the Hautes-Pyrénées and the Pyrénées-Orientales, also experienced significant population increases. In a few departments, populations were static or even at times declining, such as Calvados, the Eure, the Gers, the Jura, the Lot, Lot-et-Garonne, the Meuse, the Orne, and Tarn-et-Garonne. In general, the Paris, Lyons and Marseilles regions, and the north-east of France, were the most densely populated areas, while the Alpine region was the least densely populated.

The principal urban populations expanded as shown in the table overleaf:[3]

	1801	*1831*	*1846*
Paris	547,736	774,338	1,053,897
Marseilles	111,130	145,115	183,181
Lyons	109,500	133,715	177,976
Bordeaux	90,992	99,062	125,520
Rouen	87,000	88,086	99,295
Nantes	73,879	77,992	94,194
Lille	54,756	67,073	75,430
Toulouse	50,171	59,630	94,236
Strasbourg	49,056	49,712	71,992

Thus the demographic pre-eminence of Paris over other French cities was reinforced by the virtual doubling of its population between 1801 and 1846. In the same period, the populations of other large cities increased less rapidly – Marseilles by approximately seventy-six per cent, Lyons by sixty-two per cent, Bordeaux by forty-four per cent, and Rouen by sixteen per cent. The port and naval base of Toulon achieved the most spectacular population increase registered by any French town in this period, from 20,500 in 1801 to 62,031 in 1846. The next most spectacular population increases were gained by newly-expanding industrial centres such as Saint-Etienne, Reims and Limoges, and smaller centres such as Roubaix, Mulhouse and Tourcoing. In contrast, several towns, including Aix-en-Provence, Clermont and Troyes, recorded relatively sluggish population growths.[4]

Despite the population increase, the birth rate nationally was declining. The number of births per one thousand inhabitants fell from 32.9 in the period from 1816 to 1820 to 26.7 in the period from 1846 to 1850.[5] Consequently, the average family size declined from 4.5 children in 1801 to 3.5 children in 1846.[6] The main reason for the population increase was a decline in the death rate. Apart from the odd exceptional year such as 1832, when a cholera epidemic hit France, a slow and steady decline in the death rate occurred, so that more children survived birth and infancy; and between the periods from 1817 to 1831 and from 1840 to 1859 the average life expectancy rose from 38.3 to 39.3 years for men and from 40.8 to 41.0 years for women.[7] The rural population increased more slowly than the urban population. France's rural population rose from 24,500,000 in 1806 to 26,350,000 in 1831 and to 27,330,000 in 1846, while France's urban population rose from 5,150,000 in 1806 to 7,250,000 in 1831 and to 8,770,000 in 1846.[8] Migration from rural areas, and to some extent from foreign countries, to France's towns and cities accounted for this disparity.

By the standards of western Europe in the first half of the nineteenth century, France was a densely populated country. Although some other countries, such as Britain, experienced higher rates of population growth, France started with a relatively high population density. This had important consequences for landownership in France. Even before 1789, approximately thirty to forty per cent of French agricultural land was in peasant ownership. The sale of confiscated land during the revolution tended to increase peasant landownership, while the ending of primogeniture in revolutionary and Napoleonic legislation tended to promote the fragmentation of landholdings. Thus, in many regions of France large and compact farms were comparatively rare. In 1852 approximately sixty-eight per cent of all individual landholdings totalled less than ten hectares.[9] What constituted a viable landholding clearly varied. The profitable rearing of sheep and cattle might require considerably more than ten hectares, while orchards, vineyards and market-gardens of considerably less than ten hectares could still be profitable. However, in many regions of France a landholding of approximately ten hectares was necessary for a viable mixed farm capable of supporting a family in relative comfort. Moreover, many peasant landholdings were not only small, but also divided into separate strips and plots, sometimes at some considerable distance from each other. The combination of population growth and the prevalence of small sub-divided peasant landholdings meant that 'by the middle of the nineteenth century the [French] countryside was beginning to bulge at the seams.'[10] Land was more intensively farmed and new land was brought into cultivation, but there continued to be insufficient land to meet the demands of an expanding rural population. Peasant families went seriously into debt in order to finance land purchases which became ever more expensive. The price of agricultural land approximately doubled between 1815 and 1845. As land became more valuable, so the pressure on common land intensified, disputes often arose over boundaries and rights of way, and peasant resentment increased against restrictions limiting access to forests (often still in noble or aristocratic ownership). Since most peasants did not own sufficient land with which to support a family, they also rented land, worked as agricultural labourers for others, engaged in some rural industry, and migrated to urban centres on a seasonal or more permanent basis. In good years such strategies for economic survival usually worked but, in years of harvest failure and/or industrial recession, the economic situation of much of France's rural population was likely to be precarious.

If the French countryside was beginning to burst at the seams by the mid-nineteenth century, this was even truer of many of France's cities and towns. The influx of migrants to urban centres resulted in severe over-crowding. In some cases, urban expansion was restricted by the survival of city walls and generally there was inadequate urban investment to cope with demographic expansion. Poor inner-city neighbourhoods teemed with people. By 1848, the old quarters of Toulouse had between thirty to forty inhabitants per house.[11] In Paris approximately 14,000 people lived clustered around the cathedral of Nôtre Dame on the Ile de la Cité, while Lyons in 1846 had 180,955 inhabitants who formed 65,603 households which in turn occupied just 8,744 dwellings.[12] On the fringes of some cities, working-class suburbs expanded dramatically. The population of the suburb of Saint-Denis to the north of Paris increased from 140,181 in 1836 to 193,611 in 1841.[13] The provision of housing, sewerage, water, public transport, and medical and leisure facilities in working-class suburbs tended to be very unsatisfactory. The situation was not much better in the city centres. In 1848 only 5,300 houses in Paris were supplied with piped running water, and fewer than 150 houses had running water above the first floor.[14] The uncertainties of employment, the loosening of family and community ties, and the extreme disparities between rich and poor promoted an unstable social situation. This in turn encouraged prostitution, high rates of illegitimacy, vagrancy, begging, and various forms of criminal activity. Even for the rich, urban centres tended to be unhealthy and dangerous places, as crime rates and cholera epidemics testified. However, the rich enjoyed reasonable standards of housing, hygiene and nutrition, and could usually escape to the countryside for at least part of the summer. For the urban poor, usually denied such advantages, life was often a desperate struggle to cope with low wages, precarious job prospects, rising rents, minimal and expensive public transport, and an unhealthy, dangerous and over-crowded environment.

Economic progress and economic problems

Significant improvements, affecting both the economy and people's everyday lives, did occur during the July monarchy, particularly in the field of communications. A law of 21 May 1836 obliged local authorities for the first time to maintain local roads, the condition of which was vastly improved. Altogether, 22,550 kilometres of road were constructed in France between 1831 and 1847 (an average of 1,326 kilometres per year), whereas only 6,781 kilometres of road had been constructed between 1814 and 1830 (an average of 399 per year).[15] By 1843, 242 steamboats were plying France's inland waterways and by 1847 over half of France's canal system had been built since 1830.[16] France's first railway line on which locomotives were operated, connecting St Etienne to Lyons, opened to freight traffic in 1832 and to passenger traffic in 1834. By 1847 Paris was linked by rail to Amiens, Lille and Brussels, to Rouen and Le Havre, and to Orléans and Tours. A total of 1,830 kilometres of railway track was by then in use and a further 2,872 kilometres were under construction.[17] As communications became cheaper and faster, so the volume of goods and passengers transported increased. Such progress was, however, patchy. Most of France still depended on slow and expensive horse-drawn vehicles. Water transport, also slow and expensive as well as unreliable, continued to be depended upon in areas served by the sea, canals or navigable rivers.

Another area in which significant progress was made during the July monarchy was that of banking. In Paris, in particular, a cluster of merchant bankers including Blount, Davillier, Huttinguer, Laffitte, Pereire and Rothschild, was able to finance industrial development and railway construction. Private banks also existed in most important provincial centres and for more modest customers there was a proliferation of savings banks. Yet again, though, the progress achieved had its limits. National banks with networks of branches covering the entire country had yet to be established, and borrowing remained difficult and expensive for most French citizens.

French agriculture did to some extent respond to the demands imposed by a rising population. There was a certain amount of specialisation, an increase in the average output of cereals, a more widespread cultivation of the potato, a considerable rise in sugar beet production, the introduction of systems of crop rotation, the gradual elimination of the practice of leaving land fallow, greater use of agricultural machinery, and generally a slow trend towards more efficient and productive forms of agriculture. As a result, an expanding French population was fed without significant recourse to imported foodstuffs, and the average rate of per capita food consumption rose slowly during the July monarchy. On the other hand, a number of factors inhibited any really substantial improvement in French agricultural production. The fragmentation of landholdings militated against the introduction of new techniques and capital investment generally while at the same time encouraging disputes over boundaries and rights of way. The peasant obsession with landownership meant high land prices, high agricultural rents and peasant indebtedness. The perceived shortage of agricultural land meant conflicts over common land, rights of grazing, forest codes and, in southern France, water. The expansion of cattle and sheep farming was restricted by a shortage of grazing land and fodder, as well as by the shortage of capital for agricultural investment, so that meat remained relatively scarce and expensive. The orientation towards subsistence farming and towards supplying local markets discouraged specialisation and any dramatic increase in production. The relative absence of a national market for agricultural products could also lead to significant price variations from region to region and to the simultaneous incidence of scarcity and plenty of essential foodstuffs in different parts of France. While the system was basically in equilibrium, any sudden catastrophe, such as harvest failures, could not easily be coped with.[18]

Delayed by the revolution and the Empire, the 'take off' of France's industrial revolution began around 1820 and accelerated from 1840, due partly to the boom in railway construction. New technology and factory production transformed the French textile and iron and steel industries, with production clustering in specific geographical centres. Rouen, Reims, Lille, Roubaix, Armentières, Saint-Quentin and Mulhouse developed as centres for the mass-production of cotton, linen and woollen goods, while coal-mining concentrated in the Loire and Nord basins. Other industries, such as the paper, glass, crystal and porcelain industries, were similarly modernised, while new industries were developed, such as the manufacture of gas lamps and chemicals. In terms of value, industrial production in Paris and the surrounding region was particularly important. Factory production often meant working days of between twelve and fourteen hours, the imposition of harsh work disciplines, the toleration of high industrial accident rates, and the employment of women and children as cheap labour. Also, pay was normally related to output, with no compensation for time lost when machines broke down; and workers often had to contribute indirectly towards the high costs of installing and running steam-driven machinery. From the late 1830s, strikes became a feature of French industrial life, particularly in the coal and textile industries.[19] Large industrial firms emerged, so that, for example, by 1840 the Anzin company produced 79.1 per cent by value of the total coal production of the area.[20] The power of such big companies was reinforced by alliances formed between banks and steel, metallurgical, railway and coal-mining companies. At the same time, family firms and small-scale craft production remained important, especially in the Paris region, where numerous craft workshops produced luxury goods.

The beginning of the economic crisis

After a period of relative economic prosperity from approximately 1838 to 1845, which featured a speculative boom in railway construction and the achievement of unprecedentedly high rates of output in the mining, metallurgical, chemical and textile industries,[21] France endured a prolonged and exceptionally severe economic crisis or series of crises from 1845 until 1852. International developments helped to undermine financial confidence. Anglo-French relations worsened over the arrangement of a marriage between the youngest son of Louis-Philippe (the duc de Montpensier) and the heiress presumptive to the Spanish throne (August to October 1846). The repression of a rising in Cracow and Russian Poland (February to March 1846) and the Habsburg annexation of the Cracow Republic in November 1846 (a violation of the Vienna Treaties of 1815) caused an international outcry. At the same time there were liberal stirrings in the German and Italian states; and civil wars in Portugal (May 1846 to July 1847) and Switzerland (October to November 1847) had a divisive and disruptive impact on European diplomatic relations.

Bad harvests, though, principally caused the beginning of the economic crisis, demonstrating yet again the preponderant role still played by agriculture in French economic life. As a result of disease, the potato harvest in most parts of France was poor in 1845 and almost non-existent in 1846. This immediately placed extra pressure on cereals, and in 1846 the cereal harvest was also disastrous. While cereal harvests were generally good in 1847, the potato crop tended to be disappointing and indeed the potato crop continued to be below average until 1852. Exceptionally high levels of rainfall occurred during the autumn of 1846. Agricultural land was flooded and water transport disrupted. There followed an unusually severe winter in 1846–7. Construction work had to be suspended, reportedly causing 80,000 masons and carpenters to become unemployed in Paris alone.[22] At sea, storms sank or wrecked several ships, including ships transporting foodstuffs, and ice interrupted communications with the Baltic, the Black Sea and North America, from which France imported cereals. During January and February 1847 the river Loire flooded. In contrast, the summers of 1846 and 1847 were unusually dry, so that fodder for livestock became scarce and expensive in parts of France between the summer of 1846 and the summer of 1848. This resulted in large numbers of sheep and cattle being sold at low prices, particularly during the winter of 1847–8. Ironically, the same climatic factors produced an abundant grape harvest in 1847. Over-production led to a slump in wine prices from the autumn of 1847. Thereafter reduced consumer demand helped to keep wine prices at a low level.

Poor harvests, accentuated by interruptions in communications and some hoarding and speculation, led to high prices of essential foodstuffs, particularly cereals. Of all agricultural prices, wheat prices were the most politically sensitive. Wheat prices normally varied significantly from market to market. According to the highest prices given in Le Moniteur over a three-week period, the price of wheat in May 1845 ranged from 24.09 francs a hectolitre in Marseilles to 14.11 francs a hectolitre in Metz.[23] Prices were rising markedly by August 1845 in the markets of Mulhouse (24.49 francs a hectolitre), Strasbourg (24.33 francs a hectolitre) and Metz (18.60 francs a hectolitre).[24] By November 1845, prices ranged from 32.34 francs a hectolitre in Marseilles to 21.03 francs a hectolitre in Nantes.[25] Some markets, such as those of Marseilles and Toulouse, then experienced a degree of price stability, but not the markets of Bordeaux, Lyons, Metz, Mulhouse, Nantes, Paris, Rouen, Strasbourg and Verdun. By April 1847, prices had risen most dramatically in the markets of north-eastern France, with the price of a hectolitre of wheat reaching 50.03 francs in Strasbourg, 48.93 francs in Mulhouse, 45.53 francs in Metz and 44.92 francs in Verdun.[26] High prices were also recorded in other markets in northern France, with a hectolitre of wheat costing as much as 46.26 francs in Caen and 44.30 francs in Lisieux in May 1847.[27] Only in 1812 and 1817 had such price levels been exceeded during the first half of the nineteenth century. Prices thereafter generally declined, with a sharp fall in July 1847 after a relatively good harvest. By January 1848, prices were not unduly high, with the price of a hectolitre of wheat ranging from 26.56 francs in Marseilles to 17.51 francs in Metz.[28] The prices of other essential food-stuffs also experienced dramatic rises. For instance, in March 1847 a hectolitre of potatoes cost fourteen francs at Saint-Pierre-sur-Dives (Clavados), instead of the normal price of between three francs and three francs and fifty centimes.[29] With bread and potatoes scarce and expensive ('Le pain est rare et il est cher', observed La Patrie on 26 January 1847), any further disaster could have a cata-strophic impact on the poor. After sardines had disappeared off the Brittany coast in the autumn of 1846, Prosper Mérimée reported that in Saint Paul de Léon the poor were fighting over the blood from butchers' shops and living off boiled seaweed.[30]

High prices for bread and potatoes, which featured prominently in the diets of the poor, resulted in a rapid decline in consumer spending, especially on clothes. Although food prices fell in 1847, the economic situation for most industrial concerns continued to deteriorate, and a general crisis in business confidence developed. Railway companies, which had recently boomed, were particularly hard hit: investments in railways were withdrawn, railway company shares fell drastically in value on the Paris Bourse and the demand for metallurgical products associated with railways dried up. The Société Talabot, engaged in the construc-tion of the Lyons–Avignon railway line, declared itself to be bankrupt in October

1847.[31] By the end of 1847, some 700,000 workers employed in the construction of railways and in associated metallurgical industries had been laid off,[32] and those still in work were often on part-time work and reduced wages. The slow-down in the construction of new railway lines adversely affected the transport of cereals and other foodstuffs. Other major casualties were the labour-intensive construction industry and small businesses generally. The number of bankruptcies in France rose to 1,139 between 1 August 1847 and 31 July 1847, whereas in the same period the totals were 931 for 1846–7 and 691 for 1845–6.[33] All this and a parallel loss of confidence in England helped to create a financial crisis, with an outflow of gold and silver abroad, an increasing shortage of gold and silver coin, and a run on the banks, which forced some banks to suspend payments.

Social consequences

For many peasant households, harvest failures led to indebtedness. Urban workers, who normally spent nearly half the household budget on bread, vegetables and potatoes, had to cope not only with exceptionally high food prices, but also with wage cuts, part-time working and unemployment. Even urban workers in full-time employment could have great difficulty in balancing their household budget by 1847, and those who were partially or totally unemployed became dependent on assistance. Very serious social consequences followed. In most parts of France in 1847 the death rate began to rise and the birth rate began to fall, with the number of deaths exceeding that of births in Lille and Strasbourg. Demands for public and private assistance reached unprecedented levels. By January 1847 Toulouse, with a population of approximately 95,000, had, according to its mayor, 14,000 indigent people and a further 6,000 workers and artisans requiring assistance,[34] while approximately a third of the adult male population of Perpignan was unemployed.[35] By May 1847 over half the textile workers in Roubaix were unemployed and by November 1847 the wages of workers in Seine-Inférieure had been reduced by approximately thirty per cent.[36] Vagrancy and begging became serious problems. Between 1843 and 1846 in one rural commune in the Corrèze, the number of beggars increased from ten to 101, and there were comparable increases in neighbouring communes.[37] Bands of beggars appeared in the rural hinterland of Rouen during the winter of 1845–6. Day and night they knocked at the doors of rich farmers, asking for bread.[38] In January 1847 it was reported that bands of beggars were circulating in the area around Harcourt (Eure) and that every day the bands were becoming angrier and more demanding. One band, 350-strong, went from house to house demanding and seizing bread.[39] Similarly, in February 1847 it was reported that in the area around Soissons (Aisne), bands of beggars, many of whom came from outside the department, daily besieged farmhouses, demanding bread in a threatening manner from terrified farmers.[40] Begging in Tours had also reached alarming proportions by February 1847, with poor women surrounded by children and elderly invalids shouting at passers-by and insistently demanding money.[41] According to prison records for 1847, begging was the crime for which most people were imprisoned in Toulouse.[42] Such widespread and visible evidence of human desperation meant that fear of violent crime and of the impoverished masses began to haunt the possessing classes in urban and rural France.

Government, official and individual responses to the crisis

The Guizot government and the prefects were reluctant to intervene in the crisis, sticking to doctrines of *laissez-faire* liberalism. In January 1847 the collection of tolls on cereals was suspended, but in the same month the Bank of France raised interest rates from four to five per cent, the first time that this had happened since 1817. Many claimed that this just increased the cost of borrowing while failing to reverse the withdrawal of gold and silver coinage from circulation. In contrast, many local authorities adopted a variety of initiatives to combat the scarcity and high price of cereals, the growing problem of unemployment, and the destitution facing individuals and families.

In Paris, under the authority of the mayor of each *arrondissement* and in accordance with guidelines issued by the prefect of the Seine, the *bureaux de bienfaisance* issued coupons to the indigent and families in difficult circumstances, enabling them to purchase bread from bakeries at a slightly reduced price (in January 1847, forty centimes per kilogramme instead of forty-seven centimes per kilogramme).[43] A sum of 600,000 francs was allocated to this scheme just for the first two weeks of March 1847; the scheme cost 1,460,000 francs to run for the month of April 1847; and by mid-March 1847, 489,000 people in Paris (approximately half the city's population) were in receipt of bread vouchers.[44]

In the provinces, similar bread-voucher schemes were introduced by the municipal councils of Bayonne, Bordeaux and Toulouse, though restricting the bread vouchers scheme to the indigent was criticised as 'a badge of misery in the eyes of the baker'.[45] Some local authorities tried, usually unsuccessfully, to block the movement of cereals out of their area. Other local authorities supplied their local markets with cereals which they had purchased. The mayor of Saint-Malo, with the agreement of the municipal council, bought 800 tons of wheat in London and Marseilles for resale in the port. In Toulouse, the municipal council allocated 36,000 francs to subsidise the price of bread for the poor (January 1847) and 10,000 francs to public works projects to provide employment (February 1847).[46] Several other municipal councils spent significant sums on subsidising the price of bread and financing special public works schemes, including Caen (56,000 francs), Chartres (26,000 francs), Chateaudun (10,000 francs), Metz (10,000 francs) and Valenciennes (20,000 francs). The municipal councils of Autun, Châlons-sur-Marne and Rennes opened public subscriptions to raise funds with which to buy cereals for their municipal markets.[47] The mayor of Bléré (Indre-et-Loire) organised a subscription which raised 600,000 francs. With this sum 500 sacks of wheat were purchased in Paris and sold at cost price 'aux plus nécessiteux du pays'.[48] Subscriptions to finance the purchase of wheat for local distribution were organised by the *bureau de charité* in Vierzon (Cher) and by the *bureau de bienfaisance* in Angers.[49] A 60,000-franc loan provided the municipal council of Arras with assistance funds for the poor, and a 150,000 franc loan financed work schemes for the unemployed run by the municipal council of Rouen. The municipal council of Angers set aside an extraordinary sum of 100,000 francs for charitable relief. To help provide assistance to the Loire flood victims, the Prefect of Loir-et-Cher organised a lottery to which artists including Horace Vernet, Ary Scheffer and Eugène Isabey contributed prizes.[50] Another lottery raised 11,180 francs for the poor in Toulouse.[51] A ball in the Prefecture of the Haute-Marne featured a collection for a bread distribution for the poor.[52]

There were also many private initiatives, especially during and after the winter of 1846–7. The owners of the porcelain works at Vierzon had a bakery constructed in their factory site from which they sold bread to their employees at a subsidised price, and the owners of the iron works at Hyange and Moyeuvre operated a similar scheme.[53] Eugène Schneider, the owner of the important ironworks at Le Creusot, bought large quantities of flour at Marseilles. The flour was then distributed to his workers at a reduced price, with priority to 'familles nombreuses', the cost being deducted from the workers' wages.[54] The Anzin Coal Company began a similar scheme in March 1847.[55] Private subscriptions were organised in Arras and Noirmoutiers to collect funds for food subsidies and public works schemes.[56] A regiment of dragoons, garrisoned at Thionville in Lorraine, organised a daily soup and vegetable delivery to thirty-six '*indigents*'. The officers of the Second Light Infantry Regiment in Metz for three months provided food for twenty poor people selected by the local *bureau de bienfaisance*.[57] At the end of March 1847, the boarders (*internes*) of the Royal College of Toulouse subscribed to a lottery to benefit the local poor.[58]

Motivated by pity, paternalism or a concern for public order, landowners, especially noble and aristocratic landowners, also provided various forms of charitable relief. Like Eugène Schneider, the comtesse de Tournon bought large quantities of wheat in Marseilles and then resold the wheat at a subsidised price.[59] Baron James de Rothschild subsidised the bread-coupon system in Paris.[60] A bread-coupon system was similarly subsidised by the marquis d'Aligre in Bourbon-Lancy.[61] At Saint-Dié, near Chambord (Loir-et-Cher), the comte de Chambord arranged for the sale of bread to the poor at one franc fifty centimes, as opposed to the then current price of two francs fifty centimes.[62] Similarly, in March 1847 the marquis de La Moussaye gave instructions for 1,000 hectolitres of wheat to be sold in small quantities at below market prices, while the vicomte de Villèle released cereals from his own reserves in order to supply the Toulouse market.[63] A loan from the marquis de La Guiche enabled a public grain warehouse to be established at Saint Bonnet de Joux (Saône-et-Loire).[64] The vicomte de Bonneval sent 10,000 francs to the mayor of Bourges for the establishment of *ateliers de charité*.[65] The comte and comtesse de Montblanc provided a soup kitchen for the poor at Ingelmunster.[66] In two communes in the *arrondissement* of

Mayenne, the marquis and marquise de Hauteville distributed firewood and clothes to the poor and offered work to those who wanted to work.[67] A landowner called Delafontaine made available some land at La Haie-Malherbe so that the poor of the commune could grow their own potatoes, beans and turnips.[68] The scale of all this relief was staggering. For instance, by 1847 in the department of the Nord 268,000 people, nearly a quarter of the population, were in receipt of some form of public assistance.[69] In one industrial town in the Nord, Tourcoing, the local *bureau de bienfaisance* was feeding more than half the population by the beginning of March 1847.[70]

Popular protests

The social and economic crisis inevitably led to protests. As early as 25 November 1845, at Saint-Angel in the canton of Tulle (Corrèze), a 300-strong crowd formed to obstruct the movement of a cart loaded with grain.[71] Violent protests by workers against unemployment occurred in the industrial towns of Saint-Etienne on 30 March 1846 and Elbeuf on 22 May 1846. During August and September 1846 there were disturbances in the Charollais district of Burgundy, with carts transporting grain being ambushed. The disturbances continued during the autumn, including forced sales of grain at relatively low prices, opposition to the movement of cereals, and some violence, or threats of violence, directed against those suspected of hoarding and exporting cereals or of selling cereals at unreasonably high prices. By November 1846, soldiers were being regularly used to escort grain convoys. During the morning of Saturday 7 January 1847, in Laval a crowd consisting of women, children and some men forced wheat to be sold at a reduced price and looted a house in which cereals had been stored. Soldiers had to be called in to restore order.[72] Women and children were also prominent in disturbances during the night of 14 to 15 January 1847 at Saint-Paul-de-Léon.[73] On 30 January at the market held in the cloisters of the ruined abbey of Cluny, wheat was forcibly sold at five francs the double decalitre after the price had risen to eight francs the double decalitre.[74] Earlier that month at Fougères (Ille-et-Vilaine) about 200 woodcutters and charcoal-burners threatened to prevent any local export of cereals if the price of cereals rose at the next market, and attempts were made to block the movement of grain along the river Vilaine with huge rocks.[75] Woodcutters also featured in a disturbance at Jury-sur-Bois in the Loiret on 18 March 1847, when a barge transporting grain along the canal of Châteauneuf had its cargo successfully raided, despite the presence of a detachment of soldiers.[76] Previously, there had been demonstrations in Rouen over the loading of potatoes for export onto a British boat.[77]

One of the most serious disturbances occurred in the department of the Indre. On 13 January 1847 a crowd in the small town of Buzançais seized carts loaded with grain and dragged them to the town hall where, despite the mayor's protests, it was announced that the confiscated grain would be sold the next day at three francs a double decalitre, instead of the current price of seven francs.

The mayor, the *juge de paix* and some sixty local notables complied with this proposal and, on 14 January, a market was held in the name of the municipal council at which grain was sold at three francs the double decalitre. However a M. Chambert refused to sell his grain at this price and, in resisting the crowd, killed one person and wounded another. Chambert was then beaten to death and his house ransacked, as were a grain mill and several other properties. For about four days, *châteaux*, grain mills and properties in the region around Buzançais and the nearby departmental capital, Châteauroux, were attacked. In Châteauroux itself the grain market was disrupted on 16 January by an 'irruption en masse' of railway workers. Armed with picks and shovels, and urged on by a crowd of women, they sang the Marseillaise and attacked National Guardsmen and property-owners until dispersed by a cavalry charge.[78]

On 9 March, *Le Constitutionnel* reported that nearly thirty departments had experienced 'tristes soulèvements' occasioned by the cereals crisis over the previous three months. A number of towns had also experienced disturbances, including Nantes, Rennes, Boulogne, Dunkirk, Périgeux, Rouen, Tours, Le Mans, Agen and Montauban.[79] The same paper reported on 15 May that serious disorders had occurred in Cambrai and Lille. In Cambrai on 9 May a black flag had been paraded in the streets to cries of 'Bread at twenty *sous* or death!' In Lille on 12 May large crowds, including many women, had pillaged nearly all the bakeries in the city and distributed bread while shouting a bizarre mixture of slogans – 'A bas Louis-Philippe! Vive Henri V! Vive la République! Vive le roi d'Angleterre!'[80] High bread prices also led to the looting of bakeries, wine merchants and grocery shops in Mulhouse on 26 June. Troops had to be called in and there were eight deaths.[81]

Falling standards of living, caused by high food prices, wage cuts, part-time working and unemployment, and for a time the threat of famine, politically radicalised many workers. In local elections, lower income men could vote and in Rouen, a city with an important textile industry, republicans secured a majority on the city council in 1846.[82] The number of industrial disputes reached exceptionally high levels in the years 1845–7,[83] and strikes and demonstrations over economic and social grievances could acquire a political complexion. When workers at the spinning factory of Albert Ménage in Elbeuf suffered wage cuts in October 1847, they went on strike and demonstrated outside the factory, singing the Marseillaise. The strikers then turned violent when Ménage tried to break the strike by hiring workers from the Louviers area who would accept the reduced wages.[84] Apart from popular protests which might have a political character, the Guizot government was widely condemned for tolerating hoarding and speculation, for subservience towards large banks and railway companies, for food shortages and high food prices, and for doing too little to alleviate human suffering and to revive the economy. 'We do not hold the government innocent of the famine which decimates our populations', declared on 26 February 1847 *L'Impartial*, a Legitimist newspaper published in Rouen.

The continuation of the crisis

Newspapers began to report significant falls in cereal prices in some markets towards the end of March 1847.[85] Thereafter, reports of plentiful supplies and falling prices in cereal markets continued,[86] a trend sustained by imports of foreign-produced cereals and the prospects of a good cereal harvest in France. Consequently, the withdrawal of troops stationed along the canal between Dunkirk and Cambrai, to protect convoys of barges laden with cereals, was announced at the beginning of June 1847.[87] As expected, the cereal harvests were generally good in 1847, and other crops such as grapes, apples and beans also did well. From the autumn of 1847, falling prices, while benefiting consumers, could hit producers, especially those engaged in the cultivation of grapes for the wine trade, since an abundant grape harvest had coincided with a decline in demand for wine. Also, farmers who reared livestock were still experiencing difficulties securing fodder, which resulted in large numbers of sheep and cattle being sold at low prices during the winter of 1847–8. Nevertheless, to many contemporaries it seemed as though France's economic crisis was coming to an end. Food was no longer scarce and expensive, and a modest recovery even occurred in the French textile industry at the end of 1847. The regents of the Bank of France decided on 27 December 1847 to restore the four per cent interest rate and the authoritative *Revue des Deux Mondes* claimed in December 1847 that the only serious problem confronting France was the situation in Switzerland.[88] At the beginning of 1848, according to Philippe Vigier, 'a near total political calm' reigned in the Alpine region, as in the rest of provincial France.[89]

The crisis, though, was far from over. In the countryside, agricultural workers were often still unemployed or underemployed, and urban unemployment remained at unprecedently high levels. The number of electors qualified to vote through their tax contributions had declined because of the economic crisis and because of a reform of the business tax known as the *patente*. For instance, in Paris there were 18,138 electors in 1842 but only 15,991 in 1846, so a significant number had suffered a loss of political rights and of the social status associated with those rights.[90] Moreover, this loss had occurred at a time when France was entering a period of political crisis.

The loss of moral authority

By February 1848, the government headed by François Guizot, and even King Louis-Philippe and the Orleanist regime, had to a substantial degree lost their moral credibility and their legitimacy as far as French public opinion was concerned. From 1830, the July monarchy had been repeatedly challenged in political caricatures, novels and historical works. The Guizot government, grain merchants and the rich generally were widely thought to be at least partly responsible for the economic crisis of 1845–8 and for its social consequences, while Guizot's foreign policies were repeatedly branded as 'unpatriotic'. Meanwhile, support for parliamentary reform gathered momentum and found expression in the extraordinarily successful reform banquet campaign of 1847–8. A series of scandals, which suggested that corruption and decadence characterised not just the political system, but the entire Orleanist elite, intensified the impact of this campaign. Hence, when the reform banquet campaign led to the popular explosion in Paris of 22–4 February 1848, the July monarchy collapsed like a house of cards.

Disappointment with the relatively conservative outcome of the July 1830 revolution in France, and the repressive character of government policies between 1830 and 1835, encouraged political caricaturists such as Charles Philipon and Honoré Daumier to undermine Louis-Philippe's moral credibility. For instance, they depicted the king as an assassin of French liberty, as a doctor bleeding the French nation, as a Judas betraying the French constitution and France, as a pear tree watered by blood and surrounded by piles of corpses, and as a bloated 'Gargantua' seated on a toilet-throne and gorging on the tributes of his subjects while excreting honours, decorations and positions to miniature officials. Similarly, Daumier personified the July monarchy in the fictional character of Robert Macaire who, in his various guises of corrupt banker, feverish speculator, hypocritical politician, quack doctor and dishonest lawyer, allegedly represented the immorality of the regime.[91] The 1835 Press Laws restrained such attacks, but in that year publication began of Alexis de Tocqueville's *De la Démocratie en Amérique*. This highly influential work by implication drew attention to the relative lack of personal liberty and democracy in France. The novels of Eugène Sue, notably *Les Mystères de Paris* (1842–3) and *Le Juif errant* (1844–5), provided more direct critiques of contemporary French society by focusing on current social problems and by suggesting socialist remedies. While no socialist, Honoré de Balzac, in such novels as *Splendeurs et misères des courtisanes* (1846) and *Le Cousin Pons* (1847), portrayed the cynicism, corruption and ruthless ambition which he saw all around him.[92] Cheap editions and serialisation in newspapers gave these and other works a wide readership.

Histories of the revolutionary and Napoleonic periods helped to keep the revolution and Napoleon alive in the national memory, and to suggest that in comparison the July monarchy lacked idealism, patriotism and glory. Between January and March 1847 publication began of histories of the French Revolution by Louis Blanc, Jules Michelet and Alphonse de Lamartine. Contemporaries almost unanimously regarded these histories, and their impact on French public opinion, as having been one of the causes of the February 1848 revolution.[93]

The economic crisis which hit France from 1845 was widely blamed on government policies, on speculation and hoarding by grain merchants, and more generally on the egoism of the rich. The government stood accused of having encouraged speculation in railway shares[94] and of having failed to respond to the economic crisis in an effective and humane manner. According to popular assumptions, essential food items had a moral or 'just' price. It was generally assumed that the poor, like everybody else, had a fundamental right to live, a right to subsistence. Human suffering, particularly on the part of women and children, and the participation of women and children in many economic protests and disturbances, were considered by many to be both shocking and shameful. Relief efforts by employers, private individuals, local authorities and charitable organisations contrasted with the alleged inaction and indifference on the part of the government and the reigning dynasty.

Foreign policy

The revolutionary and Napoleonic periods had bequeathed France an ambiguous legacy in the field of foreign affairs. Memories of revolutionary wars of liberation, of glorious military victories, and of 'la Grande Nation' dominating most of the European continent clashed with memories of the stupendous human and material costs of war, of the popular resistance to the French in the Iberian peninsula, Russia and elsewhere, and of France's eventual defeat and humiliation at the hands of a coalition of conservative European powers. After 1815, the Vienna Treaties were rejected virtually unanimously across the French political spectrum. It was claimed that France had been unjustifiably deprived of her 'natural frontiers' by the loss of the left bank of the Rhine, Savoy and Nice, that the national aspirations of the peoples of Europe had been ignored, and that the 1815 principles of legitimacy and the balance of power were ideologically opposed to the revolutionary principles of liberty and popular sovereignty. Such attitudes encouraged hostility towards the victors of 1815 (Austria, Britain, Prussia and Russia), rejection of the territorial settlement of 1815, and sympathy for the so-called oppressed nations, especially the Poles and the Italians. The status of their country as a great power, and its ability to accomplish territorial expansion comparable to that of Russia, Britain or the United States, also became sensitive issues for the French. Yet at the same time a widely-held view prevailed that peace was a precondition for economic prosperity and would prevent the country's domination by the army. Also, wars and rumours of war were associated with the political violence and social upheaval of the 1790s. The revolution of July 1830 added another dimension, by apparently aligning the Orleanist regime with the forces of liberalism, if not of revolution. French diplomatic and military support for the secession of Belgium from the United Kingdom of the Netherlands, 1830–2, seemed to confirm this alignment, but thereafter the foreign policies of Louis-Philippe's governments remained resolutely pacific, with the exception of French military conquest and expansion in Algeria and of the Middle East policy of Thiers in 1840.

With left-wing parliamentary support, Thiers formed a government with himself as Minister of Foreign Affairs on 1 March 1840. He attempted to pursue a 'nationalist' foreign policy by supporting Mehemet Ali, the ruler of Egypt, in his bid to wrest control of Syria from the Turkish Sultan. The other main European powers, Austria, Britain, Prussia and Russia, backed Turkey by signing a convention in London on 15 July 1840 which threatened Mehemet Ali with military action unless he withdrew from northern Syria. In an atmosphere of mounting national hysteria in France, Thiers continued to back Mehemet Ali and instituted various war measures. However, the diplomatic isolation of France, the military weakness of Mehemet Ali, and the apparent prospect of France having to fight Austria, Britain, Prussia, Russia and Turkey simultaneously, led a frightened Louis-Philippe to force Thiers to resign and to replace him with François Guizot.

In the government formed on 29 October 1840, Guizot, besides in effect being the Prime Minister, was also Minister for Foreign Affairs, a post he retained until 23 February 1848. Between those dates, Guizot thus assumed the responsibility and the blame for France's foreign policies. Guizot opposed the policy of Thiers in the Middle East: it had caused France's diplomatic isolation and had threatened French military action in a conflict in which France's true national interests were not directly involved. Also, he considered that the increasing reliance of Thiers on extreme nationalist and left-wing parliamentary support had potentially threatened French political stability, while the belligerence of Thiers had dangerously inflamed the French newspaper press and French public opinion. Arguably, this was a sensible and realistic analysis, but critics claimed that Guizot had betrayed an ally, capitulated to the conservative European powers, and been swayed by conservative fears of the economic cost and revolutionary potential of war. In contrast to Thiers, Guizot presented himself as a man of peace, and he deliberately cultivated good relations with Britain, symbolised by his unusually cordial personal relations with the British Foreign Secretary, Lord Aberdeen, and by the success of three meetings between Queen Victoria and Louis-Philippe in 1843, 1844 and 1845. However, the so-called Franco–British *entente cordiale* was not popular in France. French opinion tended to view Britain as the hereditary enemy, the principal economic and colonial rival, the chief architect of the French defeats of 1814 and 1815, and as the most oppressive example in western Europe of aristocratic rule and capitalist exploitation. In any case, the *entente cordiale* was never very cordial, as was amply testified by Franco–British rivalry in Spain, Portugal, Greece, Egypt and North Africa. Guizot refused to ratify a treaty granting British warships the right to search French ships suspected of involvement in the slave trade. Also, Britain and France failed to co-operate over such issues as a war between Montevideo and Buenos Aires and relations with the United States. Any suspicion of subservience to Britain, notably over Guizot's agreement in September 1844 to pay an indemnity to George Pritchard (a British missionary allegedly mistreated by the French authorities in Tahiti), provoked a storm of outraged protest in France. The *entente cordiale* effectively ended in June 1846, when Lord John Russell succeeded Sir Robert Peel as Prime Minister and Lord Palmerston succeeded Aberdeen at the Foreign Office. At the British Embassy in Paris, Russell and Palmerston replaced Lord Cowley, a supporter of the *entente cordiale*, with the Marquess of Normanby, who willingly shared Palmerston's robust attitudes towards France. What finally ended the *entente cordiale*, though, were the so-called 'Spanish marriages'.

After a marriage between Queen Isabella of Spain and Prince Leopold of Saxe-Coburg had been discouraged by the British government so as not to damage Anglo-French relations, in August 1846 Guizot and Louis-Philippe arranged with the Spanish Court two marriages: a marriage between Queen Isabella of Spain and her cousin the Duke of Cadiz, and a marriage between the queen's sister, the Infanta Luisa Fernanda, heiress presumptive to the Spanish throne, and the duc de Montpensier, the youngest son of Louis-Philippe. Guizot believed the 'Spanish marriages' represented a great triumph, scoring revenge for 1840, consolidating French predominance in Madrid, and personally winning him political prestige. However, in Britain politicians and newspapers condemned the 'Spanish marriages' as a betrayal of the *entente cordiale*, as contrary to previous French undertakings and as a threat to British influence and interests in Spain, while in France the opposition press attacked the marriages as an example of old-fashioned dynastic diplomacy in which the family ambitions of the House of Orléans counted for more than the national interests of France. It was also pointed out that the Guizot government, having boasted for years that it had achieved good relations with Britain, now apparently gloried in the rupture of the British alliance.[95]

For months the question as to whether or not the offspring of Montpensier and the Spanish Infanta might have succession rights to the Spanish throne disrupted Anglo-French relations and influenced French diplomacy. Guizot's anxiety that Austria, Prussia and Russia should not side with Britain against France over the Montpensier marriage led him to align France diplomatically with those states which French public opinion generally associated with repression, political backwardness and the dismemberment of Poland. Thus Guizot protested in the mildest possible terms against the Austrian annexation of Cracow in November 1846. The treaties of 1815 had recognised Cracow as an independent and separate state, and in France Cracow was generally viewed as the last remnant of an independent Poland and as the potential nucleus of a reconstituted and free Poland. Guizot's tacit acceptance of the annexation of Cracow was therefore condemned almost universally in France as condoning the breach of an international treaty, as betraying the cause of Polish independence, and as stemming from the rupture in Anglo-French relations. Anglo-French relations further deteriorated in February 1847, when Guizot in a parliamentary debate misrepresented the content of one of Normanby's diplomatic despatches concerning the Montpensier marriage.[96]

In addition to the breakdown of the *entente cordiale* between Britain and France, Guizot could also be blamed for arranging a marriage for Queen Isabella which rapidly turned out to be disastrous, and for aligning France with the most conservative elements in Spanish politics who, from October 1847, ruled Spain under Narvaez through a virtual military dictatorship. Similarly, Guizot's policies towards Switzerland coincided with those of Metternich, the Austrian Chancellor, who personified political reaction for the French Left. Like Metternich, Guizot backed the league of conservative Swiss cantons known as the *Sonderbund* in their opposition to Swiss radical demands for a strong Federal Diet and the expulsion of the Jesuits from Switzerland. Guizot attempted to support the *Sonderbund* through Great Power mediation or a Great Power conference, but Palmerston successfully sabotaged Guizot's initiatives and, after a brief civil war (October to November 1847), the radical cantons defeated and dissolved the *Sonderbund*, expelled the Jesuits and eventually established a stronger federal constitution in Switzerland. In France the Catholic Swiss cantons were supported only by Legitimists and Catholic conservatives and by such newspapers as *Le Journal des Débats* (conservative), *L'Union monarchique* (Legitimist) and *L'Univers* (Catholic). The two latter newspapers organised subscriptions in aid of the *Sonderbund*. Contributors included Catholic bishops and clergy together with Letgitimist grandees such as the duc de Blacas, the vicomte de Chateaubriand, the vicomte de Falloux, the baron Hyde de Neuville, the comte de Montalembert and the duc de Noailles. Otherwise, Guizot's support for the *Sonderbund* antagonised French public opinion, aligned himself and his government once again with the forces of reaction at home and abroad, further strained France's diplomatic relations with Britain, and ended in total failure. Hence Guizot's policy towards Switzerland was attacked in a wide range of French newspapers and in a series of speeches in the Chamber of Deputies.[97]

Setbacks in foreign policy might have been compensated by successes in Algeria, such as the capture on 23 December 1847 of Abd-el-Kader, who for years had led a series of daring and successful attacks against the French. He was brought to France at the end of December 1847 and in January 1848 was imprisoned with his family in Fort Lamalgue. However, this triumph excited a muted response in France. Apart from the official government newspaper, *Le Moniteur*, which stressed the 'glorious' contribution of Louis-Philippe's sons to what France had achieved in North Africa, and the consistently pro-government *Journal des Débats*, *Le Courrier français* alone among Paris newspapers expressed joy that the rebel leader had been captured.[98] The French conquest of Algeria had been stained by too many atrocities, such as the incident on 19 June 1845 when French troops under Colonel Pélissier, attempting to smoke out Arabs who had hidden in caves, killed over five hundred men, women and children, or the massacre on 24 April 1846 of nearly three hundred French soldiers who had been captured by Abd-el-Kader.

Marshal Bugeaud (Governor General of Algeria, December 1840 to June 1847) and the French military authorities in Algeria had made the situation worse by their unapologetic and unrepentant defence of their tactics and behaviour and by their resistance to the introduction of an independent civilian administration in the colony. The human and material costs of the seemingly endless military operations in Algeria further dampened enthusiasm in France for Algeria. Opponents of the Orléans dynasty criticised the prominent Algerian roles of Louis-Philippe's sons, particularly the duc d'Aumale, who eventually succeeded Bugeaud as Governor General in September 1847. Hence French policies in Algeria were condemned in parliament, not just by republicans, but also by relatively moderate opposition deputies, notably Alphonse de Lamartine and

Alexis de Tocqueville. Thus French policies in Algeria, as well as Guizot's conduct of foreign policy, contributed substantially to the unpopularity of the Guizot government and of the July monarchy.

The reform banquet campaign

The general parliamentary election of August 1846 gave the Guizot government a secure majority in the Chamber of Deputies. With the government still very unpopular, dissatisfaction with the existing electoral and parliamentary system came to a head. During the autumn of 1846 a majority in thirteen *conseils généraux* voted declarations of support for electoral and parliamentary reform.[99] In January 1847, a former supporter of Guizot who had become an opposition deputy, Prosper Duvergier de Hauranne, published a pamphlet, *De la Réforme parlementaire et de la réforme électorale*, which claimed: 'Representative government is in danger. It is no longer, as in 1830, threatened by violence, but undermined by corruption.'[100] He argued that the main problem was the number of 'députés fonctionnaires', for as long as they formed two-thirds of the government's majority among the deputies, the Chamber of Deputies could never be 'indépendante et pure'.[101] A further problem was the restriction of the parliamentary electorate to those who fulfilled the high tax qualifications, a problem which a recent reduction in the *patente* business tax had exacerbated.[102] The solutions were to decrease the number of 'députés fonctionnaires' and to increase the number of electors, since allegedly the larger the electorate, the more difficult it would be to corrupt.

On 6 March 1847 Duvergier de Hauranne formally proposed in the Chamber of Deputies that the tax qualification for parliamentary voters should be halved (payment of 100 rather than 200 francs in direct taxes per year) and that the range of non-fiscal voter qualifications should be expanded, which would have approximately increased the electorate from 241,000 to 441,000. At the same time, the number of deputies was to be increased from 459 to 538. The Guizot government opposed even discussion of this comparatively modest proposal, but was overruled. On 23 March Duvergier de Hauranne defended his proposals in the Chamber of Deputies and was supported by, among others, Gustave de Beaumont and Odilon Barrot. In reply, Duchâtel (Minister of the Interior) argued that the country did not want these reforms, which anyway could be adopted only immediately before parliamentary elections. Guizot was even more dismissive: it was much better that the right to vote should be based on political ability ('capacité politique') rather than on numbers, and universal (manhood) suffrage was not on the agenda ('Il n'y a pas de jour pour le suffrage universel'). Guizot simply did not believe in universal manhood suffrage, but instead maintained throughout his life that political power should be in the hands of the wealthy, the educated and those with specific qualifications or 'capacités'.[103] At the end of the parliamentary debate, the proposals for electoral reform were rejected on 26 March by the unprecedentedly high figure of 252 votes to 154. The same day

Charles de Rémusat tabled a motion that deputies should be disbarred from becoming 'fonctionnaires' while they were deputies and for a year thereafter. Debated between 19 and 21 April, this motion was similarly rejected, though by a smaller margin, 219 voting for (of whom 129 were *fonctionnaires*) and 170 voting against (of whom 34 were *fonctionnaires*).[104] This was the eighteenth failed parliamentary attempt since 1830 to secure the exclusion of 'functionnaires' from parliament.[105] As far as the opposition was concerned, the Guizot government was now the victim of inertia and immobilism, totally rejecting all reform proposals. One opposition deputy summed up the situation on 27 April with the words, 'Nothing, nothing, nothing!' ('Rien, rien, rien!'). Opposition newspapers seized on this phrase and gave it a wide currency.

Following the defeat of the two parliamentary reform bills, liberal and moderate republican deputies met during May 1847 to organise a campaign outside parliament. In order to evade restrictions on public meetings, they adopted the idea of public-subscription banquets. Influenced by the recent success of Richard Cobden's Anti-Corn Law League in Britain, the aim of these banquets was to unite different elements of the opposition in a single-issue campaign for parliamentary reform, provide a public platform for speeches, and attract nationwide publicity and a nationwide mobilisation of public opinion.[106] On 8 June, at a meeting attended by both opposition deputies and by editors of opposition newspapers (*Le Charivari*, *Le Constitutionnel*, *Le Courrier français*, *La Démocratie pacifique*, *Le National* and *Le Siècle*), it was agreed to form a Comité central des électeurs de l'opposition du département de la Seine, which would organise a reform banquet in Paris in early July and a subsequent series of reform banquets in the provinces.[107]

The first reform banquet was held in Paris during the evening of 9 July 1847 in a marquee situated in a public garden near Montmartre known as Château Rouge. Members of the left-wing opposition, who wanted an extension of the parliamentary franchise (Odilon Barrot, Gustave de Beaumont, Duvergier de Hauranne and Léon de Malleville), and republicans, who wanted the introduction of manhood suffrage (Hippolyte Carnot, Louis-Antoine Garnier-Pagès, Charles Pagnerre and Athanase Recurt), launched the campaign. To avoid any public disorder, invitations to the banquet were sent out only to parliamentary deputies sympathetic to reform and to those already qualified to vote, and the subscription was set at the relatively high level of ten francs. Nearly twelve hundred people, including eighty-six deputies, attended the banquet. The Marseillaise and other revolutionary songs were sung, toasts were proposed and speeches delivered. Instead of a toast to the king, which was notionally obligatory at public meetings, there were toasts to the sovereignty of the nation, the revolution of 1830, electoral and parliamentary reform, the city of Paris, and to the improvement of the condition of the working classes. Among the speakers, Barrot claimed that the ideals of July 1830 had been betrayed and that the Guizot government was corrupt; and Pagnerre appealed to all who wanted reform to join the campaign and for committees to be formed all over France to organise similar banquets. Duvergier de Hauranne compared the situation in France in 1847 with that at the end of the Restoration monarchy, while Beaumont demanded social as well as political reforms. The proceedings attracted widespread publicity in the newspapers and provided a good start to the reform banquet campaign. There were, however, a number of notable absentees, including opposition deputies such as Dufaure, Lamartine, Rémusat, Thiers and Tocqueville, all of whom had personal reservations about the reform banquet campaign,[108] and radical republicans such as Louis Blanc, Marc Caussidière, Ferdinand Flocon and Alexandre Ledru-Rollin, who feared that the occasion would be too moderate.

After the Château Rouge banquet, numerous reform banquet committees were formed in the provinces, usually with some contact with the Comité central in Paris, which could recommend a speaker and advise on organisation. The first provincial reform banquet was held at Colmar on 8 August 1847, and until February 1848 there followed some sixty provincial reform banquets. The banquets were generally held in the afternoon in a variety of places, including a *château* (Pas-de-Calais, 15 November), a hotel (Compiègne, 21 November) and industrial premises (Saint-Denis, 14 December). The committees which organised the banquets usually included local notables who opposed the Guizot government and supported reform such as members of the departmental *conseil général*, mayors, municipal councillors, National Guard officers, newspaper editors and lawyers. Several of the organisers of the Château Rouge banquet participated in the provincial banquet campaign – Beaumont, Duvergier de Hauranne, Garnier-Pagès, Pagnerre, Recurt and, most prominently, Odilon Barrot. Also prominent were two opposition deputies, Isaac Crémieux, a champion of Jewish causes, and Drouyn de Lhuys, a former diplomat who had attacked Guizot over the Pritchard indemnity.[109] Politically, participants in the reform banquet campaign included members of the constitutional or Dynastic Left and of the Centre Left, moderate and left-wing republicans and, at least in one instance (Condom, 28 November), Legitimists.

Republicans and Legitimists did sometimes co-operate politically out of a common hostility to Orleanism, for instance in the August 1846 parliamentary elections in the Pyrénées-Orientales. However, the association of republicanism with radicalism and even socialism meant that such alliances were fragile and easily broken, as in Toulouse during 1846 and 1847; and the reform banquets were generally too radical for most Legitimists.[110] In addition, either from caution, a distrust of radicalism or a desire for political independence, several leading politicians refused to chair or even attend reform banquets. Invitations from banquet organisers were rejected by Lamartine (Saint Quentin, Autun, Lyons, Amiens and Rouen), Monier de La Sizeranne (Valence), Léon de Malleville (Albi) and Dufaure (Saintes), which could lead, as at Autun and Albi, to radicals taking over the banquet.[111]

The more radical banquets included those of Le Mans (10 August), Autun (27 October), Lille (7 November), Dijon (21 November), Chalon-sur-Saône (19 December) and Limoges (2 January 1848). At Le Mans there were several references to the overthrow of the monarchy on 10 August 1792, the Marseillaise was sung and money was collected for French political prisoners. At Autun, Ulysse Pic, editor of a left-wing republican newspaper, *L'Union libérale* of Nièvre, in a fiery speech denounced in turn monarchy, aristocracy, moderate as well as conservative politicians, the Jesuits and even private property. The speech was so extreme that it attracted an energetic rebuttal from Lamartine in his Mâcon newspaper, *Le Bien public*, on 14 November. At Lille the inclusion on the platform of the republican, Ledru-Rollin, and the absence of a toast to the constitutional monarchy, led Odilon Barrot and other more moderate speakers to withdraw at the last minute. Consequently, Ledru-Rollin could unopposed deliver a speech in favour of granting political rights to the workers, a speech which, rather surprisingly, Lamartine warmly endorsed.[112] At Dijon, the organisers ensured an exclusively radical banquet by inviting only radicals to attend and by fielding a list of republican speakers, including Etienne Arago, Ferdinand Flocon, Louis Blanc and Ledru-Rollin.[113] Louis Blanc outlined his socialist schemes for the organisation of labour while Ledru-Rollin declared his commitment to the introduction of direct manhood suffrage.[114] At Chalon-sur-Saône, Flocon elaborated on the declaration of the rights of man drawn up by Robespierre in 1793 and collectively condemned Thiers, Barrot and Guizot ('all accomplices of the same crime'), while Ledru-Rollin repeated his commitment to manhood suffrage, castigated those who wanted to retain some sort of property franchise, and defended the Jacobin Terror of 1793–4.[115] Finally, at Limoges a series of relatively obscure speakers, apart from the radical lawyer Théodore Bac, demanded a national system of education, manhood suffrage and the organisation of labour.[116]

The reform banquet campaign rapidly took hold in many parts of France. Attendance figures ranged from a few hundred to approximately 1,700 (Rouen, 25 December).[117] In aggregate, over 20,000 attended the reform banquets, and in addition there were thousands of spectators. According to the moderate republican Paris newspaper *Le National*, 107 deputies in some way publicly declared their support for the reform banquet campaign.[118] Accounts of the proceedings and texts of the speeches were normally published in newspapers and sometimes in pamphlets as well, thereby reaching a wider audience. Local opposition newspapers often played a key role in organising the banquets, such as *Le Courrier de la Sarthe* (Le Mans), *Le Courrier du Bas-Rhin* (Strasbourg), *L'Echo de Vésone* (Périgueux), *L'Union libérale* (Autun), *Le Messager du Nord* (Lille), *Le Patriote des Alpes* (Grenoble), *Le Journal de Rouen* (Pétit-Quevilly) and *Le Patriote de Saône-et-Loire* (Chalon-sur-Saône). Among Paris newspapers *Le National*, *La Patrie* and *Le Siècle*, in particular, provided extensive reports of most of the banquets. Altogether, the reform banquet campaign gave a fresh impetus to the political role and influence of newspapers. It was a nationwide campaign, though more banquets were held in eastern than in western France, with a particular concentration in the north-east, the Paris region, and the regions of the Rhône and the Saône, reflecting local strengths of the opposition press. Reform banquets were held in Paris, Lyons, Rouen and Lille, but not in Marseilles, Bordeaux or Nantes. Radicalism emerged as early as 10 August, with the reform banquet at Le Mans, but became much more prominent from the end of October. Figures such as the republican Ledru-Rollin, the socialist Louis Blanc and the Fourierist Victor Considérant, who had at first viewed the campaign as too conservative, began to attend banquets and give speeches. This sharpened and publicised the division between those who wanted to reform the existing constitution, and those who wanted universal manhood suffrage and possibly a republic and socialist measures as well.

Enthusiasm for the reform banquet campaign was not universal. The novelist Gustave Flaubert wrote privately of the Rouen reform banquet of 25 December 1847: 'Quel gout! Quelle cuisine! Quels vins! Et quels discours!' [119] Yet the reform banquet campaign mobilised public opinion behind the cause of electoral and parliamentary reform as well as publicising more radical demands for manhood suffrage, a republican constitution, and measures to improve the lives of workers and peasants. Hence the reform banquets have been described as 'the *cahiers de doléances* of democracy'.[120] In the longer term, participation in the reform banquet campaign related to political participation in 1848. All members of the Provisional Government (24 February to 9 May 1848) had had some involvement in the campaign, except François Arago (who had been ill) and a worker known as Albert. One hundred and thirty-four members of the Constituent Assembly, the national parliament elected in 1848, had delivered a speech to at least one reform banquet, and many of those appointed to official posts at both a national and local level during 1848 had also participated in the campaign.[121]

Corruption, scandals and the parliamentary session

Corruption featured as a recurring theme in the speeches of the reform banquet campaign. Corruption was said to have characterised the general parliamentary election of August 1846, and where these cases were pursued in the courts, some defendants had been found guilty. During 1847 a series of scandals erupted which seemed to confirm the view, long held by critics and opponents of the July monarchy, that the whole system in France was corrupt. On 12 May *La Presse* revealed that Guizot had been secretly subsidising a newspaper, *L'Epoque*, with over a million francs. On 17 July the Chamber of Peers found Lieutenant-General Despans-Cubières and Jean-Baptiste Teste guilty of corrupt practices in connection with an application for a government concession to exploit a salt mine. The newspapers were transfixed – both Despans-Cubières and Teste were peers and former government ministers, while Teste in addition was a senior judge in the Civil Court of Appeal. Even more sensational was the murder on 18 August of the duchesse de Choiseul-Praslin by her husband and his death in prison six days later from self-administered poison. The newspapers gave prolonged and saturation coverage to the unfolding of this drama, and to all the associated documents. There were verbatim accounts of interrogations, medical reports, police and witness statements, and pronouncements by Chancellor Pasquier. The Choiseul-Praslin affair was exceptional, but throughout 1848 a series of court cases, reported in the newspaper press, revealed greed and immorality among members of the grandest families of France. There were also some spectacular family tragedies, such as the suicide on 2 November of the comte Bresson, the recently-appointed French ambassador to Naples. Altogether, by the end of 1847 public respect for the Orleanist regime and its elite had been substantially eroded while the elite itself had lost much of its collective self-confidence, as the regime and its personnel seemed to be drowning in a sea of corruption and immorality.[122] The prevailing 'malaise des esprits' is illustrated by the reflections on 1847 of a friend of the Guizot government, the baron de Viel-Castel, in his private journal on 31 December:

> A sad year, marked by so many disasters, so many catastrophes, so many public and private crimes, and which will go down in history as having been more sombre than years witnessing the outbreak of great and bloody revolutions, because during this year the festering sores of a corrupt society have been revealed.[123]

The new parliamentary session opened on 28 December 1847 with the opposition greatly encouraged by the success of the reform banquet campaign, while reverses in foreign policy, the economic crisis, scandals and corruption, and mounting evidence of the unpopularity of the Guizot administration, had undermined the morale of government supporters. Louis-Philippe's speech to the assembled members of both chambers, amidst the customary banalities, implied that the existing constitution was perfectly satisfactory and that the reform banquet campaign had stirred up 'blind or hostile passions' ('des passions ennemies ou aveugles'). This phrase, 'blind or hostile passions', was taken out of context and given maximum publicity so as to suggest that the attitude of the king and his ministers towards electoral and parliamentary reform was totally dismissive. After the success of the reform banquet campaign and the votes of the *conseils généraux* of twenty-three departments in favour of reform, this dismissive attitude seemed to the opposition to be provocative and gratuitously insulting, and to involve the monarch one-sidedly in partisan politics.[124]

At this time a number of individuals, including the comte de Montalivet (*Intendant* of the Civil List), Marshal Gérard, the baron Dupin and the comte de Rambuteau (prefect of the Seine) conveyed their fears and concerns to the king. Louis-Philippe, however, continued to support Guizot and his policies, firmly believing that Guizot should stay in office as long as a majority of the deputies backed him, and recoiling at the prospect of an administration headed by a leading member of the opposition, such as Thiers or the comte Molé. Louis-Philippe also believed that as long as he acted constitutionally he should be safe, and he discounted suggestions that the Paris National Guard might be unreliable. Seventy-four years old and not in the best of health, Louis-Philippe was further disadvantaged by the death on 31 December of his sister, Mme Adélaïde, who had, for many years, been a devoted confidante and adviser. The Court went into mourning and social isolation until 25 January 1848, while the cancellation of balls and receptions added to the economic despondency of Paris.[125] The remains of Mme Adélaïde were buried at Dreux on 5 January, so that a royal funeral, appropriately enough, marked the beginning of the year 1848 in France.[126]

Louis-Philippe's speech from the throne was first discussed by the Chamber of Peers in no less than eight sessions (10–18 January 1848). Guizot's Italian policy was attacked as allegedly too pro-Austrian, too lukewarm towards Pope Pius IX (then regarded as a liberal) and as a betrayal of the July monarchy's liberal origins; and in an emotional and well-received speech (11 January), Montalembert deplored the triumph of radicalism in Switzerland and warned of the dangers of a resurgent radicalism within France.

The Chamber of Deputies began its session on 21 January by discussing yet another personal and financial scandal associated with the Guizot administration, the so-called Petit affair. On 27 January Tocqueville delivered a famously prophetic speech. He enlarged on his fears for the future, on account of the embrace of socialist ideas by the working class, the degradation of public morality, and the wind of revolution that he discerned blowing throughout Europe. 'We are at this moment sleeping on a volcano', he told his fellow-deputies; and he urged Guizot and his ministerial colleagues: 'in God's name, change the spirit of the government; for, I repeat, that spirit will lead you to the abyss.'[127]

Two days later, Lamartine roundly condemned Guizot's foreign policies: 'Since the Spanish marriages, France has had to become, contrary to her nature and to centuries of tradition, papal in Rome, clerical in Berne, Austrian in Piedmont, Russian in Cracow, French nowhere, counter-revolutionary everywhere!'[128] Several newspapers praised Lamartine's 'eloquent condemnation'[129] and his accusations were repeated by Hippolyte Carnot (31 January), Thiers (2 February) and Odilon Barrot (3 February). The attack then switched to the reform banquet campaign. Speaker after speaker argued that the campaign had been a perfectly legal form of protest and had not threatened public order, that the allegation of 'blind and hostile passions' had been unjustified and irresponsible, and that public opinion supported the objective of eliminating political corruption through electoral and parliamentary reform. Again, the big guns of the opposition blazed away – Duvergier de Hauranne and Crémieux on 7 February, Odilon Barrot on 8 February, Ledru-Rollin on 9 February and Lamartine on 11 February.

In contrast to the divisions which had emerged during the reform banquet campaign, the diverse strands of the parliamentary opposition were now remarkably united. A motion on 12 February to suppress the words 'blind' and 'hostile' from the text of the speech from the throne attracted 185 votes, including those of Legitimists (Berryer, Falloux, Genoude, La Rochejaquelein), liberals (Dufaure, Emile de Girardin, Tocqueville), members of the Dynastic Left (Odilon Barrot,

Bethmont, Chambolle, Crémieux, Drouyn de Lhuys, Léon Faucher, Georges and Oscar Lafayette) and Centre Left (Duvergier de Hauranne, Ferdinand de Lasteyrie, Léon de Malleville, Rémusat, Thiers), and republicans (François Arago, Carnot, Courtais, Dupont de l'Eure, Garnier-Pagès, Ledru-Rollin, Marie), as well as independent opposition deputies such as Lamartine. Guizot bravely and patiently attempted to answer his critics, but the sustained and relentless onslaught exhausted him, demoralised his supporters and fed the opposition newspaper press with an abundance of anti-Guizot material. Meanwhile, trouble was looming on another front.

The reform banquet of the twelfth *arrondissement*

The reform banquet campaign had begun to run out of steam by the end of December 1847. Nevertheless, during that month a group of radical officers of the Twelfth Legion of the Paris National Guard decided to organise a reform banquet to be held in the twelfth *arrondissement* of Paris, one of the poorest districts of the capital. On 16 December a meeting of supporters of the proposed banquet elected an organising committee, mostly composed of National Guard officers. Two weeks later, on 30 December, the Prefect of Police rejected an application to hold the banquet. The organising committee decided to go ahead regardless and hold the banquet on 19 January 1848. Invitations to attend were sent out to opposition deputies representing the department of the Seine. Although some members of the organising committee were reluctant to defy the authorities, on 10 January the Prefect of Police was informed that the banquet would take place nine days later. When the Prefect of Police, on behalf of the government, repeated his prohibition, the organising committee published a protest in the moderate republican Paris newspaper, Le National, on 18 January. The protest claimed that the proposed banquet did not contravene any law and that the committee regarded the prefect's decision as a purely arbitrary act with no legal validity. At the same time a radical peer who supported the twelfth *arrondissement* banquet, the comte d'Alton-Shée, asked Duchâtel, the Minister of the Interior, in the Chamber of Peers if the government recognised that citizens had a right to hold political banquets and if the holding of previous political banquets had simply been tolerated. Duchâtel replied that the government did indeed have the right to prohibit or to permit reform banquets, that previous reform banquets had been tolerated by the government, and that it was on his orders that the Prefect of Police had forbidden the twelfth *arrondissement* banquet. The organising committee responded by maintaining their determination to hold a reform banquet and by enlisting the support of opposition deputies, including Garnier-Pagès, Odilon-Barrot, Duvergier de Hauranne and Ledru-Rollin. The issue rapidly became a cause célèbre.

On 13 February approximately one hundred opposition deputies met in a room in the Café Durand in the Boulevard de la Madeleine. Marie, Chambolle, Drouyn-de-Lhuys and others argued for a mass resignation of opposition deputies, a proposal which Armand Marrast had suggested and which Emile de Girardin had supported in *La Presse*. Such action would have forced the government to have dissolved parliament and to have held new elections. However, Duvergier de Hauranne, Lamartine, Garnier-Pagès and Odilon Barrot opposed the idea, and the meeting agreed instead to form a new organising reform banquet committee, composed overwhelmingly of parliamentary deputies. The committee wanted to exclude working-class Parisians from the banquet, so at a meeting the following day it decided to double the banquet subscription from three to six francs, not to hold the banquet in the working-class twelfth *arrondissement*, and to restrict admission to those who were parliamentary electors. Subsequently, the committee arranged that the banquet should be held in premises in Chaillot, a suburb of Paris, on Tuesday 22 February (a working day, rather than a Sunday).

On 19 February a second meeting of opposition deputies, this time attended by over two hundred, rejected a proposal to abandon the banquet but agreed to the drafting and publication of a declaration designed to reduce the likelihood of violence. The declaration, drafted principally by Armand Marrast, was published on 21 February in the main opposition Paris newspapers (*Le Courrier français*, *La Démocratie pacifique*, *Le National*, *La Réforme* and *Le Siècle*). It stated that the objective was the legal and peaceful exercise of a constitutional right, namely the right of public assembly, and 'des dispositions qui éloignent toute cause de trouble et de tumulte' were proposed. The march before the banquet would take place in a district of Paris with broad streets, starting at the Place de la Madeleine and proceeding via the Champs Elysées to the site of the banquet at Chaillot. The procession was to be policed by unarmed members of the National Guard, and demonstrators were instructed not to shout any slogans or to wear any badge or symbol, so as to ensure a legal and peaceful protest. The committee even expressed the hope that every demonstrator would consider himself to be in the position of an official and responsible for the maintenance of order.

All this suggested the banquet committee wanted to avoid any violence, though the declaration was also an act of defiance likely to appeal to republicans such as Ledru-Rollin and left-wing radicals generally. Certainly, the government considered the invitation to National Guardsmen to participate in the demonstration in uniform, albeit unarmed, as provocative, since it constituted a usurpation of the government's sole responsibility to police demonstrations and to deploy the National Guard. The banquet committee was informed of the government's continued determination to prohibit the banquet. The committee responded by issuing another statement, which appeared in the evening edition of *La Patrie* on 21 February, insisting that it had no intention of usurping the government's authority over the National Guard. Nevertheless, the Prefect of Police issued an edict prohibiting the planned banquet and demonstration while General Jacqueminot, commander of the Paris National Guard, reminded guardsmen that they should not assemble as guardsmen without orders from their superiors.

During the late afternoon of 21 February, after the adjournment of proceedings in the Chamber of Deputies, opposition deputies met at Odilon Barrot's Paris residence. On 21 February *Le National* and *La Presse* had published a letter signed by ninety-two opposition deputies publicly declaring their intention to attend the twelfth *arrondissement* banquet. Now Odilon Barrot, supported by Chambolle, Thiers, Bethmont and Rémusat, urged them not to attend in order to avoid the risk of violence. The meeting agreed first that deputies would not attend the banquet and then that the banquet and the accompanying demonstration would be called off altogether. Only seventeen out of more than a hundred parliamentarians, including Alton-Shée, Duvergier de Hauranne, Lamartine and Malleville, voted for the banquet and the demonstration to go ahead.

Thus, having since July 1847 'tolerated' over sixty reform banquets, all of which had passed off peacefully, in December 1847 the Guizot government refused permission for a reform banquet in the twelfth *arrondissement* of Paris. Clearly, a reform banquet organised by a group of radical National Guard officers and held in a working-class district of Paris would have constituted a provocative challenge to the government. Yet the government maintained its prohibition even after the organisation and character of the projected banquet had become much less radical and threatening. The government claimed that it had a duty to preserve law and order and that it had every right to prohibit the banquet, while the supporters of the banquet argued that, in denying the right of peaceful protest, the government was acting illegally and unconstitutionally. The opposition deputies certainly wanted to avoid violence, as their arrangements for the proposed demonstration and banquet, and their ultimate decision to abandon the banquet, indicate. Similarly, the left-wing republicans associated with *La Réforme*, following the leadership of Louis Blanc and Ledru-Rollin, agreed that any provocative or violent action should be avoided; and *La Réforme* itself on 22 February urged its readers to be cautious and not to give the authorities any excuse for 'a bloody victory' ('un succès sanglant'). Even members of the revolutionary group, the Society of the Seasons, were ordered by their leaders, Albert and Lucien de La Hodde, not to take up arms.[130] However, this commitment to non-violence, so characteristic of French political culture prior to February 1848, was not shared by the working-class militants of Paris. They claimed a right of popular resistance to oppression as part of the revolutionary tradition of Paris since 1789.

Chapter 3

The February Revolution and the Provisional Government

The February Days

The February Days constituted, to a substantial extent, an insurrection of the Paris working class and of elements of the Paris petty bourgeoisie. Crucial roles were also played by the Paris National Guard and by Paris university students. Apart from the relatively weak Municipal Guard and the Paris military garrison, in Paris the defence of the government and ultimately of the regime itself depended upon the part-time militia known as the National Guard. The Paris National Guard was organised into twelve legions, one for each of the *arrondissements* of Paris, together with one cavalry legion. Each infantry legion tended to reflect the predominant political attitudes of its *arrondissement*. Thus the First, Tenth and Eleventh Legions, and the Cavalry Legion, mainly recruited from wealthy Parisians, tended to be conservative, whereas the Third, Eighth and Twelfth Legions, from working-class *arrondissements*, tended to be quite radical, the remaining legions having less pronounced political loyalties. Many guardsmen did not qualify to vote in parliamentary elections and had come to support an extension of the parliamentary franchise and the reform banquet campaign. Indeed, a group of radical Paris National Guard officers had provided the original initiative for the twelfth *arrondissement* banquet. Guard officers and many guardsmen had planned to participate in the reform banquet and demonstration, wearing their uniforms. The cancellation of the banquet and demonstration left many guardsmen feeling angry, betrayed and in no mood to defend the Guizot government or even the regime of Louis-Philippe.

Many Paris students felt equally betrayed and angry, and equally hostile to the Guizot government and the regime of Louis-Philippe. In contrast to Guizot, Paris students tended to identify with the allegedly oppressed nations of Europe, the Poles, the Italians and the Irish, and to revile the conservative regimes in Austria, Prussia, Russia and, to a lesser extent, Britain. According to the Paris student newspaper, *La Lanterne*, over 1,200 students on 22 February 1847 commemorated the anniversary of the Cracov insurrection.[1] Student enthusiasm had also come to focus on three professors at the Collège de France, Jules Michelet, Adam Mickiewicz and Edgar Quinet. Their radical ideas and treatment by the government had earned them the status of student heroes, and they had become the focus of a series of student protests. In May and June 1843 a course of lectures by Quinet and Michelet critical of the Jesuits occasioned student disturbances. Further student disturbances occurred the following year after the suspension of Mickiewicz by the government, which regarded his anti-clericalism, his idealisation of Napoleon and his fervour for Polish independence as subversive. In 1845 it was the turn of Quinet and Michelet to be branded as subversives for their radical lectures on Christianity and the French Revolution. When on 13 July 1845 the faculty of the Collège de France voted by seventeen to seven to back the two professors, students held a large demonstration in their honour. Quinet's course of lectures was nevertheless eventually cancelled in December 1845 by Salvandy, the Minister of Public Instruction, prompting more student demonstrations. In 1847, when a substitute delivered Quinet's lectures, student disruption forced the abandonment of the lecture programme. On 16 December 1847 Michelet began a new course of lectures on the French Revolution. After just three lectures, his ill-concealed anti-clerical and republican sympathies led the ministry to cancel his lectures and dismiss him from his chair on 2 January 1848. The following day some 3,000 students marched in protest to the Chamber of Deputies.[2] Michelet also issued protests, which were published in Paris newspapers,[3] and student demonstrations continued. On 5 January, nine Paris newspapers representing four different political views – republican, Fourierist, liberal and Legitimist – published the text of a student protest against the dismissal of Michelet, indicating support for the students on this issue across much of the political spectrum.[4] One of the newspapers, Le Siècle, commented that to dismiss a professor on account of student disorders was absurd, that the real reason was the radical content of Michelet's lectures, and that such arbitrary government action would be self-defeating. The newspaper subsequently argued that the administration of the Collège de France, not an individual professor such as Michelet, should be responsible for student discipline.[5]

During the afternoon of 6 January some two thousand students, shouting 'Vive Michelet!', marched from the Place du Panthéon to the Hôtel Flavacourt in the Rue des Postes (where Michelet lived), the Institut de France and to the editorial offices of Le National, La Réforme, Le Courrier français and La Démocratie pacifique. The editors of La Réforme sent Michelet a public letter the next day, protesting against his 'brutal', 'iniquitous', 'arbitrary' and 'provocative' dismissal, and expressing support and solidarity in his fight for 'liberty, truth and the rights of all'.[6] Michelet composed his own protest against his expulsion, which newspapers publicised.[7] Another march occurred during the afternoon of 3 February, when reportedly over three thousand students, organised by the two radical Paris newspapers, L'Avant-Garde and La Lanterne, proceeded from the Place du Panthéon to the Chamber of Deputies. They presented Adolphe Crémieux, a left-wing deputy, with a petition demanding justice in the name of educational freedom, which they considered to have been violated in the cases of Mickiewicz, Quinet and Michelet. The demonstrators returned to the Place du

Panthéon via, once more, the editorial offices of the four main Paris left-wing newspapers sympathetic to the students.[8]

Many students had welcomed the reform banquet campaign, and some had attended reform banquets, so it was not surprising that in December 1847 a group of Paris students tried to organise their own banquet, partly to demonstrate their solidarity with Quinet and Michelet. Police action frustrated student attempts to find a suitable locale for the proposed banquet, so eventually the students abandoned the project and backed instead the twelfth *arrondissement* banquet, for which they were given a certain number of tickets.[9] Some of the more radical students, associated with the editor of *L'Avant Garde*, fretted at what they saw as the over-cautious conservatism of the banquet's organisers after 15 February, and the eventual cancellation of the banquet on 21 February caused much student dismay, but Michelet's dismissal and the climax of the reform banquet campaign had brought student radicalism to a fever pitch. When a group of students meeting at the editorial offices of *L'Avant Garde* learnt after midnight that the banquet had been cancelled, they decided to go ahead with a demonstration anyway.

On the morning of 22 February, despite heavy rain, students assembled in the Place du Panthéon in the Latin Quarter prior to marching to the Place de la Madeleine to protest against the cancellation of the banquet. Joined by workers and several militants, the students set off after 10 am, singing the Marseillaise and the chorus from a currently popular opera, 'Les Girondins'. Arriving at the Place de la Madelaine at approximately 11 am, when the banquet demonstration had been planned to start, they joined a crowd of about fifteen hundred, many of whom had not realised that the demonstration and banquet had been cancelled. The demonstrators, now several thousand strong, moved off towards the Place de la Concorde and the Pont de la Concorde, the bridge across the Seine in front of the Chamber of Deputies. Brushing aside a few Municipal Guards and National Guards, they reached the Palais Bourbon, but the chamber was not yet in session and General Sébastiani, commander of the Paris military garrison, was able to force the crowd back to the Place de la Concorde with a squadron of cavalry and two battalions of infantry. However, violence broke out, particularly when mounted Municipal Guards charged demonstrators in the Place de la Concorde and demonstrators responded by throwing paving stones at soldiers and guardsmen. The Place de la Concorde was eventually cleared, but the demonstrators fanned out to other parts of Paris, throwing stones at guardsmen and soldiers and breaking into gunsmiths' shops as they passed. In the Champs-Elysée district, wooden chairs and omnibuses were set alight, gas street lights were smashed, and police stations and guard posts were attacked. At the same time, the construction of barricades began in the streets near the Place de la Concorde. Railings were torn down and used as missiles or as instruments for ripping up paving stones which, with other missiles, were thrown at buildings such as the Ministry of the Marine in the Rue de Rivoli and the Ministry of Foreign Affairs in the Boulevard des Capucines. Several contemporary observers emphasise the prominence, at least initially, of *gamins* or young males aged between about eleven and seventeen in the violence, though their role has tended to be downplayed by historians, presumably because *gamins* do not feature in official statistics.[10]

By 22 February the political initiative was passing from politicians to the street. Around 11 am opposition deputies met once more at Odilon Barrot's house to draw up a statement. They accused the government of having betrayed France's honour and interests, violated the constitution, perverted parliamentary government by systematic corruption, deprived citizens of a constitutional right and, through openly counter-revolutionary policies, of having called into question the achievements of two revolutions and of having provoked a 'perturbation profonde'. *Le National* published the text of the statement on 23 February but to no discernible effect. Similarly, when deputies met for their afternoon parliamentary session they discussed, not the crisis situation in Paris, but the draft of a bill concerning the Bank of Bordeaux. After the session, a group of deputies tried to persuade the Prefect of the Seine, the comte de Rambuteau, to convene a meeting of Paris municipal councillors, mayors, National Guard colonels and parliamentary deputies to tackle the crisis, but Rambuteau declined, stressing his allegiance to the king and his determination not to re-establish a revolutionary Paris commune.

Louis-Philippe himself remained confident that the disorders would not assume serious proportions and that all necessary security measures had been taken. Units of the National Guard were indeed ordered early in the afternoon of 22 February to occupy strategic points throughout Paris. However, many guardsmen failed to turn out, and some of those who did indicated their political sympathies by shouting 'Long live reform!', 'Down with Guizot!' and 'Down with Louis-Philippe!' This permitted disturbances to continue. The closure of Paris workshops freed thousands of workers to demonstrate and riot. Large crowds milled around singing revolutionary songs. Once more, gunsmiths' shops were raided and railings were dismantled to provide weapons and instruments with which to rip up paving stones from the streets. Many of the customs barriers surrounding Paris were set on fire. Street barricades were erected and several people were killed or injured in clashes between rioters and either regular soldiers or members of the National Guard.

Early in the morning of 23 February, a cold and rainy day, soldiers and guardsmen were once more ordered to occupy strategic positions throughout Paris. Again, many guardsmen refused to turn out, and those who did wanted to prevent bloodshed rather than defend the Guizot government. A company of National Guards from the fourth *arrondissement* even presented Crémieux (who lived in the *arrondissement*) at the Chamber of Deputies with a declaration stating that they were prepared to maintain public order but not the Guizot government. They further declared that they totally rejected the politics and policies of the Guizot government, described as 'a corrupting and corrupted ministry' which should be dismissed immediately and put on trial.[11] Other guardsmen shouted 'Long live reform!' and other anti-government slogans and usually refused to support military action by regular soldiers and municipal guards against rioters. By the late morning of 23 February General Jacqueminot, commander of the Paris National Guard, was being informed by his subordinate officers that the loyalty and effectiveness of the National Guard could not be relied upon without major concessions, such as the resignation of the Guizot government.

Sébastiani, the duc de Nemours and the king himself rapidly became aware of the situation. Under pressure from all his advisors, including the queen, Louis-Philippe with great reluctance decided to dismiss Guizot and to call upon the comte Molé to form a new government. Guizot had a personal interview with Louis-Philippe in the Tuileries and then at around half past three in the afternoon announced in the Chamber of Deputies that the king had invited Molé to form a new government. Greeted with astonishment and anger by many conservative deputies, and with delight by members of the opposition, this news had an electrifying impact. However, a reluctant Molé failed to persuade opposition deputies such as Dufaure, Rémusat and Thiers to serve under him, so at this extremely critical moment Louis-Philippe had deprived himself of a government and had left the army and National Guard without clear orders, which increased their demoralisation and disorganisation. The fall of Guizot appeared to be a victory for the rioters, and was widely celebrated as such. Houses and shops blazed with candles. At the same time it also became clear that the appointment of Molé was deeply unpopular. With Guizot gone, Louis-Philippe was now in the frame, the slogan 'Down with Louis-Philippe!' replacing 'Down with Guizot!' During the late afternoon and evening of 23 February, rioters began to target the Municipal Guard rather than the army or the National Guard. Municipal Guard posts were attacked and in some cases their armouries were pillaged by rioters. The socialist Louis Blanc drew up a demand for the dissolution of the Municipal Guard and the democratisation of the National Guard, which he argued should have sole responsibility for the maintenance of public order in Paris.

The next escalation of violence, however, occurred as a result of action by regular soldiers, not Municipal Guards. An officer in charge of soldiers guarding the Ministry of Foreign Affairs in the Boulevard des Capucines refused to allow a column of demonstrators to advance. In the subsequent stand-off, a gun was discharged, probably accidentally, whereupon several soldiers fired at the demonstrators, killing fifty-two and wounding seventy-four. These were the official figures – higher figures of approximately sixty-five dead and eighty wounded may be more accurate.[12] This massacre rapidly created a revolutionary situation. Sixteen corpses of those killed were loaded onto a cart which, illuminated by men carrying torches and surrounded by a crowd calling for vengeance and weapons, processed to the editorial offices of Le National and eventually to the mairie of the fourth arrondissement. This macabre spectacle produced a frenzied response. Amidst cries of 'Vengeance!', 'To arms!' and 'We are being assassinated!', street lamps were smashed, church bells were rung to sound the alarm, street barricades were constructed or reinforced, and house-to-house searches for weapons were conducted. Inevitably, all this led to further clashes with the army, the National Guard now generally siding with the crowd.[13]

The king was informed of the massacre of the Boulevard des Capucines at about 10 pm, and around two hours later he learnt that Molé had been unable to form a government. Convinced that in this emergency the power vacuum had to be filled immediately, Louis-Philippe appointed Marshal Bugeaud commander-in-chief of both the regular army and the National Guard in Paris and summoned Thiers to the Tuileries Palace to invite him to form a government. Bugeaud was not a good choice. A Napoleonic veteran who had gained a reputation as an able military commander in Algeria, he suffered from the double misfortune of being hated by both the Legitimists, as the jailer of the duchesse de Berry, and the republicans, as the officer ultimately responsible for the massacre of the Rue Transnonain. Bugeaud rapidly devised a plan of attack, to be effected early in the morning of 24 February, while Thiers assembled a team of potential ministers from among leading opposition deputies, including Duvergier de Hauranne, Odilon Barrot, Malleville and Rémusat.

However, by the morning of 24 February, the situation in Paris had become much more serious. Many believed that the government had treacherously deceived Parisians by announcing the resignation of Guizot and then massacring unsuspecting demonstrators in the Boulevard des Capucines. Trees were cut down, carts and omnibuses commandeered, and paving stones and iron railings ripped up. Old barricades were strengthened and new ones erected. Broken glass and china were scattered on the *pavé* to stop the cavalry. Soldiers and Municipal Guards found themselves cut off from orders, reinforcements and supplies of food and ammunition, while subject to violent attack in the streets and squares. In their barracks and guard posts, they were under threat of arson. The Abbaye military prison was attacked and the prisoners released. Many of the rioters were now armed with weapons seized from armouries, gunsmiths' shops, private homes, and disarmed soldiers and guardsmen, and they could now generally count on the active support of the National Guard. The popular insurrection was largely spontaneous, but some direction was supplied by republicans such as Etienne Arago and Louis Blanc and by the editors of the left-wing republican newspaper, *La Réforme*. Similarly, those associated with the radical student newspapers, *L'Avant-Garde* and *La Lanterne du Quartier latin*, provided student leadership. The columns of soldiers which Bugeaud had ordered to dismantle barricades in a series of offensive sweeps through the streets of Paris made very little headway and eventually had to retreat, so that around midday he ordered them to end all hostilities and to hand over responsibility for policing Paris to the National Guard. Shortly before 1 pm Rambuteau, the Prefect of the Seine, was persuaded to resign, after which the crowd peacefully invaded the Hôtel de Ville.

The failure of this policy of repression forced Louis-Philippe to attempt a policy of conciliation. There was to be a new ministry, headed by Thiers and Odilon Barrot and including supporters of parliamentary reform such as Duvergier de

Hauranne, Malleville and Rémusat; General Lamoricière, reputedly more popular than Bugeaud, would command the Paris National Guard; parliamentary reforms would be promised; and the policing of Paris would be the responsibility of the National Guard. Difficulties arose immediately. For a start, there was no effective means of communicating this programme to the people of Paris. In any case, since the massacre on the Boulevard des Capucines apparent conciliation from Louis-Philippe encountered deep suspicion, and more radical programmes were now being advanced. *La Démocratie pacifique* produced a poster demanding a general amnesty, a dissolution of parliament and new elections with a wider franchise and parliamentary reform, the right to work guaranteed, equal educational opportunities for all, and various social reforms.[14] Other, more radical, posters urged rejection of a Thiers-Barrot ministry and even a popular assault on the Tuileries Palace ('Aux armes! Aux Tuileries!').[15]

As crowds began to assemble near the Louvre and the Tuileries Palace, soldiers manning the Château d'Eau guard post facing the Place du Palais Royal and the Palais Royal came under popular pressure to surrender their weapons. The soldiers refused, shots were fired and a serious confrontation developed. The noise of the fighting attracted more demonstrators and National Guards to the area around the Place du Palais Royal while in the Tuileries Palace the king and his advisers began to panic. Urged on by the queen, Louis-Philippe decided to review the soldiers and National Guards in the Cour des Tuileries and the Place du Carrousel within the Tuileries–Louvre complex. He chose to display his regal authority with full pomp and military glory. Mounted on a horse, wearing the uniform of a lieutenant-general, he was accompanied by a grand entourage including his sons, the duc de Nemours and the duc de Montpensier, his military commanders, Marshal Bugeaud and General Lamoricière, and his ministers, Montalivet, Thiers and Rémusat. Looking pale and as though petrified, he then proceeded to review the defenders of his palace, who amounted to approximately 4,000 men. At first he was greeted with a few shouts of 'Vive le Roi!' by members of the first legion of the Paris National Guard, but members of the Fourth Legion not only shouted 'Vive la Réforme!', but also broke ranks and surrounded the king's horse. Alarmed, the king broke off the review and galloped back to the palace. There he desperately made further concessions, replacing Thiers with Barrot and Marshal Bugeaud with Marshal Gérard.[16]

Once again, concessions could not effectively be communicated to Parisians, by now converging in their tens of thousands on the Tuileries Palace. Their demands had shifted radically: they wanted the abdication of Louis-Philippe and the proclamation of a republic. Louis-Philippe was made fully aware of the situation and advised that he could save the monarchy only by abdicating in favour of his grandson, the comte de Paris. Emile de Girardin, the journalist-proprietor of the Paris liberal newspaper, *La Presse*, seems to have finally made up Louis-Philippe's mind. He came to the Tuileries Palace with proposals for the abdication of the king, the regency of the duchesse d'Orléans, the dissolution of the Chamber of Deputies and a general amnesty. The queen protested but Louis-

Philippe, urged on by the duc de Montpensier, Girardin and Crémieux, duly wrote out his abdication.[17] Shortly afterwards, accompanied by members of his family, Louis-Philippe hurriedly left the Tuileries Palace and proceeded to the Place de la Concorde, where three carriages awaited them. Protected by a cavalry escort, Louis-Philippe and his entourage slipped out of Paris for Saint-Cloud and the royal château at Dreux, where they spent the night. They eventually reached England via Honfleur.[18]

As the king left Paris, the crowd smelt victory. For a while the soldiers defending the Château d'Eau guard post continued to resist, but their resistance ended when the guard post was set on fire. Threatened with being burnt out, soldiers and guardsmen defending the Prefecture of Police on the Ile de la Cité evacuated the building. With the Château d'Eau guard post and the Prefecture of Police dealt with, thousands of demonstrators converged on the Tuileries Palace. The abdication and flight of Louis-Philippe had demoralised the defenders of the palace. Louis-Philippe's son, the duc de Nemours, was in overall command at the palace, but, anxious to avoid any unnecessary bloodshed, he abandoned the palace to invading crowds of demonstrators. During the afternoon of 24 February successive waves of demonstrators penetrated all the palace apartments. The rooms were ransacked, their contents vandalised, and the royal throne was carried off in triumph to be burnt in the Place de la Bastille. The palace itself might have been burnt down if the initiative had not been taken to write on the walls of the building, 'National Property, Civilian Hospital'. Little else was saved; even the swans in the basins of the Tuileries Gardens were killed.[19] The royal apartments in the Palais Royal were similarly vandalised. [20]

There was one last hope for the monarchy. On foot, the duchesse d'Orléans and her two sons courageously made their way to the Chamber of Deputies to plead for parliamentary approval for the accession of the comte de Paris and for the regency of the duchesse d'Orléans.[21] In the chamber they were almost immediately joined by the duc de Nemours. Dupin and Odilon Barrot tried to persuade the chamber to proclaim the regency, but demonstrators had begun to invade the parliament building, and a succession of speakers (Marie, Crémieux, Ledru-Rollin and Lamartine) urged the rejection of the regency and the proclamation of a Provisional Government. Demonstrators kept pushing their way into the debating chamber, causing many deputies to flee and the duchesse d'Orléans, the duc de Nemours and the two princes to withdraw to Les Invalides. Lamartine's speech was interrupted but eventually sufficient calm was restored to enable first Dupont de l'Eure and then Ledru-Rollin to read out a list of names of those who would compose a Provisional Government: Lamartine, Ledru-Rollin, François Arago, Dupont de l'Eure, Garnier-Pagès, Marie and Crémieux. This list had essentially been agreed upon at an earlier meeting held in the editorial offices of Le National. Meanwhile Lamartine and a crowd of followers set off for the Paris Hôtel de Ville, where the Provisional Government was to be proclaimed and installed. The list of Provisional Government members drawn up by the moderate republicans associated with Le National was communicated by

Louis Blanc and Martin de Strasbourg to the editorial offices of *La Réforme*, where about forty left-wing republicans had gathered, including Etienne Arago, Marc Caussidière, Ferdinand Flocon and Joseph Sobrier. They decided on a slightly different list for a future Provisional Government: the leader of the Dynastic Left, Odilon Barrot, whose name had appeared on the original *National* list, was excluded; François Arago, Garnier-Pagès, Lamartine, Ledru-Rollin, and Marie, were included, as in the *National* list, but so, too, were an additional four left-wing republicans or socialists, Louis Blanc, Flocon, Armand Marrast and (at Louis Blanc's insistence) a worker known as Albert. The meeting also decided that two key buildings should be occupied, the Hôtel des Postes (the Paris head post office) and the Prefecture of Police. Etienne Arago was to take charge of the former while Caussidière and Sobrier were to take charge of the latter. At the Hôtel de Ville, municipal councillors rejected an attempt to transform the Paris municipal council into a revolutionary government or commune but did decide to re-establish the post of mayor of Paris, with Garnier-Pagès as the new mayor and Laurent-Antoine Pagnerre and Athanase Recurt as the new deputy mayors (they had all been members of the organising committee for the banquet of the twelfth *arrondissement*).

Crossing numerous barricades and penetrating the dense crowds which now filled the Place de Grève, Arago, Crémieux, Dupont de l'Eure, Lamartine, Ledru-Rollin and Marie eventually arrived from the Palais Bourbon to join Garnier-Pagès at the Hôtel de Ville at around 4 pm. Lamartine drafted a proclamation announcing that the heroism of the people of Paris had overthrown a reactionary and oligarchic government, that a Provisional Government had been formed as proclaimed in the Chamber of Deputies, and that the Republic had been provisionally adopted.[22] Government posts were then distributed: the presidency to Dupont de l'Eure, Public Works to Marie, Foreign Affairs to Lamartine, the Ministry of the Interior to Ledru-Rollin, Justice to Crémieux, the Navy to Arago, Public Instruction to Hippolyte Carnot, Commerce to Eugène Bethmont, Finance to Michel Goudchaux and War to General Lamoricière (who declined the appointment and was replaced by General Subervie).[23] The latter four were not full members of the Provisional Government. Other important appointments made included those of General Cavaignac as Governor General of Algeria and General Courtais as Commander-in-Chief of the Paris National Guard. Only after all these decisions had been made, by which time night had fallen, did Louis Blanc, Flocon and Marrast arrive at the Hôtel de Ville from the editorial offices of *La Réforme*, claiming membership of the Provisional Government on the basis of their nominations at the *Réforme* meeting and their subsequent public acclamation. Against opposition from Arago, Garnier-Pagès successfully proposed that they and Albert should be appointed secretaries.

Louis Blanc and the insurgents who had invaded the Hôtel de Ville insistently clamoured for the unequivocal proclamation of the Republic. Lamartine managed to give a short speech in one of the principal rooms of the Hôtel de Ville, explaining that the Provisional Government wanted the Republic, but that the final decision lay with the national electorate formed on the basis of manhood suffrage.[24] Among members of the Provisional Government, Ledru-Rollin and Flocon supported Louis Blanc in urging an immediate proclamation of the Republic, while Dupont de l'Eure, Arago and Marie were more cautious. They argued that Paris was not France, that royalists might regard the Republic as an accident, that the Republic would lack moral influence abroad, and that the electorate defined by manhood suffrage should decide. Eventually, the Provisional Government approved a formula, suggested in its original version by Crémieux: 'The Provisional Government wants the Republic, on condition that it is approved by the people, who will be immediately consulted.' This sentence appeared in the first decree formally issued by the Provisional Government.[25]

As in July 1830, just three days sufficed to transform France from being a conservative, oligarchic monarchy to being a revolutionary, democratic republic. The insurrection succeeded because it simultaneously involved all districts of Paris. The over-confident authorities were caught entirely by surprise and the Paris National Guard was at first unreliable and then largely sided with the insurrection. By that stage, the Guizot government and even the regime of Louis-Philippe had become so hated that tens of thousands of Parisians were prepared to fight and die in the revolutionary cause. The parliamentary opposition clearly initiated the crisis which led to the February Days, with the reform banquet campaign, culminating in the proposed twelfth *arrondissement* banquet. However, there would have been no revolution but for the popular protests which began on 22 February and which rapidly escalated into a largely unplanned and leaderless insurrection. In the fighting, approximately fifty regular soldiers and twenty-two municipal guards were killed, as against 289 insurgent dead, including fourteen women.[26] The spontaneity, popularity and violence of this insurrection can be attributed not just to the deep and widespread detestation of Guizot and Louis-Philippe, but also to the high unemployment and other social consequences arising from the exceptionally severe and prolonged economic crisis which had begun in 1845. Prominent among the February insurgents were those employed in the construction, clothing, textile, furniture and metallurgical industries, all of which had been particularly badly hit by the economic crisis.[27] Once again a monarchy in France had succumbed to a coincidence of political and economic crises.

Republicanism and socialism

By the morning of 24 February 1848, the revolutionary crowds in Paris were demanding the proclamation of a Republic and the lists of names of those who emerged as members of the Provisional Government were being drawn up in the editorial offices of the two main Paris republican newspapers, *Le National* and *La Réforme*. After the Provisional Government had been formed, its first decree declared its intention to re-establish the French Republic, provided the electorate agreed. Republicanism had thus come to the top of the political agenda in

France. The First French Republic (1792–1804) had been tarnished by its association with Jacobin dictatorship and terror and by its capitulation to Napoleon. Yet romanticised memories of the First Republic, a tradition of republicanism in some families, the secret political societies of the 1820s, the association of republicanism with Bonapartism and liberalism, and the publication of the socialist ideas of Saint-Simon and of Buonarroti's writings on Babeuf, all helped to ensure that republicanism did not disappear. Nevertheless, it was liberalism rather than republicanism which had constituted the main ideological ingredient in the opposition to Charles X and Polignac.[28]

When the July 1830 revolution occurred, French republicanism was so relatively weak that proclaiming a Republic was not a serious option. However, after 1830 French republicanism experienced a rebirth owing to a number of factors. The alleged 'betrayal' of the revolution of July 1830, the relatively undemocratic and repressive character of the Orleanist regime, and disappointments over government jobs and official favours, meant that republicanism came to be seen by some as an attractive alternative. Etienne Cabet, one of the organisers of the popular insurrection in Paris of July 1830 who rapidly became disenchanted with Orleanism, soon emerged as an influential republican publicist, with his account of the 1830 revolution (*Révolution de 1830*, 1831 and later editions) and his newspaper, *Le Populaire* (founded in September 1833, forced to close in 1834, revived in 1841). Other republican newspapers included Armand Carrel's *Le National* (from 1832), Armand Marrast's *La Révolution de 1830* and François Raspail's *Le Réformateur*, though *Le Réformateur* and several other republican newspapers did not survive the application of the September 1835 press laws. However, a number of republican newspapers did manage to survive in the provinces;[29] and in Paris *Le National* and *La Réforme*, from its foundation in 1843, circulated republican ideas and sustained editors and journalists, notably Etienne Arago, Louis Blanc, Ferdinand Flocon and Ledru-Rollin. During the 1830s and 1840s, the memory of the Great Revolution was revived and in several cases rehabilitated through the publication of numerous memoirs, collections of documents and speeches, and historical works. Catering more to the popular imagination, pamphlets, songs, prints and almanacs performed a similar role.[30]

The various republican conspiracies and urban insurrections which punctuated the life of the July monarchy, and the much-publicised trials of those held responsible, kept the flame of a martyred Republic alive in the political consciousness. Political trials could also provide a public platform for republican lawyers such as Emmanuel Arago and Ledru-Rollin. The Chamber of Deputies provided another such platform for a small group of republican deputies, including François Arago, Eugène Bethmont, Carnot, Cormenin, Dupont de l'Eure, Garnier-Pagès, Ledru-Rollin and Alexandre Marie. Thus, as journalists, lawyers, parliamentary deputies and writers, a sufficient number of republicans had gained national prominence before 1848 to enable a national republican leadership to be formed when the July monarchy collapsed. At a local level, republican newspapers, clubs and societies similarly produced a local republican leadership after

24 February 1848, as did municipal councils, particularly those with a significant republican membership, such as the municipal councils of Grenoble, Rouen, Strasbourg and Toulouse.

Despite official repression, republicanism achieved a modest expansion in France during the July monarchy. The economic and social transformation of France after 1830 favoured the spread of republicanism. The threat to the livelihoods of skilled artisans posed by industrialisation made this social group particularly susceptible to radicalism and republicanism. Concepts of working-class honour and masculinity, especially in Paris, became embedded in a radical and sometimes violent brand of republicanism; and the exceptionally high levels of unemployment experienced by the beginning of 1848 in the construction, metallurgical, textile and clothing industries provided ready recruits to the republican cause. Republicanism could also flourish in certain rural areas, where traditional rural grievances over forest laws, communal rights and taxation, together with forms of rural sociability and the existence of a rural working class such as the Var cork workers, promoted rural radicalism.[31] In both Paris and the provinces, republicanism was sustained by republican secret societies, masonic lodges, electoral associations, social clubs and informal café gatherings, which could offer a political culture which embraced not just republicanism but also masculine camaraderie, male bonding, secrecy and ritual.[32] Fertile soil for republicanism could also be found in university faculties, such as the Law Faculty at the University of Grenoble.[33] Membership of republican circles included middle-class professionals, students, soldiers, artisans, tradesmen, and even some peasants.[34] Public manifestations of republicanism ranged from public commemorations of republican anniversaries to public funerals of republican heroes such as Armand Carrel (editor of *Le National*, mortally wounded in July 1836 in a duel with Emile de Girardin).[35]

Republicanism during the July monarchy became linked, at least for many workers, with socialism. Before 1830, the renegade aristocrat Saint-Simon had developed and publicised his conviction that, in an efficient and modern state, status and wealth should depend upon the value of the individual's contribution to society, rather than on inherited privilege and wealth or the holding of some unproductive office. He particularly stressed the role that scientists, artists, engineers and industrialists could play in improving the lot of humanity. He also believed that the State should promote infrastructure projects, such as the construction of canals, which would have economic benefits, and that all members of society should be encouraged to fulfil their individual potential. Thus the social hierarchy would be dominated by a natural elite of the capable and useful, wealth-creation would be promoted by the State, and personal satisfaction and social harmony would be achieved through economic prosperity and individual fulfilment. Saint-Simon opposed violence, believed in the power of persuasion and, before he died in 1825, argued that society should be governed by Christian principles such as the principle of brotherly love. Saint-Simon's ideas were publicised and developed by his disciples, notably Enfantin, Michel Chevalier and

Olinde Rodrigues, but the Saint-Simonian movement never really recovered from the trial of leading Saint-Simonians in August 1832.

While the Saint-Simonians hoped to achieve a moral revolution in humanity, Charles Fourier accepted human beings as they were, creatures of passion and desires. According to Fourier, industrialisation and capitalism were wasteful and inefficient, and failed to cater satisfactorily for human needs and aspirations. The same was true, Fourier argued, of the prevailing character of the institution of the family, with its emphasis on patriarchy, monogamy and child-rearing within individual families. To achieve economic, social and personal harmony, people should live in ideal communities or 'phalanstères' of 1,700 persons, in which individuals would do only the jobs which they enjoyed doing, adults would couple solely according to their desires, and children would be brought up collectively by those who wanted to be child-carers. Individuals would be able to change their occupations and partners, while work would be made as attractive as possible. Fourier's ideas were publicised in a series of newspapers, Le Phalanstère in 1832, La Phalange in 1836 and, from August 1836, La Démocratie pacifique, edited by Victor Considérant. The latter, in particular, was influential in developing a critique of capitalism while emphasising the desirability of change without violence and without the destruction of private property.[36]

Another influential socialist newspaper was L'Atelier, which appeared on a monthly basis between 1840 and 1850. Influenced by the ideas of Philippe Buchez, it also opposed violent insurrection, instead campaigning for a new society founded on a combination of Christian morality, manhood suffrage, public education and worker co-operatives. More radical, in the sense that he believed in the collective ownership of property, was Etienne Cabet. He also believed in an egalitarian and highly regimented society; he regularly condemned the iniquitous consequences of unregulated capitalism; and he is often described as a communist. However, he was a pre-Marxist communist. Like most other French socialists at this time, his means were persuasion and example, rather than violent revolution; he hoped to attract followers voluntarily and to run his utopian communities through direct democracy; and he maintained that communism was really Christianity in practice. To propagate his ideas and to attract followers, Cabet began to publish a monthly newspaper, Le Populaire, in March 1841. It achieved a print run of 5,000 copies in January 1848, which made it the highest circulation popular newspaper in France, with an urban working-class readership, particularly in Paris and Lyons.[37] By the beginning of 1848 Cabet had become preoccupied with establishing an ideal community in the United States, and Louis Blanc was replacing him as the most influential socialist in France.

Louis Blanc's reputation as a socialist rested particularly on L'Organisation du travail, first published in 1839 and in its fifth edition by 1847. Like other socialists, Blanc blamed poverty on the class exploitation which he saw as an inevitable feature of capitalism. His solution was State intervention in the economy, for instance, the State ownership and operation of railway companies, the development of State-owned agricultural estates, and the establishment of State-owned banks which would lend capital on favourable terms to groups of individuals so that they could set up co-operative workshops.[38] In contrast, Pierre-Joseph Proudhon rejected the State-dominated socialism of Louis Blanc, arguing instead for the establishment of producers' and consumers' co-operatives or associations. These co-operatives or associations would promote fraternal ties among workers via education and would give workers control over the productive process by a barter system, whereby the co-operatives or associations would exchange their products with each other.[39]

Although the ideas of these individual socialist thinkers varied, they shared a considerable amount in common. They tended to oppose revolutionary violence, support Christian morality and be restrained in their anti-clericalism,[40] and to believe in patriarchy and the institution of the family. They were opposed to the forcible expropriation of property-owners, apart from a limited nationalisation programme of, for instance, banks, insurance companies, canals, railways and mines. Of course, there were exceptions. Auguste Blanqui maintained a life-long commitment to secret conspiracies and political violence, but his imprisonment after the abortive 1839 rising in Paris limited his influence.[41] Proudhon became anti-religious and notorious for his claim, 'God is evil' ('Dieu, c'est le mal!'). Fourier's ideas on free love attracted few supporters and were an embarrassment to most French socialists, though Fourierists such as Constantin Pecqueur opposed the indissolubility of marriage. Proudhon was also notorious for the phrase, 'Property is theft' ('La propriété, c'est le vol!'), but what he objected to was not property per se, but surplus wealth, such as land which the owner could not cultivate and so rented out. The concept that individuals were entitled to own the fruits of their labour was widely shared by French socialists, even by those who, like Louis Blanc, wanted significant State ownership of the means of economic production and significant State direction of the economy. Similarly, French socialists, apart from Blanqui, were almost universally opposed to the forcible expropriation of property-owners without compensation.

Before the February Days, the over-confident Guizot government had taken no action against republicans or socialists in Paris, although a handful of foreigners, including the Russian revolutionary Bakunin and Friedrich Engels, the friend and associate of Karl Marx, had been expelled.[42] Thus on 24 February 1848 prominent republicans and socialists were able to form the Provisional Government almost immediately. However, from the start the balance of power was substantially in the hands of the moderate republicans. Initially, the leading figure in the Provisional Government was Lamartine, the Minister for Foreign Affairs. A publicly-declared left-wing opponent of the July monarchy since January 1843, Lamartine had in effect made a last-minute conversion to moderate republicanism by his intervention in the Chamber of Deputies on 24 February 1848 opposing the regency of the duchesse d'Orléans and demanding the formation of a Provisional Government. With the exception of the left-wing republican Ledru-Rollin (Minister of the Interior), moderate republicans were allocated all the other main posts in the Provisional Government: François Arago (Minister of the Navy), Adolphe Crémieux (Minister of Justice), Dupont de l'Eure (President), Michel Goudchaux, soon replaced by Louis Antoine Garnier-Pagès, (Minster of Finance), and Alexandre Marie (Minister of Public Works). Similarly, those from outside the Provisional Government appointed to important posts were also moderate republicans: Eugène Bethmont (Minister of Commerce), General Bedeau, soon replaced by General Subervie, (Minister of War), Hippolyte Carnot (Minister of Public Instruction), Armand Marrast (who succeeded Garnier-Pagès as Mayor of Paris), and Laurent-Antoine Pagnerre (Secretary General of the Provisional Government). The exceptions were Etienne Arago (Minister of Posts), one of the founders of La Réforme, and Marc Caussidière (Prefect of Police), a survivor of the 1834 workers' rising in Lyons. Albert, Louis Blanc and Ferdinand Flocon were given no ministerial portfolios at all, but were simply designated as secretaries. Left-wing republicans and socialists, many of whom were associated with La Réforme, were therefore in a minority and controlled few positions of power or influence.

Reactions to the February Revolution in Paris

The February Days largely took members of the French elite in Paris by surprise.[43] It had been widely assumed that the worst of the economic crisis was over, that the reform banquet campaign did not seriously threaten the July monarchy, that the Guizot government was secure in its parliamentary majority, and that the army and National Guard could be relied upon to maintain order in Paris.

Elite social life, on hold during the period of mourning for the Princess Adélaïde, had resumed at the end of January. The queen held a reception on 26 January attended by members of the diplomatic corps. There followed balls hosted by the comtesse Apponyi (wife of the Austrian ambassador) on 8 February, by the marquise de Lauriston on 10 February, by Lady Normanby (wife of the British ambassador) on 11 February, and by both the duchesse d'Estissac and the princesse de Ligne (wife of the Belgian ambassador) on 21 February.[44] The Turkish ambassador also hosted a ball shortly before the February Revolution.[45] Meanwhile, the celebrated composer and pianist, Frédéric Chopin, had given a piano recital on 16 February in the salons of Messers Pleyel and Company to an audience of Paris society ladies.[46] Only as the revolution began was the social life of Paris high society disrupted. A ball arranged at the Austrian embassy for the evening of 22 February was cancelled at 2 pm that afternoon, the food being distributed to the poor of the arrondissement; and Tocqueville, invited out to dinner that evening by a fellow deputy, recorded: 'The meal was magnificent, but the table was deserted; of twenty invited guests, just five appeared.' Nevertheless, the comtesse Pozzo held a reception on the evening of 23 February.[47]

Before the eve of the February Revolution, the political crisis had penetrated the ballroom. It was reported that, at the Austrian embassy ball, Legitimists (the

Faubourg Saint-Germain) had literally turned their backs on those who had rallied to Louis-Philippe, while at the British embassy ball the opposition deputies Thiers and Odilon Barrot attended but not the government ministers Guizot and Duchâtel.[48] At the ball given by the duchesse d'Estissac on 21 February, resistance and agitation were allegedly the sole topics of conversation.[49] The princesse de Ligne recalled that at her ball, at which guests danced until 6 am, Guizot and Duchâtel excused themselves, Rambuteau (Prefect of the Seine) expressed anxiety about the security situation, and some women were too frightened to wear their jewellery. Guests from the Faubourg Saint-Germain feared that they would not get home if demonstrators had occupied the bridges over the Seine.[50]

Members of the Paris elite were in fact terrified, though desperately trying to pretend otherwise. 'Fear was the great goddess.'[51] Balzac, who personally witnessed the pillaging and destruction of the contents of the Tuileries Palace during the afternoon of 24 February, wrote the next day to a personal friend: 'Nothing could be more terrifying than what is happening at this moment.' The sacking of the Orléans apartments in the Palais Royal and the burning of the royal château at Neuilly led him to predict to the same correspondent on 26 February a class war in France or a war between France and Europe; and, having learnt that fire had totally devastated the Rothschild château at Suresnes, he reported the next day: 'People in the elevated ranks of society are everywhere in the depths of despair.'[52] Another novelist and dramatist, Mme Ancelot, recalled: 'The Tuileries sacked, the Palais-Royal devastated and Neuilly consigned to the flames, recalled [the Terror of 17]93. People were afraid.'[53] 'I shall never forget the figures green with fear whom I saw during those [February] days,' wrote the princesse de Ligne.[54] The comtesse d'Armaillé similarly recorded: 'Everyone was terrified. Each individual shared a belief in personal threat, proscription and ruin.'[55] The royalist and Romantic novelist, Alfred de Vigny, in his memoirs described Paris at this time as 'a city stricken with fear and madness.'[56]

The wealthy owner of Le Constitutionnel, Dr Véron, remembered how, the day after the February Revolution, the Paris bourgeoisie trembled for their heads, and how, once they were reasonably certain of keeping their heads, they trembled for their money.[57] Public displays of wealth in Paris disappeared. People dressed soberly and often wore something red to indicate support for the revolution. Silver, jewellery and other valuables were concealed. Representations of coats of arms were removed from carriages. Upper-class entertaining dramatically ceased. Messages such as 'Armes données' or 'Armes rendues' were written on the doors and walls of private houses, to indicate that any privately-owned weapons had been handed over to the insurgents. The wealthy made well-publicised donations to the collections and subscriptions for the victims of the February Days,[58] and bourgeois and upper-class men of military age rushed to join the Paris National Guard. Others escaped from Paris – according to a British observer, 'the nobility sneaked out of the capital.'[59] Alfred de Vigny later recorded:[60]

The principal streets, the boulevards and the avenues, were covered with carriages driven at full gallop, their lanterns swinging in all directions. I saw them full of women, children, mattresses, trunks, everywhere an improvised house clearance . . . To pass the barrier [the customs barrier surrounding Paris] was the hope of each family and the objective bought with the weight of gold.

Baroness Bonde wrote to a friend on 5 March, doubtless with some exaggeration: 'You can have no idea of the ludicrous means of escape to which terror has driven many women of society; Madame de Valin and Madame de St Priest were so frightened that they dressed as peasants, got a barrowful of eggs and left Paris, shouting the Marseillaise out of tune.'[61] A similar state of panic seized wealthy foreigners resident in Paris:[62]

The foreigners [resident in Paris] are blinded as if by fear. They are emigrating in caravans. The Russians have to leave, the British want to leave, and whoever remains only does so because the banks are not giving out any travel money. The British Embassy has issued five thousand passports recently.

Those members of the wealthier classes who remained in Paris soon began to recover at least some of their composure, while remaining anxious about the future. Prosper Mérimée wrote on 3 March to the comtesse de Montijo: 'Until now, things have not gone too badly. There have been individual misfortunes, instances of financial ruin, but nothing to indicate that people are physically in danger. We must live from day to day and rejoice when the day passes without mishap.'[63] To the enormous relief of the wealthier classes in particular, Paris did not experience significant looting or acts of violence after 24 February. In the same letter, Merimée reported: 'The people who seized the Tuileries and who did not have a *sou* in their pockets, have stolen nothing. I have seen workers in rags bring back priceless objects and mount guard in the midst of rooms filled with porcelain and jewellery.'[64] Rémusat observed of Paris as early as 25 February: 'The city was, one could say, at the mercy of the working masses. Everywhere they demonstrated a remarkable calm and gentleness.'[65] The same day a British woman resident in Paris wrote in a private letter: 'I cannot tell you how civil the mob is; I do not think it prudent to take a servant, and the groups give me the inside of the pavement, saying, 'Vive la République madame!'[66] The entries in the diary of an Austrian diplomat convey a similar impression:[67]

We are perfectly tranquil in Paris. The Provisional Government has expended enormous efforts to give us peace. . . . I circulated yesterday very easily in a hackney cab. The barricades still exist, but gaps sufficiently large for the passage of vehicles have been created [27 February]. . . . Vehicles circulate once more in Paris, shops are open, workers have returned to their workshops, everything in fact is in an unbelievable and miraculous state of calm, given current circumstances [28 February]. . . . Order is completely re-established in Paris. We do not even have a guard any more at our gate [1 March].

Conservative Paris newspapers were equally astonished and appreciative. 'Shops have re-opened everywhere. Paris presents almost its ordinary appearance' (*Le Journal des Débats*, 29 February 1848). 'The admirable good sense of the workers of Paris has preserved France from anarchy' (*L'Union*, 3 March 1848). Not just the absence of looting and popular violence, but the politeness of Paris workers and even beggars continued to amaze Paris residents and visitors. A German female writer recorded her experience of Paris on 17 March:[68]

> We have crossed Paris by day and night, on foot and by coach, almost always without a male companion and often in full formal dress, and have never encountered the slightest problem. Everyone has been courteous and has begged for alms in the most modest way, although their need is probably very great.

Instead of looting and violence, there was almost a carnival atmosphere, with numerous peaceful parades and demonstrations, and ceremonies at which trees of liberty were planted. Flags, speeches, songs, music, uniforms, fancy dress, the participation of women and children, and the involvement of Roman Catholic clergy could give such events a festive air. Even the public funeral on 4 March of the victims of the February Days was turned into a celebration of the Republic characterised by joy, euphoria and unity,[69] as well as by order, decency, reverence and mutual politeness. This led George Sand to comment: 'The people of Paris are the first people of the world.'[70]

The February Days and the provinces

About 9 pm on the evening of 24 February 1848, Alexandre Andryane, a veteran of Buonarotti's secret societies and a former inmate of the notorious Spielberg prison, whom Lamartine had instructed to precede Ledru-Rollin at the Ministry of the Interior, sent out an official dispatch to the prefecture of each department, announcing the formation of the Provisional Government.[71] Prefectures had generally been kept informed as the situation in Paris had developed. For instance, the Prefecture at Besançon (Doubs) received the following dispatches by telegraph on 24 February: 8.30 am – Thiers had been invited by the king to form a government; 1 pm – Odilon Barrot had been invited to form a government and calm and conciliation prevailed ('Tout ici marche vers le calme et la conciliation'); 1.30 pm – the king had abdicated and the duchesse d'Orléans had been appointed regent; 10 pm – a Provisional Government had been formed. On 25 February at 11 am a final message arrived, 'The Republican government is constituted.'[72] There was inevitably some variation in the rapidity with which news of the overthrow of Louis-Philippe and of the proclamation of the Republic reached prefectures, for example, the morning of 25 February in the case of Perpignan (Pyrénées-Orientales) and 26 February in the case of Rodez (Aveyron). In many cases, the news was confirmed by the arrival of stage-coaches, sometimes decorated with red flags, bringing reports of the events in Paris. It took time, though, for the outcome of the February Days to become generally known in provincial France. On 26 February L'Abeille de la Vienne of Poitiers announced as the latest news the formation of an Odilon Barrot ministry. In the absence of reliable and up-to-date information, rumour and fear could flourish.[73]

Most provincials seem to have been astonished and shocked, though republicans and workers often publicly demonstrated their delight. According to L'Aveyron républicain (1 March 1848), crowds gathered in central Rodez and expressed their joy at the news by singing the Marseillaise and the 'Chant du départ' and by shouting 'Vive la République!', 'Vive l'ordre!' and 'Vive l'union!'. Often in the context of crowd invasions of prefectures and town halls, in the chef-lieu or administrative capital of approximately thirty departments, a group composed mainly of local moderate republicans with perhaps a few radicals quickly formed a committee, named variously comité révolutionnaire, comité or commission départementale, préfectorale, administrative, républicaine, or provisoire. These committees took over the administration of the department from the Orleanist prefect, who immediately either resigned or abandoned his post (seven departments) or was forced out (four departments), or collaborated with the republican commission (seven departments). In the remaining twelve departments, all that is known is that the committee operated with or without the agreement of the prefect. In most of the other departments, where republicans were too weak to stage a mini revolution, the Orleanist prefect seems to have continued to function in the name of the Provisional Government.[74] In towns and cities, mayors and existing municipal councils were usually replaced by commissions municipales. The republican Pierre Joigneaux describes how in Châtillon-sur-Seine on 25 February the municipal council dissolved itself and the mayor 'to his great regret coldly proclaimed the Republic in a room in the town hall facing a portrait of Louis-Philippe.'[75] Alternatively, the new republican committee might for a time co-exist with the municipal council, even, as at Lons-le-Saunier, meeting in the same building as the municipal council.[76]

The change-over could take some time. The sub-prefects of Autun (Saône-et-Loire) and Châtillon-sur-Seine (Côte-d'Or) remained at their posts until 13 and 17 March respectively.[77] The administrative personnel of the July monarchy remained in post in the department of the Basses-Alpes, except for the town of Manosque, until 10 March.[78] In Perpignan (Pyrénées-Orientales), the municipal council was not dissolved until 6 April and a new commission municipale not formed until 8 April, while the Orleanist prefect rather than local republicans and radicals appointed the interim mayor of Perpignan, Théodore Guiter. The July monarchy conseil général of the Pyrénées-Orientales survived until

11 April,[79] while the July monarchy *conseil municipal* of Bayonne (Basses Pyrénées) survived until the municipal elections of 30 July.[80]

The most pressing objectives of the new self-appointed committees were to avoid a power vacuum, to ensure a peaceful transition of power and thereafter to maintain law and order. One of the first actions of these committees was usually, therefore, to reconstitute the local National Guard; and when the Republic was officially proclaimed in public ceremonies a few days later, local National Guard units and, where available, soldiers from the local regular army garrison invariably participated in a prominent manner, so that the ceremonies resembled military reviews in which military force legitimised the new regime and the new authorities. Some committees went further. For instance, at Limoges the committee, besides reorganising the National Guard, ordered that items, worth ten francs or less and deposited in pawn shops, should be returned to their owners and set up new works projects for the *chantiers municipaux*. They also instituted basic welfare services by distributing relief to the indigent. To promote republican fraternity, they organised a 'grande fête' at Limoges on 27 February, they set free those imprisoned for the disturbances at Buzançais in 1847, and they supported the establishment in Limoges of a *Société* populaire, which eventually had nearly six thousand members.[81]

The composition of the *commissions départementales* and *commissions municipales* often included moderate republicans who held some public or official post, for example, an association with a local republican newspaper, officer rank in a local National Guard unit, or membership of a local *arrondissement*, municipal or departmental council. In some instances, quite a well organised group assumed power, for instance the 'parti Arago' in Perpignan and the 'parti Lamartine' in Mâcon. An individual's reputation could immediately catapult him to revolutionary office. In Toulouse on 25 February Jacques Joly, a republican lawyer and former deputy, became president of the *commission municipale et centrale* of the Haute-Garonne on account of his local fame in having won a recent and notorious court case.[82] Socially, moderate republicans tended to be middle class – lawyers, doctors, professors, journalists, pharmacists, merchants and bankers – whereas more radical republicans might be artisans or even unskilled workers. The main exception to this was in Lyons, France's second city, which had a strong and autonomous radical political tradition. Radical crowd pressure in Lyons forced the creation of an exceptionally large Central Committee of ninety-four members, over half of whom belonged to previously illegal associations. A raft of radical measures rapidly followed – flying the red flag over the Hôtel de Ville, encouraging workers to join the National Guard, sending radicals out into the suburbs to organise revolutionary councils and to democratise the National Guard, and issuing bread vouchers to the indigent. Meanwhile, members of a radical workers' group, the Voraces, seized the fortifications around the working-class Croix-Rousse district, thereby acquiring munitions and artillery, an operation virtually unopposed by the Lyons army garrison. Similarly unopposed was a wave of machine-breaking directed principally at church and charity workshops, which allegedly threatened the livelihoods of workers with their looms and cheap labour.[83]

There was virtually no resistance anywhere in France to the overthrow of Louis-Philippe and proclamation of the Second Republic. Indeed, most officials of the former regime, holders of any kind of public office and members of the Orleanist elite generally were almost embarrassingly eager to profess their support for the new order and their willingness to serve the Republic. Instances of passive resistance or of a refusal to co-operate by Orleanist officials were very rare. In the Drôme between 26 February and 9 March the Orleanist prefect even co-operated with a republican committee in the administration of the department.[84] As in Paris after 24 February, troop withdrawals ordered by the relevant military commanders prevented serious clashes between workers and soldiers, for instance in Lyons and Rouen.[85] A decree released soldiers from their oath of allegiance to Louis-Philippe, and senior military commanders such as Bedeau, Bugeaud and Lamoricière, by immediately rallying to the Second Republic, helped to persuade the rest of the French army officer corps to do likewise. General Castellane briefly dreamt of resisting the February Revolution from a Normandy redoubt, but resigned on 28 February. In Algeria, the Governor General and son of Louis-Philippe, the duc d'Aumale, could possibly have organised a counter-revolutionary invasion of southern France. General d'Hautpoul, commander of the military garrison in Marseilles, claimed in his memoirs that he would have supported Aumale and Aumale's brother Joinville (the naval commander at Algiers) in any such attempt.[86] Another supporter might have been General Changarnier, commander of the military garrison of Algiers. However, Aumale handed over his authority to General Cavaignac, whom the Provisional Government had appointed on 29 February Governor General of Algeria. At the same time, Aumale urged the officers of the Army of Africa to maintain peace and order and the union of the army with the 'Patrie'. With Joinville, he then went into exile. While some officers must have harboured a sense of loyalty towards the Orleanist regime, the example of their seniors, the absence of any sign of counter-revolution, and the fear of social upheaval and European war kept them loyal to the Second Republic.[87] In a small number of regiments, mutinous soldiers forced, or attempted to force, the dismissal of their colonels.[88]

Other elements of the French elite similarly accepted the new order. Most of the Roman Catholic clergy had never enthusiastically supported Louis-Philippe. Indeed, several bishops and parish priests publicly welcomed the revolution. For instance, the Bishop of Dijon, in a circular of 29 February 1848, celebrated 'the miraculous manner in which have been accomplished the great events that have just changed the face of France.'[89] In his circular of 1 March, the Bishop of Digne instructed the priests of his diocese to support the new government with all their authority.[90] A Latin text for blessing liberty trees was circulated on 12 April by the Bishop of Quimper to the priests of his diocese.[91] Early fears that the Republic was synonymous with political extremism were rapidly allayed: the relatively moderate composition of the Provisional Government had not led to radical decrees and policies, while the maintenance of law and order had not collapsed. Those who had felt excluded from official positions and patronage were delighted to find that the passing of the July monarchy ended, at least temporarily, the local power and influence of families identified with the Orleanist regime. Some of the Legitimists hoped that circumstances would now favour a restoration of Henri V, and some Roman Catholic clergy believed that Church–State relations might now improve: they welcomed the overthrow of the July monarchy. Former Orleanists had supported the July monarchy because they believed it favoured their class interests rather than out of a sense of dynastic loyalty, so they were not predisposed to make any sacrifices for a regime that had fallen. A class war might conceivably have broken out in Lyons, but many members of the Lyons elite fled the city after 24 February.[92] Elsewhere, an illusion of national solidarity was promoted by the organisation of numerous 'patriotic' subscriptions for the victims of the February Days and for the local unemployed.

While the political situation was beginning to settle, the economic and social crisis continued and in many cases was deteriorating. The February Revolution provided for some disaffected workers an inspiration and an opportunity to resort to violent or lawless behaviour. In Rouen on 25 February crowds of workers surged through the town singing the Marseillaise and shouting 'Vive la République!' and 'A bas les Anglais!' In the evening the crowd attacked the railway station and then set fire to the wooden bridges serving the Paris to Le Havre railway line. Arsonists also attacked railway bridges at Asnières, Bezons and Oissel, and station installations at Epone, Meulan and Mantes. These attacks were blamed on the rivalry between French and British railway workers and on dockworkers and river-boat workers, whose livelihoods were threatened by competition provided by the new railway line. On 27 February a new linen mill was attacked at Petit Quevilly, near Rouen. Again xenophobia was a factor, since the mill employed English and Irish workers.[93] The property of railway companies was attacked in many places. At Valenciennes (near Lille in the department of the Nord) the line was vandalised, possibly to prevent Louis-Philippe from escaping by train to Brussels. Less pragmatic and more ideologically motivated reasons may have provoked these attacks: the railway symbolised industrial capitalism and capitalists such as the Rothschilds, and it represented a form of modern technology which could make workers redundant.[94] In Lille and elsewhere there were several instances of Luddite attacks on industrial machinery, blamed for increasing unemployment. In Reims on 26 February a mill which had recently installed the first steam-powered looms in the region was burned down.[95] Even convents came under attack, particularly where nuns engaged in some form of economic production and were alleged to undercut other producers. Five people were killed in an attack on convent workshops at Saint-Etienne on 13 to 14 April 1848.[96] Another alleged cause of unemployment, and another target of popular violence, were foreign workers – Belgian miners and glass-workers, British and Irish textile workers, English and Piedmontese workers on the railways and in the coal mines, and Sardinian fishermen.

Over seven thousand British workers were reportedly forced to leave France after February 1848. In many cases, they and their families returned home 'in the greatest state of destitution', having been rescued from the ports of Boulogne, Calais, Le Havre and Dieppe by ferries belonging to British companies.[97] At Douai several hundred workers from the Anzin mines attempted to force the dismissal of Belgian workers from a local glass works.[98] In the Bas-Rhin, soldiers were used to end attacks against Jews, and Jews were also attacked in the Haut-Rhin.[99] The difficult employment situation, coupled with the expectation that the Republic would improve the lot of industrial workers, prompted a rash of strikes and industrial disputes. During March 1848 there were strikes in the Saint-Etienne coal-mining region and at the mining and engineering complex at Le Creusot, and during March to April 1848 in the Alès coal-mining centre in the department of the Gard. Workers in traditional occupations, such as bakers, tailors, carpenters and stonemasons, also agitated for higher wages and a shorter working day, sometimes forming local associations to press their claims and occasionally also organising strikes.

In rural areas, the change of regime meant that for several weeks the police and judicial systems barely operated. Advantage was sometimes taken of this situation to attack and pillage *châteaux* and appropriate communal land. Peasants asserted alleged grazing rights and agitated for higher wages for agricultural labourers. They stopped paying taxes and tried to destroy tax records; they refused to pay rents and engaged in smuggling; they transgressed against the Forest Codes; and they harassed individuals including tax collectors, forest guards and unpopular parish priests.[100] Despite all this, except in a few specific places such as Rouen and Lyons, violence in the provinces soon ceased to be a major concern. Instead, public confidence was rapidly restored. Regime change had encountered virtually no opposition. The local administrative system had soon been re-established and local National Guard units reconstituted. The Provisional Government was perceived to be moderate. The holding of peaceful communal events such as republican banquets and the planting of liberty trees also helped to reduce fears.

Nevertheless, seeds of disaffection from the new regime already existed. Members of the former Orleanist elite rallied to the new regime only for opportunistic reasons. Their continued support was contingent on the Republic's moderation and maintenance of law and order; and the republican purge of Orleanists from official posts caused some resentment. Unusually large withdrawals from banks and a general unwillingness to spend money or invest capital indicated that the fears of the elite had not yet subsided. At the same time, such action contributed to a crisis of economic confidence, to a drying up of credit and a shortage of money in circulation, to bank failures and company bankruptcies, to increasing urban unemployment, and to a paralysis of the economy. This compounded an already difficult economic and social situation for workers already experiencing high unemployment and for farmers and peasants experiencing, especially from April 1848, low agricultural prices.

The domestic policies of the Provisional Government

The Provisional Government had several immediate domestic policy objectives. Primarily, it had to restore law and order in Paris and throughout France and ensure the supply of adequate food for the population of Paris. It needed to impose a new national and local administration. While France had to be republican in spirit as well as in name, it had to establish a clear distinction between the Second Republic and its predecessor of 1792, and its associations with war, terror and dictatorship. It had to reduce urban unemployment quickly and improve the government's financial position through the achievement of a substantial increase in tax revenues. Finally, it needed to acquire legitimacy through national parliamentary elections based on manhood suffrage, so as to produce a new national parliament and government.

Different members of the Provisional Government had, of course, different priorities. The radicals – Albert, Flocon, Louis Blanc, Ledru-Rollin – were particularly concerned with republicanising France and with meeting the demands and needs of urban workers. More conservative members of the Provisional Government, such as Dupont de l'Eure, François Arago, Crémieux, Garnier-Pagès, Marie and Marrast, tended to focus instead on the restoration of law and order and of government finances. Inevitably, members of the Provisional Government disagreed among themselves. On 21 April Albert insisted that his opposition to the summoning of five infantry regiments to Paris should be recorded in the minutes of the meetings of the Provisional Government.[101] Moreover, the Provisional Government had to operate in very difficult circumstances. It initially lacked significant and reliable military forces to defend itself, at a time when it was virtually besieged in the Paris Hôtel de Ville by radicals and workers. The effectiveness of the Paris National Guard could not at first be guaranteed and, under Bedeau's orders, units of the regular army progressively evacuated Paris from 25 February. To a significant extent, the Provisional Government had to rely on students from the Ecole polytechnique and military cadets from Saint-Cyr, both given authority by their uniforms and neutrality by their youth.[102] The Provisional Government also had to deal with a constant stream of delegations and deputations, anxious either to demonstrate publicly their support for the Second Republic or to bring their demands and complaints to the government's attention.

On 24 February 1848 the Provisional Government publicly declared that now all adult male citizens were members of the National Guard ('Aujourd'hui tous les citoyens font partie de la garde nationale'), while at the same time the existing Paris National Guard was to be reorganised.[103] This reflected both the desperate security situation in Paris and the unwillingness of the Provisional Government to trust absolutely the loyalty and reliability of the Paris National Guard inherited from the Orleanist regime. Colonel Courtais, a Napoleonic veteran who since 1842 had been a left-wing parliamentary deputy, was promoted to the rank of general and appointed commander of what was to become the reorganised Paris National Guard. Also on 24 February, special precautions were taken to protect the art treasures in the Louvre and the building of the Tuileries Palace (the contents of which had, of course, been pillaged). To help prevent any further damage being inflicted on the Tuileries, the palace was declared to be a shelter for those suffering from injuries sustained in work. Later, on 22 March a credit of 500,000 francs was allocated to the conservation of the Louvre, the Tuileries and the Palais National (formerly the Palais Royal), as well as to the former royal and imperial palaces at Versailles, Trianon, Saint-Cloud, Fontainebleau and Compiègne. It is striking that the Provisional Government gave the protection of France's royal and imperial heritage such immediate concern and high priority, notwithstanding the many financial demands on a much-depleted government treasury. Regular army soldiers, released from their oath of loyalty to Louis-Philippe, were urged to rally to the Republic, while severe penalties were threatened on those who deserted. On 25 February the Provisional Government decreed the creation of a twenty-four battalion-strong *garde nationale mobile*, a paid and full-time Paris National Guard, in contrast to its unpaid and part-time counterpart. Enrolments were to start at once in each of the twelve Paris *arrondissements*. The daily rate of pay was one franc fifty centimes and uniforms and equipment were provided free. Working-class Parisians were thus enabled to join the *garde mobile*, whereas previously the Paris National Guard had been a bastion of the bourgeoisie. The period of enlistment was to be one year and one day. The Ministry of War and the Paris National Guard jointly assumed responsibility for the establishment of this new paramilitary force.[104] At the same time, the Paris Municipal Guard, which had generally fought the insurgents, was dissolved.

Reports of arson attacks suffered by railway companies and of other instances of the destruction of property prompted a stern condemnation of such incidents by the Provisional Government (27 February). All public and private property was placed under the protection of the Republic, while in the current situation the destruction of property was declared to be the equivalent of treason. In the provinces National Guard units were widely deployed to deal with any outbreak of popular disorder, so that the provincial National Guard became in effect a counter-revolutionary force. The reorganisation of the Paris National Guard involved elections for new officers. The elections were originally to be held on 18 March but were later postponed to 5 April. All male citizens aged between twenty-one and fifty-five were entitled to vote, so long as they had not been deprived of their civic rights. The Provisional Government wanted to make the Paris National Guard more democratic in another respect, by dissolving elite companies. These recruited from the wealthier districts of Paris, had better equipment than the other guardsmen and wore special uniforms, including bearskin headgear. Their dissolution, decreed by the Provisional Government on 14 March, provoked on 16 March the first significant counter-revolutionary demonstration in Paris.

So far as the regular army was concerned, between 7 and 8 March a new

Committee of National Defence was formed with six generals, representing the cavalry, artillery, engineers and infantry, who were presided over by François Arago, the Minister of War. To strengthen the French army within France, the Provisional Government decided on 12 March to recall 15,000 veteran soldiers from Algeria. A further 12,000 veterans were recalled on 29 March, reservists replacing them in Algeria. At the same time, troops on leave were called up. Meanwhile on 22 March General Cavaignac succeeded François Arago as Minister for War, General Changarnier in turn succeeding Cavaignac as Governor General of Algeria. The reorganisation of the Paris National Guard and of the regular army garrison of Paris had gone sufficiently well for a grand military review to be staged in Paris on 20 April. Members of the Provisional Government crowded onto a dais in front of the Arc de Triomphe, accompanied by a large assemblage of judges, senior army and naval officers, members of the Conseil d'Etat and top civil servants. In a solemn public display of loyalty to the new Republic, the soldiers and guardsmen paraded and new regimental colours were presented to the sound of artillery salutes.

Besides ensuring security of life and property, the most immediate concern of the Provisional Government was the food situation in Paris. Nearly three days of street-fighting had severely disrupted the commercial life of the city, and the erection of numerous street barricades obstructed the free movement of people and vehicles. However, food prices were still relatively low and on 25 February the Provisional Government announced that Paris bakers had sufficient flour for thirty-five days. The same day Ecole polytechnique students were specifically instructed to ensure that bakers were adequately supplied with flour and were empowered to use military force if necessary. Special efforts were also made to keep the bakers supplied with charcoal for their ovens by at least partially dismantling Paris street barricades to permit the circulation of vehicles.[105] Since the feeding of national guardsmen was a top priority, bakers were ordered to supply the Paris National Guard with up to one-fifth of their total output.[106] The absence of any resistance to the revolution after 24 February, and the rapid acceptance of the Republic by the garrisons of the forts surrounding the capital, helped the Provisional Government to persuade workers first to make significant gaps in the barricades and then to dismantle them altogether. Once the barricades had been removed, and with continuing low food prices, the food situation in Paris ceased to be a major problem. Further relief came when the Provisional Government abolished or reduced taxes on the movement of foodstuffs and alcoholic drinks.

The formation of the Provisional Government, and the allocation of ministerial posts to members of that government, was just the start of a long process of purging the ranks of office-holders – judicial, military, naval, diplomatic and administrative. In some cases, of course, resignations or popular pressure removed incumbents from their posts. Their replacements generally possessed, at least supposedly, republican credentials, though other factors influencing appointments included the personal preferences of those making the appointments, the need for relevant expertise and experience, and the need for the appointees to be accepted. As early as 25 February new judicial appointments were being made, and thereafter long columns in Le Moniteur listed those appointed to the Conseil d'Etat, to the post of public prosecutor (procureur général), to the judicial bench and to the magistracy.[107] Out of approximately 3,000 justices of the peace (juges de paix), 798 were replaced between 29 February and 21 April.[108] The new appointees had often identified themselves with the opposition to the Guizot government,[109] though professional competence and likely acceptance could also be important. Thus the new public prosecutor of the Paris Court of Appeal, Auguste Portalis, was a liberal rather than a republican besides being a member of a distinguished legal family and a baron. Top personnel in government ministries, particularly the Ministry of Finance, were largely replaced. Numerous army officers publicly declared their willingness to serve the Second Republic. However, identification with either the Bourbon or Orléans dynasties or with the Guizot ministry earned early retirement, as did old age and perceived incompetence. Financial constraints and a desire to promote younger, more active and more politically loyal officers were further factors. A decree of 11 April transferred from the reserve list to the retired list 172 generals, whose individual annual salaries were thereby reduced by 2,000 francs to 5,000 francs. Another decree (17 April) retired thirty-eight major-generals (généraux de division), twenty-seven brigadier-generals (généraux de brigade), twenty-five colonels and five lieutenant-colonels. Some of the resulting vacancies in the most senior ranks in the army were not filled since, on 3 May, the number of major-generals on the active list was cut from eighty to sixty-five and the number of brigadier generals from 160 to 130.[110]

The February Revolution had less impact on the naval officer corps, presumably because the French navy was considered to be less influenced by politics than the French army. Probably the most important new appointment was that of Admiral Baudin, whose naval career had begun under Napoleon but had been interrupted by the Restoration. He became the new commander of French naval forces in the Mediterranean. The French diplomatic corps, on the other hand, experienced massive changes of personnel. Nearly all French diplomats serving abroad were dismissed as were most of the senior officials in the Ministry of Foreign Affairs in Paris.[111] Some of the replacements were moderate republicans, notably, in the Ministry of Foreign Affairs itself, Jules Bastide (general secretary) and Sain de Boislecomte (chef du cabinet). Bastide had edited Le National between 1836 and 1846, had contributed to the Histoire parlementaire de la Révolution française of Buchez and Roux, and had founded the Revue nationale (1847), while Sain de Boislecomte had similarly contributed to the Histoire parlementaire de la Révolution française and the Revue nationale. Yet many of the diplomats Lamartine chose to represent France abroad seem to have been selected, not for their republican credentials, but for their acceptablilty to the regime to which they were accredited, for instance the marquis de Boissy (Florence), the comte de Circourt (Berlin), the duc d'Harcourt (the Holy See), Edouard de Lacour

(Vienna), the vicomte Sérurier (Brussels), the marquis de Tallenay (London) and the comte de Thiard (Berne).[112]

Between 26 February and 9 March the Orleanist prefects and the self-appointed committees which had taken over the local administration in thirty departments were replaced, not by prefects, but by *commissaires*, the new title deliberately evoking the official terminology of the First Republic. Ledru-Rollin as Minister of the Interior made most of the appointments, though the Provisional Government had to give its approval, which it did with some reluctance in the cases of Frédéric Deschamps (Seine-Inférieure) and Charles Delescluze (Nord and Pas-de-Calais). Deschamps was a radical lawyer and republican activist in Rouen, while Delescluze, another radical lawyer and a left-wing journalist, could claim participation in the 1830 revolution, former membership of various secret societies and personal friendship with Ledru-Rollin. Altogether, Ledru-Rollin, unlike Lamartine with many of his diplomats, deliberately selected men of the left, though not necessarily left-wing republicans. Of the first batch of 110 *commissaires* despatched to eighty-five departments, the political affiliations of thirty are unknown, fourteen belonged to the Dynastic Left, twenty-two to the liberal republicans like Lamartine, twenty-two to the moderate republicans of *Le National*, and just twenty-two (approximately a quarter) to the left-wing republicans of *La Réforme*.[113] For those in official positions who were not dismissed, life was made easier both by their release from their oath of loyalty to Louis-Philippe and by the absence, unlike after 1789, of any new oath of loyalty.

The Second Republic did, however, follow the precedent of the revolution of 1789 in attempting to republicanise French political culture and discourse, reflecting Karl Marx's famous accusation that the French Revolution of 1848 'knew no better than to parody at some points 1789 and at others the revolutionary traditions of 1793–5.'[114] Children who had lost a parent or parents in the February Days were officially adopted by the State and designated as 'enfants de la patrie' (25 February). The institution of monarchy was formally abolished in France (26 February) and the next day the Republic was ceremonially proclaimed in the Place de la Bastille, site of the storming of the Bastille on 14 July 1789 and of the July Column commemorating the heroic dead of July 1830. The Chamber of Peers was suppressed, its members were forbidden to meet (24 February), and all titles of nobility, and all privileges attached to titles of nobility, lost their legal status (29 February). Numerous trees of liberty were planted as a result of both official and popular initiative, in the revolutionary tradition of 1789 or, in Balzac's opinion, 'the saddest parody of 1793.'[115] On 4 March the dead of the February Days were in turn buried in the tomb beneath the July Column in a ceremony which featured a chariot transporting a papier maché goddess representing the Republic, in accordance with a tradition dating back to the 1790s by which a young woman symbolised the Republic.

Another official ceremony took place on 20 May, to celebrate the opening of the National Assembly, which again consciously harked back to the Festival of the Federation of 14 July 1790 and to the republican pageants of David.[116] On

17 March 1848 the Provisional Government announced a competition for the submission of a painted symbolic image of the Republic.[117] The annual exhibition of paintings in the Louvre, known as the *Salon*, which opened on 21 March, was transformed. A hanging committee chosen by the artists themselves replaced the traditional jury; a record number of over five thousand works of art were accepted; and, at least in the opinion of one critic, 'republican art' was on display.[118] Republican drama was also on display. At the beginning of April, the plays being performed in Paris included 'William Tell' at the Théâtre de la Nation, 'Robert Macaire' at the Porte Saint-Martin and 'The Three Revolutions' at the Ambigu Comique. For the representatives elected to the National Assembly, the Provisional Government even prescribed an official form of dress inspired by male fashions of the First Republic, 'l'habit et le gilet à la Robespierre', in the words of the royalist comte de Falloux.[119]

France's revolutionary and republican heritage was resurrected in other ways. In the army, the ranks of *général de division* (*lieutenant général*) and of *général de brigade* (*maréchal de camp*) were re-established. Similarly, ambassadors became ministers, prefects and sub-prefects became *commissaries* and *sous-commissaires* respectively, *procureurs du Roi* became *commissaires de la République*, and governors of former royal *châteaux* became administrators. Prominent buildings in Paris were renamed, including the Palais National (formerly the Palais Royal), the Palais du Peuple (formerly the Louvre), the Bibliothèque Nationale (formerly the Bibliothèque Royale) and the Assemblée Nationale (formerly the Palais Bourbon). Similarly, in Paris the Place Royale became the Place de la République and the Place de la Concorde became the Place de la Révolution. The same process occurred in the provinces. For instance, in Givors, a small town south of Lyons in the department of the Rhône, the Rue Saint-Jean became the Rue de la République and the Place du Marché became the Place de la Fraternité.[120] Outside France, the French colonial island in the Indian Ocean, Ile Bourbon, resumed its republican name of Ile de la Réunion.

The Napoleonic as well as the revolutionary eras were recalled. On 18 March the Provisional Government decided that a monument should be erected in honour of Marshal Ney on the site of his execution (though the famous statue was not inaugurated until December 1853). At the same time, a statue of the duc d'Orléans, the late eldest son of King Louis-Philippe, was removed from its pedestal in the courtyard of the Louvre, to the astonishment and regret of Alexandre Dumas.[121] *Collèges royaux* were renamed *lycées* and the provincial town of Bourbon-Vendée was rechristened Napoléon-Ville, as under Napoleon. Government competitions were opened for 'patriotic songs' and for the design of a new coinage.[122] At least officially, individuals were addressed as 'citizens', in self-conscious imitation of the 1790s; and historic republican greetings, such as 'salut et fraternité', 'salut fraternel', 'salut et respect' and 'salut et dévoûment', were officially revived.[123]

The new Minister of Public Instruction, Hippolyte Carnot, was very aware of the need to 'make' republicans and of the republican tradition that ideally education should be free, obligatory and secular. In a circular on primary schools, published on 6 March 1848, he stressed that hitherto primary school education had neglected the formation of children as citizens. The rights and duties of citizenship, and the benefits of the Republic, should be taught, particularly in rural areas. 'France requires new men. A revolution should not only renew institutions, it is essential that it should also renew men.'[124] To help teachers with civic education, Carnot commissioned two republican manuals, *Manuel de l'instituteur pour les élections* by Henri Martin and *Manuel républicain de l'homme et du citoyen* by Charles Renouvier, both published by Charles Pagnerre in 1848. This well-intentioned initiative did, however, lay Carnot open to the charges of attempting the political indoctrination of primary school teachers and of their use as political propagandists.[125] A large proportion of schools in France were church schools, run mainly by the Roman Catholic Church, historically opposed to revolution and republicanism. In a circular to the French bishops of 11 March, Carnot announced a new system of State inspection of church schools and a new requirement that nuns who opened schools should have a certificate of teaching competence (*brevet de capacité*). Carnot planned new *lycées* or State secondary schools and a new system of State scholarships at the *lycées*. Fees were abolished and students were put into uniform at the Ecole Normale Supérieure, to make the institution more democratic and more republican. Recruitment was also to be more democratic at the Ecole polytechnique by attracting able candidates from less privileged backgrounds through scholarships.[126]

Carnot believed that a new institution was needed to train a new generation of republican administrators. A committee on literary and scientific education, formed on 27 February and chaired by Jean Reynaud, approved Carnot's proposal on 6 March. Two days later the Provisional Government decided to establish an Ecole d'administration along the lines of the Ecole polytechnique.[127] Lacking the money to found a new institution, the Provisional Government combined the Ecole d'administration with the Collège de France. There Carnot's republican broom even swept five professors from their chairs, including Michel Chevalier, the distinguished advocate of free-trade theories. When the Provisional Government announced twelve new professorial appointments on 9 April, they included those of Garnier-Pagès, Lamartine, Ledru-Rollin and Marrast. A three-year course of study was proposed, with an annual intake or promotion of 220 students. Eight hundred and sixty-five candidates took the entrance examinations in May and June and the school officially opened on 8 July. However, ridicule and disbelief had greeted the appointed of members of the Provisional Government to professorial chairs;[128] and the school lasted only six months, a victim of the combined hostility of professors, bureaucrats and politicians.[129]

A concern to distance the Second Republic from the dictatorship and terror associated with the years 1792–4 tempered the Provisional Government's republicanising zeal.[130] The adoption of the title Provisional Government on 24 February emphasised that the government was a temporary caretaker administration which would be replaced as soon as possible once national parliamentary elections had been held. On 25 and 26 February demonstrators at the Hôtel de Ville demanded that the Provisional Government should adopt the red flag as France's national flag. The precedents of 1789, 1814, 1815 and 1830 all suggested that regime change should be accompanied by a change in the national flag, and radical republicans believed that a new society required a new flag ('à une société nouvelle il faut un drapeau nouveau').[131] However, the official adoption of the red flag, which had become the symbol of popular revolt,[132] would have been regarded as a capitulation to popular militancy and as the precursor of extreme left-wing government policies. Therefore Provisional Government members, notably Lamartine, successfully insisted that the *tricolore* should remain the official flag of the French nation.[133]

Lamartine also played a prominent part in securing the abolition of capital punishment for political offences, which the Provisional Government announced on 26 February.[134] Louis Blanc subsequently commented: 'The still lasting terror created by the events of 1793 and 1794 being the most serious obstacle we had to contend with, the best way of removing it was to fling down the guillotine.'[135] The royal family were allowed to leave France unharmed to avoid any repetition of the imprisonment, trials, executions and prison deaths suffered by Louis XVI and his family between 1792 and 1795.[136] The former ministers of Louis-Philippe were similarly allowed to escape before any formal proceedings were brought against them. Whereas the Roman Catholic Church had suffered from severe persecution during the revolution of 1789, in contrast the Provisional Government invited representatives of the Roman Catholic Church to participate officially in public ceremonies such as the planting of liberty trees.[137]

While anxious to avoid Jacobin excesses, the Provisional Government was subject to considerable pressure to take a more radical turn. It had inherited a very serious economic and social situation, and pressure for the adoption of radical economic and social policies came from socialists within and outside government and from popular demands and demonstrations. Moreover, moderate republicans who dominated the Provisional Government appreciated the need to placate unemployed Paris workers, socialists and left-wing republicans, at least until a new national parliament had met. As early as 24 February the Provisional Government decreed that items worth ten francs or less deposited at any State pawnshop since the beginning of the month should be returned to their owners. The next day the Provisional Government pronounced that it guaranteed work to all male citizens, that workers had a right to form the equivalent of trade unions (prohibited by the Chapelier Law of 1791 and subsequent legislation) and that workers would now be allocated the civil list (which had formerly covered the expenses of Louis-Philippe and his family).[138] An attempt to realise the ambitious promise of full employment was made on 26 February with the decree immediately establishing National Workshops. Unemployed male workers resident in Paris were invited to register at the *mairie* of their *arrondissement*. If work could be found for them (usually preparing ground for construction work), they would be paid at the rate of two francs per day, the average daily wage for Paris workers then being approximately three francs and fifty centimes. Otherwise they would qualify for the equivalent of unemployment benefit of just one franc and fifty centimes per day.

Despite these indications that the Provisional Government was prepared to act in the interests of the Parisian working class, militant workers continued to press for further concessions. During the morning of 28 February a large demonstration of workers marched on the Hôtel de Ville demanding a 'Ministry of Progress' and the 'Organisation of Labour'. Lamartine and the majority of the Provisional Government were unsympathetic to these demands, but Louis Blanc vigorously defended them and threatened to resign along with Albert if they were not met. Unwilling to inflame the mood of militant Paris workers, the members of the Provisional Government agreed on a compromise whereby a Government Commission for the Workers meeting in the Luxembourg Palace (the former Chamber of Peers) would be concerned with the condition of the working class. The Luxembourg Commission, as it became known, with Louis Blanc as its president and Albert as its vice president, first met on 1 March. The ushers of the former Chamber of Peers, still wearing their old uniforms (plus a tricolore armband), now looked after between one hundred and fifty and two hundred workers' delegates, a startling change from their previous duties.[139] Initial topics discussed included the length of the working day and the abolition of *marchandage* or the expoitation of workers by sub-contractors, a practice then particularly prevalent in the construction industry. The commission agreed that the maximum legal working day should be reduced by one hour to ten hours in Paris and eleven hours in the provinces and that the practice of *marchandage* should be abolished. Louis Blanc secured the consent of representatives of Paris employers to these measures the following day, when they were immediately decreed by the Provisional Government.[140] On 21 March a scale of fines was introduced for those found guilty of having exploited workers through *marchandage*. The Luxembourg Commission also helped to negotiate the end of a strike by Paris public carriage drivers. In addition to the National Workshops, the reduction of unemployment was attempted by allocating special funds for the maintenance and conservation of former royal palaces and important government-owned buildings and by outlawing unfair competition from workers in prisons, charitable institutions and religious communities.

In Paris and in the provinces the Provisional Government authorised municipal and departmental authorities to borrow money to finance labour-intensive public works projects. The nationalisation of French railway companies and coal mines was also considered. However, any further moves towards socialism were blocked by the anti-socialist majority in the Provisional Government. Louis Blanc had urged the creation of a Ministry of Progress which would develop and implement socialist policies, a proposal strongly supported by the workers in the Luxembourg Commission. However, on 16 April an attempt to impose a Ministry of Progress on the Provisional Government failed. A huge demonstration took a petition for a Ministry of Progress to the Hôtel de Ville, only to be confronted by the massed ranks of the Paris National Guard. The guardsmen stood firm, the petition was rejected, and the demonstrators eventually dispersed.[141]

Employment schemes cost money, as did other government initiatives such as the creation of the *garde nationale mobile*. At the same time, the economic crisis had decreased tax revenues and the February Revolution had made the collection of taxes more difficult. On 29 February the Provisional Government decided to confiscate and melt down the royal silver, except those items classified as 'objets d'art', while all the other property belonging to members of the royal family was provisionally impounded. Even the diamonds from the royal crown were later removed and sold, and arrangements were made, though never acted upon, for the sale of forests and agricultural land formerly belonging to the French Crown.[142] Meanwhile, all existing taxes continued to be collected as far as possible, citizens being urged, 'in the name of patriotism', not to delay their tax payments.[143] The main exceptions were the stamp tax on newspapers and periodicals, which was abolished, and the salt tax, which was due to be cancelled on 1 January 1849. An attempt was made to borrow with the flotation of a new government loan offering an interest rate of five per cent. A huge shortfall between government income and expenditure still remained so, on 16 March, Garnier-Pagès, who had succeeded Goudchaux as Minister of Finance on 5 March, persuaded the Provisional Government to raise the property tax by a massive 45 per cent in 1848 only. Garnier-Pagès and his government colleagues were desperate to avoid State bankruptcy. They were distrustful of the introduction of a paper currency and reluctant to sell public assets such as State forests. At the same time they found themselves unable to borrow money because of the collapse of financial confidence, yet they had to cope with debts contracted under Louis-Philippe, falling tax revenues and increased expenditure on the military and the National Workshops.[144] What became known as the forty-five centimes tax (in fact a forty-five per cent increase to the existing property tax) came into immediate effect and was immensely unpopular with all property-owners and particularly with peasant landowners. In Paris special taxes were also introduced payable by the owners or tenants of property worth more than 800 francs per year, by the owners of luxury carriages, by those who employed more than one male domestic servant, and even by dog-owners, so that, insultingly, domestic servants could be taxed like dogs.[145]

The National Assembly elections of 23 April 1848

The measures taken by the Provisional Government were not as drastic as some had hoped and others had feared, partly because the Provisional Government always saw itself as a temporary administration. The first proclamation, issued on 24 February, referred to a provisional government 'momentarily invested with the responsibility of assuring and organising the national victory', and declared that the people would be 'immediately consulted'.[146] The same day the Provisional Government publicly referred to a forthcoming National Assembly.[147] The vicomte Cormenin, appointed Vice President of the Conseil d'Etat on 29 February, was responsible for drawing up proposals for the elections to what was now styled the National Constituent Assembly. Having served both Napoleon and the Restoration monarchy as a civil servant, Cormenin had become a left-wing opposition deputy after the 1830 revolution and he was the author of numerous legal and political publications.[148] He first submitted his proposals to the Provisional Government on 2 March.

The principle was unanimously agreed that the parliamentary vote should be on the basis of direct manhood suffrage, without any tax qualification (unlike the Restoration and July monarchies). However, at its meeting on 4 March the Provisional Government decided to withhold the vote from French soldiers, since they would not be able to vote in their communes without dispersing the army in a manner which would be arbitrary and dangerous for national security. General Lamoricière's vigorous objections subsequently removed this exclusion.[149] On the other hand, it was at once agreed that domestic servants should have the vote (in contrast to the constitution of 1791). On 4 and 5 March the Provisional Government further agreed that 9 April should be the date for the National Assembly elections with the National Assembly meeting for the first time on 20 April. They decided that the total number of elected representatives of the people should be 900 and that departments should return a varying number of representatives, according to their populations (one representative for every 40,000 inhabitants). The franchise was extended to all male French citizens who were aged at least twenty-one, if they fulfilled a six-month residence requirement and were in full possession of their civic rights. Potential parliamentary candidates had to be aged at least twenty-five and in possession of their civic rights. It was further agreed that voting should be secret, in the *chef-lieu* of each canton and according to the system of *scrutin de liste*. According to this system, the department was the constituency, so voters voted for a list of candidates to represent the whole department, whereas under the July monarchy voters had elected one candidate to represent their *arrondissement* (*scrutin d'arrondissement*).[150]

The introduction of manhood suffrage for national parliamentary elections, and later for local elections, was the Provisional Government's most audacious and significant achievement. As Rémusat put it, it was 'le fait capital de l'année 1848'.[151] Manhood suffrage had featured in the Jacobin constitution of 1793, but possibly just for propaganda reasons and in any case the 1793 constitution was never enforced. Before 1848, no significant European state had ever adopted manhood suffrage for national parliamentary elections; and the electoral decree of 5 March expanded the French electorate from approximately 246,000 to approaching ten million, in itself an astonishing increase with unpredictable political consequences. During March, mayors all over France drew up lists of those qualified to vote.

Almost immediately, left-wing republicans and socialists began to argue that more time was needed to educate public opinion and to prepare for a general election. They feared that many of the newly enfranchised lacked political awareness and would be subject to the conservative influences of landowners, employers and Roman Catholic clergy. Also, except in Paris and a handful of provincial cities, they knew that they lacked effective electoral organisations and supportive newspapers. Assuming that left-wing republican and socialist candidates would not win many seats in the forthcoming National Assembly elections, they wanted to impose a radical programme on the Provisional Government before the National Assembly met. On 7 March Blanqui, on behalf of the Société Républicaine Centrale (the first and initially the most prestigious of the Paris revolutionary clubs of 1848), presented the Provisional Government with a petition demanding absolute freedom of the press and association, postponement of the National Assembly elections, suppression of the magistrature, and the arming, organising and payment of all unemployed workers by the government. As spokesman of the Provisional Government, Lamartine replied that the September Press Laws had already been abolished (on 5 March), that the National Assembly elections could not be postponed, and that the right of association had to be restricted by considerations of public order. He said nothing about suppressing the magistrature or about arming, organising and paying all unemployed workers. However, he did say that he and his colleagues considered their first duty, after what they had done to safeguard liberty, was to restore as soon as possible to the nation itself the powers they had seized in the national interest, and not postpone for another minute the quasi-dictatorship that circumstances had compelled them to assume.[152]

Blanqui nevertheless kept up the pressure. On 12 March he persuaded the Société Républicaine Centrale to adopt a motion inviting other Paris clubs to join a campaign to pressure the Provisional Government to postpone the elections for both the National Assembly and for the Paris National Guard.[153] Other Paris clubs, such as the Société Démocratique Centrale, proceeded to demand that the National Assembly elections should be postponed, at least until all the mayors and *juges de paix* appointed under the July monarchy had been replaced.[154] On 14 March, Blanqui himself, representing the Société Républicaine Centrale, issued a second protest against holding the National Assembly elections on 9 April. He argued that the political education of the people would take time, that only the conservatives, the 'parti royaliste', were prepared for the elections, and that if the elections were held soon the reactionaries would triumph. He predicted that this would lead to civil war, because Paris, 'the heart and the brain of France', would not submit to a return to the past.[155]

However, the left was divided. Blanqui wanted an indefinite or at least a three-month postponement of the elections, but the utopian communist leader, Cabet, proposed instead that the army should remain outside Paris, while the National Guard elections should be postponed until 5 April and the National Assembly elections until 31 May. The Luxembourg Commission and several radical clubs accepted Cabet's proposal and tried to impose it on the Provisional Government. At the same time, elite regiments of the Paris National Guard mounted a protest on 16 March against their dissolution. Furious at this demonstration of right-wing muscle, the next day no less than 200,000 demonstrators took to the streets of Paris and marched to the Hôtel de Ville to demand that the National Assembly elections be postponed. However, the Provisional Government refused to commit itself, and the demonstrators eventually marched off peacefully.

Members of the Provisional Government also held different views with regard to political campaigning. Ledru-Rollin, as Minister of the Interior, issued a circular, published on 12 March 1848, informing the *commissaires* who had been sent out into the departments that their powers were unlimited. They should promote republican sentiments by entrusting public positions to the politically reliable ('hommes sûrs et sympathiques') and encourage the formation of republican electoral committees. They should also vet the political credentials and the republican appeal of prospective parliamentary candidates. 'Let election day be a triumph for the revolution.'[156] Understandably, this circular caused much alarm and provoked immediate criticism,[157] while at the same time revealing a split in the Provisional Government. When, on 15 March, a deputation from the conservative Club Républicain pour la Liberté Electorale complained to the Provisional Government about this circular, Lamartine publicly replied that the government did not want to influence the elections. As individual citizens, members of the government could support particular candidates, but collectively the government would not imitate the Guizot ministry by engaging in electoral corruption.[158] Also on 15 March, presumably persuaded by Lamartine, the Provisional Government agreed that individual members of the government, but not the government collectively, could endorse candidatures to the National Assembly.[159] A declaration published in the *Bulletin des lois* on 18 March confirmed that the Provisional Government would not imitate previous governments, which, it was suggested, had usurped the sovereignty of the people, corrupted the electors and bought the country's conscience at an immoral price.

Lamartine had argued that popular sovereignty would be usurped if the government imposed itself on France, and even threatened resignation when Louis Blanc urged postponing elections for a month.[160] Many left-wing republicans and socialists like Louis Blanc continued to consider that the elections should be delayed, to give more time for the spread of republicanism, especially in the countryside. As George Sand observed: 'The elections come too quickly, above all for the peasant who does not think quickly.'[161] A partial victory was gained when, after Albert and Louis Blanc had threatened to resign over the issue, the Provisional Government on 26 March postponed the National Assembly elections to 23 April and the first meeting of the National Assembly to 4 May. Concern that lists of those eligible to vote would not be ready by 9 April, as well as left-wing pressure, accounted for this delay. Blanqui was still not prepared to accept this compromise and organised a second demonstration against the Provisional Government on 16 April. Well defended by the Paris National Guard, the Provisional Government refused to postpone the 23 April election date, and this second demonstration also passed off peacefully.

Despite Lamartine's objections, and the publicly-declared neutrality of the Provisional Government, Ledru-Rollin exploited his position at the Ministry of the Interior to try to secure a republican victory in the National Assembly elections. The ministry commissioned republican propaganda from Alfred Delvau, Jules Favre, Clarles Lecointe, Elias Regnault and George Sand which appeared in twenty-five numbers or issues of the *Bulletins de la République* between 13 March and 6 May. The thirteenth *Bulletin* posed the question: 'Should the Government intervene in the electoral campaign, or should it simply ensure that the electoral process operates satisfactorily?' The answer was that the government should enlighten France and work openly to confound the intrigues of the counter-revolutionaries. The *commissaires* sent out into the departments should act like 'noble missionaries of new ideas' by serving as the government's electoral agents. The sixteenth *Bulletin* even threatened that, if the elections were not satisfactory, Paris would take the defence of the Republic into its own hands by launching a second insurrection.

Meanwhile, Ledru-Rollin began a new purge of those holding official posts. Whereas moderate republicans had predominated in the first appointments of *commissaires*, between 17 March and 16 April many were replaced by left-wing republicans and a new category of *commissaires généraux* was created. The *commissaires* in turn 'republicanised' the ranks of mayors, *juges de paix* and tax collectors. They also drew up lists of republican candidates, often including their own names and those of *sous-commissaires*. They promoted the opening of republican clubs and instructed mayors and local civil servants to use their influence to secure the election of republican candidates. They also proceeded to spend public money on printing posters, lists of approved republican candidates and voting bulletins.[162] Ledru-Rollin himself spent 123,000 francs from his secret funds on political activities, notably sending out between 400 and 450 delegates from the Paris clubs to spread republican propaganda throughout France, an operation which he entrusted to the Paris Club des Clubs, which represented most of the Paris republican clubs.[163] Non-commissioned officers performed a similar role in army regiments. These activities could not be concealed. In any case, Ledru-Rollin issued a public statement in *Le Moniteur* on 7 April that the government should enlighten France and openly work to foil the intrigues of the counter-revolutionaries.[164]

Ledru-Rollin's efforts were supplemented by those of Hippolyte Carnot and Lamartine. As Minister of Public Instruction, Carnot attempted to use school teachers, and particularly primary school teachers (there were not many State secondary schools), as republican propagandists and electoral agents. He organised courses of lectures on civic duties for teachers; he encouraged the publication of manuals on republicanism, which often took the form of catechisms; he promoted the formation of committees of teachers to organise republican political activities; and he arranged for the circulation to teachers of lists of approved republican candidates, for whom teachers were supposed to vote.[165] Lamartine tried to influence the elections by publicly endorsing individual candidates. At a time when he was uniquely popular and influential, he sent letters of support and encouragement to at least thirty candidates, letters which were invariably reprinted in newspapers and electoral manifestos.[166] Those favoured by such letters included republicans (Alexandre Bixio, Ledru-Rollin) and even Fourierists (Félix Cantagrel, Victor Considérant, Victor Hennequin), but also Legitimists (Charles de Chamborant, Henri Roch-Dupuys). If a 'parti Lamartine' did exist at this time, its members did not possess much political coherence other than some sort of personal tie with Lamartine, but they clearly believed that this tie would count in their favour, if only to rescue them from obscurity. Charles Alexandre, a candidate in Finistère, disarmingly acknowledged his inadequacies ('Je suis bien jeune et bien obscur. Derrière moi je n'ai nulle oeuvre.'), before producing his trump card, a letter from Lamartine.[167] The belief in the potency of a letter of endorsement from Lamartine seems to have been shared. Thus Le Franc-Comtois of Besançon (Doubs) on 11 April described a letter by Lamartine endorsing the candidature of Alexandre Bixio as 'a certificate of honour and patriotism'; and L'Avenir national of Limoges (Haute-Vienne) on 19 April gushed that Arthur de La Guéronnière had 'the honour to hold aloft the banner of M. de Lamartine', who was referred to as 'the illustrious statesman' and 'the hope of France'.

Outside the Provisional Government, the Luxembourg Commission and republican clubs and newspapers campaigned for the republican cause. On 5 March a committee was formed at the Luxembourg Commission to vet candidates for the National Assembly elections. It reported to the Luxembourg Commission which agreed on a list of candidates on 17 April.[168] Most of the republican Paris clubs, except the most militant, such as the Club de la Révolution, sent delegates to a Comité Central pour les Elections Générales which, by 15 April, had endorsed 850 republican candidates for the 900 seats in the National Assembly. The president or chairman of this Central Committee was Athanase Recurt, the deputy mayor of Paris, and committee members included Alton-Shée, Jacques-Alexandre Bixio, Pierre-François Bocage, Bois-le-Comte, Félix Cantagrel (journalist on La Démocratie pacifique), Michel Goudchaux, Lamennais (editor-in-chief of Le Peuple constituant), Jules Michelet, Edgar Quinet, Alexandre Rey, Charles Ribeyrolles (editor-in-chief of La Réforme), Clément Thomas, and Achille Vaulabelle.[169] They represented nearly all shades of the French Left, except the extreme socialists and radical militants. The latter, who included Armand Barbès, Amable Longepied, Joseph Sobrier and other members of the Club de la Révolution, mounted their own separate electoral campaign from 18 March through a Comité Révolutionnaire and the radical Paris newspaper, La Commune de Paris.[170] A list of candidates supported by the Comité Révolutionnaire and the Club des Clubs was published in La Commune de Paris on 19, 20 and 22 April.[171]

Republican newspapers in Paris and throughout France published lists of approved candidates for whom their readers were urged to vote. The lists were drawn up either by the newspaper's editorial team or by a club or electoral committee politically aligned with the newspaper. Thus at the end of March the Comité Central des Elections Générales, composed of moderate republicans, met and chose by vote a list of thirty-four approved candidates for the department of the Seine.[172] Members of the Provisional Government and those holding official positions predominated, but socialists such as Etienne Cabet and Pierre Leroux were excluded. This so outraged Cabet that the final list published on 22 April in his newspaper, Le Populaire, included just four radical members of the Provisional Government (Albert, Louis Blanc, Flocon and Ledru-Rollin), as well as Cabet himself, Leroux, Proudhon, Raspail, Barbès, Blanqui, Caussidière, Agricol Perdiguier and various workers. Apart from Raspail, Barbès and Blanqui, these names also featured on the list issued by La Démocratie pacifique on 22 April, together with Fourierists such as Victor Considérant, César Daly and Jules Lechevallier. La Réforme (23 April) and Le Représentant du peuple printed the list of the Comité Révolutionnaire and the Club des Clubs, with slight variations. For the thirty-four National Assembly seats for the department of the Seine, only the candidatures of Albert, Louis Blanc, Flocon and Ledru Rollin received the backing of the six key Paris left-wing newspapers – La Commune de Paris, La Démocratie pacifique, Le National, Le Populaire, La Réforme and Le Représentant du peuple, though Caussidière, Pierre Leroux and Agricol Perdiguier were supported by all the newspapers except Le National.

Tocqueville famously asserted in his memoirs, with reference to the Provisional Government and the National Assembly elections of April 1848: 'There have been more wicked revolutionaries than those of 1848, but I do not think that there were ever any more stupid; they neither knew how to make use of universal suffrage nor how to do without it.'[173] In fact, members of the Provisional Government did try to influence the elections, and they were helped by figures such as George Sand and by the Paris republican club movement. Their efforts, though, were not very successful. Many considered that the government should not even try to influence parliamentary elections, so as to avoid one of the 'crimes' of the Guizot administration, but should instead allow genuinely free and fair elections to take place. In any case, republican propaganda could backfire. The political role of the commissaires, and Ledru-Rollin's circular of 12 March, caused much resentment in the provinces and may have been counter-productive.[174] Certainly in Paris Emile de Girardin, editor of the influential Paris newspaper, La Presse, was so outraged that he switched from firm support to belligerent criticism of the Provisional Government. [175] Some commissaires, such as Ulysse Trélat in the Limousin, were not very effective,[176] though a significant number of commissaires and former commissaires did gain election on 23 April. Underpaid, under-appreciated and in some cases anti-clerical, many primary school teachers were ideologically sympathetic to republicanism and hoped that the Second Republic would improve their lot.[177] On the other hand, primary school teachers were not necessarily either republican or willing to exert themselves in the republican cause, nor could they always successfully counteract local conservative influences. Conservatives, of course, condemned as entirely improper Carnot's attempts to convert primary school teachers into republican missionaries and to persuade them to stand as parliamentary candidates.[178] Also, republicans could sometimes badly mishandle electoral campaigning. For instance, in the Vaucluse, which had been assigned six representatives in the National Assembly, the local republican newspaper published a list of eight candidates.[179]

The Provisional Government and the republicans also had competition. The February 1848 revolution had temporarily eclipsed, but by no means totally eradicated, the political influence of the traditional ruling class in the provinces. Approximately a third of the *commissaires* appointed in early March had previously served as parliamentary deputies, mayors or city councillors; and their social background, as well as their concern to maintain law and order, could lead them to establish cordial relations with local notables.[180] Similarly, wealthy landowners could be found in the new *commissions municipales* even, as at Blois, being in the majority; and conservative mayors sometimes remained in post, for instance at Rennes.[181] The National Guard, which might have become the armed militia of the Republic and the revolution, instead recruited significantly from the wealthier classes and almost at once began to play a counter-revolutionary role as the upholder of law and order. Moreover, economic power remained largely unchanged, with no serious challenge to the ownership or control of banks, businesses or land. The abolition of restrictions on newspapers and public meetings could be exploited by the right as well as by the left. Legitimists were now able to operate politically more freely than under the July monarchy. New conservative newspapers were founded, such as *L'Assemblée nationale* of Paris on 1 March and *La Liberté* of Arras before 25 March, and they found a ready audience. By 30 April the print run of *L'Assemblée nationale* had reached an impressive 27,000.[182] Liberal and conservative newspapers enjoyed total freedom to attack the Provisional Government. Ledru-Rollin's circular of 12 March informing *commissaires* that their powers were unlimited ended an initial honeymoon period, with critical articles in *L'Assemblée nationale* (14 March), *Le Siècle* (15 March) and numerous conservative newspapers in the provinces. The first important Paris newspaper to break openly with the Provisional Government was *La Presse*. In a leading article on 28 March, Emile de Girardin announced a complete change of attitude towards the government and subsequently became one of its severest critics.

Conservatives, like republicans, radicals and socialists, could form political clubs. In Paris a Club Républicain pour la Liberté Electorale, closely associated with the Paris newspaper, *L'Assemblée nationale*, first met on 10 March. At its second meeting it agreed to protest against Ledru-Rollin's circular of 12 March and elicited Lamartine's response of 15 March critical of Ledru-Rollin. Conservative newspapers in Paris and the provinces widely reproduced this disavowal by Lamartine of Ledru-Rollin's Jacobin tendencies. Like the republicans and socialists, conservative Paris clubs agreed on lists of approved candidates, the list of the Club Central de la Garde Nationale being one of the most widely circulated and reproduced. The Liberté d'Enseignement or Comité pour la Défense de la

Liberté Religieuse, an electoral committee formed in 1846 principally by Montalembert to defend the interests of the Roman Catholic Church, met as early as 26 February to begin planning for the forthcoming elections. On 10 March the committee sent a private letter to the bishops, encouraging them to work with their clergy to identify potential pro-clerical candidates. Some bishops, on their own initiative, drew up lists of recommended candidates and distributed them to the clergy in their diocese and to local newspapers.[183] Similarly, some parish priests turned their churches into political clubs and, more commonly, used sermons and the confessional to spread anti-republican propaganda. The postponed election date, 23 April, coincided with Easter Sunday, and there are many reports of parish priests leading the voters in their parish to the polling booth, having celebrated together an early service of Mass and having distributed lists of candidates which served as ballot papers.[184] The conservative political influence of the Roman Catholic Church in provincial France was widely reinforced by the activities of local conservative electoral committees, often linked to a local conservative newspaper;[185] and conservative newspapers collectively were more numerous, better funded and had larger circulations than their republican counterparts, particularly in rural and provincial France. Conservatives could also afford to print ballot papers listing the names of conservative-approved candidates.[186]

It might have been thought that the April 1848 elections for the National Assembly would have involved a conflict essentially between the left and the right, between republicans of whatever tendency on the one hand and their conservative opponents on the other. In fact, Legitimists, Orleanists, other conservatives and moderate republicans often tended to form an informal alliance, backing, and voting for, many of the same parliamentary candidates, rallying round a political ideology which stressed the importance of order, property, family and religion, and uniting in their opposition to the candidatures and ideologies of the left-wing republicans and socialists. Thus in Paris two liberal-conservative newspapers, Le Constitutionnel and Le Siècle, joined the main Paris moderate republican newsaper, Le National, to form the Comité Central des Elections Générales, which promoted an electoral list combining moderate republicans with conservatives. The other main conservative Paris newspaper, Le Journal des Débats, backed a very similar list. Both lists included all members of the Provisional Government, except Albert, Louis Blanc, Flocon and Ledru-Rollin, the four members in all the left-wing republican and socialist lists. Even Legitimists often included in their electoral lists at least some moderate republicans, notably moderate republican members of the Provisional Government. In Seine-Inférieure, twelve out of a total of nineteen candidates featured on both the moderate republican list and the conservative list.[187] Similarly, in, for example, the departments of Maine-et-Loire, Nord and Loir-et-Cher, Legitimists included moderate republicans in their electoral lists.[188]

Moderate republicanism, without any association with conservatism, had some electoral appeal, particularly in urban areas. Identification with the increasingly unpopular Provisional Government, though, restricted this appeal. Left-wing republicanism and socialism had a very limited electoral appeal, except in Paris and a handful of towns and cities with significant urban working-class populations, such as Lyons, Rouen and Saint-Etienne. However, in these urban constituencies left-wing republicans and socialists tended to back too many candidates, whereas the moderate republicans successfully concentrated their vote on a limited number of candidates.[189] In any case, republicanism of any description still remained a minority enthusiasm in most of rural France, where the traditional influences of landowner and priest tended to prevail. There were, of course, exceptions, such as the Pyrénées-Orientales, where the three Arago brothers – Emmanuel, Etienne and François – were all elected, reflecting the unique influence this republican family dynasty had gained in the department.

Most candidates in the April 1848 National Assembly elections issued *professions de foi* or electoral manifestos. Unsurprisingly, they usually proclaimed, honestly or otherwise, a commitment to the Second Republic and to republicanism. Those who could claim a republican past usually advertised it. Adolphe Thiers was atypical: he declared that he had neither desired nor wanted the Republic, that he had considered French liberties adequately safeguarded by the constitutional monarchy, and that he believed the British constitutional example should not be spurned.[190] Another exception was Montalembert, a candidate in the Doubs, who promised support for the Second Republic only if it guaranteed religion, property and family.[191] Rémusat adopted a more philosophical position in his electoral manifesto:[192]

> Under the Republic as under the [July] Monarchy, France is always France; she has eternal rights and eternal interests, which I will always strive to defend. I asked of the consitutional monarchy order, liberty and the grandeur of France; I ask the same of the Republic.

Candidates generally proclaimed their commitment to traditional liberal freedoms: freedom of conscience and of religious worship, liberty of the press, freedom of association and assembly, the right to petition. The general encouragement of agriculture, the improvement of the condition of the working class, the provision of free primary education for all, and the protection of private property, were widely supported. More specific demands, reflecting individual interests, included the abolition of capital punishment, the wider use of trial by jury, the abolition of the practice of avoiding military service through replacements, the creation of agricultutral colonies, and improved public provision of libraries, savings banks, crèches, wash houses and public baths. Left-wing republicans and socialists tended to emphasise democracy and manhood suffrage, progressive income and wealth taxes, the reduction or abolition of taxes (such as the salt tax) which fell particularly on the poor, public health and social provision including a Ministry of Public Health, care for the elderly and the infirm, the promotion of mutual benefit societies, and State intervention in the economy so as to guarantee employment to workers. One candidate wanted uniform postal charges throughout France.[193] The architect and editor of *La Revue de l'architecture et des travaux publics*, César Daly, championed low-cost and salubrious housing for workers.[194] Rescanière-Lange promised to campaign for the election of bishops, parish priests and army officers and for the revision of the forest codes.[195] Clément Dulac even maintained that hunting should be free on Sundays for those too poor to be able to afford a hunting licence.[196]

Some candidates produced quite comprehensive political manifestos as their *professions de foi*, for instance Victor Hennequin (the Fourierist editor of *La Démocratie pacifique*), who, like Thiers, was a candidate in the Bouches-du-Rhône. Hennequin first outlined his constitutional programme: France forever a Republic, with a single chamber legislature and guaranteed rights of assembly, association, employment, press freedom, secular education and religious toleration. On a more conservative note, he wanted the institutions of the family and property to be respected. In foreign affairs, France should be the natural ally of all peoples, providing an example to the world but not imposing its institutions on anybody and respecting existing French frontiers. At a time when the revolutionary and nationalist tide seemed to be sweeping across Europe, Hennequin looked forward to an era of universal peace and to the creation of a European congress or parliament, where delegates from all European nations would publicly debate world issues. Improved communications, a single currency and a uniform system of weights and measures would promote European unity, and throughout Europe agriculture, industry, trade and culture would be encouraged. Within France, State schools would prepare candidates for all branches of public service; a new Ministry of Industrial Progress and Social Welfare and a new Ministry of Agriculture would be established; railway, canal, mail-coach and insurance companies would be nationalised, with compensation for the owners; a new national bank would be founded; an ambitious public works programme would be launched; and encouragement would be given for the provision of crèches and old peoples' homes.[197]

What is perhaps most striking is the repetition in so many *professions de foi* of a commitment to the protection of order, property and family, very often religion as well, and, in at least one instance, 'heritage'. With royalism discredited and Bonapartism not yet fully revived, conservatives needed a new political creed which would have mass appeal. In a country in which peasant landowners composed a large proportion of the electorate, an emphasis on order, property, family and religion was bound to have a wide appeal. Left-wing candidates usually shared this commitment to property and family, if not religion.[198] Of course, these concepts did not have quite the same meaning for conservatives as for those on the left, and left-wing candidates may have tried to present themselves as more conservative than they really were in order to win votes. Nevertheless, more of a political consensus existed in France in April 1848 than might be supposed.

Before the elections, at least some contemporaries predicted that the election results would not be too radical. Tocqueville reported from Normandy on 3 April

1848: 'The rural inhabitants are full of good sense and, up till now, of steadfastness, and, since they form the great majority, presumably they will impose their choices.'[199] The following day Gustave de Beaumont wrote privately to Tocqueville: 'It is extremely probable that I will be re-elected along with my former colleagues from the Sarthe.'[200] Such predictions proved accurate. An analysis of the election results suggests that the elected representatives included seventy-five ex-peers or nobles and 439 former monarchists, compared to just 230 moderate republicans and only fifty-five left-wing republicans and socialists.[201] Left-wing republicans and socialists did not perform well. Even in the department of the Seine, leading socialists such as Barbès, Blanqui, Cabet, Raspail and Sobrier failed to gain election, though Barbès was elected in his native department of the Aude; and of the twenty-one workers endorsed by the Luxembourg delegates, the Comité central and *Le Représentant du peuple*, only Agricol Perdiguier was successful. In contrast, of the thirty-four candidates endorsed by *Le Constitutionnel* in the department of the Seine, twenty-one were elected.

What was true of the department of the Seine was even more true of most provincial departments, with the exception of the Allier, Aude, Bas-Rhin, Corsica, Côte-d'Or, Haute-Garonne, Hautes-Alpes, Isère, Pyrénées-Orientales and Var. The electorate generally rejected left-wing republicans and socialists, except in a few major urban centres, and even moderate republican candidates did not attract as many votes as might have been expected. Legitimists, on the other hand, staged a minor political comeback, especially in Brittany, the Vendée and the poorer departments of the Massif Central, with at least fifty-six elected,[202] including grandees such as Berryer, Falloux and La Rochejacquelein. Also elected were numerous politicians who had been prominent during the reign of Louis-Philippe, even conservatives such as Dupin, Montalembert and Sallandrouze, but more especially opponents of the Guizot adminstration such as Odilon Barrot, Gustave de Beaumont, Duvergier de Hauranne, Rémusat and Tocqueville (though not Thiers). Candidates in holy orders also did surprisingly well. Sixteen members of the Roman Catholic clergy were elected, including Lacordaire. The Bishop of Quimper headed the list of successful candidates in the department of Finistère, the Bishop of Langres was elected in the Morbihan and the Bishop of Orléans in the Lozère.[203]

Perhaps the most striking feature of the elections, though, was the extraordinary success of Lamartine's candidature. Ten departments elected Lamartine – Bouches-du-Rhône, Côte-d'Or, Dordogne, Finistère, Gironde, Ille-et-Vilaine, Nord, Saône-et-Loire, Seine and Seine-Inférieure.[204] Within those ten departments were major population centres, such as Paris, Marseilles, Bordeaux, Lille, Rouen, Dijon, Rennes and Le Havre; and the departments were geographically representative with the Nord in the north, Bouches-du-Rhône in the south, Finistère in the west, and Saône-et-Loire in the centre. Lamartine headed the list of successful candidates in five departments (Gironde, Nord, Saône-et-Loire, Seine and Seine-Inférieure), and was elected either second or third in four more departments (Bouches-du-Rhône, Dordogne, Finistère and Ille-et-Vilaine). In the Côte-d'Or, where he was the tenth and last candidate to be elected, apparently many electors did not vote for him because they assumed he would, if successful, opt for another department, and they did not want to go to the polls a second time.[205] The ten departments returned Lamartine with 1,283,501 votes, a number far greater than that obtained by any other candidate; and in the Seine he came ahead of every other member of the Provisional Government.

Altogether, the election results for Lamartine amounted to a personal plebiscite in his favour, and he seemed to be the most popular and influential political figure in France. For conservatives, his aristocratic origins, his long official and political career, his status as a major landowner, and his literary reputation offered reassurance to those frightened by his more obviously radical and revolutionary colleagues; and, although Lamartine had become a republican and a revolutionary, he had consistently opposed socialism. He had rejected the red flag, the death penalty for political offences, foreign wars of liberation, and government interference in the elections. At this time, Lamartine could also appeal to republicans and even to radicals. He had openly broken with Guizot and the conservatives in 1843 and thereafter had championed liberal and humanitarian causes such as the abolition of slavery and the improvement of the working and living conditions of the working classes. More recently, he had established republican credentials: his *Histoire des Girondins*, published in 1847, had portrayed Robespierre and the Jacobins relatively favourably; he had been one of the most determined supporters of the twelfth *arrondissement* reform banquet; on 24 February he had intervened decisively in the Chamber of Deputies to reject the regency and to support the formation of a Provisional Government; and after 24 February he had cultivated contacts with left-wing political leaders and clubs and worked for an inclusive republicanism.[206]

Polling day on 23 April seems to have been remarkably peaceful throughout France, and a massive eighty-four per cent of those eligible cast their votes. Direct intimidation of voters did not occur to any significant extent. Nevertheless, the election was far from being completely free and fair. Since many voters were illiterate, economically dependent upon their employer or landlord, and had never voted in any election before in their lives, they could in many cases be influenced or manipulated. Some workers complained of having encountered difficulties in enrolling on the electoral lists, due to *mairies* withholding birth certificates and landlords six-month residence certificates.[207] In rural communities, all the eligible males often marched as a group to the polling station, sometimes led by their priest, mayor or local notable.[208] Voting was public, and ballot papers were not provided, so many voters just used a printed list of candidates issued to them by a priest, employer, landowner, political club or local newspaper. In addition, a number of factors tended to benefit conservative rather than left-wing candidates. In many departments, as a result of the divisions between moderate republicans, left-wing republicans, radicals and socialists, there was a bewildering proliferation of left-wing candidates. In contrast, conservative electoral committees and newspapers often backed fewer candidates and, by including at least some moderate republicans in their electoral lists, achieved quite a broad appeal. The delay of twenty-four days achieved through postponing the elections from 9 to 23 April did not give republicans significantly more time to try to win over the electorate, but may have advantaged conservatives who were often better placed to exploit the postponement.[209] It was, in the words of Louis Blanc, 'too much or too little.'[210]

Moreover, delay allowed more time for a number of factors to sap support for republicanism. Voters objected to the alleged excesses of the *commissaires* and *sous-commissaires* and the Jacobin-style attempts by Ledru- Rollin and Carnot to influence the elections. The National Workshops were widely thought to be a waste of public funds, while at the same time there was dismay over the announcement of the forty-five centimes tax. The economic, financial and social crises seemed to be never ending and there remained the continuing threat of socialism, communism and violent revolution. To counter-balance such negative factors, the Provisional Government failed to develop a sufficiently positive pro-gramme, particularly for the peasantry. Peasant indebtedness had reached record levels, agricultural prices had fallen, and wine sales had sustained a dramatic slump. As Tocqueville and others have pointed out, the Provisional Government should have addressed such issues as peasant indebtedness and the provision of credit to farmers and peasants, as well as peasant grievances over forest codes and communal lands and the need for improved communications in rural areas.[211]

Very little violence accompanied the National Assembly elections. But as soon as voting was over violent rioting broke out in Rouen on 27 and 28 April and thirty-four people died.[212] After it had become clear that left-wing republi-cans had performed badly in the elections, the Société populaire of Limoges decided on 26 April to disarm the National Guard and form a new municipal council. The following day workers destroyed the ballot papers of soldiers, who had all voted separately, and took over the Hôtel de Ville. By the evening of 27 April a newly-formed provisional committee was in occupation of the prefec-ture. This committee tried to create a new radical military force, a *garde mobile ouvrière*, but was forced to dissolve itself at the insistence of the local *commissaire*, Ulysse Trélat, on 30 April.[213] In Nîmes clashes occurred between Protestant republicans and royalist Catholics, after it became clear that Protestant voters had refused to vote for Catholic Legitimist candidates. Catholics retaliated by largely taking over the local National Guard, which led to further trouble.[214] There were also disturbances in the textile manufacturing town of Elbeuf.

After the election results had become known, many republican felt cheated, believing that the elections had not been free and fair. They frequently directed their anger at the Roman Catholic Church. Even before the elections, *Le Progrès du Pas-de-Calais* of Arras complained on 21 April that 'The reaction had no more zealous and active agents than the clergy.' On 28 April *Le Républicain du Jura* issued an appeal to its readers: 'We invite republicans to give us all the necessary information to establish the scandalous manoeuvres of the jesuitico-royalist faction, and to denounce to us the public officials who have employed against the Republic the influence and authority which they exercise.' [215] The same newspaper referred on 30 April to 'the burlesque *dénouement* of the electoral farce which has just been played out in the Jura'; and on 7 May it complained '[The] clergy have waged, before and during the elections, a relentless war against the republicans'. *Commissaires* had complained that priests were supporting conservative candidates in the April 1848 elections;[216] and complaints of clerical influence in the elections were rife in Britanny.[217] Nor were such complaints unjustified. In Ille-et-Vilaine, seventy-two per cent of those who voted, voted for the bishop's list.[218] Other complaints included the allegation that voters in the department of Saône-et-Loire had been pressured to vote for Ledru-Rollin.[219] Altogether, the National Assembly election results tended to divide France politically into the left-wing socialists and republicans versus the rest, with the former harbouring sentiments of bitterness and revenge.

Chapter 4

The Executive Commission and the June Days

The formation of the Executive Commission

There was a general expectation that the National Assembly elections of 23 April 1848 would unite France. For the first time, a new parliament had been elected on the basis of manhood suffrage and therefore represented all adult male French citizens. A strong parliament, and a government endowed with authority and legitimacy by the newly-elected National Assembly, would be able to bring France out of its current state of crisis.[1] The reality, however, was rather different. By isolating the left-wing republicans and socialists, the election campaign had been divisive; and the poor performance of the left-wing republicans and socialists in the elections encouraged them to believe that the elections had been unfair and that they had been cheated. At the same time, the general economic situation continued to be exceptionally difficult. The persistence of the slump in demand meant that the prices of property and of agricultural products remained low and that unemployment rates remained high. Financial confidence further weakened, with consequent falls on the Paris stock exchange. Members of the French urban working class suffered particularly severely. They became more and more exasperated and increasingly concerned about government policies regarding unemployment and job creation schemes. An explosion of strikes and workers' demonstrations, and opposition, sometimes violent, to the forty-five centimes tax, testified to this discontent, which left-wing agitators and Bonapartist propagandists attempted to exploit.

The National Assembly first met in Paris on 4 May in a hastily-constructed chamber in the courtyard of the old parliament building. After a ceremonial opening,[2] the Assembly confirmed the proclamation of the Republic and then heard reports from Lamartine and other members of the Provisional Government justifying their tenure of office, reports which won a congratulatory vote from the Assembly. The principal legislative task facing the Assembly was the drawing up of a new constitution for France, but its most immediate task was to approve another interim government. In the course of discussions and meetings held between 4 and 9 May, the issue polarised around two main proposals: were members of the government to be elected by the entire Assembly or should the

Assembly elect an Executive Commission, which would in turn appoint government ministers? The moderate republicans, who had predominated in the Provisional Government, wanted to remain in power, and thus favoured an Executive Commission which they could monopolise and which would enable them to fill most of the ministerial posts. Conservatives tended to prefer a government directly elected by the Assembly and to demand the exclusion of all radicals and socialists from office. However, conservatives were not yet ready to exploit their majority position in the Assembly; and they had to take account of Lamartine, who had come first in the Seine elections and who had polled some 1,283,500 votes in ten departments. Like the moderate republicans, Lamartine wanted an Executive Commission, but unlike most of them he insisted that the Executive Commission should include Ledru-Rollin, the most prominent left-wing republican. Among others, Marie, Marrast and Dupont de l'Eure opposed the inclusion of Ledru-Rollin. Executive Commissions consisting of Arago, Garnier-Pagès, Lamartine, Marrast, Marie or Dupont de l'Eure, or of just Arago, Garnier-Pagès and Lamartine, were proposed.[3] Ledru-Rollin had other supporters besides Lamartine, such as the republicans Jules Bastide, Sain de Boislecomte and Marc Caussidière,[4] but Lamartine's support was almost certainly crucial. The unrivalled number of votes which he had received in the April elections made him uniquely influential; and in the National Assembly, in a persuasive speech delivered on 9 May, he urged unity and conciliation and the formation of a politically representative executive commission. Consequently, on 10 May the National Assembly elected to the Executive Commission, besides Arago, Garnier-Pagès, Marie and Lamartine, the controversial Ledru-Rollin.

Ledru-Rollin came from a relatively prosperous bourgeois background. He had become a left-wing lawyer, and in 1841 had gained election to the Chamber of Deputies in the Sarthe. As a deputy, Ledru-Rollin had immediately gained notoriety as a champion of manhood suffrage and as the only significant parliamentary representative of left-wing republicanism. In addition, in 1843 he had become one of the principal founders of the left-wing republican Paris newspaper, La Réforme. During the reform banquet campaign, Ledru-Rollin had made radical and much publicised speeches at Lille (7 November 1847) and Dijon (21 November 1847); he had effectively criticised Louis-Philippe's speech from the throne in the Chamber of Deputies (9 February 1848); and during the afternoon of 24 February he had intervened decisively to demand the formation of a Provisional Government. In the Provisional Government, Ledru-Rollin naturally allied himself with Flocon, chief editor of La Réforme after the death of Godefroy Cavaignac (May 1845), but also with the socialists Albert and Louis Blanc. As Minister of the Interior, Ledru-Rollin alienated many through appointing alleged radicals as commissaires and sous-commissaires, informing commissaires that their powers were unlimited in his circular of 12 March, and attempting to support the candidatures of left-wing republicans and radicals in the April elections. As early as 16 March, when elite companies of the Paris National Guard demonstrated to protest against their dissolution, conservative and anti-republican hostility focused on Ledru-Rollin. The reputation of Ledru-Rollin also suffered from the attempt by radical clubs to impose more left-wing policies on the Provisional Government by organising a massive demonstration in Paris on 16 April. Ledru-Rollin was accused of having encouraged this demonstration, when in fact, as Minister of the Interior, he had called out the National Guard, thereby saving the Provisional Government from having to make concessions in response to popular pressure. The April elections revealed the fears aroused by Ledru-Rollin. In the Department of the Seine he came twenty-fourth, in Saône-et-Loire (despite support from Lamartine) he came thirteenth, and in Algeria he came third, while he failed to gain election in the Côte-d'Or, Loire-Inférieure, the Nord, Seine Inférieure, or even in his former constituency of the Sarthe.

For Lamartine, Ledru-Rollin was someone to be kept on board. As early as 1843 Lamartine's personal relations with Ledru-Rollin were close to the extent that he had served as a witness at Ledru-Rollin's wedding. After 1843 their political positions became increasingly similar, as they both publicly declared during the reform banquet campaign;[5] and on 24 February 1848 Ledru-Rollin read out a list of prospective members of a Provisional Government, a list which included Lamartine's name. Lamartine very publicly opposed Ledru-Rollin's circular informing *commissaires* that their powers were unlimited, which suggested he was Ledru-Rollin's major opponent within the Provisional Government, but their relationship survived this disagreement. Throughout the revolution of 1848 Lamartine feared that the Second Republic might slide into anarchy, a new Terror, and the dictatorship of a Paris revolutionary movement. He apparently calculated that Ledru-Rollin could exercise a significant moderating influence over the left and the Paris popular movement, and that he would support the government in a crisis, as he had done on 17 March and 16 April, provided that he had not been alienated. The inclusion of Ledru-Rollin in the Executive Commission was therefore one way of preparing for an extremist Paris uprising.[6]

Lamartine's support for Ledru-Rollin also stemmed from his passionate belief in an inclusive Second Republic. On 26 February 1848 Lamartine told the comte de Carné: 'The Republic will be everybody's government: it will seek out all those with ability, wherever they may be found.'[7] To a deputation of the Fraternité Society, he declared on 19 March: 'Previous republics were, in effect, partisan republics; we want this republic to be the republic of the entire nation.'[8] In the National Assembly on 9 May, he argued that the people had not entrusted its destiny to one party alone, but to all the main parties which then formed the basis of public opinion, and to all those who had inspired the people.[9] Factional and partisan was how he described the revolutionary government which temporarily occupied the Paris Hôtel de Ville on 15 May.[10] After the June Days, he emphasised that 'concorde' was the only foundation on which the Republic could be built; and in 1850 he claimed to have won support for the idea of 'this unanimous Republic', in which no party monopolised power.[11]

Lamartine's vision of the Second Republic, and of his personal political role, may well have been laudable, but it was based on a number of misjudgements and misunderstandings. He failed to appreciate how polarised political opinion had become in France and the extent to which Ledru-Rollin and the left-wing republicans and socialists had been successfully demonised. Lamartine could not, as he seems to have imagined, be all things to nearly all people and court virtually every shade of political opinion. His popularity, so strikingly demonstrated in the April elections, was not personal but due to his reputation as the most effective moderate republican and opponent of radicalism within the Provisional Government.[12] His threat to resign if Ledru-Rollin were not included in the Executive Commission therefore struck many conservatives as a betrayal.[13] Altogether, the moderation and conciliation which Lamartine offered seemed increasingly unattractive to the majority of Frenchmen, who instead began to think in terms of a showdown with the left, their war-cry being 'Il faut en finir!'. Lamartine's support of Ledru-Rollin therefore had an enormous impact. According to Tocqueville, 'an indescribable disappointment, terror and anger seized the Assembly and the nation.'[14] Representatives in the Assembly indicated their views by voting the transference of power to the Executive Commission by only 411 votes to 385, and by giving Lamartine fewer votes than any other commission member besides Ledru-Rollin.[15]

Le Constitutionnel on 13 May expressed the opinion of a substantial section of French editorial opinion. People had voted for Lamartine because they opposed Ledru-Rollin and because they viewed Lamartine as the political antithesis of Ledru-Rollin. When the Provisional Government commissaire in the Haute-Vienne, Charles Montagut, had proposed a toast to Ledru-Rollin after a banquet to which he had been invited at Nontron, the spontaneous response had been a shout of 'Vive Lamartine!'[16] On 15 April Le Courrier de la Gironde of Bordeaux declared its support for Lamartine in the forthcoming National Assembly elections because in the Provisional Government he represented a principle. He was a symbol of order and of respect for property and genuine liberty, whereas Ledru-Rollin was a symbol of violence, communism and the oppression of all honourable citizens. It was 'a duty to elect Lamartine in order to protest energetically against Ledru-Rollin.' Le Courrier français on 27 April argued that in the Provisional Government there were two camps, two flags and two men representing very different 'passions', Lamartine and Ledru-Rollin. However, Lamartine had used his popular mandate, which was largely based on the public perception that he was Ledru-Rollin's most significant opponent within the Provisional Government, to force the majority in the National Assembly, against its will, to include Ledru-Rollin in the Executive Commission. He was therefore guilty of a complete betrayal of public confidence. Having been considered the most eminent member of the Provisional Government, 'l'homme de la situation', the counter-weight to Ledru-Rollin, his insistence was astonishing.[17] As Le Courrier de la Gironde (12 May) succinctly and bitterly complained: 'We are threatened with having Ledru-Rollin; Lamartine is responsible!'

Members of the Executive Commission did not hold ministerial portfolios.

Instead, ministerial portfolios were allocated at the first meeting of the Executive Commission held on 11 May. Carnot was reappointed Minister of Public Instruction and Crémieux was reappointed Minister of Justice. New appointees included Jules Bastide as Minister of Foreign Affairs (with Jules Favre as his Under-Secretary), Athanase Recurt as Minister of the Interior, Ulysse Trélat as Minister of Public Works, Ferdinand Flocon as Minister of Agriculture and Commerce, Charles Duclerc as Minister of Finance, and Eugène Bethmont as Minister of Religious Worship. Laurent-Antoine Pagnerre was appointed secretary to the Executive Commission. With the exception of Flocon, they were all moderate republicans. The two socialists, Albert and Louis Blanc, were the only members of the former Provisional Government not appointed to any official post in the new government.

The Paris *journée* of 15 May 1848

The Executive Commission suffered from severe handicaps from the date of its formation on 10 May. The conservative majority in the National Assembly had little reason to support a government in which conservatives remained totally unrepresented. Moreover, many conservatives felt Lamartine had betrayed them over Ledru-Rollin. Also, the Executive Commission appointed the left-wing republican Flocon to be Minister of Agriculture and Commerce, and allowed the radical Caussidière to retain the Prefecture of Police. At the same time, the radical left felt equally betrayed and frustrated: the hopes aroused by the February revolution had been dashed with the intensification of urban unemployment, the cautious moderation of government policies and the conservative successes in the April elections. Radical anger at the election results had exploded into popular violence in Rouen, Limoges and Nîmes at the end of April, while in Paris a major confrontation became virtually inevitable.

Exaggerated reports of 'the massacre of Rouen'[18] intensified the widespread sense of grievance and frustration among Paris radicals and workers, as did the exclusion of Albert and Louis Blanc from the new administration. Furthermore, the Assembly on 10 May had rejected Louis Blanc's proposals for a Ministry of Progress. Equally telling, for radicals, was the Assembly's simultaneous rejection of Wolowski's pleas for help for the beleaguered Poles. The cause of Polish independence, popular in France since 1815, had after February 1848 been enthusiastically embraced by the radical Parisian Left. Reports of Prussian repression of Posen and of an Austrian bombardment of Cracow prompted the Committee of Polish Emigration in Paris to appeal to the Paris clubs at the beginning of May to support a mass lobbying of the National Assembly for French arms and assistance for the Poles. The left-wing Club des Amis du Peuple agreed to petition the National Assembly for help for the Poles, and by 11 May radical members of Paris clubs had decided to organise a pro-Polish demonstration for 13 May. On that particular day relatively small numbers of demonstrators marched to the bridge over the Seine facing the National Assembly. Meanwhile it had been decided to postpone the main demonstration to 15 May, when the Polish issue and other foreign policy matters were due to be discussed in the National Assembly. Radicals recognised not only that Poland was a popular cause, but also that a pro-Polish demonstration could serve as a means of reviving their flagging political influence and of challenging the government and the Assembly. However, concern over the possible consequences of the demonstration and fears that the anarchist Blanqui would participate led the Club de la Révolution to vote against the demonstration on the eve of 15 May. Even the extreme radical Barbès was sufficiently concerned to vote for cancellation.[19] The radicals, however, were split. A group of radicals around the club leader Joseph Sobrier, publisher of La Commune de Paris, seems to have plotted a coup d'état to coincide with the Polish demonstration, though La Commune de Paris itself called on 15 May for a calm and peaceful demonstration. Similarly, Aloysius Huber, president of the Club des Clubs and one of the most influential figures involved in the demonstration, consistently opposed violence so as not to provoke a crackdown by the Paris National Guard.[20] In the event, the large crowd of demonstrators which marched from the Place de la Bastille to the Assembly on 15 May was largely unarmed. They were, nevertheless, determined to make their point. Owing to a series of miscalculations and misunderstandings, the National Guard failed to prevent the demonstrators from invading the National Assembly.[21]

For three traumatic hours, graphically described in Tocqueville's memoirs,[22] hordes of demonstrators paralysed the Assembly and intimidated the representatives. Raspail tried to address the Assembly after it had been invaded by the crowd, although he was not an elected representative. After protests and interruptions, but with the support of Louis Blanc, Raspail read out a proclamation demanding that France should support the re-establishment of a Polish nation state, if necessary by military force. Barbès then demanded that the Assembly should approve Raspail's demands and that the demonstrators should be allowed to file past the representatives. He claimed that the demonstrators were exercising their right to petition the Assembly.

At this juncture, the sound of the rappel being beaten to mobilise the National Guard reached the Assembly. Demonstrators forced the President of the Assembly to give instructions that the rappel should not be beaten, but the National Guard ignored his undated and unsealed instructions. Blanqui made a speech demanding that Poland be restored within its pre-1772 frontiers and that France should not sheathe its sword until this objective had been achieved. He also demanded the release of political prisoners and the adoption of policies to provide employment, and he complained about the composition of the Executive Commission. Ledru-Rollin intervened in an attempt to calm the demonstrators, but there followed a period of uproar and confusion. Demands were made for a Ministry of Labour, for a social committee to watch over the government, for the punishment of those responsible for the Rouen massacres, for war against the oppressors of Poland, and for the resignation of government ministers. The Assembly was brought to a halt. Amidst the din, Huber declared that the Assembly was dissolved and lists of members of a new Provisional Government were read out. The lists included the names of Barbès, Louis Blanc, Ledru-Rollin, Blanqui, Huber, Raspail, Caussidière, Etienne Arago, Albert, Cabet, Pierre Leroux, Considérant and Proudhon. This was to no avail: National Guardsmen began to arrive in large numbers and the demonstrators fled from the Assembly building in panic.

When General Courtais, the commander of the Paris National Guard, finally appeared in the Assembly he was given a very hostile reception from the representatives, who blamed him for the failure to protect them from the invasion of demonstrators. Courtais withdrew, whereupon Lamartine stood to propose a vote of thanks to the Paris National Guard. He condemned the invasion of the Assembly, and described the self-styled Provisional Government as a factional and partisan government, which had momentarily usurped the sovereignty of the people. Albert and Barbès had led a mass of demonstrators off to the Hôtel de Ville to establish a self-proclaimed Provisional Government, while other radicals had tried to occupy various other government buildings. This attempt to repeat the events of 24 February rapidly ended in failure as the National Guard cleared the Assembly and the Hôtel de Ville and generally restored order.[23]

While virtually no loss of life occurred in Paris on 15 May, the events of that day had a profound political impact. The government, shaken by what had happened and desperately concerned to restore its authority and credibility, openly resorted to repression in Paris for the first time since 24 February. In the late afternoon of 15 May, the offices in the rue de Rivoli of the radical newspaper, *La Commune de Paris*, were surrounded by members of the National Guard. The National Guard subsequently broke into and occupied the offices, confiscated papers and arrested the editors of the newspaper. On 22 May the Executive Commission dissolved the left-wing Paris clubs, the Club Raspail and the Club Blanqui. Radical leaders, such as Albert, Barbès, Blanqui, Raspail and Sobrier, were arrested and imprisoned, while Huber went into hiding. To strengthen its military capabilities, the government reorganised the command structure of the National Guard and reintroduced a large regular army garrison into central Paris. The conservative majority in the National Assembly, furious at the attack on their dignity and sovereignty, blamed the invasion of the Assembly on the incompetence of the Executive Commission and on the treasonable behaviour of various left-wing figures: they forced Caussidière to resign as Prefect of Police; they in effect put Louis Blanc on trial and they ceased to treat members of the Executive Commission with respect. Conservative provincial newspapers similarly blamed and criticised Lamartine and the Executive Commission for the outrage committed against their representatives. They also had their prejudices against the Paris popular movement confirmed and their determination not to make further concessions to it strengthened.[24] For the Paris popular movement itself, 15 May represented yet another defeat; and its aftermath – the harassment of left-wing clubs, the imprisonment of radical leaders, the dissolution of the Luxembourg Commission, and the proceedings against Louis Blanc (who was almost certainly innocent of any complicity in the events of 15 May)[25] – further angered and alienated Paris radicals and workers.

The National Assembly by-elections of 4 June 1848

By early June crowds of disgruntled workers were regularly gathering in the Paris boulevards of Saint-Denis and Saint-Martin, where they sang revolutionary songs and shouted slogans such as 'Vive Barbès!' and 'Vive Louis Blanc!'[26] Forty Assembly by-elections on 4 June, largely occasioned by the multiple candidatures in April, confirmed how polarised the electorate had become, not just in Paris but in the provinces as well. In relatively low polls, approximately six moderate republicans as against seven left-wing republicans were elected, with most of the remaining seats going to conservatives. The Seine elected just one moderate republican but at the same time the socialist Proudhon and three other left-wing candidates (Leroux, Lagrange and Caussidière), and five conservatives, including Thiers, whom three provincial departments also returned. Political reaction was now in full swing, with moderate republicanism and the compromises and conciliation which it represented squeezed out as French politics increasingly became a confrontation between conservative reaction on the one hand and left-wing republicanism and socialism on the other. Popular support for the latter was expressed in Paris by large crowds which continued to form in the evenings in the boulevards Montmartre, Poissonnière, Bonne Nouvelle, Saint-Denis and Saint-Martin. The crowds milled around, singing patriotic and republican songs, chanting 'A bas Thiers!', 'Vive Barbès!', 'Vive Louis Blanc!', and 'Vive la république démocratique!', and demonstrating outside the Paris residence of Thiers in the Place Saint-Georges.[27]

In the Assembly by-elections of 4 June, one of the successful candidates in the Seine, and in three other departments, was Louis Napoleon Bonaparte. Immediately after the February Revolution, Louis Napoleon Bonaparte had arrived in Paris from England, where he had lived in exile since his escape in 1846 from imprisonment in the fortress of Ham. On 28 February he wrote a letter to the Provisional Government, announcing his arrival and pledging his support.[28] Having been requested by the Provisional Government to leave France, he obediently returned to London, prompting the comte Apponyi to record in his diary: 'Louis Bonaparte, who flattered himself that he was an embarrassment for this government, has been sent back. He is nothing for this country.'[29] In London he enrolled as a special constable to defend the Houses of Parliament during the Chartist demonstration of 10 April. Meanwhile in the National Assembly elections of 23 April three of his cousins gained election, Napoleon Bonaparte (son of Jérôme Bonaparte) and Pierre Napoleon Bonaparte (son of Lucien Bonaparte) in Corsica and Lucien Murat (son of Joachim Murat and Caroline Bonaparte) in the Lot. These electoral successes coincided with a resurgence of Bonapartism. Ageing veterans of the Napoleonic wars paraded in their old uniforms at ceremonies such as the commemorations of the anniversaries of the deaths of Napoleon (5 May) and of the Empress Joséphine (29 May).[30] Bonapartist newspapers suddenly appeared while images of the Emperor Napoleon and other forms of Bonapartist propaganda became much more common. Various clubs and associations revived memories of the Napoleonic Empire and Bonapartist agents began to associate Bonapartism and Louis Napoleon Bonaparte with promises of peace, order, reduced taxes and the restoration of French national glory.[31] Partisans of Louis Napoleon Bonaparte put forward his candidature in the by-elections of 4 June, apparently without his prior knowledge or consent, in several departments. The Seine, three provincial departments (Charente-Inférieure, Sarthe and Yonne), and subsequently Corsica as well, elected him. In Le Mans and Paris he attracted considerable working-class support, while in the Yonne and Charente-Inférieure conservatives and peasants voted for him. Since he could appeal both to those who wanted to wage wars of liberation and who were impressed by his interest in poverty and the social question, and to those for whom he represented the army, national glory, an ordered society and a conservative and authoritarian state, he could attract votes from across the political spectrum. His electoral successes were also presented as a patriotic protest against the 1815 Settlement, which nearly all French people opposed, whether conservative, liberal or left-wing.[32]

Alarmed, on 12 June, a day on which large crowds participated in Bonapartist demonstrations in Paris, the Executive Commission ordered all prefects to arrest Louis Napoleon Bonaparte should he set foot on French territory. In the Assembly Lamartine, a long-standing opponent of Bonapartism, proposed that an 1832 law of exile should be applied to the prince. However, the next day the Assembly by a large majority rejected this proposal, which had been attacked by Clément Thomas (commander of the Paris National Guard), Louis Blanc and Jules Favre (a moderate republican who had resigned from being Under Secretary at the Ministry of Foreign Affairs on 6 June).[33] Only Ledru-Rollin had defended the proposal. Louis Napoleon Bonaparte on 24 May had protested to the National Assembly against any attempt to exclude him, but, claiming that he did not want any disorder, on 14 June sent a letter of resignation to the Assembly.[34] This saved the government some embarrassment, but the attempt to exclude Louis Napoleon Bonaparte attracted hostile press criticism from across the political spectrum, and especially from the newly-founded Bonapartist newspapers.[35]

At the same time, the government's parliamentary defeat and the public divisions among republicans led to widespread rumours that the members of the Executive Commission itself would resign.[36] In fact on 14 June, at a meeting of the government and the Executive Commission, Lamartine did indeed suggest that the entire Executive Commission should resign. Although this proposal was rejected by thirteen votes to four, Lamartine and Ledru-Rollin still wanted to resign, and the same day instructed Pascal Duprat to announce their resignations to the Assembly. The President of the Assembly, however, refused to allow Duprat to interrupt parliamentary proceedings until 15 June, by which time Lamartine and Ledru-Rollin had been persuaded to change their minds.[37]

The Paris National Workshops

The eventual resignation of the Executive Commission was occasioned, not by Bonapartism and Louis Napoleon Bonaparte, but by the Paris National Workshops and the outbreak of a Parisian insurrection on 23 June. After proclaiming on 25 February that the Provisional Government promised to guarantee workers the right to existence through employment, the following day the establishment of the Paris National Workshops was decreed. In doing so, the Provisional Government was responding to the unemployment problem in the capital and to the demands of the revolutionary crowds for radical measures. Louis Blanc had previously advocated that workers in the same trade should be encouraged to set up co-operative workshops with the assistance of State loans, but the Provisional Government entrusted the implementation of the decree on the National Workshops not to Louis Blanc, but to Marie, the Minister of Public Works and an opponent of the ideas of Louis Blanc. Marie did not want to preside over a socialist experiment. Instead, he simply saw the National Workshops as a pragmatic response to radical demands and as a means of keeping unemployed Paris workers out of mischief. Emile Thomas, the Minister of Public Works, shared Marie's views, and at the suggestion of Thomas the unemployed workers enrolled in the National Workshops were organised into labour brigades and, where possible, set to work on largely futile manual jobs. When Sir Edward Blount, a British banker based in Paris, asked a worker enrolled in the National Workshops what he would do next, he was told: 'Probably put the Seine into bottles.'[38]

Despite the discipline of the labour brigades and the evident pointlessness of much of the work on offer, the number of those enrolled in the workshops rose remorselessly: by mid-June the total had reached nearly 118,000, approximately half the adult male working-class population of Paris. Workers were attracted by the equivalent of unemployment benefit, and the mayors of the Paris *arrondissements*, who were responsible for enrolments, seem to have been willing to register almost anybody. The number of those enrolled in the National Workshops soon far exceeded official expectations. Work projects were never provided for more than about 10,000 of those enrolled; and even the little work on offer mainly took the form of labouring jobs, such as preparing land for construction work, which were unsuitable for the skilled artisans who constituted a major part of the Paris workforce.[39] Consequently, most of the workers enrolled in the National Workshops remained in an enforced state of idleness. This situation inevitably attracted much criticism. Workers disliked the discipline of the labour brigades, and they resented the absence of sufficient useful and appropriate work. They also regarded the subsistence wage offered by the National Workshops as inadequate (a daily wage of one franc and fifty centimes for those who worked, just one franc for those who did not work, and nothing at all on Sundays, when before 1848 eighty per cent of all male workers in Paris had earned between three and five francs a day).[40] They increasingly believed that the government was failing in its promises and obligations towards unemployed male workers.

Conservatives, on the other hand, claimed that the National Workshops were too expensive, too unproductive and too dangerous, since they concentrated large numbers of idle workers in Paris at the taxpayers' expense. Consequently, conservatives increasingly believed that the National Workshops should be closed down.[41] By the end of May, even moderate republican opinion had come to regard the National Workshops as unproductive and expensive.[42]

The Executive Commission, under pressure from the conservative majority in the National Assembly but at the same time reluctant to abandon completely the unemployed in Paris, planned to scale down the National Workshops while simultaneously creating job opportunities, particularly outside Paris. On 13 May the Executive Commission accepted a proposal from Garnier-Pagès to close enrolment in the National Workshops, and instead invite workers aged between eighteen and twenty-five to enlist in the army. Those who refused were to be sent back to their place of origin. At the same meeting Lamartine suggested replacing the National Workshops with a scheme for the clearance of uncultivated land in France and in Algeria by unemployed workers, who would be paid partly in money and partly in the land they had cleared.[43] The events of 15 May, and the presence of large numbers of workers from the workshops among the demonstrators, hardened the government's resolve and reinforced conservative fears within the Assembly. On 17 May the Executive Commission repeated to Paris mayors the order to cease enrolments in the National Workshops, while simultaneously accepting a proposal from Ulysse Trélat (Marie's successor as Minister of Public Works) for a committee to examine the current situation regarding the workshops. Just when the Executive Commission appeared to be moving rightwards, as evidenced by its attitude towards the National Workshops, it was also prepared to countenance radical measures to nationalise the railways. On that very same day, the Finance Minister, on behalf of the Executive Commission, introduced a bill in the National Assembly for railway nationalisation. It was proposed to nationalise all railway lines of commercial and strategic national importance, leaving private companies to run minor railway lines. The bill was referred to the National Assembly's finance committee and eventually discussed by the Assembly on 22 June.

The committee on the National Workshops presented its report on 19 May. The Executive Commission decided to suppress the report, probably because it emphasised both the principle of the right to work (which the conservative Assembly would have found provocative) and also recommended public works projects in Paris (which would have continued many of the problems associated with the National Workshops). The same day Trélat appeared before the National Assembly. He described the National Workshops as temporary; he suggested that those enrolled were receiving disguised charity for carrying out useless projects; and he indicated that the Executive Commission wanted the workshops closed as soon as possible. However, in the same parliamentary session, Duclerc, the Minister of Finance, introduced a measure for State nationalisation of railway companies, with a view to drafting workers enrolled in the Paris National Workshops to railway-related work projects in the provinces.

On 23 May Trélat and the Executive Commission agreed on the following measures concerning the National Workshops: workers with less than six months' residence in Paris prior to 24 May to be sent back to their place of origin; employment offices to be opened for employers seeking workers, with immediate dismissal for those workers refusing employment in private industry; workers to be sent into the departments to be organised into labour brigades; and workers to be supplied to the Lyons Railway Company (which had asked for them), the State advancing their wages. The same day the Minister of Agriculture and Trade announced a proposal for the creation of several agricultural colonies for unemployed workers.[44]

The orders actually sent to the Director of the National Workshops were harsher than those originally agreed on by the Executive Commission. In particular, unmarried workers aged between eighteen and twenty-five were to enlist in the army or be dismissed from the workshops. When the relatively conservative Director of the National Workshops, Emile Thomas, resisted such drastic proposals as compulsory army enlistment, he was abruptly dismissed on 26 May and forced to leave Paris for Bordeaux, where he was briefly arrested and treated like a common criminal.[45] His successor, Léon Lalanne, was much less sympathetic to the workers. Shortly afterwards, on 29 May, the dominating figure of the Assembly's Labour Committee, the Legitimist comte de Falloux, in introducing a measure in parliament for the deportation to their home departments of all those enrolled in the National Workshops with less than three months' residence in the Department of the Seine, argued that the workshops encouraged idleness among workers and provided the State with a very poor return for its outlay. He claimed that the National Workshops were a 'permanent strike' and an active centre of dangerous discontent ('foyer actif de fermentation menaçante'), which cost 170,000 francs per day and which corrupted the morality of the workers.[46] The same day a leading article in the main Paris moderate republican newspaper, Le National, claimed that the National Workshops had been a temporary necessity but that they were now a financial and economic liability.

The dismissal of Thomas and the comments of Falloux, together with the by-election results of 4 June and the outbreak of Bonapartist agitation, led to renewed popular unrest in Paris at the beginning of June. The Executive Commission responded by further strengthening its military resources in Paris, by forbidding gatherings of armed civilians, and by prosecuting opposition newspapers and political clubs. However, the Executive Commission tempered repression with constructive proposals for tackling the unemployment problem. For instance, on 12 June the Minister of Public Works was authorised to spend two million francs on railway-related projects, so as to employ the largest possible number of workers from the National Workshops. However, Pierre Leroux's speech in the National Assembly on 15 June arguing for socialist solutions to the economic and social crisis was followed by a speech from Michel Goudchaux arguing that the remedy instead lay in the immediate dissolution of the National Workshops; and on 16 June the Executive Commission agreed that within five days workers enrolled in the National Workshops and aged between eighteen and twenty-five would have to enlist for two years in the army or be dismissed from the workshops.[47]

The National Assembly discussed the National Workshops on 20 June. The novelist Victor Hugo asserted that the National Workshops had been a waste of public money and had transformed Paris workers into potential rioters ('prétoriens de l'émeute'); and even the moderate republican Léon Faucher argued that, since those enrolled in the National Workshops could not be provided with useful work, it would be preferable to dissolve the workshops and give the unemployed workers charity. It was left to the Legitimist La Rochejacquelein to argue that financial assistance to the construction industry could create thousands of jobs in Paris, and to the Fourierist Considérant to suggest that the unemployed could help to clear uncultivated land in Corsica or could be drafted to work in export industries.[48] The outcome of the debate was agreement that a plan for the dissolution of the workshops should be drawn up. With this encouragement, on 21 June the Executive Commission finally decided to enforce its decree compelling young men aged between seventeen and twenty-five enrolled in the workshops to enlist in the army or be dismissed. The same day the commission agreed to allocate six million francs for the completion of the Paris–Lyons railway line between Chalon-sur-Saône and Collonges; and on 22 June it received the draft of a bill on agricultural colonies from the Minister of Agriculture and Trade.[49] Meanwhile the National Assembly considered a bill for railway nationalisation, which Montalembert vigorously opposed. The Executive Commission and government ministers thus tried to dissolve the National Workshops in a humane way, by attempting to provide viable alternatives to enrolment in the workshops. However, their hand was to a large extent forced by the conservative majority in the National Assembly, which was increasingly alarmed by the mounting discontent of Paris workers and which was constantly egged on by reactionaries such as Falloux and Montalembert and even by the occasional sniping of moderate republicans such as Favre and Goudchaux.[50]

The June Days

Among the poorer classes, great hopes of change and improvement had accompanied the February Revolution, hopes which the government itself had helped to encourage. Those hopes signally failed to materialise. After February, the economic situation deteriorated, which for the poor meant rising unemployment. The government, despite its initial promises, did little to ameliorate conditions for the poor. Two gestures had been made: it had decreed that articles worth ten francs or less should be returned free of charge by the State pawnshops, and it had reduced the maximum working day by one hour to ten hours in Paris and eleven hours in the provinces. On the other hand, Louis Blanc's speech in the

National Assembly on 10 May in favour of the establishment of a Ministry of Work or Progress fell on deaf ears. Hence the view held by many that the needs and grievances of the workers had largely been ignored. *L'Accusateur public*, a Paris newspaper edited by the socialist Alphonse Esquiros, charged the moderate republicans: 'The worker is for you an obstacle, an embarrassment, an inconvenience, as he was for the [July] Monarchy.'[51]

This failure to respond to the needs of the urban working class and to the demands of socialists such as Louis Blanc was partly due to the preoccupation of the Provisional Government and the Executive Commission with their political survival. They also regarded the social question as the responsibility of the Luxembourg Commission and the National Workshops. Moreover, conservatives, who had done so well in the April 1848 parliamentary elections, were determined to close the National Workshops. Conceivably, the Luxembourg Commission might have emerged as a Soviet-style workers' parliament and government. However, starved of resources and denied any real authority, it never amounted to much more than a debating chamber, and its short life ended on 16 May after the Assembly had voted its dissolution. The demonstrations in Paris on 15 May and their aftermath (the dissolution of the Luxembourg Commission, the arrest and imprisonment of Albert, Blanqui and Raspail, the occupation of the houses of Sobrier and Cabet, and the threat of legal proceedings against Louis Blanc) finally destroyed the myth of national unity and further alienated left-wing republicans and socialists.[52] Paris workers were further antagonised by the Assembly's hostility towards the National Workshops. They were also annoyed by the closure of Paris political clubs and by the debate surrounding the right of Louis Napoleon Bonaparte to take up his seat in the Assembly. Sporadic demonstrations and outbreaks of violence ensued, and, in response, a new law restricting the right of public assembly was introduced on 7 June. This added fuel to the potential fire. Two weeks later, on 22 June, *Le Moniteur* announced that the National Workshops were effectively closed down. The National Workshops offered only minimal financial relief and boring manual work to less than a tenth of those enrolled, who finally numbered about 120,000.[53] Yet they represented the one major concession to unemployed Paris workers, and they held out the hope of a restructuring of society on socialist rather than capitalist principles. With thousands of workers suddenly being confronted with the choice of army enlistment or immediate deprivation of all financial support, resistance was almost inevitable. On 21 June leaders from the National Workshops, possibly delegates from the Luxembourg Commission, and representatives of the revolutionary clubs attended a meeting in the Faubourg Saint-Marceau. Together they made arrangements for a workers' protest the following day.

Early in the morning of 22 June workers demonstrated outside the Petit Luxembourg, where the Executive Commission met. Marie, the only member of the government who had arrived in his office, agreed to see a five-man delegation led by Louis Pujol, a revolutionary militant who was a member of Blanqui's club and who had played a prominent role in the invasion of the National Assembly on

15 May.[54] To the dismay and anger of Pujol and the demonstrators, Marie was adamant that the government would not change its policies on the National Workshops.[55] The workers came away determined to hold a massive workers' protest in the Place du Panthéon that evening. From all parts of Paris, thousands of workers began to assemble in the Place du Panthéon. From there they proceeded to the Place de la Bastille, shouting 'Work! Work! Bread! We will not leave!' The demonstration rapidly turned violent: the first street barricades were erected in the Rue Saint-Denis early in the morning of 23 June. Despite attempts at conciliation by, among others, François Arago,[56] insurgents and guardsmen exchanged shots around noon at the Porte Saint-Denis. A full-scale insurrection then rapidly escalated throughout the working-class districts of eastern Paris, with the ninth and twelfth *arrondissements* being the principal strongholds of the insurgents. On the morning of 25 June the army, supported by members of the Paris National Guard and the *garde mobile*, counter-attacked. Street barricades were blasted with artillery fire and, in costly house-to-house fighting, the 'forces of order' had regained control of the city by the morning of 26 June.[57]

Why did this insurrection fail so miserably? It was partly a question of numbers. The total number of insurgents was probably between 40,000 and 50,000, whereas enrolment in the National Workshops had reached approximately 118,000, and the adult male working-class population of Paris numbered over 200,000. The insurgents thus constituted a minority of Paris workers. This may partly be explained by the fact that those enrolled in the National Workshops continued to be paid. Against the insurgents were ranged approximately 45,000 regular soldiers and Mobile and Republican Guards. The Paris National Guard had a nominal strength of over 200,000, but when mobilised on 23 June few guardsmen responded in working-class areas, and even in the wealthier districts the response was poor, with, at best, guardsmen being prepared to defend, and maintain order in, their own neighbourhoods. In fact it has been calculated that only some 12,000 Paris National Guards made themselves available for combat operations.[58] In contrast, the *garde mobile*, which by this time numbered approximately 16,000 young men, mobilised and took up their positions quickly on 23 June. Altogether, initially some 40,000 to 50,000 insurgents confronted nearly 60,000 members of the 'forces of order'. The latter were better trained, equipped and commanded than the former, and were rapidly reinforced. Soldiers and national guardsmen were summoned from the provinces and in some cases were deployed within a day through the use of railway transport.

A further factor was morale. While many of the insurgents, at least at the start of the June Days, fought bravely and even recklessly, so too did the 'forces of order'. Soldiers and guardsmen knew they were fighting in the name of the first regime and national parliament in French history given legitimacy and authority by manhood suffrage. Also, soldiers were doubtless determined to avenge their humiliation during the February Days; and soldiers and guardsmen of provincial origin must, in many cases, have harboured a powerful animus against Paris workers. Although the *garde mobile* had been formed only since 25 February

1848, its military performance during the June Days greatly impressed contemporaries and confounded fears that the *garde mobile* might identify, on class lines, with the insurgents. As Lord Normanby, the British ambassador, put it: 'Through the whole of the four days, the *Garde Mobile* fought with fury on the side of order.'[59] This conspicuous challenge to the concept of class solidarity led Karl Marx to suggest that the members of the *garde mobile* were not genuinely working class, but instead belonged to the *lumpenproletariat*, a debased and depraved subgroup of the working class. More convincing explanations of *garde mobile* behaviour during the June Days lie elsewhere. The *garde mobile* were much better paid than ordinary soldiers, earning per day one franc fifty centimes as opposed to twenty-five centimes. The *garde mobile* had also already demonstrated their loyalty by their support of the authorities during the Paris demonstrations of 16 April and 15 May and by their contribution to various policing operations in the capital. Mostly young, with an average age of between twenty-one and twenty-two, unmarried and therefore without wives or families to support, they lived largely isolated from the working-class population of Paris in barracks, where they developed their own collective *esprit de corps*. They elected their own officers, whose ranks thereby gained legitimacy in the eyes of their men. In addition, their security of employment and relatively satisfactory material circumstances, and the military routines and disciplines of their lives, cut them off from other Paris workers, particularly the Paris unemployed. Hence they were prepared to risk their lives by fighting so energetically against their fellow workers during the June Days.[60]

General Cavaignac's leadership and tactics were also important. On 23 June the Executive Commission appointed Cavaignac supreme commander of all government forces in the Paris region. The following day the National Assembly proclaimed martial law in Paris, despite opposition from some liberals and republicans, notably Tocqueville and Jules Grévy. Shortly afterwards the Executive Commission resigned and the Assembly voted to invest all executive powers in Cavaignac, with only one representative (Charles Beslay) dissenting.[61] Thus, in addition to being the supreme commander of all government forces in the Paris region, Cavaignac became the head of the government as well, with the near unanimous support of members of the National Assembly; and the resignation of the Executive Commission, and the proclamation of martial law, meant that he could operate without concerning himself with civilian interference or legal niceties. Only too aware how isolated units of the army and the Municipal Guard had been cut off during the February Days, Cavaignac decided to concentrate his forces and then launch a series of massive attacks against the street barricades and buildings held by the insurgents. At the outset of the fighting several attempts were made to parley with the rebels, but these attempts failed and the insurrection was suppressed with considerable bloodshed. The government forces lost about 1,000 killed, while the insurgents almost certainly suffered a higher casualty rate. Army casualties were 708 killed or wounded out of a total deployment of approximately 25,000. Relatively, the *garde mobile* suffered more severely, with 195 killed and over 700 wounded out of a total combat deployment of approximately 13,000 to 13,500.[62]

The insurgents seem to have been prepared to risk their lives partly through desperation and hatred of the rich. While the trigger for the insurrection had been the dissolution of the National Workshops, Paris workers also felt frustrated in their longer-term objectives of social reform and of a 'democratic and social Republic'. With little to lose, they hoped to repeat their success of the February Days, and were under the illusion that the working-class *garde mobile* would side with them and that the largely bourgeois Paris National Guard would be too scared to fight.

An analysis of those arrested almost certainly provides some indication of the collective character of those who joined the insurgents during the June Days. Some caution is needed, though, since those arrested may not have accurately represented the insurgents in general. The authorities singled out known radicals for arrest and imposed repression more severely in some districts of Paris than in others, and many of the two-thirds of those arrested who were subsequently released had probably not participated in the insurrection. Nevertheless, it is clear that construction workers, metalworkers, those employed in the clothing and shoe industries, labourers, navvies, and furniture workers were particularly prominent, reflecting those Parisian professions most severely hit by unemployment. The June insurgents seem to have been more exclusively working class than their counterparts of the February Days. A significant proportion of those arrested were young men aged between 25 and 29, with over seventy per cent aged between 18 and 40. The majority of them were married, often with young families, and were migrants from the provinces rather than native-born Parisians. In so far as the insurrection had any leadership or organisation, it was provided by the National Workshops (in which nearly half of those arrested had been enrolled), by a handful of Paris working-class associations and by disaffected working-class elements of the Paris National Guard.[63]

The end of the fighting was followed by house-to-house searches for arms and suspected insurgents, the detention of nearly 12,000 suspects and the summary execution of hundreds of prisoners, as Louis Blanc described:[64]

> After the victory the reprisals were terrible. Prisoners huddled together in the vaults beneath the terrace, in the garden of the Tuileries, which faces the Seine, were shot at random through the air-holes in the wall: others were shot in masses in the Plaine de Grenelle, in the cemetery of Mont Parnasse, in the quarries of Montmâtre, in the cloister of Saint Benoit, in the court[yard] of the Hôtel de Cluny.

Suspected insurgents who were not executed were incarcerated in various improvised prisons. Thousands more melted away. Some even sought refuge in the catacombs of Paris until hunger forced them out of their hiding places.[65] The suspected insurgents incarcerated in the vaults beneath the terrace of the Tuileries

Gardens referred to by Louis Blanc were perhaps the worst treated. Some 850 prisoners were detained there. The corpses of those shot and killed were not at first removed and therefore putrified in the summer heat, which helped to drive some prisoners virtually insane and threatened an outbreak of typhoid fever.[66]

The dictatorial powers vested in Cavaignac by the National Assembly were used not only against the insurgents and suspects but also against newspapers which had allegedly incited the insurrection. On 25 June the publication of eleven Paris newspapers critical of the Cavaignac government was suspended and their editors arrested. The most important newspaper affected was *La Presse*. From 25 June to 6 August this leading liberal newspaper was prevented from appearing, while its distinguished editor, Emile de Girardin, suffered eleven days' imprisonment. The other newspapers banned between 25 June and 6 August included the satirical *Le Lampion*, the conservative *L'Assemblée nationale*, the Bonapartist *Le Napoléon républicain*, and several left-wing and socialist newspapers (*Le Journal de la Canaille*, *La Liberté*, *L'Organisation du Travail*, *Le Père Duchêne*, *Le Pilori*, *La Révolution*, *La Vraie République*).

There are many similarities between the February Days and the June Days. They were both predominantly working-class insurrections in Paris. They both exploded in highly volatile situations as a result of what were considered to be acts of extreme provocation – the boulevard des Capucines massacre in February, the dissolution of the National Workshops in June. They were both largely spontaneous and leaderless. They both took the same form – the construction of street barricades and the transformation of mainly working-class districts of the city into defended urban areas. They both lasted approximately the same time, roughly three days. However, their outcomes were strikingly different. By February 1848, the Guizot ministry, Louis-Philippe and the Orléans regime for most Parisians had all become morally discredited and hated politically, so that the cry that Louis-Philippe was murdering the people of Paris instantly ignited a massive and violent popular response. The loyalties of the Paris National Guard were uncertain, and many guardsmen eventually joined the insurgents. The Municipal Guard did on the whole fight, but they were too few and too isolated. In terms of numbers and supplies of food and ammunition, the army was not prepared for serious street-fighting in February, was unable to take effective offensive action, and was poorly led. Thus the insurgents were able to capture key buildings, notably the Tuileries Palace, and to overrun the Chamber of Deputies. As a result, Louis-Philippe was panicked into abdication and flight and the rejection of the regency of the duchesse d'Orléans and the proclamation of the Republic became almost inevitable. In contrast, by June national elections on the basis of manhood suffrage had produced the National Assembly and had sanctioned the establishment of the Second Republic, which could therefore command legitimacy and authority. Only unemployed workers in Paris were likely to be violently opposed to the dissolution of the Paris National Workshops, which many provincials and members of the bourgeoisie positively welcomed. The possibility of street-fighting in Paris was anticipated and prepared for by the

Executive Commission. After 15 May the Paris Republican Guard was reorganised, the expansion of the Paris National Guard continued, and the Paris *garde mobile* was developed into a formidable fighting force. The Executive Commission discussed military matters on 20 May, and agreed to concentrate a large regular army garrison in the Paris region. Further, on 1 June the Executive Commission accepted a proposal from Lamartine to create three hundred reserve battalions of the *garde mobile* in the provinces;[67] and between 5 and 7 June the Executive Commission gained the National Assembly's approval for a law drastically restricting the right of public assembly and facilitating the use of force to disperse crowds. After the June Days Cavaignac's tactics were criticised by Ledru-Rollin and others on the grounds that he should have ordered attacks on every barricade as soon as it had been erected to stop the insurrection from spreading.[68] However, Cavaignac's tactics certainly secured the rapid crushing of the insurrection, though at considerable cost. Indeed, the conflict was so one-sided, and the outcome so inevitable, that Paris workers as well as Marx believed that the insurgents had been deliberately provoked into launching a civil war which they could not win.[69]

The aftermath of the June Days

The violence of the June Days was not confined to Paris. A few outbreaks of violence occurred in the provinces, the most serious being a clash in Marseilles on 22 June which resulted in twelve deaths. Generally, though, the provinces remained quiescent and the authorities were able to dissolve provincial National Workshops without any significant resistance. In the provinces the collection of the forty-five centimes tax was a more inflammatory issue than the closure of the National Workshops, and a number of provincial riots over this issue occurred during the summer of 1848. For some provincials the June Days could be explained only in terms of a conspiracy, in which agitators had persuaded Paris workers to resort to violence with provocative speeches and distributions of gold coins and banknotes,[70] an explanation which had already been advanced by Armand Marrast, the mayor of Paris.[71] The suggestion that 'British gold' had contributed to the insurrection led to protests from the British ambassador.[72] Some provincial newspapers similarly gave credence to stories, which had already circulated widely in Paris, that the insurgents had cut off the hands of their prisoners and that women sympathetic to the insurgents had acted as ammunition-carriers and had given poisoned food and drink to soldiers and National Guardsmen.[73] Reports of dreadful atrocities allegedly committed by male and female insurgents, as well as accounts of such incidents as the killings of Geberal Bréa (who had been kidnapped while negotiating with the rebels) and of the Archbishop of Paris (who had attempted to mediate on a barricade),[74] contributed to a climate of fear in which the most absurd rumours flourished, confirmed provincial prejudices against the Paris working class, and morally justified what was seen as a victory of provincial France, 'la France des départements', over Paris.[75]

Meanwhile Paris resembled a city under foreign military occupation. Martial law still remained in force. Those moving around the city were constantly inspected for arms and ammunition.[76] Suspects continued to be arrested and buildings searched. National Guards who had not fought on the government side in the June Days were disbanded, while tens of thousands of soldiers and loyal guardsmen bivouacked in public spaces, patrolled the streets and squares, and guarded the main public buildings. The Grande Orangerie of the Louvre was converted into a huge barracks and tents covered the Tuileries Gardens. A contemporary described Paris after the June Days as resembling both an army camp and a city captured by assault.[77] This situation continued well into the summer. A British visitor to Paris recorded on 19 July: 'Everywhere enormous numbers of National Guards are to be seen in possession of great public buildings, as so many garrisons in an enemy's land.'[78]

Despite this large military presence, revenge attacks occurred. Isolated soldiers, guardsmen and members of the *garde mobile* were chased and stoned, and in some cases killed.[79] It was alleged on 12 July that workers in many workshops received letters offering them fifty francs for every *garde mobile* killed, forty francs for every soldier, thirty francs for every National Guard, and twenty francs for every *gardien de Paris*.[80] Four days later a Paris newspaper reported that a soldier guarding the military camp of Saint-Maur had been seized during the night and horribly mutilated.[81] This in turn made soldiers and guardsmen jittery and vengeful, resulting in cases of prisoners being shot and a number of accidental shootings. Many provincial guardsmen did not have uniforms, which could lead to confusion, sometimes with fatal consequences.[82] The large number of wounded severely stretched the resources of the Paris hospitals, which had to rely on women volunteering to work as nurses, who thus performed the female equivalent of National Guard duty.[83]

The continuing security problem led to the requirement that all those who entered Paris had to have a *laisser-passer* and to the arrests of editors of left-wing republican newspapers hostile to the Cavaignac government (Alphonse Esquiros of *L'Accusateur public*, Théophile Thoré of *La Vraie république* and Grandmesnil of *La Réforme*). In this grim environment, thousands of Paris families were in mourning for the loss of loved ones during the June Days, while many Paris buildings still bore the scars of the recent fighting. The elaborate public funerals of the soldiers and guardsmen killed during the June Days (6 July) and of the Archbishop of Paris (7 July) added to the general air of gloom in the capital.[84] At the same time, fears continued to persist of some fresh insurrection or of some terrorist outrage, possibly coinciding with the anniversary of the 1789 storming of the Bastille on 14 July[85] or of the 1792 Paris prison massacres on 2 September.[86] By August 1848, however, the perception was that law and order were slowly being restored and consequently the military presence in Paris was reduced.

Provincial National Guardsmen had first appeared in Paris after the invasion of the National Assembly on 15 May. Their presence in large numbers among the ranks of those fighting the insurgents during the June Days and subsequently occupying Paris emphasised the conflict between Paris and the provinces, while their role in the defeat of the insurgents boosted provincial morale. *Le Journal de Rouen* commented on 3 July: 'The most important political fact at the moment, that which dominates the situation, is the march of the departments on Paris at the first news of the danger which threatened the capital, the Government and society.' The newspaper might have added that this provincial 'march on Paris' had been greatly facilitated by France's embryonic railway system, which had permitted the rapid concentration in Paris of thousands of provincial guardsmen. The 'march on Paris' must also have constituted something of a culture shock. For many provincial guardsmen it was their first visit to Paris, while Parisians suddenly found themselves swamped and ordered about by provincials speaking a huge variety of patois.[87]

Provincial opinion did not universally back the suppression of the June insurrection. National Guards from Coutances in Normandy had stones thrown at their carriage roofs while travelling up in the train to Paris on 27 June.[88] Generally, though, since events in Paris had determined French national politics between February and June 1848, provincial distrust and hostility towards Paris had intensified. When a conference of mainly conservative provincial newspapers assembled journalists at Tours between 15 and 19 September 1848, among the principal issues discussed were the alleged 'tyranny' of Paris, the dependence of the provincial newspaper press on Paris newspapers, and the need for decentralisation, a traditional Legitimist obsession. Paris, it was claimed, capriciously disrupted French life, threatened governments and political liberties, and arrogantly assumed that it represented France ('La France, c'est moi').[89] The February Revolution, Ledru-Rollin's circulars and *commissaires*, the Paris demonstrations of 17 March, 16 April and 15 May, and the Paris insurrection of 24 June, had provided ample ammunition for those holding such views.

Chapter 5

Cavaignac and Louis Napoleon Bonaparte

The Cavaignac government

On 28 June the National Assembly confirmed the executive authority of General Cavaignac, the commander of the forces which had suppressed the June insurrection. The government he formed included four members who, like himself, had been involved in the suppression of the insurrection: Generals Bedeau (Foreign Affairs) and Lamoricière (War) had commanded forces against the insurgents, Sénard (Interior), as President of the National Assembly, had organised parliamentary support for Cavaignac, while Goudchaux (Finance) had chaired the Assembly committee on the National Workshops.[1] Cavaignac's ministerial appointments had to receive parliamentary approval, for, although the National Assembly had voted to grant Cavaignac exceptional powers, the regime remained very much a parliamentary regime.

Many of the representatives in the Assembly had by this time formed 'réunions', or loose-knit groups of more or less like-minded representatives who met regularly to discuss issues and to decide on common positions. The most important of these 'réunions' was the Réunion de la Rue de Poitiers, established at the end of May and named after the street in which the members met.[2] It was a broad conservative alliance, often described as the Party of Order, which soon attracted Legitimists (Berryer, Falloux, Larochejaquelein and Montalembert), conservatives (Bugeaud, Dupin, Fould and Molé), members of the former Centre Left or Third Party (Beaumont, Dufaure, Duvergier de Hauranne, Léon de Malleville, Rémusat, Thiers and Tocqueville), members of the former Dynastic Left, notably Odilon Barrot, and the odd moderate republican such as Joseph Degousée.[3] During the summer and autumn of 1848 the Réunion de la Rue de Poitiers tended to become more right-wing, losing moderate republicans and gaining more conservatives, a reactionary trend which was reflected in public opinion nationally and in the results of local elections and of parliamentary by-elections. As many as 400 representatives could attend meetings, so the Réunion de la Rue de Poitiers possessed considerable political influence. Since Cavaignac had alienated the left-wing republicans through his suppression of the June insurrection and his policies of political repression, and since he even lacked sufficiently strong support among moderate republicans, he had to take into account the Réunion de la Rue de Poitiers. This was demonstrated at the time of the formation of Cavaignac's first government. A deputation of six members from the réunion saw Cavaignac and indicated their approval of the appointments of Bedeau, Lamoricière, Sénard and Goudchaux, and also of those of Eugène Bethmont (Justice) and Antony Thouret (Agriculture). However, they strongly objected to the retention of the republican Hippolyte Carnot as Minister of Education and eventually, with the support of other conservative representatives in the Assembly, secured his dismissal (5 July) and the dismissal of his undersecretary, Jean Reynaud, blamed for the notorious circular to primary school teachers.[4]

While conservative representatives joined the Réunion de la Rue de Poitiers, most moderate republicans divided between the Réunion du Palais National (pro-Cavaignac) and the Réunion de l'Institut (anti-Cavaignac). Following a meeting held on 25 May, representatives including Pascal Duprat, Flocon, Marrast (who later joined the Réunion de l'Institut), Bernard Sarrans and Vaulabelle formed the Réunion du Palais National, while François Arago, Bixio, Cormenin, Duclerc, Dupont de l'Eure, Garnier-Pagès, Malleville, Marie, Pagnerre and Barthélemy Saint-Hilaire joined the Réunion de l'Institut.[5] The Réunion de la Rue de Castiglione, later known as the Réunion Taitbout, attracted between thirty and forty left-wing republicans and socialists, such as Etienne Arago, Caussidière, Louis Blanc, Ledru-Rollin, Pierre Leroux and Proudhon. It traced its origins back to a Cercle démocratique et social founded by Albert, Etienne Arago and Barbès around 10 May.[6] These 'réunions' debated new legislative proposals. For example, during the evening of 8 August the Réunion de l'Institut and the Réunion du Palais National both debated what became the press laws of 9–11 August 1848.[7] Similarly, a meeting of the Réunion du Palais National held on the evening of 18 August decided that its candidate for the presidency of the National Assembly would be Armand Marrast. A significant proportion of representatives, estimated between fifty to sixty and two hundred, formed a 'masse flottante' of those who did not join any of the *réunions*.[8]

The predominantly moderate republican character of the Cavaignac government did not correspond with the predominantly conservative character of the National Assembly, so Cavaignac could never rely on a parliamentary majority. However, most conservative representatives were prepared to accept Cavaignac, for the time being, as the suppressor of the June insurrection and as the upholder of law and order, though their tolerance of Cavaignac did not extend to Carnot. By closing political clubs, suspending the publication of eleven Paris newspapers, dissolving politically suspect National Guard regiments, ending the National Workshops experiment, and maintaining martial law in Paris until 19 October, Cavaignac consolidated his reputation as a conservative man of order. There followed the imposition of legal restrictions on political clubs (28 July), the re-introduction of caution money for newspapers (9 August) and of libel laws (11 August), the suspension of *Le Lampion*, *Le Père Duchêne*, *Le Représentant du peuple* and *La Vraie République* (21 August 1848), and a government-supported attempt to prosecute Louis Blanc and Caussidière for their alleged complicity in the *journée* of 15 May. Meanwhile, radicals in the prefectoral corps appointed by Ledru-Rollin, radical school teachers encouraged by Carnot, and other radicals holding public posts, were purged and replaced by possessors of more moderate political credentials.

Cavaignac did not attempt to introduce any radical republican measures. His government did provide relief for the unemployed in Paris, at the modest rate of thirty-five centimes per person per day. Salaries for teachers in State schools were increased. Several railway companies were granted State financial support, but earlier proposals to nationalise the French railway system were abandoned. State financial assistance and tax incentives stimulated the construction industry in Paris, and work began on the demolition of buildings in front of the church of Saint-Eustache in order to create a site for a new central food market for Paris. Colonisation in Algeria also benefited from State financial assistance, according to a government plan accepted by the Assembly on 19 September.[9] A law of 9 September established a legal maximum working day in all mills and factories of twelve hours. Postal reforms followed the British example by introducing pre-payment by an adhesive stamp and a low uniform rate based on weight for the postage of letters (law of 24 August 1848). There were proposals to help agriculture with agricultural training and education and with institutions offering cheap credit to farmers. Such measures were acceptable to conservatives but, as the fear of further violent upheaval receded, so conservative support for Cavaignac ebbed away. At the same time, the conservatism of the Cavaignac government alienated many of those on the left.

During the summer of 1848, local elections based on manhood suffrage again provided an early indication of the collapse of popular support for Cavaignac and for moderate republicanism and of the general disillusionment with the Second Republic. In the municipal elections held from 23 July many voters failed to vote, but those who did tended to vote for conservative candidates, including a surprising number of Legitimists, who often combined with former Orleanists and moderate republicans to present a common front of 'Friends of Order' ('Amis de l'Ordre'). In a political climate dominated by fears of another working-class rising and by repression of the radical left, moderate republicanism tended to be absorbed into a conservative-Legitimist alliance, leaving left-wing republicans and socialists isolated. High abstention rates also featured in the *conseil général* elections held during the last two weeks of August. In some departments three-quarters of those enrolled on the electoral list did not vote. This low turn-out may help to explain why a surprisingly large number of former *conseillers généraux* were re-elected. Altogether, the *conseil général* elections marked a return to power at a local level of the *notable* class. Of the eighty-five *conseil général* chairmen elected for the November session, at least sixty-one had been *conseillers généraux* under the July monarchy and nearly all belonged to the *notable* class. As part of the *notable* class, again Legitimists often benefited. For instance, in the elections for the *conseil général* of the department of the Eure, successful Legitimist candidates included the duc d'Albuféra, the marquis de Blosseville, the duc de Broglie, the comte de Lagrange, d'Osmoy, the comte de Valon and the comte de Vatimesnil.[10] Legitimists were also prominent in the departments of the Deux-Sèvres and the Vendée. Generally, conservatives of one sort or another gained control of the *conseils généraux*, an exception being the department of the Var, where left-wing republicans were successful.[11] The *conseil général* deliberations of the October and November sessions often confirmed the emergence of a consensus among the representatives of the *notable* class, as they rallied behind the agenda of the 'Party of Order'.[12]

The National Assembly debates on the constitution

The National Assembly had elected a committee on 17 and 18 May to draw up proposals for a new republican constitution for France. Membership of this committee included Odilon Barrot, Beaumont, Considérant, Cormenin, Dufaure, Dupin, Marrast, Tocqueville and Vaulabelle. The committee rapidly drew up its proposals and presented them to the Assembly on 19 June. However, the crisis surrounding the National Workshops, and the June Days and their aftermath, meant that parliamentary discussion and debate of the constitutional proposals had to be postponed until the end of August.

After an introduction, the proposed constitution listed a number of guaranteed civil rights. These included freedom from arbitrary arrest, freedom of religious worship, freedom of association, freedom of assembly, freedom of the press, and the inviolability of private property. On 6 September Lamartine in the National Assembly argued that the constitution should contain a declaration of general principles rather than of specific rights. The latter varied according to different times and circumstances; they were incapable of precise definition; and property was inviolable because it was a divine institution, and not because of any human law.[13] The issue of the freedom of the press was particularly controversial, with Victor Hugo in a parliamentary speech on 11 September claiming that freedom of the press was as essential and as sacred as manhood suffrage. When the National Assembly came to vote on maintaining the existing restrictions on the newspaper press, the motion was carried by the moderate republican majority (457 to 276), against a combination of Legitimists (Falloux, Montalembert, La Rochejaquelein), liberals (Victor Hugo), some republicans (Crémieux, Garnier-Pagès, Jules Grévy, Ledru-Rollin) and socialists (Pierre Leroux, Proudhon, Raspail). On the equally controversial issues of the organisation of labour and the role of the State in the economy, Tocqueville on 12 September presented the liberal case for a free market economy, arguing that any State guarantee to provide work for all unemployed workers would lead to communism, and that any State interference in the distribution of labour and the regulation of industry would lead to socialism. Such outcomes, he suggested, would be disastrous, since communism and socialism were materialist, hostile to private property, illiberal, illogical and undemocratic. Ledru-Rollin tried to counter Tocqueville's arguments by maintaining that the right to work was not so much socialist as in the traditions of the revolution, that labour needed to be directed from the cities to clear uncultivated land in the countryside, and that new credit banks were also needed to provide cheap loans. Lamartine on 14 September attempted something of a compromise, arguing for limited State intervention, but strictly on humanitarian grounds. The citizens of the Second Republic had a right not to starve to death, and in cases of extreme hardship the government had a moral obligation to provide the basic necessities of life. The National Workshops had therefore been a temporary institution, made necessary by circumstances, to save people from hunger and pauperism. This alleviation of the suffering of the masses had been a moral obligation for the Provisional Government; and it had been in accordance with the February Revolution's fundamental principle, which was 'L'idée du peuple'.[14]

The list of guaranteed civil rights became, with only minor modifications, part of the constitution accepted by the National Assembly on 4 November. Lamartine's speeches, in particular, made a considerable impact[15] and his arguments had some effect: when finally adopted, the constitution recognised that the State should provide public works for the unemployed and help those unable to help themselves. Crucially, though, the principle of the right to work was not specifically endorsed. An amendment to this effect was successfully opposed by, among others, Thiers and Tocqueville, and rejected by 596 votes to 187. Similarly, on education a conservative compromise was achieved. After a debate (18 and 20 September) in which Montalembert and Falloux had championed Catholic education, and Jules Simon had defended republican educational ideals, the National Assembly agreed that primary education should be compulsory but not free, and that the curriculum should include 'moral, religious and civic instruction' with theology taught by priests.

One of the major constitutional questions raised in the Assembly debates was whether there should be a single or two-chamber legislature. Lamartine on 27 September pointed out a number of practical objections to a bicameral system. No group or class existed in France which could satisfactorily form a second chamber, so that a method of determining the membership of a second chamber would be difficult to devise. Also, in a crisis there would be conflict over which chamber possessed sovereignty.[16] Lamartine was not opposed to a second chamber on principle. The previous April he had reportedly favoured both a single and a double chamber legislature; and he is supposed to have told his chief adversary in the debate, Odilon Barrot: 'You will be right later, but not at present.'[17] Lamartine's speech was well received,[18] but it was probably not decisive in convincing the representatives that they should reject Barrot's arguments. Tocqueville and Thiers supported Barrot, but they were vigorously opposed by Dufaure and Dupin, and a majority in the constitutional committee had eventually recommended a single chamber legislature. This recommendation was in line with majority opinion in Paris and in nearly all the departments.[19] Moreover, agreement would not have been easily reached as to the character and composition of a second chamber; it was thought that the Conseil d'Etat would serve as a counterweight to the Assembly; and it was feared that two chambers rather than one would be a source of weakness when confronted by an elected president. A single Legislative Assembly was therefore adopted, with 750 members.

At the end of May the constitutional committee agreed with Cormenin's proposal that the president should be elected by the electorate. Marrast had wanted the president to be elected by the National Assembly, while Tocqueville had suggested a complicated system whereby the president would be elected indirectly by delegates elected by the electorate. Failing an absolute majority of votes for any one presidential candidate, the National Assembly would then choose the president.[20] The constitutional committee also agreed that the president should possess executive powers. These proposals obviously followed the example of the constitution of the United States, met the perceived need for a strong executive authority, and accorded with the newly-orthodox principle of popular sovereignty as expressed by manhood suffrage. However, by September the opponents of Bonapartism and of Louis Napoleon Bonaparte were beginning to have second thoughts. When Assembly by-elections were held in thirteen departments on 17 September, four departments (Charente-Inférieure, Corsica, Seine and Yonne) re-elected Louis Napoleon Bonaparte.[21] His candidature was also successful in the Moselle and attracted a considerable number of votes in the Nord, Orne and Rhône. This time no attempt was made to prevent his return to France, and he took his seat in the Assembly as a representative of the Seine on 26 September. The plebiscitary nature of the prince's electoral successes, and the demonstration of his nationwide appeal in both rural areas and in cities such as Paris, clearly indicated that the French electorate might vote for him to be president of the Second Republic.

This striking demonstration of the popular appeal of Louis Napoleon Bonaparte and of the declining popularity of the moderate republicans alarmed those who were distrustful of Bonapartism.[22] As a result, Jules Grévy introduced an amendment proposing that instead of a president there should be a head of a council of ministers, appointed and dismissed at the will of the Assembly. Lamartine vigorously opposed this (6 October). There was, he argued, a need for a strong executive authority. In a republic, sovereignty lay with the people, who should consequently elect the president. A president elected by the Assembly would inevitably share the Assembly's unpopularity, which might lead to a paralysis of government. Such a president would also be the choice, not of national opinion, but of political parties. National opinion should decide who was to be the president, since circumstances in France did not favour the establishment of a Napoleonic dictatorship. A presidential election by the electorate would rally the population to the Republic. Votes in the Assembly might be bought with offers of patronage, whereas the entire electorate could never be corrupted.

Above all, the people had the right to select their rulers, even if they wanted a Bourbon restoration.[23]

At least four contemporaries, and several historians, have considered Lamartine's speech to have been mainly responsible for the defeat of the Grévy amendment, and the further defeat of an amendment introduced by Leblond that there should be a president, though elected by the Assembly.[24] This was certainly one of Lamartine's most powerful speeches, and its impact partially explains why the Grévy and Leblond amendments were defeated so overwhelmingly (by, respectively, votes of 643 to 158 and 602 to 211).[25] There were, however, other factors. The conservative successes in the parliamentary elections of 23 April, and in the various local elections between July and September, meant that recourse to manhood suffrage did not alarm the Assembly's conservative majority – indeed, some Legitimists believed that the operation of manhood suffrage would lead to a restoration of the Bourbon monarchy. At a meeting of the Réunion de la Rue de Poitiers held at the end of September, only Degousée had argued for the National Assembly to elect the president.[26] A majority of the Réunion de l'Institut wanted the president to be elected by manhood suffrage,[27] as did most Paris and provincial newspapers .[28] In addition, Louis Napoleon Bonaparte's initial interventions in the proceedings of the Assembly had been so unimpressive as to encourage representatives to underestimate him.[29] Lingering doubts nevertheless remained. While the Assembly defeated a proposal to review the 1832 law exiling members of former ruling families from France, the Assembly was persuaded by, among others, Beaumont and Tocqueville, to limit the presidential term of office to four years and to debar any president from serving for a second consecutive term.

When the National Assembly finally voted to accept the entire text of the new constitution, the representatives who voted against acceptance were a mixture of Legitimists such as Berryer, Montalembert and La Rochejacquelein, left-wing republicans such as Félix Pyat, socialists such as Greppo, Leroux, Proudhon and Raspail, and a few independents such as Victor Hugo. The constitution was officially proclaimed at a grand ceremony in the Place de la Concorde in Paris on Sunday 12 November by Armand Marrast, President of the National Assembly. The new Archbishop of Paris, Sibour, assisted by four bishops, attended, along with the members of the National Assembly, the government, the diplomatic corps and other official bodies. A review of the Paris National Guard and of provincial guardsmen followed the ceremony. Despite the cold and the falling snow, it was reportedly an impressive occasion.[30]

The French Left after the June Days

The rejection of socialism by the National Assembly's conservative majority did not pass unchallenged. In a speech to the Assembly on 31 July, Proudhon bravely argued that the February 1848 revolution had been fundamentally socialist in character. He also proposed a number of practical measures: a lowering of interest rates; the establishment of a new national bank to provide interest-free loans to encourage ambition and industry; the introduction of a thirty per cent income tax; and a guarantee by the State to producers to find consumers for their products in return for a ten per cent commission. Proudhon tried to convince his fellow-representatives that such measures would not undermine private property, the family or inheritance rights, and would not involve nationalisation or bankruptcies. Instead, he claimed that they would make property and society more secure by ending the division of society into a working class and a bourgeois class. By guaranteeing employment, the State could restore public confidence, which martial law, restrictions on political clubs and newspapers, and disarming the workers served only to undermine. Totally unconvinced, the Assembly passed a motion condemning Proudhon's proposals as 'an odious attack on the principles of public morals', a violation of property, an appeal 'to the most wicked passions', and a slander against the revolution of February 1848. Only Jean-Louis Greppo (left-wing republican representative for the Rhône) voted with Proudhon.[31] Undeterred, Proudhon continued to advocate his socialist ideas in speeches, and in his newspaper, *Le Peuple*.

Olinde Rodrigues also challenged the prevailing political climate of conservatism and reaction by drafting and publishing an alternative constitution for the Second Republic. Work, intellectual or physical, he declared, was the fundamental condition of the moral and physical existence of individuals. The work of all was useful to all. Work should be allocated according to ability, and income should be work-determined, while those injured in work and the elderly should be cared for. All men and women, resident in France for at least a year and economically independent, should qualify for the full rights of citizenship, including the right to vote. Nine hundred representatives should be elected annually by all citizens to a National Assembly. All careers in the sciences, arts and industry should be open equally to men and women. Husbands and wives should enjoy the same rights, while brothers and sisters should possess equal inheritance rights. The post and telegraph system, all roads, railways and public transport, street lighting, water supplies, museums, art galleries, gymnasiums, theatres and concert halls should be in public ownership. Capital punishment, forced labour and life prison sentences should be abolished. Divorce should be possible, subject to the approval of a family council.[32] Influenced by figures such as Proudhon and Olinde Rodrigues, left-wing republican newspapers campaigned during the autumn of 1848 for free, secular State education, State support for co-operative workshops, the right to work, a progressive income tax, and the abolition of usury.

At a grass roots level, left-wing political activity during the autumn of 1848 largely took the form of holding banquets. Following the example set by the reform banquet campaign of 1847–8, a number of republican banquets had been organised in the provinces since February 1848. These usually combined popular sociability with listening to left-wing speeches and singing revolutionary songs. They could be family occasions, and they were often held on Sundays, which for many was not a working day. Thus, for example, on Sunday 3 September two hundred workers with their wives and children assembled for a 'democratic banquet' in a field by the river Saône in the commune of Belligny near Villefranche. The families picnicked, listened to a series of left-wing speeches, and joined in the communal singing of patriotic and revolutionary songs.[33] Left-wing republicans commemorated the proclamation of the First Republic in 1792 with a banquet held on 22 September in Paris near the Champs Elysées. Ledru-Rollin, the principal speaker, argued that the right to work was a republican rather than a socialist principle, that indirect taxes on foodstuffs should be abolished and taxes on the rich increased, and that France should intervene militarily in Italy.[34] Commemorative banquets were also held in the provinces, for example at Louhans (Saône-et-Loire). At a 'democratic banquet' held in Montpellier on 9 October the participants sang revolutionary songs, waving revolutionary and republican emblems as they sang. They shouted a mixture of anti-masonic, anti-clerical, Jacobin and socialist slogans.[35]

In Paris the first banquet of 'the Democratic and Social Republic' took place on Tuesday, 17 October. Alton-Shée spoke, and argued that the February revolution could not be exclusively political but had to have a social dimension as well. Among those present were Cabet, Greppo, Pierre Leroux and Proudhon. They also attended another 'democratic banquet' at Passy on 22 October.[36] Meanwhile the Fourierists had organised a banquet in Paris at the Jardin d'Hiver on 21 October. Further 'socialist banquets' or 'democratic and social banquets' were held on Sunday 22 October at Dijon, on Sunday 5 November at Mâcon, and on Sunday 26 November at Lyons. Over four thousand attended the Dijon banquet. The local National Guard band played while money was collected for those deported after the June Days. The diners signed petitions for a political amnesty. They also signed petitions for the abolition of the alcoholic drink tax, and drank toasts to the organisation of labour and to the Democratic and Social Republic.[37] A more modest turn-out of five or six hundred attended a 'democratic banquet of the Seine-Inférieure' at Graville on 1 November. Toasts were proposed to the Republic, to the martyrs of the democratic cause, to the liberation of oppressed peoples, to Ledru-Rollin, to the Mountain and to universal peace.[38] Sex equality could also be on the agenda on these occasions. About 1,200 men, women and children attended a 'womens' social and democratic banquet' on Sunday 19 November in the Jardin de la Gaieté, by the Maine barrier on the outskirts of Paris. Many of the women were elegantly dressed in satin dresses and wore hats. Pierre Leroux opened the proceedings by reading an extract from the writings of Condorcet on the rights of women. There followed a series of toasts proposed by women, including Mme Desirée Gay ('To the political union of men and women!') and Mme Jeanne Deroin, the feminist ('Honour to every intelligent and courageous man who has understood and proclaimed the civil and political equality of women!'). The usual republican songs were sung and those attending contributed to a collection for the transportés.[39]

The same Sunday on the other side of Paris at Château Rouge, Lamennais presided over a banquet for the radical newspaper press. It attracted left-wing representatives such as Théodore Bac, Martin Bernard, David d'Angers, Greppo, Pierre Joigneaux, Ledru-Rollin, Raspail and Victor Schoelcher, as well as over two thousand other diners, each paying three francs and twenty-five centimes. The participants sat down to their meal in a huge tent and heard a series of speeches and a selection of patriotic tunes. The main speaker was Ledru-Rollin, who denounced the failure of the Second Republic to assist foreign revolutionary movements.[40] Five days later, at a banquet organised by Paris wine merchants, Ledru-Rollin not surprisingly spoke against taxes on wine. Pierre Leroux was again in action at a 'banquet of families' of the twelfth *arrondissement* of Paris on 26 November and at a banquet organised by the corporation of shoemakers on 27 November.[41] Three more left-wing banquets were held in Paris on Sunday 3 December: at Grenelle, where Alton-Shée presided, at the Sèvres barrier, where the speakers included Ledru-Rollin and Proudhon, and at the Maine barrier, where the subscription was as low as seventy-five centimes and nearly half of those who attended were women.[42] The same day in the provinces a 'democratic and socialist banquet' was held at Nevers, at which Ledru-Rollin was adopted as the favoured presidential candidate.[43] On 8 December about 1,800 people attended a 'democratic and social banquet' of the third *arrondissement* of Paris in the concert hall in the Rue Saint-Honoré. Greppo, Pierre Leroux, Proudhon and Félix Pyat were there, and Mme Pauline Roland delivered a feminist speech calling for equality between the sexes.[44] Some of these banquets probably helped Ledru-Rollin's presidential campaign, but the banquets lacked any central organisation or uniform character and could expose the divisions among French republicans and socialists. Also, exaggerated reports of their revolutionary character served to alarm conservatives. Yet these banquets performed an important role in keeping alive a left-wing political culture in a French environment now increasingly hostile to the French Left.

The presidential candidates

Six candidates emerged to fight the presidential election campaign – Louis Napoleon Bonaparte, General Cavaignac, General Changarnier, Lamartine, Ledru-Rollin and Raspail (still imprisoned in Vincennes for his role in the *journée* of 15 May). The left-wing vote was split between Cavaignac (moderate republican), Ledru-Rollin (left-wing republican) and Raspail (socialist). Changarnier stood as a Legitimist and Lamartine represented, if anything, the Provisional Government and the Executive Commission.

Louis Napoleon Bonaparte was, of course, the Bonapartist candidate, but he was much more than that, since at one and the same time he could appear to be the unofficial candidate of the Party of Order, the anti-establishment candidate, and the symbol of a radical, even revolutionary, tradition of Bonapartism. The Réunion de la Rue de Poitiers did not, however, officially endorse the candidature of Louis Napoleon Bonaparte. At a meeting held on Saturday, 4 November, Thiers indicated his lack of enthusiasm for either Cavaignac (accused of having 'une politique indécise') or Louis Napoleon Bonaparte. Yet he opposed the idea of promoting an additional conservative candidate, and he recognised the prince's appeal:

> France, wounded, frightened, impoverished, seeks the name which would appear to it to be the greatest antithesis to everything which we see, and it is for this reason that it adopts Louis Bonaparte. The fault does not lie with us, but with those who have governed France for the last eight months.
>
> (*Le Constitutionnel*, 7 November 1848)

Those attending the meeting agreed with Thiers that the Réunion de la Rue de Poitiers should not support any candidate, but only by fifty-two votes to thirty-seven with sixty-one abstentions. This vote prompted the moderate republican Joseph Degousée (a representative for the Sarthe) to resign from being vice president of the Réunion de la Rue de Poitiers. In his letter of resignation, he complained that recent meetings of the Réunion revealed that the Republic was tolerated as a temporary necessity rather than upheld as the only form of government which could assure the country's welfare, and that the reason they had been unable to adopt a single candidate was because they were so divided over Louis Napoleon Bonaparte.[45] Eventually most members of the Party of Order, including Thiers, rallied behind Louis Napoleon Bonaparte.

Changarnier and Raspail were both relatively unknown and could appeal only to relatively small constituencies at opposite ends of the political spectrum. Now that so many Legitimists had rallied to the Party of Order and hence mostly to Louis Napoleon Bonaparte, Changarnier's constituency was reduced to just a fraction of the Legitimist camp. There were cases of local meetings of Legitimists adopting Louis Napoleon Bonaparte's presidential candidature.[46] Also, most Legitimist newspapers eventually backed Louis Napoleon Bonaparte, with rare exceptions such as *La Gazette du Bas-Languedoc* of Nîmes and *La Gazette du Midi* of Marseilles. The Comité central électoral des républicains démocrates et socialistes adopted Raspail as its official presidential candidate. Raspail's supporters included Proudhon and his newspaper *Le Peuple* and the odd provincial newspaper, such as *Le Peuple de la Haute-Vienne* of Limoges and *Le Peuple souverain* of Lyons.[47] Socialism, though, had as yet few converts outside Paris and a handful of provincial cities such as Lyons, so Raspail's constituency, though larger than that of Changarnier, was similarly circumscribed.

Lamartine's candidature was more problematic. Historians have generally dismissed Lamartine's presidential candidature as hopeless from the start, but the full extent of Lamartine's loss of popularity was not immediately apparent to contemporaries. In the National Assembly elections of 23 April 1848 Lamartine had received 1,283,501 votes in ten departments, and had been elected ahead of every other member of the Provisional Government in the department of the Seine. Since then his determination to include Ledru-Rollin in the Executive Commission, his alleged responsibility for the failure to protect the Assembly from invasion by demonstrators on 15 May, and his share in the responsibility for the hated forty-five centimes tax, the continuing economic and social crisis, and the catastrophe of the June Days in Paris, had all drastically eroded his popular standing, particularly among conservatives. At the same time, many on the left felt that he had betrayed revolutionary and nationalist movements abroad by his non-interventionist policies as Minister of Foreign Affairs, just as he had allegedly betrayed the workers at home through his opposition to socialism, his acceptance of the closure of the National Workshops, and his failure to prevent the slaughter and repression associated with the June Days. Moreover, Lamartine's vision of national unity and harmony could not survive in France's political climate after the June Days, with conservative reaction uncompromisingly triumphant, left-wing republicanism and socialism defeated and embittered, and a resurgent Bonapartism waiting in the wings.

Yet at first Lamartine's political eclipse was partially disguised. He could still receive favourable press coverage, as in a long article by Daniel Stern (the comtesse d'Agoult) in Le Courrier français of 20 July and by his portrayal as a progressive politician in La Démocratie pacifique on 31 July.[48] On 30 July he was elected to the municipal council of Mâcon and on 27 August he was re-elected in two cantons to the conseil général of Saône-et-Loire, of which he was elected chairman for the autumn session. With Armand Marrast's presidency of the National Assembly due to expire on 19 August, the moderate republican Réunion du Palais National and Réunion de l'Institut both proposed Lamartine's candidature, though, probably realising that his chances of electoral success were slim, Lamartine publicly declined to stand (17 August) and Marrast was re-elected.[49] In September Lamartine published a vigorous defence of his role in government in 1848 in a pamphlet entitled Lettre aux dix départements (the ten departments which had elected him in April), which received considerable publicity in the press. In the National Assembly, his speeches on the constitution of 6, 14 and 27 September also received considerable press publicity, much of it favourable.[50] More favourable publicity surrounded his return to Mâcon and the surrounding area in October and November, and the deceptively enthusiastic reception which he was then accorded. Lamartine himself promoted much of this favourable publicity by feeding newspapers with the texts of his speeches and writings; and, responding to France's changed political climate, Lamartine now presented himself as a resolute defender of order, property, family and religion, and an equally resolute opponent of socialism, communism, anarchy and violence.

Lamartine's sudden repudiation of his all-too-recent radical and revolutionary past alienated the left while conservatives remained sceptical and unconvinced.[51] Moreover, his failure to intervene on 25 August in the Assembly debate on the report of the official enquiry into the events of 15 May and the June Days seemed to some an admission of guilt. He equally failed to issue a clear statement that he was a presidential candidate or to publish an electoral manifesto – his newspaper, Le Bien public, claimed on 4 December that his name was a manifesto and his life since 24 February a programme. Absent from Paris from 16 October to 24 November, the Assembly debate on the June Days on 25 November prompted his return to the capital, but again he did not speak in the debate or even vote, for which he was publicly criticised.[52] Finally, Lamartine's presidential election campaign lacked organisational and newspaper support. A committee backing Lamartine's candidature reportedly met on 25 or 26 November. Members included moderate republicans who were opposed to Cavaignac and who had been Lamartine's former colleagues in government: Dupont de l'Eure (President of the Provisional Government), Garnier-Pagès (member of both the Provisional Government and the Executive Commission), Duclerc (Minister of Finance, 11 May – 28 June 1848), Barthélemy Saint-Hilaire (head of the secretariat of the Provisional Government), and Pagnerre (general secretary of both the Provisional Government and the Executive Commission). There were also three journalists sympathetic to Lamartine – Xavier Durrieu (editor of Le Courrier français), Arthur de La Guéronnière (editor of Le Bien public) and Charles Lesseps (former editor of Le Commerce) – and Leblanc de Prébois (a representative for Algeria in the Assembly).[53] However, it is not at all clear what, if anything, this committee achieved.

Only two Paris newspapers promoted Lamartine's presidential candidature, his own newspaper, Le Bien public, and Le Courrier français, which described him as the candidate of 'la concorde' (5 November) and as the man who had saved France in February 1848 (19 November). Victor Hugo's L'Evénement was at first quite favourable to Lamartine, but in the end firmly supportive of Louis Napoleon Bonaparte. In the provinces just a handful of relatively obscure newspapers backed Lamartine – L'Ami du Peuple of Hazebrouck (Nord), La Démocratie of Béziers (Hérault), L'Eclaireur des Pyrénées of Bayonne (Basses-Pyrénées), Le Glaneur d'Eure-et-Loire of Chartres, Le Loing of Montargis (Loiret) and La Tribune lyonnaise of Lyons. Another provincial newspaper, Le Conciliateur of Limoges (Haute-Vienne) at first came out for Lamartine but then switched to Louis Napoleon Bonaparte; and Le Patriote jurassien of Lons-le-Saunier (Jura) suggested to its readers that, if they did not want to vote for Cavaignac, they should vote for Lamartine.[54]

Ledru-Rollin stood as a left-wing republican with the endorsement of the Réunion de la rue Taitbout.[55] He was described by a provincial newspaper as the candidate of democratic republicans, in other words of those who were not content with just republican structures but who wanted the substance of republicanism and institutions which were genuinely democratic.[56] For Le Républicain de Lot-et-Garonne, he was the true founder of the republic of 1848, the personification of 'la République républicaine'.[57] He would finally realise the promises of the February 1848 revolution, such as the right to work and a fairer system of taxation.[58] La Réforme and La Révolution supported his candidature, as did left-wing republican newspapers in the provinces,[59] and eventually the Fourierist Paris newspaper, La Démocratie pacifique. He could hope for the votes of skilled artisans and shopkeepers in Paris, in provincial cities such as Marseilles and Lille, and in smaller towns with left-wing traditions such as Narbonne, as well as of peasants in the few rural areas in which left-wing republicanism had taken root. However, his appeal was largely restricted to these minority groups, particularly since he was saddled with the conservative-inspired reputation of being a dangerous revolutionary and with at least some of the responsibility for the failures of the Provisional Government and of the Executive Commission. Thus it soon became clear that the only serious contenders for the presidency were Cavaignac and Louis Napoleon Bonaparte. Appreciating this, the republican George Sand wrote despairingly in a private letter on 20 November that the choice was between 'the bloody sabre of Algeria' (Cavaignac) and 'the rusty sword of the Empire' (Louis Napoleon Bonaparte). She added: 'I do not know, in truth, for whom I would vote if I were a man.'[60]

Unusually for a senior career officer, Cavaignac was a staunch republican, both by family tradition and by personal conviction: his father had been elected to the Convention parliament of 1792; his brother had been a prominent figure in the republican movement before a premature death in 1845; and he himself displayed a firm commitment to a rather limited brand of moderate republicanism. As the defender of the conservative Republic, Le National (moderate republican) and Le Siècle (liberal) backed him, along with a clutch of lesser known and mainly moderate republican Paris newspapers (Le Crédit, L'Ere nouvelle, Le Moniteur du matin, Le Moniteur du soir and La Voix de la vérité).[61] Most left-wing republicans, socialists and members of the urban working class, of course, hated Cavaignac, and often opposed his candidature more vigorously than that of Louis Napoleon Bonaparte. They were alienated by Cavaignac's military career and by his military rank; they blamed him for the 'butchery' of the June Days, for the severity of the subsequent repression, and for the imposition of martial law in Paris; and they considered that he had betrayed the Republic and the revolution through failing either to assist foreign nationalist and revolutionary movements or to tackle effectively the domestic problem of urban unemployment. Thus, Le Journal du Loiret could claim on 28 November: 'The candidature of General Cavaignac is surrounded with hatreds.' However, left-wing republicans, socialists and urban workers constituted a relatively small proportion of the electorate; and, while the moderate republican constituency was also relatively small, Cavaignac's candidature potentially had a wider appeal. The general had had a distinguished military career in Algeria; he had successfully defended the cause of 'order' and 'civilisation' during the June Days; and he represented existing authority, so his election would guarantee a reasonably safe and predictable continuity of government. Therefore Cavaignac could hope to be the choice of all those who distrusted Bonapartism and Louis Napoleon Bonaparte and who wanted a conservative, albeit republican, president and government.

A number of factors, though, limited Cavaignac's popularity. While Cavaignac enjoyed the support of several bishops and of several Catholic newspapers, including L'Ere nouvelle, many Catholics opposed the Cavaignac government's educational plans and resented its refusal to help Pope Pius IX restore his authority over the Papal states. When the Bishop of Orléans on 16 November issued a letter to the Catholic clergy, urging them to vote for Cavaignac, many, including the Bishop of Langres, criticised this initiative. The latter publicly declared that members of the clergy, like all other citizens, should enjoy complete freedom of choice in the forthcoming presidential election.[62] After the assassination of Cardinal Rossi in Rome (15 November), Cavaignac did try to win the support of Catholic voters by offering the Pope sanctuary in France, but the Pope decided to flee to the Kingdom of the Two Sicilies. Within the elite many conservatives considered that Cavaignac had been too high-handed in suppressing newspapers and in maintaining martial law, and too republican in attempting to prohibit the avoidance of military service through the use of substitutes and in awarding financial compensation to republican victims of the July monarchy. The publication of lists of those who were due to benefit from the so-called 'récompenses nationales', lists which allegedly included would-be assassins of King Louis-Philippe, angered many conservatives in the days leading up to the presidential election on 10 December.[63] Cavaignac tried to win over conservatives just as he tried to win over Catholics, but with a similar lack of success. Several prominent political figures, including Gustave de Beaumont and Antony Thouret, campaigned for Cavaignac,[64] but his stiff and irritable manner, combined with an authoritarian and brutally unsubtle approach to politics, won him few friends.

Since Cavaignac's supporters tended to be too narrowly confined to the *National* faction, attempts were made to broaden his base of support. In return for backing Cavaignac, Thiers was offered the vice presidency if Cavaignac were elected President, an offer Thiers declined.[65] Similarly, General Lamoricière, without success, clumsily sought to blackmail an employer into persuading his workers to vote for Cavaignac.[66] At a meeting held on 30 October, the Réunion du Palais National agreed to back Cavaignac's candidature, as did the Réunion de l'Institut at a meeting held on 6 November, but only against the advice of Cavaignac's former government colleagues, Barthélemy Saint-Hilaire, Duclerc, Garnier-Pagès and Pagnerre.[67] However, Cavaignac's friends (who were sometimes referred to as 'Cavaignachiens') failed to secure the endorsement of the much more influential Réunion de la Rue de Poitiers at the meeting of the réunion held on Saturday, 4 November.[68] Printed biographies of Cavaignac were distributed to army garrisons through the medium of *Le Moniteur de l'armée*, but soldiers were allegedly not impressed and instead tended to focus their political loyalties on Louis Napoleon Bonaparte.[69] According to the mother-in-law of Thiers, Cavaignac alternately bullied, flattered and threatened journalists. Dr Véron, the editor of *Le Constitutionnel*, was told that it was thanks to Cavaignac that his newspaper had not been suspended during the period of martial law, in a failed attempt to secure his support for Cavaignac.[70] Emile de Girardin, outraged rather than intimidated by Cavaignac's treatment of himself and his newspaper, led *La Presse* in a personal crusade against the general's presidential candidature.

Meanwhile, in a National Assembly debate on 25 November, Garnier-Pagès accused Cavaignac of having unfairly blamed the Executive Commission for the shortage of troops in Paris at the beginning of the June Days. Ledru-Rollin in the same debate even challenged Cavaignac's reputation as the saviour of France and of civilisation by claiming that the general had used the wrong military tactics and had himself been responsible for shortages of troops and ammunition. Such criticisms and accusations helped to undermine Cavaignac's reputation and to expose the divisions among French republicans. Above all, Cavaignac's identification with the social and administrative status quo, with the collection of the forty-five centimes tax, and with the continuing depressed state of the economy, heavily penalised him among the great mass of peasant voters.

After his re-election to the National Assembly in five departments on 17 September, Louis Napoleon Bonaparte left London for Paris, arriving on 24 September and lodging at the Hôtel du Rhin, which symbolically faced Napoleon's column in the Place Vendôme.[71] He at once summoned his cousin the Princesse Mathilde to Paris, and she proceeded to help him financially and to introduce him to influential members of the French elite.[72] On 26 September Louis Napoleon Bonaparte took his seat in the Assembly as a representative of the department of the Seine. At first he failed to impress. His physical appearance counted against him. Like his uncle, he was relatively short in stature. Some considered his moustache too luxuriant, his nose too big and his head too large for his body. His eyes also attracted unflattering comments ('yeux de cochon'). He spoke French with a slight foreign accent and in a nasal tone and monotonous manner, while his years of exile in England had given him an English air ('l'air très gentleman'), which Rémusat described as gauche. On his rare visits to the Assembly, he seldom contributed to parliamentary debates and was allegedly too busy gazing, with the aid of a pair of immense opera glasses, at women in the public gallery.[73] He spoke only to a few friends in the corridors. He remained cold, stiff and polite, and was not an easy conversationalist. His lack of formal education, and his years of exile, conspiracy, subversion, imprisonment, idleness and dissipation, suggested that he was not a political heavyweight. There were also those who were alarmed by his links, and apparent sympathy, with left-wing republicans and socialists, and yet others who professed to be scandalised by the fact that he lived openly with his English mistress, the beautiful Miss Howard. All this encouraged contemporaries to underestimate Louis Napoleon Bonaparte and even to ridicule him. They failed to appreciate his political ambition, his ruthless determination and his unshakeable belief in his own destiny.[74]

More substantial political objections could be made against the presidential candidature of Louis Napoleon Bonaparte. He was a poor imitation, even a parody, of his uncle the Emperor Napoleon ('le petit chapeau de l'empereur'). He gave the impression of being unpredictable ('l'homme des surprises'). His commitment to the Republic and republicanism was uncertain. He was all things to all people.[75] His name recalled noble victories but also terrible defeats, order but also despotism.[76] Yet Louis Napoleon Bonaparte could make the most unlikely converts. After Proudhon had visited the prince on 26 September, he privately recorded that he had seemed well intentioned.[77] After meeting him on 17 November, Thiers thought Louis Napoleon Bonaparte possessed 'a good and gentle character' and 'a cultivated mind'.[78] Throughout the autumn of 1848 Louis Napoleon Bonaparte charmed visitors of every description who besieged the Hôtel du Rhin from morning to evening.[79]

The candidature of Louis Napoleon Bonaparte in fact mixed in a complex manner a glorious legend, a Bonapartist programme and a rejection of the moderate republicanism which had dominated France since the February revolution. With the passage of time, and with the contrast of the 'inglorious' rulers of France since 1815, images of Napoleon's military victories and of a mighty and orderly French Empire presiding over continental Europe, had become powerful and persuasive. The Napoleonic legend had been kept alive in many ways: through the memories of those who had served and who remembered the Empire; through numerous publications, prints, songs, dramatic entertainments and forms of memorabilia; through actions of the Orleanist regime, such as the completion of the Arc de Triomphe and the reburial of Napoleon's remains in the Invalides; and through public commemorations, including the funerals of imperial dignitaries, the inauguration of statues to Napoleon and of his marshals, and the celebration of Napoleonic anniversaries. As the Bonapartist pretender, Louis Napoleon Bonaparte was able to appropriate and exploit this legend to further his own political ambitions. In view of the legend's near-universal and emotional appeal, this was an enormously valuable asset.

Louis Napoleon Bonaparte also developed a new Bonapartist political programme. In his electoral manifesto of 27 November he presented himself as a symbol of order and security, as a protector of the Roman Catholic Church, as an upholder of the institutions of the family and private property, as a defender of the freedom of the press, as a guardian of peace at home and abroad, and as a promoter of national prosperity.[80] Again, such a programme had a very wide appeal. Thus, *La Haute-Auvergne* saw in the manifesto 'a pronounced tendency towards the fusion of the political parties'.[81] Members of the elite, including Legitimists and Orleanists who disliked Cavaignac and republicanism, certainly saw in Louis Napoleon Bonaparte a conservative candidate who could attract mass support. Frenchmen across the political spectrum responsive to French nationalism identified Louis Napoleon Bonaparte with Napoleonic glory and grandeur, with French national institutions such as the Civil Code, the Ecole polytechnique and the Legion of Honour, with the defence of French interests particularly against the British, and with the rejection of the treaties of 1815. Catholics, by now generally alienated from the Second Republic, responded to the prince's promises to restore Roman Catholic schools and the temporal authority of the Pope in the Papal states. Army officers and soldiers were likely to be attracted by the Napoleonic legend and could be jealous of 'the Africans' such as Cavaignac and Lamoricière, who had allegedly been given too much scope in Algeria and had enjoyed too rapid promotion.[82] Peasants, suffering from low agricultural prices and relatively high taxes, welcomed the assurance of tax cuts and the chance to vote against the system. Urban workers, despairing of republican and socialist remedies for unemployment, turned to the Bonapartist pretender in substantial numbers in Rouen, Lyons, Bordeaux, Toulouse and Paris. Even republicans and socialists could be seduced into believing that Louis Napoleon Bonaparte, the author of *Les Idées napoléoniennes* (1839) and *L'Extinction du pauperisme* (1844), embodied a Bonapartist tradition of support for the principles of the revolution, defence of the oppressed nationalities of Europe, and concern for the plight of the poor.[83]

Louis Napoleon Bonaparte's allegiance to the Second Republic might be doubted. For Tocqueville, his candidature signified 'A bas la République!'[84] The increasing unpopularity of the regime of the Second Republic, however, made this an electoral asset rather than an electoral liability. Altogether, the political appeal of Louis Napoleon Bonaparte ranged from the left to the right. Appreciating this, he had published the texts of letters sent to him by Odilon Barrot, Pierre-Jean de Béranger, Louis Blanc, Armand Carrel, Chateaubriand and George Sand,[85] and a favourable review in *Le National* of his *Manuel de l'artillerie* (1835). Thus he attempted to claim political endorsement from a composer of patriotic, Bonapartist, anti-monarchical and anti-clerical popular songs (Béranger), from a Romantic author who, until his recent death (4 July 1848), had been a Legitimist and a Catholic and who had served the Restoration monarchy as a diplomat and minister (Chateaubriand), from the leader of the Dynastic Left under the July monarchy and prominent figure in the reform banquet campaign of 1847–8 (Odilon Barrot), from moderate republicans (Armand Carrel, George Sand and *Le National*) and even from a socialist (Louis Blanc).[86]

The presidential election campaign

The Napoleonic legend and the Bonapartist programme were effectively promoted among the electorate. Louis Napoleon Bonaparte's long-standing friend and supporter, Persigny, directed his campaign with the aid of substantial financial resources. Several influential political figures joined the Bonapartist camp, notably Odilon Barrot (who had been politically marginalised since his prominent role in the reform banquet campaign of 1847–8), Léon Faucher, Léon de Malleville, Molé (who switched from Cavaignac), Montalembert and Thiers.[87] A leading figure in his campaign team was the Corsican Jacques Abbatucci, a former deputy, opponent of Guizot, friend of Odilon Barrot, and representative of the Loiret in the National Assembly.[88] Louis Napoleon Bonaparte, unlike Cavaignac, was determined to charm potential supporters. Thus he pursued Thiers with dinner invitations, presentations of his publications, and requests to help draft his electoral manifesto.[89] In the provinces a number of 'Napoleon Committees' were formed either by genuine Bonapartists or by those who realised how popular Louis Napoleon Bonaparte's candidature had become. Conservative electoral committees, which had originally been formed to secure the election of conservative candidates in the National Assembly elections of 23 April, usually backed Louis Napoleon Bonaparte, for example the Comité des Amis de l'Ordre of Rennes.[90] Former officials of the July monarchy, who had been dismissed from their posts after February 1848 and who hoped to regain office under Louis Napoleon Bonaparte, were often willing recruits to the Bonapartist campaign.

While an overall majority of newspapers seem to have been pro-Cavaignac, a large minority declared for the prince, including several important Paris newspapers (*Le Constitutionnel*, *L'Evénement*, *La Gazette de France*, *La Liberté*, *La Presse*, and from 2 December *L'Assemblée nationale*) and several leading provincial newspapers (*La Bourgogne*, *Le Capitole* (Toulouse), *Le Charentais*, *Le Courrier de la Gironde*, *Le Courrier de l'Eure*, *Le Courrier de Lyon*, *Le Courrier du Havre*, *La Gazette d'Auvergne et du Bourbonnais*, *La Gazette du Languedoc*, *La Guienne* (Bordeaux), *La Haute-Auvergne*, *L'Impartial* (Rouen), *Le Journal de la Côte-d'Or*, *Le Journal de Loir-et-Cher*, *Le Journal de Maine-et-Loire*, *Le Journal de Toulouse*, *Le Journal du Loiret*, *Le Mémorial bordelais*, *Le Mémorial de Rouen*, *La Tribune de la Gironde* and *L'Union Franc-comtoise*).[91] Thiers persuaded Dr Véron that *Le Constitutionnel* should support Louis Napoleon Bonaparte,[92] and this support was made public in a leading article published in the newspaper on 15 November. Cavaignac was claimed to be too much the candidate of the moderate republicans, a minority who had monopolised the government of France and whose doctrines had produced either anarchy or dictatorship. In contrast, Louis Napoleon Bonaparte was the candidate of the moderates; and the vigorous and united opposition to his candidature from left-wing republicans, socialists and anarchists further enhanced his standing. *Le Constitutionnel* proceeded to publicise Louis Napoleon Bonaparte's election manifesto and favourable news items, such as the prince's donation of 100 francs to a workers' society at Chaillot which helped the unemployed.[93] To *La Liberté*, another Paris newspaper which decided to back Louis Napoleon Bonaparte, the prince was 'the national candidate', the patriotic choice. For instance, anybody who voted for Cavaignac would be voting for the treaties of 1815, whereas those who voted for Louis Napoleon Bonaparte would be voting against them. The newspaper summed up the candidates as follows: 'Cavaignac – dictatorship and martial law; Lamartine – weakness and indecision; Ledru-Rollin – violence and illusions; Raspail – presumption and charlatanism; Louis Napoleon Bonaparte – order and the future.'[94] Answering the question, 'Why vote for Louis Napoleon?', *Le Journal du Loiret* (7 December) emphasised that he was above the political parties, that he would be the man of France and not of a coterie, that he had personally suffered and concerned himself with the poor, that he was both a man of progress and a man of order, and that his election would be the most energetic and solemn of protests against the infamous treaties of 1815. Most left-wing newspapers, of course, vigorously opposed Louis Napoleon Bonaparte's candidature. On 2 November *La Démocratie pacifique* declared that 'The election of M. Louis Napoleon to the presidency would be a calamity for the country'; and predicted that Louis

Napoleon Bonaparte would not respect the Republic or be content with a presidency limited by the constitution.

The majority of voters were peasants, many of whom were illiterate and most of whom probably did not read newspapers. They were, however, exposed to various forms of Bonapartist propaganda, particularly at markets and fairs. The magic of the name Napoleon was successfully exploited,[95] but even if unaffected by Bonapartist propaganda, the name Napoleon was familiar to the French peasantry, whereas the other presidential candidates were largely or completely unknown, and might even be the subject of confusion (Cavaignac was allegedly identified with Polignac, while Lamartine was thought to be a woman, La Tartine, the mistress of Ledru-Rollin). After decades of relative peace, peasants seem to have forgotten the military conscription, the war casualties, and the taxation and requisitioning imposed upon them by the Emperor Napoleon, instead selectively remembering the emperor as the personification of French glory and as the martyr of St Helena.[96] Some peasants may even have thought that the Emperor Napoleon was still alive or that he had come to life again to save France from the mess which the February Revolution had created.[97] They may also have thought that Louis Napoleon Bonaparte was the son, rather than the nephew, of the Emperor Napoleon, and that his personal wealth would remove the need for taxation for many years.[98] Peasants seem also to have been motivated by a desire for revenge against the republicans and the forty-five centimes tax and against the urban working class and the National Workshops.[99]

The parliamentary election of three nephews of Napoleon in April, and Louis Napoleon Bonaparte's own electoral successes in June and September, had already indicated the force of the Bonapartist tide. By 20 October Tocqueville was writing privately to his friend Gustave de Beaumont that he considered the presidential election of Louis Napoleon Bonaparte to be 'extremely probable.'[100] *La Presse* came to a similar conclusion on 27 October. *L'Evénement* calculated on 18 November that Louis Napoleon's candidature would win an absolute majority of votes in sixty out of France's eighty-six departments. During November a victory for Louis Napoleon Bonaparte was predicted several times by Léon Faucher, who described the Bonapartist candidature as a life-raft sent by Providence to a shipwrecked France.[101] Similarly, *Le Journal de Maine-et-Loire* on 2 December compared his candidature to 'a cry of rescue in the tempest, an invocation to Providence at a time of peril.' By Sunday 10 and Monday 11 December (the polling days for the presidential election) the Bonapartist tide had become a flood. The fine weather[102] particularly encouraged peasants, most of whom had allegedly been won over by Bonapartist propaganda, to vote.[103] Some peasants reportedly even went to vote collectively as members of the same village, headed by their parish priest and with the name of Louis Napoleon Bonaparte on their hats.[104]

The polling days were apparently characterised by calm everywhere and a holiday atmosphere.[105] Voter turn-out was approximately seventy-five per cent, a considerable increase compared with the local elections of July and August and the parliamentary by-elections of September, though less than the eighty-four per cent registered in April. Including votes cast by soldiers and by electors in Algeria, the results were as follows:

Louis Napoleon Bonaparte	5,572,834
Cavaignac	1,469,156
Ledru-Rollin	376,843
Raspail	37,106
Lamartine	20,938
Changarnier	4,687

Louis Napoleon Bonaparte came first in every department of France except the Bouches-du-Rhône, Finistère, Morbihan and the Var. In other words, only Brittany and the region around Marseilles, both traditionally anti-Bonapartist, failed to deliver a landslide victory for Louis Napoleon Bonaparte but instead gave Cavaignac majorities of up to sixty per cent. Cavaignac also did quite well in the Bas-Rhin, Côtes-du-Nord, Doubs, Gard, Ille-et-Vilaine, Loire-Inférieure, Lozère, Manche, Nord, Seine, and Vaucluse. The Protestant vote tended to go to Cavaignac, which was significant in a few departments, such as the Gard, Tarn and Tarn-et-Garonne. Whereas Louis Napoleon Bonaparte won more votes in predominantly rural areas than in cities, Cavaignac performed well in cities such as Lille (Nord), Le Havre (Seine-Inférieure) and Srasbourg (Bas-Rhin), where Louis Napoleon's failed *coup* of 1840 may have been a factor. Ledru-Rollin gained a respectable share of the vote in the Allier, Bouches-du-Rhône, Gard, Garonne, Hérault, Lot-et-Garonne, Pyrénées, and Var. Lamartine's total included 2,286 votes cast in Saône-et-Loire, an astonishing decrease from the 129,879 votes, approximately 99 per cent of the total, which he had won in the department the previous April. Even in his home department his near universal appeal had vanished while his local political support group had disintegrated.[106] However, what emerged, above all, from the results of the presidential election of 10 December 1848 was that a fearful and discontented population had rallied massively to the candidature of Louis Napoleon Bonaparte, in defiance of much of France's political leadership. This dramatic demonstration of popular voting power was also, paradoxically, a blow to democracy. Manhood suffrage, hitherto seen as the key for any radical transformation of society, had instead become the agency for the triumph of reaction, for Louis Napoleon Bonaparte's electoral success had in effect given him a popular mandate to begin the task of burying the Second Republic and founding the Second Empire.

Chapter 6

Conclusion

The legacies of the *Ancien Régime*, the revolutionary decade from 1789 to 1799, and Napoleonic rule, dominated French political culture until 1848. Centuries of tradition, a popular brand of Roman Catholicism, and the political faith of royalists and Legitimists meant that the influence of the *Ancien Régime* lingered on well after 1789. However, the revolution had shattered forever the mystique of monarchy in France. The Roman Catholic Church had lost most of its wealth, power and influence, and anti-clericalism had become a significant political force. The nobility and aristocracy had survived rather better, but they remained a tiny minority, diluted and divided by Napoleonic creations. The *Ancien Régime*, moreover, had too many unpopular associations: with tithes, the seigneurial system, and privileges based on inherited social status; with 'unpatriotic' emigration and counter-revolution; with defeat, occupation and humiliation at the hands of France's national enemies; and with ultra-royalist extremes and excesses after 1815.

The legacy of the revolution was both positive and negative. Many of the abuses of the *Ancien Régime* were swept away. The administrative, judicial and financial reforms of the early 1790s created systems which were uniform, rational, efficient and long-lasting. There was also the promise of democratic government and of respect for individual liberties. Tragically, the pressures of popular discontent, foreign and civil wars, and the political dynamic of the revolution itself, led to the Jacobin dictatorship and terror. Consequently, for decades after 1799 the revolution, the Republic and even republicanism were identified with arbitrary arrests, executions and property confiscations, with the tyrannical fanaticism of Robespierre, with military conscription and heavy taxation, with a depressed economy and a devalued currency, with an unrestrained onslaught against the Roman Catholic Church, and with the stripping away and destruction of so much that made life familiar and reassuring. Nor did the poor derive much benefit from the revolution.

Napoleonic rule introduced, or re-introduced, into French political culture national pride in military victories, the grandeur of France, and French domination of continental Europe. Added to this were Napoleon's extraordinary personal charisma and popular appeal. Napoleon could also present himself as a son of the revolution, consolidating the achievements of the revolution with his various reforms and legal codes, endowing France with 'national' institutions ranging from the Legion of Honour to the Conseil d'Etat, and ending privilege by birth through opening careers in the public service to all those with the appropriate talents. Yet spectacular failures marred Napoleonic rule. Relations between Napoleon and the Pope, the Roman Catholic Church and French Roman Catholics largely failed. Individual liberties, press freedoms and effective democracy were sacrificed as the regime became more and more of a personal military dictatorship. Above all, Napoleon's seemingly endless military campaigns cost the lives of approximately a million Frenchmen, consumed an incalculable amount of French wealth, and ultimately ended with the defeats and disasters of 1814 and 1815.

The Restoration monarchy undoubtedly inherited a difficult legacy and too obviously owed its existence to French defeats and enemy victories. It nevertheless could have attempted to have won over widespread support by protecting individual liberties and press freedoms and by allowing effective parliamentary government to develop. Instead, political arrests, imprisonments and even executions, restrictions on the newspaper press, and curtailments and limitations of parliamentary democracy were all too frequent. A problem, of course, existed in that a free press and effective parliamentary democracy could mean attacks on the Bourbon monarchy. Yet the Crown could have been more of a neutral arbiter instead of being so openly partisan. Moreover, Louis XVIII, and even more so, Charles X, in so many ways demonstrated that their political sympathies and loyalties lay with the *Ancien Régime*.

The July monarchy faced much the same political challenge as the Restoration monarchy – the development of a regime which would protect individual liberties and press freedoms and promote effective parliamentary democracy. An additional challenge lay in the need to respond to the problems arising from the urbanisation and industrialisation of French society. Louis-Philippe did not revive memories or fears associated with the *Ancien Régime*. Instead, he celebrated and commemorated the Napoleonic legacy. This was a policy not without its potential dangers and could not compensate for the failure of the July monarchy to construct its own ideology. Moreover, the July monarchy repeated many of the mistakes of the Restoration monarchy. The response to popular insurrections, anarchist conspiracies, assassination attempts and political opposition was military repression, political trials, restrictions on the newspaper press, and government manipulation of a very restricted form of parliamentary democracy. Admittedly, the July monarchy faced the same problem as the Restoration monarchy: liberal press laws and more unrestricted parliamentary democracy meant more attacks on, and more opposition to, the Orleanist regime. The solution, though, was the same: Louis-Philippe should have reigned rather than governed. Admittedly, too, French political culture created difficulties for the July monarchy. Guizot's foreign policies, while clearly conservative, avoided unnecessary and expensive wars and arguably served France's national interests. Yet they jarred with the revolutionary and Napoleonic legacy of confrontaion with Britain and of French military intervention abroad. Hence Guizot was widely accused of seeking peace at any price. The July monarchy's failure to alleviate significantly workers' grievances or tackle the adverse social consequences of urbanisation and industrialisation is understandable, given the contemporary faith in *laissez-faire*. However, not addressing these issues adequately, together with losing moral authority and credibility, refusing to extend the parliamentary franchise or to introduce parliamentary reforms, and believing that a government majority in the Chamber of Deputies was all that mattered, proved fatal for the Orleanist regime in February 1848.

The introduction of manhood suffrage for national parliamentary, local government and presidential elections after February 1848 completely transformed the political landscape in France. Political success now required mass popular appeal and mass popular support; and in a new age of railways and telegraphs, as well as of universal manhood suffrage, Paris could no longer politically dominate the rest of France. The majority of the French electorate in 1848 opposed political violence and wars of liberation, believed in the inviolability of private property, was restrained in its anti-clericalism, and held traditional views on the institution of the family and the position of women. Reflecting this consensus, a broad-based Party of Order emerged in 1848. This coalition of Legitimists, Orleanists, conservatives and moderate republicans claimed that they would defend order at home, peace abroad, private property, the Roman Catholic Church, and the family. The Party of Order seemed to offer what most French people wanted and in effect represented the emergence of a new right. No longer standing for monarchy, aristocracy and privilege, no longer divided by competing dynastic loyalties, the new right adopted a conservative programme behind which all conservatives, and even many moderate republicans, could rally and which could attract mass support. The Party of Order successfully exploited the fears aroused by popular insurrection and violence in Paris and elsewhere, by Ledru-Rollin and his *commissaires*, by the proposals of Proudhon and other socialists, and by the continuing depressed state of the economy. Such fears could be intensified by misleadingly branding the entire French Left with a radicalism which it did not possess in 1848. At the same time, the Party of Order could offer reassurance by posing as the defender of morality, society and civilisation against attack and subversion from the Left. The Party of Order also benefited from possessing much greater political experience, and much greater material resources, than its left-wing opponents.

In contrast to the relatively united Right–Centre coalition represented by the Party of Order, the French Left remained disunited during 1848. Coming to power as a result of the February Revolution, the moderate republicans at once became the party of government, with a vested interest in staying in power and in maintaining law and order. At the same time, any political opposition, protest or violence was inevitably directed at least partly against them. Hence the divisions between the moderate republicans on the one hand, and the left-wing republicans and socialists on the other, intensified. Disagreements over how to tackle the problems of unemployment and economic depression, a government foreign policy of non-intervention, conservative successes in the National Assembly elections of 23 April 1848, the disbandment of the National Workshops, the threat and reality of popular insurrection, culminating in the June Days, and the post-June 1848 repression, all served to maintain, and even widen, the gulf dividing the moderate republicans from the left-wing republicans and socialists. When it came to the presidential election of December 1848, the separate and competing candidatures of Cavaignac (moderate republican), Ledru-Rollin (left-wing republican) and Raspail (socialist) demonstrated once again the divisions of the French Left.

During 1848 the French Left also failed to develop a political programme which could capture mass enthusiasm. The moderate republican Provisional Government did introduce manhood suffrage for national and local elections in France and did abolish slavery in France's colonies and overseas possessions, two major achievements. However, the newly-enfranchised for the most part did not use the ballot box to vote for moderate republican candidates. Instead, manhood suffrage provided the mechanism for the removal of the moderate republicans from power and for the electoral triumph of Louis Napoleon Bonaparte. As for the abolition of slavery, it seems to have exercised a minimal impact on French domestic politics. In other respects, the moderate republicans pursued relatively conservative policies, partly, no doubt, to demonstrate that the Second Republic would avoid the 'crimes' of the Jacobin Republic of 1793–4. In particular, no wars of liberation were launched and no serious attempt was made to redistribute wealth. Instead, a determination to uphold financial orthodoxy led to the imposition of the forty-five centimes tax. This conservatism meant that many on the left felt disappointed and betrayed while the forty-five centimes tax, and the absence of policies that might have benefited agriculture, alienated the peasantry. The left-wing republicans and socialists similarly lacked any mass appeal. Events such as the crowd invasion of the National Assembly on 15 May and the June Days in Paris recalled the Jacobin Republic of 1793–4 and its associations with terror, civil war and dictatorship. The apparent enthusiasm of the Paris radical clubs for French military intervention in Poland and Italy aroused fears of a European war. Proudhon's notorious and well-known claim that all property is theft suggested to many that the left wanted to expropriate all property-owners. Anti-clerical incidents, Carnot's vision of a republican State educational system and the killing of the Archbishop of Paris during the June Days similarly aroused fears of a new republican onslaught against the Roman Catholic Church. The emergence of a radical feminist movement in Paris after February 1848 and Crémieux's much publicised and debated divorce law proposal of May 1848 seemed to threaten the institution of the family and to alter drastically the position of women. Altogether, instead of winning mass popular support, the left-wing republicans and socialists tended to alarm the majority of the electorate and provide ammunition to those on the right who, often through exaggeration and misrepresentation, stoked up popular fears of the left.

Louis Napoleon Bonaparte could claim to be a man of the left. He had personally experienced poverty, hardship, exile and imprisonment; he had plotted against Papal rule in Rome and Habsburg rule in northern Italy; he had staged his attempted *coups* against Louis-Philippe at Strasbourg (1836) and Boulogne (1840); he had written about the extinction of pauperism and corresponded with the likes of Louis Blanc; and he could tap into a radical Bonapartism linked to hatred of priests, nobles and the rich, and to the popular radicalism and nationalism of the Hundred Days. In the presidential election he could therefore attract votes as an anti-Establishment and even radical candidate. However, Louis Napoleon Bonaparte's electoral manifesto of 27 November 1848 denied that he was an ambitious man who dreamed of empire and war or the realisation of subversive theories. Instead, he promised to re-establish order, restore national finances, protect religion, the family and property, and avoid war. The presidential election campaign of Louis Napoleon Bonaparte, in fact, brilliantly exploited the political culture of France in the autumn of 1848, though it did so by resorting to a substantial measure of misrepresentation of his rivals and opponents and of deception as to his own future intentions and policies. In a society riven by fear and politically polarised, his conservative message triumphed. As *Le Journal de la Côte d'Or* explained on 14 December 1848:

> The people do not want property to be equated with theft, they do not want sons no longer to inherit from their fathers . . ., they do not want religion, morality and the family to disappear . . .; they do not want the abominable epoch of the guillotine and the terror to be evoked. They want fraternity in word and deed, and that is why they have voted for Louis-Napoleon.

Notes

I The French Revolutionary tradition from 1789 to the July monarchy

1 D. Stern, *Histoire de la Révolution de 1848*, 3 vols, Paris, G. Sandré, 1850–3.
2 A. Delvau, *Histoire de la Révolution de février*, Paris, Blosse et Garnier, 1850.
3 A. de Tocqueville, *Souvenirs*, L. Monnier (ed.), Paris, Gallimard, 1964.
4 K. Marx, 'The Class Struggles in France: 1848 to 1850', and 'The Eighteenth Brumaire of Louis Bonaparte', in D. Fernbach (ed.), *Surveys from Exile*, Harmondsworth, Penguin Books, 1977, pp. 31–142 and 143–249.
5 Marx, 'The Eighteenth Brumaire of Louis Bonaparte', *Surveys from Exile*, p. 146.
6 F. Furet, *Revolutionary France, 1770–1880*, Oxford, Blackwell, 1988; R. Gildea, *The Past in French History*, New Haven and London, Yale University Press, 1994; P. Rosanvallon, *Le Sacre du citoyen: histoire du suffrage universel en France*, Paris, Gallimard, 1992, and ibid., *La Monarchie impossible: les chartes de 1814 et de 1830*, Paris, Fayard, 1994; R. Tombs, *France, 1814–1914*, London and New York, Longman, 1996.
7 Furet, *Revolutionary France*, p. vii.
8 Gildea, *The Past in French History*, p. 9 and p. 10.
9 Rosanvallon, *La Monarchie impossible*, p. 170 and pp. 179–80.
10 Rosanvallon, *Le Sacre du citoyen*, p. 263.
11 Tombs, *France, 1814–1914*, p. 1.
12 Ibid., p. 2.
13 Ibid., p. 9.
14 Ibid., p. 32.
15 Ibid., p. 105.
16 Furet, *Revolutionary France*, p. 288.
17 See D. Porch, *Army and Revolution: France, 1815–1848*, London, Routledge and Kegan Paul, 1974, and R. D. Price, 'The French Army and the Revolution of 1830', *European Studies Review*, 3 (1973), pp. 243–67.
18 See D. Higgs, 'Politics and Landownership among the French Nobility', *European Studies Review*, 1 (1971), pp. 105–21.
19 See S. Kent, *The Election of 1827 in France*, Cambridge, Mass., Harvard University Press, 1975, pp. 130–56.
20 D. H. Pinkney, *The French Revolution of 1830*, Princeton, New Jersey, Princeton University Press, 1972, p. 31.
21 P. M. Pilbeam, 'The Growth of Liberalism and the Crisis of the Bourbon Restoration', *Historical Journal*, 25 (1982), p. 359, and ibid., *The 1830 Revolution in France*, London, Macmillan, 1991, pp. 25–6.
22 P. M. Pilbeam, 'The Economic Crisis of 1827–32 and the 1830 Revolution in

Provincial France', *Historical Journal*, 32 (1989), p. 320, and ibid., *The French Revolution of 1830*, p. 38.

23 D. L. Rader, *The Journalists and the July Revolution in France: the role of the political press in the overthrow of the Bourbon Restoration, 1827–1830*, The Hague, Martinus Nijhoff, 1973, p. 59.

24 I. Collins, *The Government and the Newspaper Press in France, 1848–1881*, Oxford, Oxford University Press, 1959, pp. 43–6.

25 Rader, *The Journalists and the July Revolution in France*, p. 30 and p. 31.

26 Ibid., p. 213.

27 P. M. Pilbeam, 'The 'Liberal' Revolution of 1830', *Historical Research*, 63 (1990), p. 163.

28 P. M. Pilbeam, 'Republicanism in Early Nineteenth-century France, 1814–1835', *French History*, 5 (1991), p. 35.

29 R. S. Alexander, 'Restoration Republicanism Reconsidered', *French History*, 8 (1994), pp. 442–69, and ibid., *Re-writing the French Revolutionary Tradition: liberal opposition and the fall of the Bourbon monarchy*, Cambridge, Cambridge University Press, 2003.

30 See D. Skuy, *Assasination, Politics, and Miracles: France and the royalist reaction of 1820*, Montreal, McGill-Queen's University Press, 2003.

31 Alexander, 'Restoration Republicanism Reconsidered', *French History*, 8 (1994), p. 446, and ibid., *Re-writing the French Revolutionary Tradition*, pp. 175–85.

32 Pinkney, *The French Revolution of 1830*, pp. 252–7. A few foreigners also participated in the July Days. For British participants, see D. Turnbull, *The French Revolution of 1830: the events which produced it, and the scenes by which it was accompanied*, London, Henry Colburn and Richard Bentley, 1830, pp. vi–xii.

33 See E. L. Newman, 'The Blouse and the Frock Coat: the alliance of the common people of Paris with the liberal leadership and the middle class during the last years of the Bourbon Restoration', *Journal of Modern History*, 46 (1974), pp. 26–59.

34 P. Gonnet, 'Esquisse de la crise économique en France de 1827 à 1832', *Revue d'histoire économique et sociale*, 33 (1955), p. 265.

35 Pinkney, *The French Revolution of 1830*, p. 63.

36 Pilbeam, 'The Economic Crisis of 1827–32 and the 1830 Revolution in Provincial France', *Historical Journal*, 32 (1989), p. 336.

37 C. Limet, *Un Vétéran du barreau parisien: quatre-vingts ans de souvenirs, 1827–1907*, Paris, A. Lemerre, 1908, pp. 41–2.

38 J. M. Merriman, 'The *Demoiselles* of the Ariège, 1829–1831', in J. M. Merriman (ed.), *1830 in France*, New York, New Viewpoints, 1975, pp. 87–118. The new forest code was also resisted in the Doubs. See A. B. Spitzer, 'The Elections of 1824 and 1827 in the Department of the Doubs', *French History*, 3 (1989), p. 171.

39 J. M. Merriman, 'The Norman Fires of 1830: incendiaries and fear in rural France', *French Historical Studies*, 9 (1976), pp. 451–66.

40 Pilbeam, *The 1830 Revolution in France*, p. 64; Pinkney, *The French Revolution of 1830*, p. 76 and p. 102; and D. H. Pinkney, 'Pacification of Paris: the military lessons of 1830', in Merriman (ed.), *1830 in France*, p. 192.

41 J. V. A., duc de Broglie, *Mémoires du duc de Broglie*, 2 vols, Paris, Calmann-Lévy, 1938 and 1941, vol. I, p. 30.

42 R. J. Bezucha, 'The Revolution of 1830 and the City of Lyons', in Merriman (ed.), *1830 in France*, p. 121; Pilbeam, *The 1830 Revolution in France*, p. 72.

43 M. A., vicomte de Reiset, *Souvenirs du lieutenant-général vicomte de Reiset (1775–1832)*, publiés par son petit-fils le vicomte de Reiset, 3 vols, Paris, Calmann-Lévy, 1899–1902, vol. III, p. 591.

44 Porch, *Army and Revolution*, pp. 36–43.

45 Pinkney, *The French Revolution of 1830*, p. 212.

46 B. Fitzpatrick, *Catholic Royalism in the Department of the Gard, 1814–1852*, Cambridge, Cambridge University Press, 1983, pp. 99–104.

47 Pilbeam, *The 1830 Revolution in France*, p. 71.

48 G. Lubin (ed.), *Correspondance de George Sand*, Paris, Editions Garnier frères, vol. 1 (1964), p. 820.

49 See R. D. Price, 'Legitimist Opposition to the Revolution of 1830 in the French Provinces', *Historical Journal*, 17 (1974), pp. 755–78.

50 D. Higgs, *Ultraroyalism in Toulouse from its Origins to the Revolution of 1830*, Baltimore and London, Johns Hopkins University Press, 1973, p. 173 and p. 175.

51 See R. J. Bezucha, *The Lyon Uprising of 1834: social and political conflict in the early July monarchy*, Cambridge, Mass., Harvard University Press, 1974. See also P. M. Pilbeam, 'Popular Violence in Provincial France After the 1830 Revolution', *English Historical Review*, 91 (1976), pp. 278–97.

52 G. Weill, *Histoire du parti républicain en France de 1814 à 1870*, Paris, Alcan, 1900, pp. 41–2.

53 Rader, *The Journalists and the July Revolution in France*, p. 254.

54 Weill, *Histoire du parti républicain*, pp. 95–7.

55 See J. D. Popkin, *Press, Revolution, and Social Identities in France, 1830–1835*, Pennsylvania, Pennsylvania State University Press, 2002, pp. 193–228.

56 Tombs, *France, 1814–1914*, p. 358.

57 See J. B. Margadant, 'Gender, Vice, and the Political Imaginary in Postrevolutionary France: reinterpreting the failure of the July monarchy, 1830–1848', *American Historical Review*, 104 (1999), pp. 1,461–96. *Le Siècle* declared on 15 March 1847: 'On éprouve un profond sentiment de pitié en voyant le pouvoir sorti des barricades de 1830 renier son origine comme un parvenu, effacer de son front le signe du baptême populaire, et couvrir les austères insignes d'une dynastie nationale sous les oripeaux de l'*Ancien Régime*.'

58 For a description, see S. Gaudon (ed.), *Victor Hugo: Choses vues*, Paris, Robert Laffont, 1987, pp. 805–16.

59 N. W. Senior, *Conversations with M. Thiers, M. Guizot, and Other Distinguished Persons, During the Second Empire*, 2 vols, London, Hurst and Blackett, 1878, vol. I, p. 127.

60 J. J. Baughman, 'Financial Resources of Louis-Philippe', *French Historical Studies*, 4 (1965), pp. 63–83.

61 P. L.-R. Higonnet and T. B. Higonnet, 'Class, Corruption, and Politics in the French Chamber of Deputies, 1846–1848', *French Historical Studies*, 5 (1967), pp. 206–7.

62 P. Bastid, *Les Institutions politiques de la monarchie parlementaire française, 1814–1848*, Paris, Recueil Sirey, 1954, p. 201.

63 A.-J. Tudesq, *Les Grands notables en France, 1840–1849: étude historique d'une psychologie sociale*, 2 vols, Paris, Presses universitaires de France, 1964, vol. I, p. 356.

64 F. Julien-Laferrière, *Les Députés fonctionnaires sous la Monarchie de Juillet*, Paris, Presses universitaires de France, 1970, pp. 67–8.

65 H. A. C. Collingham, *The July Monarchy: a political history of France, 1830–1848*, London, Longman, 1988, p. 72; Tudesq, *Les Grands notables en France*, vol. I, p. 98.

66 Tudesq, *Les Grands notables en France*, vol. I, p. 358.

67 Rosanvallon, *Le Sacre du citoyen*, p. 270.

68 Tudesq, *Les Grands notables en France*, vol. I, p. 358.

69 L. Girard, *La Garde nationale, 1814–1871*, Paris, Plon, 1964, p. 168 and p. 184.

70 Pinkney, *The French Revolution of 1830*, p. 277.

71 See R. Magraw, *France, 1815–1914: the bourgeois century*, Oxford, Fontana, 1983, pp. 51–5.

72 N. Richardson, *The French Prefectoral Corps, 1814–1830*, Cambridge, Cambridge University Press, 1966, p. 203.

73 P.-B. Higonnet, 'La Composition de la Chambre des Députés de 1827 à 1831', *Revue historique*, 239 (1968), pp. 357–8.

74 Pinkney, *The French Revolution of 1830*, p. 195, n. 78.

75 Ibid., pp. 289–95.

76 P. M. Pilbeam, 'The "Impossible Restoration": the Left and the Revolutionary and Napoleonic legacies', in D. Laven and L. Riall (eds), *Napoleon's Legacy: problems of government in Restoration Europe*, Oxford and New York, Berg, 2000, p. 193.

77 Magraw, *France, 1815–1914*, p. 54. Cf. Tudesq, *Les Grands notables en France*, vol. I, p. 435.

78 See T. D. Beck, *French Legislators, 1800–1834: a study in quantitive history*, Berkeley, University of California Press, 1974, pp. 108–31; Higonnet, 'Class, Corruption, and Politics in the French Chamber of Deputies, 1846–1848', *French Historical Studies*, 5 (1967), pp. 204–24; Higonnet, 'La Composition de la Chambre des Députés de 1827 à 1831', *Revue historique*, 239 (1968), pp. 351–78. *Revue historique*, 239 (1968), pp. 351–78.

79 D. H. Pinkney, *Decisive Years in France, 1840–1847*, Princeton, New Jersey, Princeton University Press, 1986, p. 6; Tudesq, *Les Grands notables en France*, vol. I, p. 379, p. 188, p. 437, p. 426, pp. 430–1, and p. 323.

80 T. D. Beck, 'Occupation, Taxes, and a Distinct Nobility under Louis-Philippe', *European Studies Review*, 13 (1983), pp. 403–22.

81 Tudesq, *Les Grands notables en France*, vol. I, p. 88.

82 J. Dupâquier et al., *Histoire de la population française*, 4 vols, Paris, Presses universitaires de France, 1988–91, vol. III, p. 130.

83 A. Daumard, *La Bourgeoisie parisienne de 1815 à 1848*, Paris, SEVPEN, 1963, p. 7.

84 A. Daumard (ed.), *Les Fortunes françaises au XIXe siècle*, Paris, Mouton, 1973, p. 216.

85 Ibid., p. 228.

86 C. Aboucaya, *Les Structures sociales et économiques de l'agglomération lyonnaise à la veille de la Révolution de 1848*, Paris, Recueil Sirey, 1963, p. 24.

87 P. Lévêque, *Une Société provinciale: la Bourgogne sous la monarchie de juillet*, Paris, Editions Jean Touzot, 1983, p. 253.

88 M. Agulhon, *Une Ville ouvrière au temps du socialisme utopique: Toulon de 1815 à 1851*, Paris, Mouton, 1970, p. 45.

89 D. M. Gordon, *Merchants and Capitalists: industrialization and provincial politics in mid-nineteenth-century France*, Alabama, University of Alabama Press, 1985, p. 15.

2 The economic, social and political crises

1 C. H. Pouthas, *La Population française pendant la première moitié du XIXe siècle*, Paris, Presses universitaires de France, 1956, p. 22.

2 Dupâquier et al., *Histoire de la population française*, vol. III, p. 126.

3 Pouthas, *La Population française*, p. 98.

4 Ibid., pp. 98–9.

5 R. Price, *A Social History of Nineteenth-century France*, London, Hutchinson, 1988, p. 79.

6 Dupâquier et al., *Histoire de la population française*, vol. III, p. 353.

7 Price, *A Social History of Nineteenth-century France*, p. 49.

8 Dupâquier et al., *Histoire de la population française*, vol. III, p. 130 and p. 132.

9 R. Price, *The Modernization of Rural France: communication networks and agricultural market structures in nineteenth-century France*, London, Hutchinson, 1983, p. 352. Cf. A. Corbin, *Archaïsme et modernité en Limousin au XIXe siècle, 1845–1880*, 2 vols, Paris, Marcel Rivière, 1975, vol. I, p. 261.

10 P. M. Jones, *Politics and Rural Society: the southern Massif Central, c. 1750–1880*, Cambridge, Cambridge University Press, 1985, p. 17.

11 Agulhon, *Une Ville ouvrière au temps du socialisme utopique*, p. 57.
12 D. H. Pinkney, *Napoleon III and the Rebuilding of Paris*, Princeton, New Jersey, Princeton University Press, 1972, p. 10; Aboucaya, *Les Structures sociales et économiques de l'agglomération lyonnaise*, p. 15, n. 9.
13 Pouthas, *La Population française*, p. 144.
14 Ibid., p. 171; Pinkney, *Napoleon III and the Rebuilding of Paris*, p. 21.
15 R. Price, *The Economic Modernisation of France, 1730–1880*, London, Croom Helm, 1975, p. 8.
16 Ibid., pp. 17 and. 16.
17 Ibid., p. 21.
18 In general, see J. Vidalenc, *Le Peuple des campagnes: la société française de 1815 à 1848*, Paris, Marcel Rivière et Cie, 1969. For examples of regional studies, see Corbin, *Archaïsme et modernité en Limousin au XIXe siècle*; G. Dallas, *The Imperfect Peasant Economy: the Loire country, 1800–1914*, Cambridge, Cambridge University Press, 1982; Lévêque, *Une Société provinciale*: P. Vigier, *La Seconde République dans la région alpine*, 2 vols, Paris, Presses universitaires de France, 1963.
19 See J.-P. Aguet, *Les Grèves sous la Monarchie de Juillet (1830–1847): contribution à l'étude du mouvement ouvrier français*, Geneva, Droz, 1954; P. N. Stearns, 'Patterns of Industrial Strike Activity in France During the July Monarchy', *American Historical Review*, 70 (1965), pp. 371–94.
20 Price, *The Economic Modernisation of France*, p. 123.
21 F. Crouzet, 'Essai de construction d'un indice annuel de la production industrielle française au XIXe siècle', *Annales, E.S.C.*, 25 (1970), pp. 92–5.
22 *L'Union monarchique*, 2 January 1847, p. 3.
23 *Le Moniteur universel*, 1 June 1845, p. 1,529.
24 Ibid., 1 September 1845, p. 2,375.
25 Ibid., 1 December 1845, p. 2,761.
26 Ibid., 1 May 1847, p. 1,005.
27 E. Labrousse (ed.), *Aspects de la crise et de la dépression de l'économie française au milieu du XIXe siècle, 1846–1851*, La Roche-sur-Yon, Société d'Histoire de la Révolution de 1848, 1956, pp. 41 and p. 172.
28 *Le Moniteur universel*, 1 February 1848, p. 239.
29 M. Perrot, 'Aspects industriels de la crise: les régions textiles du Calvados', in Labrousse (ed.), *Aspects de la crise et de la dépression de l'économie française au milieu du XIXe siècle*, p. 172.
30 Mérimée to Mme de Montijo, 23 January 1847; M. Parturier (ed.), *Prosper Mérimée: correspondance générale*, vol. 5, 1847–1849, Paris, Le Divan, 1946, pp. 12–13.
31 Vigier, *La Seconde République dane la région alpine*, vol. I, p. 117.
32 A. Jardin and A.-J. Tudesq, *Restoration and Reaction, 1815–1848*, Cambridge, Cambridge University Press, 1983, p. 195.
33 A.-J. Tudesq, 'La Crise de 1847, vue par les milieux d'affaires parisiens', in Labrousse (ed.), *Aspects de la crise et de la dépression de l'économie française au milieu du XIXe siècle*, p. 27.
34 J. Godechot (ed.), *La Révolution de 1848 à Toulouse et dans la Haute-Garonne*, Toulouse, Préfecture de la Haute-Garonne, 1948, p. 126. See also R. Aminzade, *Class, Politics, and Early Industrial Capitalism: a study of mid-nineteenth-century Toulouse, France*, Albany, State University of New York Press, 1981, p. 40.
35 P. McPhee, 'The Seed-Time of the Republic: society and politics in the Pyrénées-Orientales, 1846–1852', unpublished PhD thesis (Melbourne, 1977), p. 48.
36 Price, *The Modernization of Rural France*, p. 107.
37 Corbin, *Archaïsme et modernité en Limousin au XIXe siècle*, p. 489.
38 P. Deyon, 'Aspects industriels de la crise: Rouen', in Labrousse (ed.), *Aspects de la crise et de la dépression de l'économie française au milieu du XIXe siècle*, p. 146.

39 *Le Siècle*, 31 January 1847, p. 4.

40 *L'Argus soissonnais*, cited by *L'Union monarchique*, 21 February 1847, p. 3.

41 *L'Union monarchique*, 24 February 1847, p. 3.

42 Aminzade, *Class, Politics, and Early Industrial Capitalism*, p. 40.

43 *Le Journal des Débats*, 1 January 1847, p. 2.

44 *Le Moniteur universel*, 24 February 1847, p. 371, and 1 April 1847, p. 670; *Le Journal des Débats*, 26 March 1847, p. 2.

45 *Le Courrier de la Côte-d'Or* (Dijon, Côte-d'Or), 17 November 1846.

46 Aminzade, *Class, Politics, and Early Industrial Capitalism*, p. 142.

47 *Le Journal des Débats*, 13 March 1847, p. 2; *Le Moniteur universel*, 29 March 1847, p. 637, and 1 April 1847, p. 670.

48 *Le Moniteur universel*, 18 March 1847, p. 538.

49 *Le Journal des Débats*, 16 March 1847, p. 3; *Le Moniteur universel*, 21 March 1847, p. 556.

50 *Le Presse*, 30 January 1847, p. 2.

51 *Le Moniteur universel*, 26 February 1847, p. 385.

52 Ibid., 18 March 1847, p. 538, citing *L'Echo de la Haute-Marne*, 13 March 1847.

53 *Le Journal des Débats*, 20 March 1847, p. 2; *Le Moniteur universel*, 27 February 1847, p. 390, and ibid., 21 March 1847, p. 556.

54 Lévêque, *Une Société en crise*, p. 33.

55 A. Chanut et al., 'Aspects de la crise: le département du Nord', in Labrousse (ed.), *Aspects de la crise et de la dépression de l'économie française au milieu du XIXe siècle*, p. 118.

56 *Le Moniteur universel*, 16 April 1847, p. 814.

57 *L'Union monarchique*, 1 January 1847, p. 2.

58 Godechot, *La Révolution de 1848 à Toulouse et dans la Haute-Garonne*, p. 123.

59 *Le Moniteur universel*, 24 February 1847, p. 371. Cf. Lévêque, *Une Société en crise*, p. 33.

60 *Le Constitutionnel*, 12 January and 14 March 1847, p. 2; *Le Moniteur universel*, 15 March 1847, p. 509, and ibid., 22 March 1847, p. 567; *La Patrie*, 21 March 1847, p. 2.

61 *Le Moniteur universel*, 2 March 1847, p. 418.

62 *L'Union monarchique*, 22 January 1847, p. 3.

63 *Le Journal des Débats*, 17 March 1847; *Le Moniteur universel*, 18 March 1847, p. 538; Godechot, *La Révolution de 1848 à Toulouse et dans la Haute-Garonne*, p. 86.

64 Lévêque, *Une Société en crise*, p. 33.

65 *Le Journal des Débats*, 5 January 1847, p. 2.

66 *Le Moniteur universel*, 24 February 1847, p. 371.

67 *L'Union monarchique*, 6 March 1847, p. 2.

68 *Le Moniteur universel*, 29 March 1847, p. 637.

69 R. Price, 'Poor Relief and Social Crisis in Mid-nineteenth-century France', *European Studies Review*, 13 (1983), p. 435.

70 A. Chanut et al., 'Aspects industriels de la crise: le département du Nord', in Labrousse (ed.), *Aspects de la crise et de la dépression de l'économie française au milieu du XIXe siècle*, p. 113.

71 Corbin, *Archaïsme et modernité en Limousin au XIXe siècle*, p. 498.

72 *Le Journal des Débats*, 14 January 1847, p. 2, citing *L'Echo de la Mayenne*, 14 January 1847.

73 *L'Union monarchique*, 22 January 1847, p. 4.

74 Lévêque, *Une Société en crise*, p. 27.

75 *Le Journal des Débats*, 17 January 1847, p. 2, and ibid., 31 January 1847, p. 2.

76 *La Presse*, 22 March 1847, p. 3.

77 *L'Union monarchique*, 25 January 1847, p. 3.

78 *Le Journal des Débats*, 18 and 19 January 1847, p. 2 and pp. 1–2; *L'Union monarchique*, 23 January 1847, p. 3.

79 *Le Constitutionnel*, 9 March 1847, p. 2.

80 See also Price, *The Modernization of Rural France*, p. 164.

81 Ibid., p. 164. Cf. W. M. Reddy, *The Rise of Market Culture: the textile trade and French society, 1750–1900*, Cambridge, Cambridge University Press, 1984, p. 203.

82 R. Aminzade, *Ballots and Barricades: class formation and republican politics in France, 1830–1871*, Princeton, New Jersey, Princeton University Press, 1993, p. 180.

83 See Aguet, *Les Grèves sous la Monarchie de Juillet*, pp. 291–362.

84 Ibid. and *La Presse*, 10 October 1847, p. 2.

85 See *Le Moniteur universel*, 21 March 1847, p. 556, 26 March 1847, p. 605, and 8 April 1847, p. 715.

86 Ibid., 10, 18, 20 and 22 April 1847, p. 737, p. 837, p. 851, p. 875, 26, 29 and 31 May 1847, p. 1,291, p. 1,335, p. 1,367, 4 and 21 June 1847, p. 1,415, p. 1,671.

87 *Le Siècle*, 3 June 1847, p. 2.

88 *Revue des Deux Mondes*, 19 (15 December 1847), p. 1,128.

89 Vigier, *La Seconde République dans la région alpine*, vol. I, p. 9.

90 Daumard, *La Bourgeoisie parisienne de 1815 à 1848*, p. 32, p. 55 and p. 57; R. L. Koepke, 'The *Loi des patentes* of 1844', *French Historical Studies*, 11 (1980), pp. 398–430.

91 See E. C. Childs, 'Big Trouble: Daumier, *Gargantua*, and the Censorship of Political Caricature', *Art Journal*, 51 (1992), pp. 26–37; J. Cuno, 'The Business and Politics of Caricature: Charles Philipon and la maison Aubert', *Gazette des Beaux-Arts*, 106 (1985), pp. 95–112; B. Farwell (ed.), *The Charged Image: French lithographic caricature, 1816–1848*, Santa Barbara, California, Santa Barbara Museum of Art, 1989; R. J. Goldstein, *Censorship of Political Caricature in Nineteenth-century France*, Kent, Ohio, and London, Kent State University Press, 1989; E. K. Kenney and J. M. Merriman, *The Pear: French graphic arts in the golden age of caricature*, South Hadley, Mass., 1991; D. S. Kerr, *Caricature and French Political Culture, 1830–1848*, Oxford, Oxford University Press, 2000; P. ten-Doesschate and G. P. Weisberg (eds), *The Popularization of Images: visual culture under the July monarchy*, Princeton, Princeton University Press, 1994.

92 See S. Gemie, 'Balzac and the Moral Crisis of the July Monarchy', *European History Quarterly*, 19 (1989), pp. 469–94.

93 See Stern, *Histoire de la Révolution de 1848*, vol. I, pp. 12–14, and W. Fortescue, 'Poetry, Politics and Publicity, and the Writing of History: Lamartine's *Histoire de Girondins* (1847)', *European History Quarterly*, 17 (1987), pp. 259–84.

94 See, for example, *Le Siècle*, 11 November 1845.

95 See *Le Constitutionnel*, 9 January 1847.

96 See E. Jones Parry (ed.), *The Correspondence of Lord Aberdeen and Princess Lieven, 1832–1854*, 2 vols, London, Royal Historical Society, 1938–9 (Camden Third Series, vols 60 and 62), vol. I, p. 265, p. 269, and p. 278.

97 See R. Bullen, 'Guizot and the *Sonderbund* Crisis, 1846–1848', *English Historical Review*, 86 (1971), pp. 497–526, and ibid., *Palmerston, Guizot and the Collapse of the Entente Cordiale*, London, Athlone Press, 1974; D. Johnson, *Guizot: aspects of French history*, London, Routledge and Kegan Paul, 1963, chapter 6.

98 See *Le Moniteur universel*, 3 January 1848, p. 9; *Le Journal des Débats*, 2 January 1848; *Le Courrier français*, 2 and 3 January 1848.

99 Ardennes, Aube, Corsica, Côte-d'Or, Côtes-du-Nord, Creuse, Deux-Sèvres, Ille-et-Vilaine, Mayenne, Morbihan, Nord, Saône-et-Loire, Seine-Inférieure. They were joined in 1847 by Aisne, Aveyron, Corrèze, Finistère, Haute-Loire, Haut-Rhin, Moselle, Oise and Vosges. See *Le Constitutionnel*, 7 February 1848.

100 P. Duvergier de Hauranne, *De la Réforme parlementaire et de la réforme électorale*, Paris,

Paulin, 1847, p. 1. Cf. *Le Constitutionnel*, 18 January 1847, pp. 2–3, and *Le Siècle*, 18 January 1847. *La Gazette de France* criticised the system of parliamentary suffrage in a series of articles published on 6, 7 and 8 January 1847, and on 12 February 1847.

101 Duvergier de Hauranne, *De la Réforme parlementaire et de la réforme électorale*, pp. 140–2 and p. 169.

102 Koepke, 'The *Loi des patentes* of 1844', *French Historical Studies*, 11 (1980), pp. 398–430.

103 F. P. G. Guizot, *De la Démocratie en France*, Paris, Victor Masson, 1849; P. Rosanvallon, *Le Moment Guizot*, Paris, Gallimard, 1985, pp. 55–63, 75–82 and 87–140; Senior, *Conversations with M. Thiers, M. Guizot, and Other Distinguished Persons, During the Second Empire*, 1878, vol. II, p. 373 and p. 385.

104 *Le Consitutionnel*, 24 April 1847.

105 See C. H. Pouthas (ed.), *Charles de Rémusat: mémoires de ma vie*, 5 vols, Paris, Plon, 1958–67, vol. IV (1962), pp. 115–16.

106 C. Barthélemy, *Histoire de la monarchie de juillet*, Paris, H. Gautier, 1887, pp. 240–1; L.-A. Garnier-Pagès, *Histoire de la Révolution de 1848*, 10 vols, Paris, Pagnerre, 1861–72, vol. IV (1861), pp. 97–103; P. Thureau-Dangin, *Histoire de la monarchie de juillet*, 7 vols, Paris, E. Plon, Nourrit et Cie, 1884–92, vol. VII, pp. 80–1.

107 Garnier-Pagès, *Histoire de la Révolution de 1848*, vol. IV, pp. 103–5.

108 For the reservations of Thiers, see *Notes et souvenirs de M. Thiers, 1848*, Paris, 1902, pp. 3–4.

109 Crémieux's reform banquet speeches are reprinted in I. M. A. Crémieux, *En 1848: discours et lettres de M. A. Crémieux*, Paris, Calmann Lévy, 1883. On Crémieux see G. Renauld, *Adolphe Crémieux, homme d'Etat français et franc-macon: le combat pour la République*, Paris, Detrad, 2002.

110 McPhee, 'The Seed-Time of the Republic', pp. 28–32; Aminzade, *Ballots and Barricades*, pp. 114–15.

111 Guillemin to Pagnerre, n.d. (Pagnerre Papers, AN 67 AP 2, f. 44); *Le National*, 12 October 1847, p. 2; *L'Etoile*, 24 and 26 October and 4 November 1847; *L'Eduen* (Autun, Saône-et-Loire), 31 October 1847; *Le Journal du Tarn* (Albi, Tarn), 27 November 1847.

112 E. de Lignères, comte d'Alton-Shée, *Souvenirs de 1847 et de 1848*, Paris, M. Dreyfous, 1879, pp. 62–3; C. H. O. Barrot, *Mémoires posthumes*, 4 vols, Paris, Charpentier er Cie, 1875–6, vol. I, pp. 464–5; M.-A. Chambolle, *Retours sur la vie: appréciations et confidences sur les hommes de mon temps*, Paris, Plon, 1912, pp. 454–6, 485–6; A. A. Ledru-Rollin, *Discours politiques et écrits divers*, 2 vols, Paris, Germer-Baillière et Cie, 1879, vol. I, pp. 329–39; *La Réforme*, 23 November 1847. On the Lille banquet, see L. Machu, 'L'Importance du banquet de Lille dans la campagne de réforme (7 novembre 1847)', *Revue du Nord*, 31 (1949), pp. 5–12.

113 Alton-Shée, *Souvenirs de 1847 et de 1848*, p. 69.

114 J. J. L. Blanc, *Discours politiques, 1847 à 1881*, Paris, Germer-Baillière et Cie, 1882, pp. 1–8; Ledru-Rollin, *Discours politiques et écrits divers*, vol. I, pp. 340–50.

115 Alton-Shée, *Souvenirs de 1847 et de 1848*, pp. 78–82; J. Gouache, *Lille: Dijon: Chalon: Banquets démocratiques*, Paris, Au bureau de *La Réforme*, 1848; Ledru-Rollin, *Discours politiques et écrits divers*, vol. I, pp. 351–60.

116 See *Compte rendu du banquet de Limoges. 2 janvier 1848*, Boussac, Imprimerie de Pierre Leroux, 1848, pp. 6–10; Corbin, *Archaïsme et modernité en Limousin au XIXe siècle*, vol. I, pp. 761–3, and vol. II, pp. 1,015–16.

117 See *Journal du maréchal de Castellane, 1804–1862*, 5 vols, Paris, Plon, Nourrit et Cie, 1895–87, vol. IV, pp. 8–10.

118 *Le National*, 12, 13 and 17 February 1848. Cf. *La Presse*, 15 and 16 February 1848.

119 G. Flaubert to L. Colet, December 1847 (G. Flaubert, *Correspondance*, vol. II, Paris, Louis Conard, 1936, p. 78).

120 Delvau, *Histoire de la Révolution de février*, p. 102.

121 See J. J. Baughman, 'The Political Banquet Campaign in France, 1847–1848', unpublished PhD thesis, Michigan, 1953; C. Bellanger *et al.* (eds), *Histoire générale de la presse française*, vol. 2, Paris, Presses universitaires de France, 1969, p. 192; Lévêque, *Une société en crise: la Bourgogne au milieu du XIXe siècle*, pp. 40–6; P. M. Pilbeam, *Republicanism in Early Nineteenth-century France, 1814–1871*, London, Macmillan, 1995, pp. 149–52; Thureau-Dangin, *Histoire de la monarchie de juillet*, vol. VII, pp. 78–87 and 100–114. For contemporary accounts, see Alton-Shée, *Souvenirs de 1847 et de 1848*; R. Dubail, *Campagne réformiste de 1847*, Paris, Paulin, 1848; M. du Camp, *Souvenirs de l'année 1848*, Paris, Hachette, 1876, pp. 40–4; Castellane, *Journal*, vol. IV, pp. 7–10; Gustave Flaubert to Louise Colet, December 1847 (Flaubert, *Correspondance*, vol. II, pp. 78–9). See also R. Spang, "La Fronde des nappes': fat and lean rhetoric in the political banquets of 1847', in C. F. Coates (ed.), *Repression and Expression: literary and social coding in nineteenth-century France*, New York, Peter Lang, 1996, pp. 167–78.

122 See W. Fortescue, 'Morality and Monarchy: corruption and the fall of the regime of Louis-Philippe in 1848', *French History*, 16 (2002), pp. 83–100; Thureau-Dangin, *Histoire de la monarchie de Juillet*, vol. VII, pp. 51–77 and 90–100; Tudesq, *Les Grands notables en France*, vol. II, pp. 914–25. For contemporary commentaries by a member of the Chamber of Peers, see Hugo, *Choses vues*, pp. 631–2, 637–41, 721–51, 978–85.

123 Thureau-Dangin, *Histoire de la monarchie de juillet*, vol. VII, p. 324.

124 See *Le Courrier français*, 4 January 1848, pp. 1–2.

125 Mérimée, *Correspondance générale*, vol. V (1946), p. 229 (Mérimée to the comtese de Montijo, 15 January 1848); A. Nougarède, *La Vérité sur la Révolution de février 1848*, Paris, Amyot, 1850, p. 11.

126 For a description of Mme Adélaïde's funeral, see A.-L., baron Imbert de Saint-Amand, *La Révolution de 1848*, Paris, E. Dentu, 1894, pp. 7–11.

127 *Le Moniteur universel*, 28 January 1848, pp. 211–12.

128 Ibid., 30 January 1848, pp. 228–31. See also E. Biré, *Mes Souvenirs, 1846–1870*, Paris, J. Lamarre, 1908, pp. 36–7.

129 See *Le National*, *La Presse*, *La Réforme* and *Le Siècle* for 30 January 1848.

130 See Alton-Shée, *Souvenirs de 1847 et de 1848*, pp. 197–227; Barrot, *Mémoires posthumes*, vol. I, pp. 506–16; Chambolle, *Retours sur la vie*, pp. 234–7; A. A. Chérest, *La Vie et les oeuvres de A.-T. Marie, avocat, membre du gouvernement provisoire*, Paris, A. Durand et Pédone-Lauriel, 1873, pp. 87–93; Garnier-Pagès, *Histoire de la Révolution de 1848*, vol. IV, pp. 171–262; A. de Lamartine, *Histoire de la Révolution de 1848*, 2 vols, Paris, Perrotin, 1849, vol. I, pp. 52–63; J.-B. Sarrans, *Histoire de la Révolution de février 1848*, 2 vols, Paris, Administration de librairie, 1851, vol. I, pp. 270–80; Stern, *Histoire de la Révolution de 1848*, vol. I, p. 85–100. For a secondary account, see A. Crémieux, *La Révolution de février: étude critique sur les journées des 21, 22, 23 et 24 février 1848*, Paris, Edouard Cornéby, 1912, pp. 55–75.

3 The February Revolution and the Provisional Government

1 *La Lanterne du Quartier Latin*, March 1847.

2 See *L'Avant-Garde: Journal des Ecoles*, January 1848, pp. 29–30; *La Réforme*, 4 February 1848; J. G. Gallaher, *The Students of Paris and the Revolution of 1848*, London and Amsterdam, Southern Illinois University Press, 1980, pp. 12–17; J. Pochon, 'Edgar Quinet et les luttes du Collège de France, 1843–1847', *Revue d'histoire littéraire de la France*, 70 (1970), pp. 619–27.

3 See *Le Courrier français*, 4 and 10 January 1848, p. 2; *La Démocratie pacifique*, 3 and 4 January 1848, pp. 1–2, and 9 January 1848, p. 2; *Le Journal des Débats*, 10 January 1848; *La Réforme*, 9 January 1848, pp. 1–2.

4 The nine newspapers were: *Le Commerce*, *Le Courrier français*, *La Démocratie pacifique*, *La Gazette de France*, *Le National*, *La Patrie*, *La Réforme*, *Le Siècle* and *L'Union monarchique*. See *La Lanterne du Quartier Latin*, January 1848, p. 5.

5 *Le Siècle*, 5 January 1848, p. 3, and 10 January 1848, p. 2.

6 *La Réforme*, 7 January 1848, p. 2.

7 *La Démocratie pacifique*, 9 January 1848, p. 2; *Le Journal des Débats*, 10 January 1848; *La Réforme*, 9 January 1848, pp. 1–2; *Le Siècle*, 9 January 1848, p. 3.

8 See *La Lanterne du Quartier Latin*, January 1848, pp. 5–6; *La Démocratie pacifique*, 5 January 1848, 7 January 1848, pp. 1–2, 4 February 1848, pp. 1–2; *La Réforme*, 4 February 1848; Gallaher, *The Students of Paris and the Revolution of 1848*, pp. 18–27.

9 *La Réforme*, 19 February 1848, p. 2.

10 See L. A. E. Achard, *Souvenirs personnels d'émeute et de révolution*, Paris, Michel Lévy, 1872, pp. 31–3; J. E. V. Arago, *Histoire de Paris: ses revolutions, ses gouvernements et ses événements de 1841 à 1852*, 2 vols, Paris, Dion-Lambert, 1855, vol. I, p. 340 and pp. 343–6; H. A. Barbier, *Souvenirs personnels et silhouettes contemporaines*, Paris, E. Dentu, 1883, pp. 107–9; L. Canler, *Mémoires de Canler, ancien chef du service de sûreté*, Paris, J. Hetzel, 1862, p. 82; E. Daudet (ed.), *Vingt-cinq ans à Paris, 1826–1850: Journal du comte Rodolphe Apponyi, attaché de l'ambassade d'Autriche à Paris*, 4 vols, Paris, Plon-Nourrit et Cie, 1913–26, vol. IV, p. 136; S. G. Goodrich, *Recollections of a Lifetime, or Men and Things I Have Seen: in a series of familiar letters to a friend, historical, biographical, anecdotical, and descriptive*, 2 vols, New York and Auburn, Miller, Orton and Mulligan, 1857, vol. II, p. 462; F.-L. Poumiès de La Siboutie, *Souvenirs d'un médecin de Paris, 1789–1863*, Paris, Plon-Nourrit, 1910, p. 293; C. J. Ligne, *Souvenirs de la princesse de Ligne, 1815–1850*, Brussels, G. Van Oest, 1923, p. 127; Tocqueville, *Souvenirs*, p. 51; J. P. Simpson, *Pictures from Revolutionary Paris, Sketched During the First Phases of the Revolution of 1848*, 2 vols, Edinburgh and London, W. Blackwood and Sons, 1849, vol. I, p. 31.

11 Crémieux, *La Révolution de février*, p. 128.

12 *Ibid.*, p. 196; J. Harsin, *Barricades: the war of the streets in revolutionary Paris, 1830–1848*, New York and Houndmills, Palgrave, 2002, p. 261.

13 Achard, *Souvenirs personnels*, pp. 44–8; L. D. Véron, *Mémoires d'un bourgeois de Paris*, 6 vols, Paris, Gabriel de Gonet, 1853–5, vol. V, pp. 77–9.

14 *La Démocratie pacifique* and *Le Journal des Débats*, 25 February 1848.

15 *Curiosités révolutionnaires. Les affiches rouges. Reproduction exacte et histoire critique de toutes les affiches ultra-républicaines placardées sur les murs de Paris depuis le 24 février 1848*, Paris, 1851, p. 6.

16 G. Bourgin (ed.), *Adolphe, comte de Circourt: souvenirs d'une mission à Berlin en 1848*, 2 vols, Paris, A. Picard et fils, 1908–9, vol. I, pp. 36–9.

17 'J'abdique cette couronne que la voix nationale m'avait appellée [sic] à porter, en faveur de mon petit-fils le Comte de Paris. Puisse-t-il réussir dans la grande tâche qui lui écheoit aujourd'hui. Louis-Philippe, 24 février 1848.' See R. Bazin, *Le Duc de Nemours*, Paris, Emile-Paul frères, 1907, p. 341, and E. de Girardin, *Bon sens, bonne foi*, Paris, Michel Lévy frères, 1848, pp. 16–17, and ibid., *Journal d'un journaliste au secret*, Paris, Michel Lévy frères, 1848, p. 7.

18 See Crémieux, *En 1848: discours et lettres*, pp. 109–206 and 282–311; Hugo, *Choses vues*, pp. 1,017–21; E. Kaye (ed.), *X. Marmier: journal (1848–1890)*, 2 vols, Geneva, Librairie Droz, 1968, vol. I, p. 63; Véron, *Mémoires d'un bourgeois de Paris*, vol. V, pp. 91–122.

19 Achard, *Souvenirs personnels d'émeutes et de révolutions*, pp. 60–1; Barbier, *Souvenirs personnels et silhouettes contemporaines*, pp. 124–7; Limet, *Un Vétéran du barreau parisien*, p. 163.

20 Achard, *Souvenirs personnels d'émeutes et de révolutions*, pp. 62–3; Véron, *Mémoires d'un bourgeois de Paris*, vol. V, pp. 308–22.

21 See C. Bocher, *Mémoires de Charles Bocher (1816–1907), précédés des souvenirs de famille (1760–1816)*, Paris, Flammarion, 1906, pp. 488–90.

22 Garnier-Pagès, *Histoire de la Révolution de 1848*, vol. II, p. 275.

23 Rémusat, *Mémoires de ma vie*, vol. IV, p. 262–3.

24 Lamartine, *Histoire de la Révolution de 1848*, vol. I, pp. 246–9; Sarrans, *Histoire de la Révolution de février 1848*, vol. II, pp. 66–7.

25 'Le Gouvernement provisoire veut la République sauf ratification par le peuple qui sera immédiatement consulté'; *Le Moniteur universel*, 25 February 1848, p. 499. See also J. J. L. Blanc, *1848: Historical Revelations inscribed to Lord Normanby*, London, Chapman and Hall, 1858, pp. 26–32, and Garnier-Pagès, *Histoire de la Révolution de 1848*, vol. V, pp. 339–48.

26 H. Guillemin, *La Première résurrection de la République*, Paris, Gallimard, 1967, p. 127; Thureau-Dangin, *Histoire de la monarchie de juillet*, vol. VII, p. 525.

27 M. Traugott, 'The Crowd in the French Revolution of February, 1848', *American Historical Review*, 93 (1988), p. 647.

28 On French republicanism in general, see Pilbeam, *Republicanism in Early Nineteenth-century France*, and Weill, *Histoire du parti républicain en France de 1814 à 1870*. On the opposition to Charles X and Polignac, see Alexander, *Re-writing the French Revolutionary Tradition*.

29 They included *Le Courrier de la Sarthe*, *Le Courrier de Saint-Quentin*, *L'Eclaireur de l'Indre*, *L'Emancipation* (Toulouse), *L'Indépendant d'Angoulême*, *Le Libéral du Nord*, *Le National de l'Ouest*, *Le Patriote de la Meuse*, *Le Patriote des Alpes*, *Le Peuple souverain* (Lyons), *Le Progrès du Pas-de-Calais*, and *La Sentinelle des Vosges*.

30 On republican almanacs, see R. Gosselin, *Les Almanacs républicains: traditions révolutionnaires et culture politique des masses populaires de paris, 1840–1851*, Paris, L'Harmattan, 1992.

31 See M. Agulhon, *The Republic in the Village: the people of the Var from the French Revolution to the Second Republic*, Cambridge, Cambridge University Press, 1982.

32 Aminzade, *Ballots and Barricades*, p. 33.

33 Vigier, *La Seconde République dans la région alpine*, vol. I, p. 177.

34 Pilbeam, *Republicanism in Early Nineteenth-century France, 1814–1871*, pp. 99–105.

35 On republican funerals, see A. Marrast, *Les Funérailles révolutionnaires*, Paris, Pagnerre, 1848.

36 On Considérant, see R. Van Davidson, *Did We Think Victory Great?: the life and ideas of Victor Considérant*, Lanham, University Press of America, 1988.

37 C. H. Johnson, *Utopian Communism in France: Cabet and the Icarians*, Ithaca and London, Cornell University Press, 1974, p. 147, p. 152 and p. 156.

38 See L. A. Loubère, *Louis Blanc: his life and his contribution to the rise of French Jacobin-Socialism*, Evanston, Northwestern University Press, 1961.

39 See K. S. Vincent, *Pierre-Joseph Proudhon and the Rise of French Republican Socialism*, Oxford and New York, Oxford University Press, 1984.

40 See E. Berenson, *Populist Religion and Left-wing Politics in France, 1830–1852*, Princeton, New Jersey, Princeton University Press, 1984; F. P. Bowman, *Le Christ des barricades, 1789–1848*, Paris, Les Editions du cerf, 1987; P. M. Pilbeam, 'Dream Worlds?: religion and the early socialists in France', *Historical Journal*, 43 (2000), pp. 499–515.

41 See S. Bernstein, *Auguste Blanqui and the Art of Insurrection*, London, Lawrence and Wishart, 1971.

42 See *Le National*, 12 February 1848, and *La Patrie*, 12 and 14 February 1848.

43 Cf. M. du Camp, *Souvenirs littéraires, 1822–1880*, 2 vols, Paris, Hachette, 1882–3, vol. I, p. 369: 'La révolution de Février fut une surprise'; Tocqueville, *Souvenirs*, p. 85: 'La révolution de Février fut *imprévue* pour tous'. For a contrary view, written with the benefit of hindsight, see J. Sangnier (ed.), *A. de Vigny: mémoires inédits, fragments*

et projets, Paris, Gallimard, 1958, p. 139: 'Depuis un an, tout le monde voyait une révolution s'amasser et s'avancer, excepté le roi Louis-Philippe.'

44 *Le Moniteur universel*, 26 January 1848, p. 183, and 11 February 1848, p. 347; M. C. A. La Forest, comtesse d'Armaillé, *Quand on savait vivre heureux, 1830–1850*, Paris, Plon, 1934, pp. 95–6 and p. 97; Bocher, *Mémoires de Charles Bocher*, p. 481; J. Estourmel, *Derniers souvenirs du comte Joseph d'Estourmel*, Paris, E. Dentu, 1860, pp. 2–3; Ligne, *Souvenirs de la Princesse de Ligne*, pp. 126–7; Vigny, *Mémoires inédits*, p. 147.

45 Tocqueville, *Souvenirs*, p. 44.

46 *Revue et Gazette musicale de Paris*, 20 February 1848, p. 58: 'la fine fleur de l'aristocratie des femmes les plus distinguées, des toilettes les plus élégantes, remplissait mercredi les salons de Pleyel'.

47 Apponyi, *Vingt-cinq ans à Paris*, vol. IV, p. 137 and p. 139; Tocqueville, *Souvenirs*, p. 52; Estourmel, *Derniers souvenirs*, p. 9.

48 Armaillé, *Quand on savait vivre heureux*, p. 96; *L'Union monarchique*, 13 February 1848, p. 3.

49 Armaillé, *Quand on savait vivre heureux*, p. 97.

50 Ligne, *Souvenirs de la Princesse de Ligne*, pp. 126–7. The Belgian embassy then occupied the Hôtel Flahaut in the rue d'Angoulême, near the Champs-Elysées. Cf. Thiers, *Notes et souvenirs de M. Thiers*, p. 22.

51 Achard, *Souvenirs personnels d'émeutes et de révolutions*, p. 73.

52 R. Pierrot (ed.), *Balzac: lettres à Madame Hanska*, 4 vols, Paris, Les Bibliophiles de l'original, 1967–71, vol. IV, p. 211, p. 212 and pp. 214–15.

53 M. L. V. Ancelot, *Un Salon de Paris, 1824 à 1864*, Paris, E. Dentu, 1866, pp. 154. For details of the pillage and destruction at the Tuileries, the Palais-Royal and Neuilly, see J. E. A. Chenu, *Les Montagnards de 1848, encore quatre nouveaux chapitres, précédés d'une réponse à Caussidière et autres Démocs-Socs*, Paris, D. Giraud et J. Dagneau, 1850, pp. 40–51, and Véron, *Mémoires d'un bourgeois de Paris*, vol. V, pp. 159–81, 243–58, and 308–22.

54 Ligne, *Souvenirs de la Princesse de Ligne*, p. 137.

55 Armailléé, *Quand on savait vivre heureux*, p. 98.

56 Vigny, *Mémoires inédits*, p. 147.

57 Véron, *Mémoires d'un bourgeois de Paris*, vol. VI, p. 41.

58 See *La Gazette de France*, 29 February 1848, p. 3; G. Lefrançais, *Souvenirs d'un révolutionnaire*, Paris, Editions de la Tête des Feuilles, 1972, pp. 40–1.

59 Captain Chamier, *A Review of the French Revolution of 1848: from the 24th of February to the election of the first president*, 2 vols, London, Reeve, Benham and Reeve, 1849, vol. I, p. 91.

60 Vigny, *Mémoires inédits*, p. 147.

61 C. E. Warr (ed.), *Paris in '48: letters from a resident describing the events of the revolution by Baroness Bonde*, London, John Murray, 1903, p. 33. See also ibid., p. 56.

62 H. B. Lewis (ed.), *A Year of Revolutions: Fanny Lewald's recollections of 1848*, Providence and Oxford, Berghahn Books, 1997, p. 7 (entry for 17 March 1848). Cf. Apponyi, *Vingt-cinq ans à Paris*, vol. IV, pp. 169–70 and p. 178.

63 Mérimée, *Correspondance générale*, vol. IV, p. 252.

64 Ibid., vol. V, p. 253.

65 Rémusat, *Mémoires de ma vie*, vol. IV, p. 257.

66 Bonde, *Paris in '48*, p. 17.

67 Apponyi, *Vingt-cinq ans à Paris*, vol. IV, p. 152, p. 153 and p. 156.

68 Lewald, *A Year of Revolutions*, p. 70.

69 M. Agulhon, *Les Quarante-huitards*, Paris, Gallimard, 1992, pp. 48–54.

70 George Sand to Augustine Brault, 5 March 1848 (G. Lubin (ed.), *George Sand: Correspondance*, vol. VIII, *Juillet 1847–décembre 1848*, Paris, Editions Garnier frères, 1971, p. 319).

71 Garnier-Pagès, *Histoire de la Révolution de 1848*, vol. VI (1862), p. 27.
72 *Le Franc-Comtois* (Besançon, Doubs) 26 February 1848. Cf. Josserand, *Notice historique sur l'établissement de la république dans le département de l'Ain, par un membre de la Société d'émulation de l'Ain*, Bourg-en-Bresse, Millet-Bottier, 1850, p. 4.
73 It took much longer, of course, for the news of the February Revolution to reach France's colonial territories. The Second Republic was not proclaimed in Tahiti until 24 June 1848 (*Le Journal des Débats*, 11 October 1848).
74 P. Haury, 'Les Commissaires de Ledru-Rollin en 1848', *La Révolution française*, 57 (1909), pp. 443–4.
75 P. Joigneaux, *Souvenirs historiques*, 2 vols, Paris, Marpon et Flammarion, 1891, vol. I, p. 142. Cf. M. B. E., comte de Comminges, *Souvenirs d'enfance et de régiment, 1831–1871*, Paris, Plon-Nourrit et Cie, 1910, p. 75.
76 D. Monnier, *Souvenirs d'un octogénaire de province*, Lons-le-Saunier, Imprimerie de Gauthier frères, 1871, pp. 506–8.
77 Lévêque, *Une Société en crise*, pp. 47–53. For events in Châtillon-sur-Seine, see Joigneaux, *Souvenirs historiques*, vol. I, pp. 141–55.
78 Vigier, *La Seconde République dans la région alpine*, vol. 1, pp. 191–3.
79 G. Bonet, *L'Indépendant des Pyrénées-Orientales: l'histoire d'un journal, un journal dans l'histoire, 1846–1848*, Perpignan, 1987, p. 260 and p. 276.
80 *La Sentinelle des Pyrénées*, 3 July 1848.
81 Corbin, *Archaïsme et modernité en Limousin au XIXe siècle*, vol. I, pp. 763–4.
82 Rémusat, *Mémoires de ma vie*, vol. IV, p. 275.
83 J. Godart (ed.), *Le Journal d'un bourgeois de Lyon en 1848*, Paris, Presses universitaires de France, 1924, pp. 10–28; General Le Pays de Bourjolly, *De l'armée et 40 jours de 1848 à Lyon*, Paris, J. Dumaire, 1853, pp. 17–35; Garnier-Pagès, *Histoire de la Révolution de 1848*, vol. VI, pp. 314–20; M. Treillard, *La République à Lyon sous le gouvernement provisoire*, Paris, Gabriel Roux, Lyon, Charavay frères, 1849; M. L. Stewart-McDougall, *The Artisan Republic: revolution, reaction, and resistance in Lyon, 1848–1851*, Kingston and Montreal, McGill-Queen's University Press, 1984, pp. 32–48.
84 Vigier, *La Seconde République dans la région alpine*, vol. I, p. 193.
85 For Rouen, see Castellane, *Journal*, vol. IV, pp. 24–8.
86 E. H. de Goutel (ed.), *Mémoires du général marquis Aphonse d'Hautpoul, pair de France, 1789–1865*, Paris, Perrin, 1906, pp. 300–2.
87 Garnier-Pagès, *Histoire de la Révolution de 1848*, vol. VI, pp. 274–8; F. F. P. L. M. d'Orléans, prince de Joinville, *Vieux souvenirs, 1818–1848*, Paris, Calmann-Lévy, 1894, pp. 444–51; Rémusat, *Mémoires de ma vie*, vol. IV, pp. 260–1; W. Serman and J.-P. Bertaud, *Nouvelle histoire militaire de la France, 1789–1919*, Paris, Fayard, 1998, pp. 271–2.
88 S. Commissaire, *Mémoires et souvenirs*, 2 vols, Lyons, Meton, Paris, Garcet and Nisius, 1888, vol. I, p. 172.
89 Lévêque, *Une Société en crise*, p. 55.
90 Vigier, *La Seconde République dans la région alpine*, vol. I, pp. 196–7.
91 H. Cabane, *Histoire du clergé de France pendant la Révolution de 1848*, Paris, Bloud et Cie, 1908, pp. 221–3.
92 Tudesq, *Les Grands notables en France*, vol. II, pp. 1,008–9.
93 *L'Impartial de Rouen* (Rouen, Seine-Inférieure), 2 March 1848; Aminzade, *Ballots and Barricades*, pp. 183–4; A. Dubuc, 'Frédéric Deschamps, commissaire de la République en Seine-Inférieure (février–mai 1848)', in *Actes du congrès historique du centenaire de la révolution de 1848*, Paris, Presses universitaires de France, 1948, p. 387.
94 Agulhon, *Les Quarante-huitards*, pp. 59–61. See also Garnier-Pagès, *Histoire de la Révolution de 1848*, vol. VI, pp. 80–3.
95 Reddy, *The Rise of Market Culture*, p. 219.

96 Aminzade, *Ballots and Barricades*, p. 152.
97 *Galignani's Mesenger*, 10 June 1848, p. 2.
98 *Le Monde de 1848*, 3 April 1848, p. 4.
99 Commissaire, *Mémoires et souvenirs*, vol. I, p. 170; Agulhon, *Les Quarante-huitards*, pp. 62–3. In general, see N. Isser, 'The Revolution of 1848 and Human Rights: the Jews,' in J. Sweet (ed.), *Proceedings of the Western Society for French History*, 12 (1986), pp. 343–56, and ibid., *Antisemitism during the Second French Empire*, New York, Peter Lang, 1991, pp. 7–15.
100 See A. Soboul, 'Les Troubles agraires de 1848, documents', *1848 et les Révolutions du XIXe siècle*, 39 (1948), pp. 1–20 and 39–61. On the expulsion of parish priests from their parishes, see also C. Marcilhacy, 'Les Caractères de la crise sociale et politique de 1846 à 1852 dans le département du Loiret', *Revue d'histoire moderne et contemporaine*, 6 (1959), pp. 18–19, and McPhee, 'The Seed-Time of the Republic', p. 65.
101 C. H. Pouthas (ed.), *Procès-verbaux du Gouvernement provisoire et de la Commission du pouvoir exécutif (24 février–22 juin 1848)*, Paris, Imprimerie nationale, 1950, p. xi and p. 168.
102 On Ecole polytechnique students, see C. L. de Saulces de Freycinet, *Souvenirs, 1848–1849*, Paris, Ch. Delagrave, 1912, pp. 2–17; Poumiès de La Siboutie, *Souvenirs d'un médecin de Paris*, pp. 294–5 and p. 301.
103 Ibid., p. 3 and p. 4.
104 P. Chalmin, 'Une Institution militaire de la Seconde République: la Garde nationale mobile', *Etudes d'histoire moderne et contemporaine*, 2 (1948), pp. 36–82.
105 *Procès-verbaux du Gouvernement provisoire et de la Commission du pouvoir exécutif*, p. 11; *Le Moniteur universel*, 26 February 1848, p. 503.
106 *Procès-verbaux du Gouvernement provisoire et de la Commission du pouvoir exécutif*, pp. 7–9 and p. 11.
107 See *Le Moniteur universel*, 12, 13, 15 and 16 March and 18 and 20 April 1848. Cf. *Procès-verbaux du Gouvernement provisoire et de la Commission du pouvoir exécutif*, p. 155.
108 D. R. Applebaum, 'The *Juges de Paix* and the Provisional Government of 1848 in France', unpublished PhD thesis (Wisconsin, 1973), p. 173.
109 *Procès-verbaux du Gouvernement provisoire et de la Commission du pouvoir exécutif*, pp. 10–11.
110 Ibid., p. 152, pp. 173–5 and p. 231; Serman and Bertaud, *Nouvelle histoire militaire de la France*, pp. 275–6.
111 See *Le Moniteur universel*, 9 March 1848, p. 572.
112 See ibid., 14 April 1848, p. 836; W. Fortescue, *Alphonse de Lamartine: a political biography*, London and Canberra, Croom Helm, New York, St Martin's Press, 1983, pp. 205–10.
113 P. Haury, 'Les Commissaires de Ledru-Rollin en 1848', *La Révolution française*, 57 (1909), p. 450. For a list of *commissaries*, see H. Castille, *Histoire de la Seconde République française*, 4 vols, Paris, V. Lecou, 1854–6, vol. II, pp. 322–5. See also Delvau, *Histoire de la Révolution de février*, pp. 353–4.
114 Marx, 'The Eighteenth Brumaire of Louis Bonaparte', *Surveys from Exile*, p. 147.
115 Balzac, *Lettres à Madame Hanska*, vol. IV, p. 280. Cf. du Camp, *Souvenirs de l'année 1848*, pp. 126–8, and ibid., *Souvenirs d'un demi-siècle*, 2 vols, Paris, Hachette, 1949, vol. I, p. 92; Marmier, *Journal*, vol. I, pp. 76–7.
116 Castellane, *Journal*, vol. IV, pp. 69–70; *Galignani's Messenger*, 22 May 1848, pp. 3–4; *Le Peuple constituant*, 22 May 1848; J.-Y. Guillou (ed.), *Guillaume Lejean, Charles Alexandre, correspondance (1846–1869): deux républicains bretons dans l'entourage de Lamartine et de Michelet*, Paris, Editions Jean Touzet, 1993, pp. 82–3; M. Agulhon, *Marianne into Battle: republican imagery and symbolism in France, 1789–1880*, Cambridge, Cambridge University Press, 1981, pp. 67–72.

117 *Le Moniteur universel*, 17 May 1848, p. 1,059; Stern, *Histoire de la Révolution de 1848*, vol. II, p. 348; Agulhon, *Marianne into Battle*, pp. 73–8.

118 Garnier-Pagès, *Histoire de la Révolution de 1848*, vol. VIII, p. 81; Mérimée, *Correspondance générale*, vol. V, p. 270.

119 A. F. P., comte de Falloux, *Mémoires d'un royaliste*, 2 vols, Paris, Perrin, 1888, vol. I, p. 304. Cf. Marmier, *Journal*, vol. I, p. 107.

120 J. and J. Duhart, *La Révolution de 1848 à Givors (26 février–15 juillet)*, Paris, Editions Sociales, 1973, p. 58.

121 *Le Mois*, 16 May 1848, p. 76.

122 *Le Moniteur universel*, 12 April 1848, pp. 817–18; *Procès-verbaux du Gouvernement provisoire et de la Commission du pouvoir exécutif*, p. 29 and pp. 225–8; Agulhon, *Marianne into Battle*, p. 81.

123 *Procès-verbaux du Gouvernement provisoire et de la Commission du pouvoir exécutif*, p. 91.

124 *Le Moniteur universel*, 7 March 1848, pp. 555–6; L. H. Carnot, *Le Ministère de l'Instruction publique et des cultes, depuis le 24 février jusqu'au 5 juillet 1848*, Paris, Pagnerre, 1848, p. 25: 'Des hommes nouveaux, voilà ce que réclame la France. Une révolution ne doit pas seulement renouveler les institutions, il faut qu'elle renouvelle les hommes.'

125 Carnot, *Le Ministère de l'Instruction publique*, pp. 23–33; Castille, *Histoire de la Seconde République française*, vol. II, p. 52; Stern, *Histoire de la Révolution de 1848*, vol. II, pp. 360–1. Some republicans, of course, welcomed and supported Carnot's initiative. See the article by A. Bouchet, urging *instituteurs* to educate the population as to their 'devoirs politiques', in *Le Patriote des Montagnes* (Le Puy, Haute-Loire), 25 March 1848, pp. 1–2.

126 Carnot, *Le Ministère de l'Instruction publique*, pp. 11–50.

127 *Procès-verbaux du Gouvernement provisoire et de la Commission du pouvoir exécutif*, p. 51; D. A. Griffiths, *Jean Reynaud, encyclopédiste de l'époque romantique, d'après sa correspondance inédite*, Paris, Marcel Rivière et Cie, 1965, pp. 295–9.

128 See *Le Charivari*, 11 April 1848; *Le Journal des Débats*, 12 April 1848; *Le Journal pour rire*, 15 April 1848, pp. 1–2; *Le Représentant du peuple*, 12 May 1848, pp. 1–2; Marmier, *Journal*, vol. I, p. 88; C. A. Sainte-Beuve, *Portraits contemporains*, 5 vols, Paris, Michel Lévy frères, 1869–71, vol. I, p. 381.

129 See Archives Nationales, 108 AP 3, dossier 13, f. 16, dossier 22, ff. 20 and 22; H. Boucher, *Souvenirs d'un Parisien pendant la Seconde République*, Paris, Perrin et Cie, 1908, pp. 78–83 and 94–8; Carnot, *Le Ministère de l'Instruction publique*, pp. 55–63; *Le Charivari*, 2 August 1848, p. 2; A. A. Cournot, *Souvenirs (1760–1860)*, Paris, Hachette, 1913, pp. 208–11; Fortescue, *Alphonse de Lamartine*, pp. 159–60 and n. 37; A. Louvel, 'L'Ecole d'Administration de 1848', *Etudes d'histoire moderne et contemporaine*, 2 (1948), pp. 19–36; *Le Moniteur universel*, 9 March 1848, p. 571, 8, 9, 11 and 14 April 1848, p. 785, p. 793, pp. 807–8 and p. 829; M. Saurin, 'L'Ecole d'Administration de 1848', *Politique d'aujourd'hui*, 7–8 (1964–5), pp. 105–95; R. J. Smith, 'The Students of the Ecole d'Administration, 1848–9', *History of Education*, 16 (1987), pp. 245–58; V. Wright, 'L'Ecole nationale d'administration de 1848–1849: un échec révélateur', *Revue historique*, 255 (1976), pp. 21–42.

130 See Regnault, *Histoire du Gouvernement provisoire*, p. 7: 'Ce qui préoccupait par-dessus tout les chefs républicains appelés subitement au gouvernement, c'était d'effacer les souvenirs de sang et de spoliation fatalement attachés à la première république.'

131 Ménard, *Prologue d'une révolution, février–juin 1848*, p. 59.

132 Dommanget, *Histoire du drapeau rouge*, pp. 51–9.

133 See Freycinet, *Souvenirs*, pp. 21–5; Garnier-Pagès, *Histoire de la Révolution de 1848*, vol. VI, pp. 100–3; Agulhon, *Les Quarante-huitards*, pp. 118–27. Louis Blanc subsequently claimed that he had wanted the adoption of the red flag as France's

national flag (Blanc, *Historical Revelations*, p. 74). The decree on the national flag of 26 February 1848 put the colours in an incorrect order (blue, red and white, rather than blue, white and red). See Boutin, *Les Murailles révolutionnaires de 1848*, pp. 5–6, and Delvau, *Les Murailles révolutionnaires de 1848*, vol. I, p. 67, p. 126 and p. 359.

134 Chérest, *La Vie et les œuvres de A. T. Marie*, p. 148; Blanc, *Historical Revelations*, p. 70; Garnier-Pagès, *Histoire de la Révolution de 1848*, vol. VI, p. 113; C. P. Robin, *Histoire de la Révolution française*, 2 vols, Paris, Penaud frères, 1849–50, vol. I, p. 376.

135 Blanc, *Historical Revelations*, p. 69.

136 See Fortescue, *Alphonse de Lamartine*, pp. 154–7.

137 Stern, *Histoire de la Révolution de 1848*, vol. II, p. 55–6; Duhart, *La Révolution de 1848 à Givors*, p. 70.

138 See R. Gossez, *Les Ouvriers de Paris: l'organisation, 1848–1851*, La Roche-sur-Yon, Imprimerie centrale de l'Ouest, 1968, p. 11.

139 Castellane, *Journal*, vol. IV, pp. 48–9. See also Hugo, *Choses vues*, pp. 1,033–4.

140 J. J. L. Blanc, *Pages d'histoire de la révolution de février 1848*, Paris, Bureau de Nouveau Monde, 1850, pp. 33–4, ibid., *La Révolution de février au Luxembourg*, Paris, Michel Lévy frères, 1849, pp. 3–9, and ibid., *1848: Historical Revelations*, pp. 89–94 and 127–31; Delvau, *Histoire de la Révolution de février*, pp. 374–7; *Le Moniteur universel*, 3 March 1848, p. 530; Gossez, *Les Ouvriers de Paris*, pp. 17–24.

141 P. H. Amann, *Revolution and Mass Democracy: the Paris club movement in 1848*, Princeton, New Jersey, Princeton University Press, 1975, pp. 173–84.

142 *Procès-verbaux du Gouvernement provisoire et de la Commission du pouvoir exécutif*, pp. 29–30 and pp. 54–5.

143 Ibid., p. 31.

144 L. A. Garnier-Pagès, *Un Episode de la Révolution de 1848: l'impôt des 45 centimes*, Paris, Pagnerre, 1850. See also A. Antony, *La Politique financière du Gouvernement provisoire, février–mai 1848*, Paris, Arthur Rousseau, 1909.

145 *Procès-verbaux du Gouvernement provisoire et de la Commission du pouvoir exécutif*, p. 159; Castellane, *Journal*, vol. IV, p. 62.

146 *Procès-verbaux du Gouvernement provisoire et de la Commission du pouvoir exécutif*, p. 1 and p. 2.

147 Ibid., p. 6. Cf. ibid., p. 31 (29 February 1848).

148 See P. Bastid, *Un Juriste pamphlétaire: Cormenin, précurseur et constituant de 1848*, Paris, Hachette, 1948.

149 Chérest, *La Vie et les oeuvres de A. T. Marie*, pp. 150–1.

150 *Procès-verbaux du Gouvernement provisoire et de la Commission du pouvoir exécutif*, p. 35 and pp. 39–42.

151 Rémusat, *Mémoires de ma vie*, vol. IV, p. 267.

152 *Le Moniteur universel*, 8 March 1848, p. 565; Amann, *Revolution and Mass Democracy*, pp. 89–91; M. Dommanget, *Auguste Blanqui et la révolution de 1848*, Paris, Mouton 1972, pp. 20–3; S. Wassermann, *Les Clubs de Barbès et de Blanqui en 1848*, Paris, Cornély, 1913, pp. 56–9.

153 *La Commune de Paris: Moniteur des clubs*, 14 March 1848, p. 3.

154 Ibid., 15 March 1848, p. 3.

155 E. Tersen, *Quarante-huit*, Paris, Club français du livre, 1957, pp. 127–8; Wassermann, *Les Clubs de Barbès et de Blanqui en 1848*, pp. 62–4.

156 For the text of the circular, see *Le Moniteur universel*, 12 March 1848, p. 595.

157 Apponyi, *Vingt-cinq ans à Paris*, vol. IV, p. 170; Marmier, *Journal*, vol. I, pp. 92–3; articles by Emile de Girardin in *Le Siècle*, 15 March 1848, *La Presse*, 16 and 24 March 1848.

158 *Le Moniteur universel*, 16 March 1848, p. 618–9. Cf. Chambolle, *Retours sur la vie*, pp. 259–61, where it is suggested that Lamartine's original statement was not printed in full.

159 *Procès-verbaux du Gouvernement provisoire et de la Commission du pouvoir exécutif*, p. 70.
160 Garnier-Pagès, *Histoire de la Révolution de 1848*, vol. VI, pp. 421–5.
161 Sand, *Correspondance*, vol. VIII, p. 349 (George Sand to Louis Viardot, 17 March 1848).
162 For examples, see Joigneaux, *Souvenirs historiques*, vol. I, pp. 162–97, and H. Goallou, *Hamon, commissaire du gouvernement, puis préfet d'Ille-et-Vilaine (3 mars 1848–25 janvier 1849)*, Rennes, Librairie C. Klincksieck, 1974, pp. 103–19. See also V. S. Pierre, *Histoire de la République de 1848*, 2 vols, Paris, E. Plon, 1873–8, vol. I, pp. 144–55.
163 E. Regnault, *Histoire du Gouvernement provisoire*, Paris, V. Lecou, 1850, pp. 352–3; Wassermann, *Les Clubs de Barbès et de Blanqui en 1848*, pp. 88–9.
164 See A. Cobban, 'Administrative Pressure in the Election of the French Constituent Assembly, April, 1848', *Bulletin of the Institute of Historical Research*, 25 (1952), pp. 133–59.
165 A. Cobban, 'The Influence of the Clergy and the 'instituteurs primaires' in the Election of the French Constitutent Assembly, April 1848', *English Historical Review*, 57 (1942), pp. 340–1.
166 W. Fortescue, 'Lamartine, lettres politiques 1847–1848', in C. Croisille and M.-R. Morin (eds), *Autour de la correspondance de Lamartine*, Clermont-Ferrand, Université Blaise Pascal, 1991, pp. 53–78; W. Fortescue, 'Lettres retrouvées de Lamartine, 1815–1868', in C. Croisille and M.-R. Morin (eds), *Autour de Lamartine: journal de voyage, correspondances, témoignages, iconographie*, Clermont-Ferrand, Presses universitaires Blaise Pascal, 2002, pp. 82–3 and 85–6; Fortescue, *Lamartine*, n. 61, pp. 190–1. For contemporary ironical comment on these letters, see *Le Corsaire*, 4 June 1848, p. 3.
167 *L'Océan* (Brest, Finistère), 27 March 1848.
168 Blanc, *Pages d'histoire*, pp. 135–7, and ibid., *Historical Revelations*, p. 373.
169 Garnier-Pagès, *Histoire de la Révolution de 1848*, vol. VII, pp. 122–4. See also Amann, *Revolution and Mass Democracy*, pp. 114–15.
170 A. Longepied and Laugier, *Comité révolutionnaire, Club des Clubs et la Commission*, Paris, Garnier frères, 1850, pp. 31–67; Wassermann, *Les Clubs de Barbès et de Blanqui en 1848*, pp. 18–25.
171 *La Commune de Paris: Moniteur des clubs*, 19 April 1848, p. 4, 20 April 1848, pp. 3–4, and 22 April 1848, p. 3.
172 *Le National*, 30 March 1848. *Le National* reprinted the list on 23 and 24 April 1848.
173 Tocqueville, *Souvenirs*, p. 115.
174 See Mérimée to Mme de Montijo, 26 April 1848 (Mérimée, *Correspondance générale*, vol. V, pp. 296–7); *Le Courrier de la Somme* (Amiens), 16 March 1848; *L'Indépendant* (Toulouse, Haute-Garonne), 12 and 13 April 1848; *Le Journal de Lot-et-Garonne* (Agen), 12 and 19 April 1848; *Le Journal de Rouen*, 9 April 1848; *L'Ordre* (Limoges, Haute-Vienne), 13 April 1848.
175 Girardin, *Journal d'un journaliste au secret*, p. 11.
176 Corbin, *Archaïsme et modernité en Limousin au XIXe siècle*, vol. I, p. 714. Cf. Vigier, *La Seconde République dans la Région alpine*, vol. I, p. 256.
177 M. Liu, 'Education and Revolution: the impact of 1848 on France', unpublished MA thesis, University of East Anglia, 1990, pp. 50–1.
178 *L'Assemblée nationale*, 11 March 1848.
179 *Le Républicain de Vaucluse*, 22 April 1848.
180 Tudesq, *Les Grands notables en France*, vol. II, pp. 1,029–30.
181 Ibid., vol. II, pp. 1,033–4.
182 *L'Assemblée nationale*, 30 April 1848.
183 For examples, see *Le Républicain du Jura*, 23 April 1848, p. 2, and Goallou, *Hamon, commissaire du gouvernement, puis préfet d'Ille-et-Vilaine*, p. 75.

184 Blanc, *1848: Historical Revelations*, pp. 362–3. See also P. M. Jones, 'An Improbable Democracy: nineteenth-century elections in the Massif Central', *English Historical Review*, 97 (1982), pp. 553–4.

185 Tudesq, *Les Grands notables en France*, vol. II, pp. 1,040–3.

186 *Revue d'histoire moderne et contemporaine*, 6 (1959), p. 25.

187 Aminzade, *Ballots and Barricades*, p. 188.

188 M. R. Cox, 'The Legitimists under the Second French Republic', unpublished PhD thesis, Yale, 1966, pp. 114–18.

189 Amann, *Revolution and Mass Democracy*, pp. 190–1.

190 *La Provence* (Aix-en-Provence, Bouches-du-Rhône), 30 March 1848.

191 P. Tollu, *Montalembert: les libertés sous le Second Empire*, Paris, Editions Albatros, 1987, p. 189.

192 *L'Indépendant* (Toulouse, Haute Garonne), 2 April 1848.

193 *Le Républicain du Jura*, 17 March 1848, p. 3.

194 BN 4º Le 64.952; Delvau, *Les Murailles révolutionnaires de 1848*, vol. I, pp. 473–4. For Daly's proposals to Louis Blanc for model lodging houses, see Blanc, *Historical Revelations*, pp. 142–3. On Daly, see R. Becherer, *Science plus Sentiment: César Daly's formula for modern architecture*, Ann Arbor, 1984; I. Frazer, 'La Vie secrète de César Daly: naissance illégitime, parti légitimiste, cause fouriériste', in H. Lipstadt (ed.), *Architecte et ingénieur dans la presse: polémique, débat, conflit*, Paris, 1980, pp. 233–91; M. Saboya, *Presse et architecture au XIXe siècle: César Daly et la 'Revue générale de l'architecture et des travaux publics'*, Paris, Picardy, 1991. On 22 April 1848 both *Le Courrier français* and *La Démocratie pacifique* supported Daly's candidature, but he was not elected.

195 *L'Etoile* (Pamiers, Ariège), 22 April 1848, pp. 1–2.

196 *Profession de foi du Citoyen Clément Dulac, agriculteur à Chabans, département de la Dordogne*, Périgueux, Imprimerie Lavertujon, 1848, p. 7.

197 *La Provence* (Aix-en-Provence, Bouches-du-Rhône), 6 April 1848. *La Provence* supported Hennequin's candidature, on the grounds that the presence of socialists in the National Assembly would be useful for the country, while at the same time supporting the candidatures of the Legitimist Berryer and the Orleanist Thiers. Neither Hennequin nor Thiers was elected.

198 See, for example, the *profession de foi* of the republican Jules Favre: 'Dans ma conviction profonde, la propriété, récompense du travail, la famille, foyer divin de l'âme, sont des institutions éternelles qui, tout en se perfectionnant par la rénovation sociale prête à s'accomplir, demeureront les bases de l'ordre démocratique que nous allons fonder' (*Le Mercure ségusien* (St Etienne, Loire), 19 April 1848, p. 3).

199 P. Gibert (ed.), *Correspondance d'Alexis de Tocqueville et de Francisque de Corcelle*, 2 vols, Paris, Gallimard, 1983, vol. I, p. 242 (Alexis de Tocqueville to Francisque de Corcelle, 3 April 1848).

200 A. Jardin (ed.), *Correspondance d'Alexis de Tocqueville et de Gustave de Beaumont*, 3 vols, Paris, Gallimard, 1967, vol. II, p. 9.

201 F. A. de Luna, *The French Republic under Cavaignac, 1848*, Princeton, Princeton University Press, 1969, pp. 107–15. Not enough information is available to permit the political classification of 122 of the elected representatives. See also G. W. Fasel, 'The French Election of April 23, 1848: suggestions for a revision', *French Historical Studies*, 5 (1968), pp. 287–90.

202 De Luna, *The French Republic under Cavaignac*, p. 112.

203 P. Pierrard, *1848 . . . les pauvres, l'évangile et la révolution*, Paris, Desclée, 1977, pp. 35–8.

204 Multiple candidatures had not been prohibited. Lamartine was also an unsuccessful candidate in the Rhône, where he polled 21,498 votes.

205 *Le Spectateur de Dijon*, 29 April 1848, p. 2.

206 See Fortescue, *Lamartine*, and Tudesq, *Les Grands notables en France*, vol. II, pp. 1,024–7.
207 Wassermann, *Les Clubs de Barbès et de Blanqui en 1848*, pp. 91–2.
208 Marmier, *Journal*, vol. I, p. 108; Tocqueville, *Souvenirs*, p. 114.
209 See Vigier, *La Seconde République dans la Région alpine*, vol. I, p. 219.
210 Blanc, *1848: Historical Revelations*, p. 300. Cf. *Mémoires de Caussidière*, 2 vols, Paris, Michel Lévy frères, 1849, vol. II, pp. 9–10.
211 Tocqueville, *Souvenirs*, p. 116; G. W. Fasel, 'The Wrong Revolution: French republicanism in 1848', *French Historical Studies*, 8 (1974), pp. 654–77.
212 Aminzade, *Ballots and Barricades*, pp. 188–9.
213 Corbin, *Archaïsme et modernité en Limousin au XIXe siècle*, vol. I, pp. 769–70.
214 Fitzpatrick, *Catholic Royalism in the Department of the Gard*, pp. 152–7.
215 *Le Républicain du Jura*, 28 April 1848, p. 3.
216 Pierrard, *1848 . . . les pauvres, l'évangile et la révolution*, pp. 47–9.
217 Tudesq, *Les Grands notables en France*, vol. II, pp. 1,058–9.
218 Goallou, *Hamon, commissaire du gouvernement, puis préfet d'Ille-et-Vilaine*, p. 133.
219 *Aux électeurs du département de Saône-et-Loire*, Autun, Dejussieu, 1848.

4 The Executive Commission and the June Days

1 See *L'Assemblée nationale*, 5 March 1848.
2 See X. de La Fournière (ed.), *Mémoires de la duchesse de Maillé, 1832–1851*, Paris, Perrin, 1989, p. 238.
3 See Garnier-Pagès, *Histoire de la Révolution de 1848*, vol. IX, pp. 14–21; J. Barthélemy Saint-Hilaire, 'La Commission exécutive de mai 1848', *Revue politique et parlementaire*, 51 (1907), pp. 318–24.
4 Caussidière, *Mémoires*, vol. II, pp. 80–1; Garnier-Pagès, *Histoire de la Révolution de 1848*, vol. IX, p. 9.
5 See Ledru-Rollin's speech at Lille, 7 November 1847 (Ledru-Rollin, *Discours politiques et écrits divers*, vol. I, p. 337), and Lamartine's article, 'Le Banquet de Lille', published in *Le Bien public* of Mâcon (Dumesnil Papers, Bibliothèque historique de la ville de Paris, 5712; *La Réforme*, 23 November 1847; pamphlet published by H. Robert, Mâcon, 1847).
6 See F. S. L. Babaud-Laribière, *Histoire de l'Assemblée nationale constituante*, 2 vols, Paris, Michel Lévy frères, 1850, vol. I, pp. 16–17; A. M. J., vicomte de Melun, *Mémoires du vicomte de Melun*, 2 vols, Paris, J. Leday, 1891, vol. I, p. 254.
7 *Le Correspondant*, 10 December 1873, p. 850.
8 *Le Moniteur universel*, 20 March 1848, p. 644.
9 Ibid., 10 May 1848, p. 997.
10 Ibid., 16 May 1848, p. 1,054.
11 Lamartine to the National Guard of Mâcon, 29 October 1848 (A. de Lamartine, *La France parlementaire, 1834–1851: Oeuvres oratoires et écrits politiques*, 6 vols, Paris, A. Lacroix, Verboeckhoven et Cie, 1864–65, vol. VI, p. 17), and to the *conseil général* of Saône-et-Loire, 26 August 1850 (L. Lex and P. M. Siraud, *Le Conseil général et les conseillers généraux de Saône-et-Loire (1789–1889)*, Mâcon, Belhomme, 1888, pp. 130–1).
12 See A. Weill, *Dix mois de révolution, depuis le 24 février jusqu'au 10 décembre 1848*, Paris, Les Principaux libraires, 1869, p. 146.
13 See Maillé, *Mémoires*, pp. 235–6 and p. 239.
14 Tocqueville, *Souvenirs*, p. 129. Cf. Melun, *Mémoires*, vol. I, p. 254.
15 The voting was Arago 725, Garnier-Pagès 715, Marie 702, Lamartine 643, Ledru-Rollin 458.
16 *L'Avenir national* (Limoges, Haute-Vienne), 15 April 1848, p. 2. Cf. *L'Impartial du Finistère*, 19 April 1848, p. 3.

17 *L'Emancipation* (Toulouse, Haute-Garonne), 14 May 1848. See also P. Audebrand, *Souvenirs de la tribune des journalistes, 1848–1852*, Paris, E. Dentu, 1867, pp. 232–3.

18 See Aminzade, *Ballots and Barricades*, pp. 188–9.

19 *La Vraie république*, 19 May 1848; Wassermann, *Les Clubs de Barbès et de Blanqui en 1848*, pp. 165–9.

20 Amann, *Revolution and Mass Democracy*, pp. 215–22. On Huber, see P. Amann, 'The Huber Enigma: revolutionary or police spy?', *International Review of Social History*, 12 (1967), pp. 190–203; L. L. Blaisdell, 'Aloysius Huber and May 15, 1848: new insights into an old mystery', *International Review of Social History*, 29 (1984), pp. 34–61; Stern, *Histoire de la Révolution de 1848*, vol. III, p. 21.

21 Amann, *Revolution and Mass Democracy*, pp. 205–33.

22 Tocqueville, *Souvenirs*, pp. 132–42. See also *Le Moniteur universel*, 17 May 1848, pp. 1,059–61; Barbier, *Souvenirs personnels et silhouettes contemporaines*, pp. 132–6; Hugo, *Choses vues*, pp. 1,038–9; A. Quentin-Bauchart, *Etudes et souvenirs sur la deuxième république et le second empire (1848–1870): mémoires posthumes publiés par son fils*, 2 vols, Paris, Plon-Nourrit et Cie, 1901–02, vol. I, pp. 9–17; Rémusat, *Mémoires de ma vie*, vol. IV, pp. 300–8; Wassermann, *Les Clubs de Barbès et de Blanqui en 1848*, pp. 169–84.

23 For a secondary account, see Amann, *Revolution and Mass Democracy*, pp. 233–9.

24 Tudesq, *Les Grands notables en France*, vol. II, pp. 1,077–82.

25 See J. M. Benoît, *Souvenirs de la République de 1848*, Geneva, Imprimerie Duchamp et Cie, Corraterie, 1855, pp. 121–2.

26 Castellane, *Journal*, vol. IV, pp. 76–9; *Le Mois*, 1 June 1848, p. 193.

27 *Le Monde républicain*, 8 and 10 June 1848; *La Patrie*, 10 June 1848, p. 4, and 11 June 1848, p. 3; *L'Union*, 10 June 1848, pp. 1–2.

28 See *La Patrie*, 1 March 1848, p. 4.

29 Apponyi, *Vingt-cinq ans à Paris*, vol. IV, pp. 159–60. See also Véron, *Mémoires d'un bourgeois de Paris*, vol. VI, pp. 75–6, and *La Patrie*, 3 March 1848, p. 3.

30 Castellane, *Journal*, vol. IV, p. 64; *Le Courrier français*, 2 June 1848, p. 4; *Le Moniteur universel*, 6 May 1848, p. 956.

31 Barrot, *Mémoires posthumes*, vol. II, pp. 217–8.

32 See *La Famille: Organe politique, social, littéraire et scientifique des intérêts généraux*, 17 June 1848: 'Cette nomination [of Louis Napoleon Bonaparte], qui a fait feu comme une traînée de poudre, est sortie pour ainsi dire du cœur de la patrie, comme une protestation contre les triomphes de la Sainte-Alliance'.

33 On the defence of Louis Napoleon Bonaparte by Jules Favre, see P. A. Perrod, *Jules Favre, avocat de la liberté*, Lyon, La Manufacture, 1988, pp. 132–4.

34 Barrot, *Mémoires posthumes*, vol. II, pp. 228–31; Rémusat, *Mémoires de ma vie*, vol. IV, pp. 315–21.

35 See *L'Accusateur public*, 14–18 June 1848, p. 2; *Le Bonaparte répubicain*, 17 June 1848; *La Constitution: Journal de la République napoléonienne et des vrais intérêts du pays*, 13 June 1848; *Le Napoléonien: Journal quotidien, politique et littéraire*, 14 and 15 June 1848. In general, see A.-J. Tudesq, *L'Election présidentielle de Louis-Napoléon Bonaparte*, Paris, Armand Colin, 1965, pp. 51–77.

36 *L'Assemblée nationale*, 17 June 1848; *La Caramagnole: Journal des enfants de Paris*, 1 June 1848, p. 2; *Le Courrier français*, 24 May 1848; *La France: Journal quotidien*, 16 June 1848; *La Gazette de France*, 8 June 1848, p. 4; *Le Lampion*, 7 June 1848; *Le Napoléonien: Journal quotidien, politique et littéraire*, 17 June 1848; *L'Organisation du travail: Journal des ouvriers*, 7 June 1848; *L'Union*, 16 June 1848.

37 Garnier-Pagès, *Histoire de la Révolution de 1848*, vol. X, pp. 294–301. Lamartine had reportedly talked about resigning as early as 18 May 1848 (Hugo, *Choses vues*, p. 1,039).

38 S. J. Reid (ed.), *Memoirs of Sir Edward Blount*, London, Longmans, Green and Co., 1902, p. 126.

39 See Simpson, *Pictures from Revolutionary Paris*, vol. I, pp. 256–69; E. Thomas, *Histoire des ateliers nationaux*, Paris, Michel Lévy frères, 1848, p. 376.

40 Amann, *Revolution and Mass Democray*, p. 21.

41 See Marmier, *Journal*, vol. I, p, 131.

42 See *Le National*, 29 May 1848.

43 Archives Nationales (Paris) 67 Archives Privées 7, ff. 2–3; *Procès-verbaux du Gouvernement provisoire et de la Commission du pouvoir exécutif*, pp. 253–4.

44 Archives Nationales (Paris) 67 Archives Privées 8, f. 12.

45 See A. Dumas, *Révélations sur l'arrestation d'Emile Thomas*, Paris, Michel Lévy frères, 1848; Thomas, *Histoire des ateliers nationaux*, pp. 286–99; *La Gazette de France*, 2 and 3 June 1848, p. 4, and 11 and 14 June 1848, p. 4.

46 *Le Moniteur universel*, 30 May 1848, p. 1,201.

47 Archives Nationales (Paris) 67 Archives Privées 8, f. 36; *Procès-verbaux du Gouvernement provisoire et de la Commission exécutif*, p. 385.

48 *Le Moniteur universel*, 21 June 1848, pp. 1,441–5.

49 D. C. McKay, *The National Workshops: a study in the French Revolution of 1848*, Cambridge, Mass., Harvard University Press, 1965, pp. 84–90.

50 See Falloux, *Mémoires d'un royaliste*, vol. I, pp. 328–39.

51 *L'Accusateur public*, 11–14 June 1848.

52 See *L'Accusateur public*, 11–14 June 1848, p. 2, and 18–21 June 1848.

53 McKay, *The National Workshops*, pp. 26–8.

54 Garnier-Pagès, *Histoire de la Révolution de 1848*, vol. IX, p. 166; Caussidière, *Mémoires*, vol. II, pp. 221–2; E. Denormandie, *Notes et souvenirs*, Paris, Léon Chailley, 1896, pp. 23–4.

55 Marie, *La Vie et les oeuvres*, pp. 250–3.

56 Stern, *Histoire de la Révolution de 1848*, vol. III, pp. 157–8.

57 For descriptions of the June Days, see Denormandie, *Notes et souvenirs*, pp. 25–74; Du Camp, *Souvenirs de l'année 1848*, pp. 237–97; Rémusat, *Mémoires de ma vie*, vol. IV, pp. 325–44; Stern, *Histoire de la Révolution de 1848*, vol. III, pp. 145–242.

58 De Luna, *The French Republic under Cavaignac*, p. 139.

59 C. H. Phipps, Marquess of Normanby, *A Year of Revolution: From a Journal Kept in Paris in 1848*, 2 vols, London, Longman, Brown, Green, Longmans and Roberts, 1857, vol. II, p. 90. Cf. *La Démocratie pacifique*, 1 July 1848; Mérimée to Mmes de Boigne and de Montijo, and to T. de Lagrené, 27 and 28 June 1848 (Mérimée, *Correspondance générale*, vol. V, p. 336, p. 340 and p. 342); Tocqueville, *Souvenirs*, p. 173.

60 See M. Traugott, *Armies of the Poor: determinants of working-class participation in the Parisian insurrection of June 1848*, Princeton, Princeton University Press, 1985, *passim*; P. Caspard, 'Aspects de la lutte des classes en 1848: le recrutement de la garde nationale mobile', *Revue historique*, 252 (1974), pp. 81–106; P. Chalmin, 'Une institution militaire de la seconde république; la garde nationale mobile', *Etudes d'histoire moderne et contemporaine*, vol. II (1948), pp. 36–82.

61 C. V. Beslay, *1830–1848–1870: Mes souvenirs*, Paris, Sandoz et Fischbacher, 1873, p. 196.

62 Traugott, *Armies of the poor*, p. 45 and p. 195. Cf. C. Tilly and L. Lees, 'Le Peuple de juin 1848', *Annales ESC*, 29 (1974), p. 1,070, and A. Balleydier, *Histoire de la Garde mobile depuis les barricades de février*, Paris, Pillet fils aîné, 1848, p. 128.

63 Agulhon, *Les Quarante-huitards*, pp. 32–6; R. G. Gould, *Insurgent Identities: class, community, and protest in Paris from 1848 to the Commune*, Chicago and London, University of Chicago Press, 1995; R. Price, *The French Second Republic: a social history*, London, B. T. Batsford, 1972, pp. 157–78; Tilly and Lees, 'Le Peuple de juin 1848', pp. 1,061–91.

64 Blanc, *1848: Historical Revelations*, p. 441. Cf. P. Haubtmann (ed.), *Carnets de P.-J. Proudhon*, 3 vols, Paris, Marcel Rivière et Cie, 1960–8, vol. III, pp. 65–7.

65 *Le Bien public*, 5 July 1848, p. 4.
66 *La France: Journal quotidien*, 1 July 1848; N. Truquin, *Mémoires et aventures d'un prolétaire à travers la révolution*, Paris, François Maspero, 1977, p. 81.
67 Garnier-Pagès, *Histoire de la Révolution de 1848*, vol. I, p. 438; Lamartine, *Histoire de la Révolution de 1848*, vol. II, p. 295.
68 See the depositions of Garnier-Pagès, Ledru-Rollin and Marie; *Rapport de la Commission d'enquête sur l'insurrection qui a éclatée dans la journée du 23 juin et sur les évènements du 15 mai*, 3 vols, Paris, 1848, vol. I, p. 285, p. 312 and p. 350. Cf. Marie, *La Vie et les oeuvres*, pp. 262–3.
69 Marx, *The Class Struggles in France*, pp. 57–8 and p. 60; Truquin, *Mémoires et aventures*, p. 71 and p. 81.
70 See *Le Républicain de Vaucluse* (Avignon, Vaucluse), 29 June 1848.
71 Cf. Du Camp, *Souvenirs de l'année 1848*, p. 297; M. Got (ed.), *Journal d'Edmond Got, sociétaire de la Comédie-Française, 1822–1901*, 2 vols, Paris, Plon-Nourrit et Cie, 1910, vol. I, p. 240; George Sand to Charles Poncy, 1 August 1848 (Sand, *Correspondance*, vol. VIII, p. 581).
72 Normanby, *A Year of Revolution*, vol. II, pp. 36–9, 61–3 and 86–7.
73 See *Le Courrier de Tarn-et-Garonne* (Montauban), 29 June 1848, p. 2; *Réveil du Midi*, 29 June 1848. Cf. Castellane, *Journal*, vol. IV, pp. 85–6; Mérimée to Mme de Boigne, 27 June 1848 (Mérimée, *Correspondance générale*, vol. V, p. 336); Normanby, *A Year of Revolution*, vol. II, pp. 67–8 and pp. 74–6; J. L. Nouguier, *Souvenirs et impressions d'un ex-journaliste pour servir à l'histoire contemporaine*, Paris, Michel Lévy frères, 1856, pp. 128–9. See also the report on 'la fille Thérèse', described as 'une grande et forte virago', in *Le Courrier français*, 17 July 1848, p. 3, and *La Gazette de France*, 17 July 1848, p. 3.
74 See Beslay, *Mes Souvenirs*, pp. 189–90, and Harsin, *Barricades*, pp. 305–11 and p. 313.
75 E.g., see *L'Indépendant* (Toulouse, Haute-Garonne), 5 and 6 July 1848.
76 Poumiès de La Siboutie, *Souvenirs d'un médecin de Paris*, p. 324.
77 Achard, *Souvenirs personnels*, p. 194. Cf. the Prince de Ligne, 28 June 1848: 'Paris ressemble à une immense place de guerre' (Ligne, *Souvenirs de la Princesse de Ligne*, p. 312).
78 T. W. Allies, *Journal in France in 1845 and 1848, with Letters from Italy in 1847*, London, Longman, 1849, p. 194. Cf. Cuvillier-Fleury to Mme Cuvillier-Fleury, 15 July 1848 (E. Bertin (ed.), *Journal intime de Cuvillier-Fleury*, 2 vols, Paris, Plon-Nourrit et Cie, 1900–3, vol. II, p. 453).
79 Castellane, *Journal*, vol. IV, p. 87; J. Couraye du Parc, *Au Secours de Paris: Campagne d'un Garde National coutançais*, Avranches, 1942, p. 22; Normanby, *A Year of Revolution*, vol. II, p. 70 and p. 74.
80 *La France: Journal quotidien*, 12 July 1848, p. 3.
81 *L'Avenir national*, 16 July 1848, p. 4.
82 Véron, *Mémoires d'un bourgeois de Paris*, vol. VI, pp. 59–67.
83 *Le Charivari*, 29 June 1848, p. 2. Among the volunteers was a Miss Julia Poussett, the daughter of the former British Consul-General in Haiti, who tended the wounded for four days and nights in the ambulance of the Institution Verdot, rue Culture Sainte Cathérine (*Galignani's Messenger*, 17 July 1848, p. 4).
84 Castellane, *Journal*, vol. IV, p. 89; Normanby, *A Year of Revolution*, vol. II, pp. 91–3 and 98–100.
85 Normanby, *A Year of Revolution*, vol. II, pp. 106–7.
86 Maillé, *Mémoires*, p. 263.
87 Tocqueville, *Souvenirs*, p. 176.
88 Couraye du Parc, *Au Secours de Paris: Campagne d'un Garde National coutançais*, p. 18. Cf. J. B. de Crèvecour de Perthes, *Sous dix rois: souvenirs de 1791 à 1860*,

8 vols, Paris, Jung-Treuttel, 1863–8, vol. VII, p. 67. At Ivry, south-east of Paris, railway workers tried to interrupt rail traffic (Tersen, *Quarante-huit*, p. 163).

89 *La Gazette de Cambrai, Echo du Nord et du Pas-de-Calais* (Cambrai, Nord), 21 October 1848. See also *L'Abeille de la Vienne* (Poitiers, Vienne), 25 September 1848, pp. 1–2; *Le Courrier du Pas-de-Calais* (Arras, Pas-de-Calais), 25 September 1848; *L'Opinion* (Auch, Gers), 15 and 25 September 1848. See also Tudesq, *Les Grands notables en France*, vol. II, pp. 1,145–8.

5 Cavaignac and Louis Napoleon Bonaparte

1 For a detailed discussion of Cavaignac's first government, see de Luna, *The French Republic under Cavaignac*, pp. 176–87.

2 *Le Journal des Débats*, 31 May 1848, and *Le Courrier français*, 1 June 1848, p. 3. A committee was formed on 20 June with General Baragueys d'Hilliers as president and Jean-Didier Baze and Joseph Degousée as vice presidents. Meetings were usually held in the Académie de Médicine at 8 pm on Tuesdays and Saturdays. See *La Démocratie pacifique*, 23 June 1848, p. 3; Tudesq, *Les Grands notables en France*, vol. II, pp. 1,094–6 and 1,141–4.

3 See *Le Bien public*, 21 July 1848; *La Patrie*, 21 July 1848.

4 Falloux, *Mémoires d'un royaliste*, vol. I, pp. 349–57; *Le Journal des Débats*, 29 June and 1 July 1848. For a secondary account, see de Luna, *The French Republic under Cavaignac*, pp. 193–9.

5 *L'Avenir national*, 17 July 1848; *Le Mois*, 26 May 1848, p. 186; *La Patrie*, 18 July 1848; *L'Union*, 18 July 1848; Stern, *Histoire de la Révolution de 1848*, vol. III, p. 60.

6 *La Patrie*, 21 July 1848; Babaud-Laribière, *Histoire de l'Assemblée nationale constituante*, vol. I, pp. 44–9.

7 *Le Bien public*, 9 August 1848, p. 4.

8 *Le Bien public*, 19 August 1848; *La Démocratie pacifique*, 19 August 1848, p. 4; *La Patrie*, 20 July 1848, p. 2; *L'Union*, 2 October 1848. See also de Luna, *The French Republic under Cavaignac*, pp. 189–91.

9 See Y. Katan, 'Les Colons de 1848 en Algérie: mythes et réalités', *Revue d'histoire moderne et contemporaine*, 31 (1984), pp. 177–202. See also Truquin, *Mémoires et aventures*, pp. 85–118.

10 L. Passy, *Souvenirs du marquis de Blosseville*, Evreux, C. Hérissy, 1898, pp. 249–50.

11 Rémusat, *Mémoires de ma vie*, vol. IV, pp. 354–5.

12 See Tudesq, *Les Grands notables en France*, vol. II, pp. 1,117–39.

13 *Le Moniteur universel*, 7 September 1848, pp. 2,333–4.

14 Ibid., 12 September 1848, p. 2,399 and pp. 2,406–7, 13 September 1848, pp. 2,417–9, 15 September 1848, pp. 2,453–4.

15 See *L'Evénement*, 7 September 1848; *Galignani's Messenger*, 7 September 1848, p. 3; *Le Journal des Débats*, 7 September 1848; *Le Siècle*, 7 September 1848; Quentin-Bauchart, *Etudes et souvenirs*, vol. I, p. 115.

16 *Le Moniteur universel*, 27 September 1848, pp. 2,621–2.

17 Normanby to Palmerston, 15 and 29 April 1848 (FO, 27, 806, ff. 139 and 280); A. G. P. B., baron de Barante, *Souvenirs du baron de Barante, 1782–1866*, 8 vols, Paris, Calmann Lévy, 1890–1901, vol. VII (1899), p. 309; Barrot, *Mémoires posthumes*, vol. II, p. 436.

18 See *Le Constitutionnel*, 28 September 1848; *Le Journal des Débats*, 29 September 1848; Quentin-Bauchart, *Etudes et souvenirs*, vol. I, p. 146.

19 Tocqueville, *Souvenirs*, p. 185.

20 Ibid., pp. 188–90.

21 For the Yonne by-election, see H. Forestier, 'Le Mouvement bonapartiste dans l'Yonne en 1848: la presse et l'opinion', *Annales de Bourgogne*, 21 (1949), pp. 114–34.

22 See A. de Tocqueville to G. de Beaumont, 24 September 1848 (*Correspondance d'Alexis de Tocqueville et de Gustave de Beaumont*, vol. II, p. 51), and the comtesse d'Agoult to Henri Lehmann, 1 October 1848 (M. de Flavigny, comtesse d'Agoult, *Une Correspondance romantique: Madame d'Agoult, Liszt, Henri Lehmann*, Paris, Flammarion, 1947, pp. 235–6).

23 *Le Moniteur universel*, 7 October 1848, pp. 2,737–9.

24 Beslay, *Mes souvenirs*, p. 199 and p. 217; Falloux, *Mémoires*, vol. I, pp. 380–1; Melun, *Mémoires*, vol. I, p. 260; O. E. Ollivier, *L'Empire libéral: études, récits, souvenirs*, 18 vols, Paris, Garnier frères, 1895–1918, vol. II, p. 100. The same is implied in Barrot, *Mémoires posthumes*, vol. II, pp. 450–1. Cf. *Galignani's Messenger*, 7 October 1848, p. 3; *Le Journal des Débats*, 7 October 1848; *Le Mois*, 7 October 1848, p. 358; *La Patrie*, 8 October 1848; *Le Siècle*, 7 October 1848; *L'Union*, 7 October 1848; *L'Univers*, 7 October 1848; P. Bastid, *Doctrines et institutions politiques de la Seconde République*, 2 vols, Paris, Hachette, 1945, vol. II, pp. 111–13; P. de La Gorce, *Histoire de la Seconde République*, 2 vols, Paris, E. Plon, Nourrit et Cie, 1904, vol. I, p. 453; Quentin-Bauchart, *Etudes et souvenirs*, vol. I, pp. 152–4; C. Seignobos, *La Révolution de 1848 – Le Second Empire*, Paris, A. Colin, 1921, p. 123.

25 See *L'Evénement*, 8 October 1848: 'Le splendide discours de Lamartine n'a pas été pour peu dans ce résultat.'

26 *Le Journal des Débats*, 29 September 1848; *L'Union*, 29 September 1848.

27 *L'Union*, 6 October 1848, p. 3.

28 See Tudesq, *L'Election présidentielle de Louis-Napoléon Bonaparte*, pp. 106–9.

29 See *L'Union*, 27 September 1848: 'C'est un représentant de plus, un républicain de plus, qui vient prendre place au milieu de ses collègues . . . En un mot, il est impossible d'être à la fois plus simple, plus modeste, plus convenable que le citoyen Bonaparte.'

30 See Castellane, *Journal*, vol. IV, pp. 111–12; H. Malo (ed.), *Mémoires de Madame Dosne, l'égérie de M. Thiers*, 2 vols, Paris, Plon, 1928, vol. I, pp. 273–6; *Le Moniteur universel*, 13 November 1848, p. 3,185.

31 *Le Moniteur universel*, 1 August 1848, pp. 1,826–30. See also G. Delmas, *Curiosités révolutionnaires: Le citoyen Proudhon devant l'Assemblée nationale, par Junius (Gaëtan Delmas). Exposé de la doctrine du citoyen Proudhon, son projet de désert, son discours à la Chambre des Représentants du peuple, rapport du citoyen Thiers. Compe rendu de la séance du 31 juillet 1848*, Paris, Bureau central, 1848.

32 B. O. Rodrigues, *Projet de Constitution populaire pour la République française*, Paris, Napoléon Chaix et Cie, 1848.

33 *Le Peuple souverain* (Lyons, Rhône), 7 September 1848, p. 3.

34 *Discours de M. Ledru-Rollin prononcé au banquet du Chalet le 22 septembre 1848 suivi des remerciements de F.-V. Raspail*, Paris, Georges Dairnvael, 1849.

35 *Le Journal des Débats*, 15 October 1848, p. 2, citing *L'Echo* (Montpellier), 10 October 1848.

36 *Premier banquet de la République démocratique et sociale, du mardi 17 octobre 1848*, Paris, Félix Malteste et Cie, 1848; *Le Journal des Débats*, 18 October 1848.

37 Lévêque, *Une Société en crise*, p. 221.

38 *Le Constitutionnel*, 4 November 1848.

39 *La Démocratie pacifique*, 16 November 1848, p. 4, and 20 November 1848, p. 3; *Le Journal des Débats*, 20 November 1848; *La République*, 20 November 1848, pp. 1–2.

40 *Le Journal des Débats*, 20 November 1848, p. 2.

41 *Le Peuple*, 29 November 1848.

42 *Le Journal des Débats*, 4 December 1848, p. 2.

43 *La Réforme*, 8 December 1848, p. 3.

44 *Le Peuple*, 10 December 1848, p. 2.

45 *Le Constitutionnel*, 7 November 1848; *Le Journal des Débats*, 5 November 1848; *La Patrie*, 6 November 1848; *L'Union*, 6 November 1848.

46 See Goallou, *Hamon, commissaire du gouvernement, puis préfet d'Ille-et-Vilaine*, p. 195.

47 *Le Peuple*, 8–15 November 1848, p. 1 and p. 3, and 6 December 1848, p. 2; *Le Peuple souverain*, 5–11 December 1848.

48 Cf. *Le Bien public*, 2 August 1848, p. 2.

49 *La Presse*, 17 August 1848, p. 3; *Le Spectateur républicain*, 18 August 1848, p. 2.

50 *Le Courrier du Bas-Rhin* (Strasbourg, Bas-Rhin), 9 September 1848: 'L'événement de la séance avait été un magnifique discours de M. de Lamartine, une de ces admirables improvisations, comme le grand orateur savait en trouver dans son cœur aux beaux jours de ses triomphes populaires'.

51 See *La Démocratie pacifique*, 20 November 1848, pp. 1–2, and 24 November 1848.

52 *Le Courrier français*, 28 November 1848; *L'Evénement*, 26 November 1848. Cf. Hugo, *Choses vues*, p. 1,117.

53 See *Le Courrier français*, 16 November 1848, p. 2, and 30 November 1848, pp. 1–2; *L'Evénement*, 27 November 1848, p. 3; *La Gazette de France*, 28 November 1848, p. 3.

54 See W. Fortescue, 'Lamartine et l'élection présidentielle du 10 décembre 1848', in S. Bernard-Griffiths and C. Croisille (eds), *Relire Lamartine aujourd'hui*, Paris, Librairie Nizet, 1993, pp. 133–41.

55 *L'Univers*, 25 October 1848, p. 2.

56 *L'Echo de la République* (Nantua, Ain), 16 November 1848.

57 *Le Républicain de Lot-et-Garonne*, 1 and 7 December 1848.

58 *Le Patriote de Saône-et-Loire*, 10 December 1848.

59 These included *Le Citoyen de Dijon*, *Le Citoyen de la Côte-d'Or*, *Le Courrier de Loir-et-Cher*, *Le Courrier de la Sarthe*, *L'Echo de l'Aude*, *La France républicaine d'Auch*, *La Fraternité d'Aude*, *Le Haro de Caen*, *Le Journal du Peuple* (Bayonne), *Le Messager du Nord*, *Le National de l'Ouest*, *Le Paysan de l'Aisne*, *Le Patriote de Saône-et-Loire*, *Le Républicain de l'Allier*, *Le Républicain de Lot-et-Garonne*, *Le Républicain de Vaucluse*, *Le Républicain des Ardennes*, *Le Républicain du Havre*, *La Ruche de la Dordogne*, *La Sentinelle de Saint-Etienne*, *La Sentinelle du Peuple* (Bordeaux), *Le Travailleur de Nancy*, *L'Union républicaine de la Somme*, *La Voix du Peuple* (Marseilles).

60 George Sand to Charles Poncy, 20 November 1848 (Sand, *Correspondance*, vol. VIII, pp. 710–11).

61 Provincial newspapers which supported Cavaignac included *L'Abeille de la Vienne*, *L'Ariégeois*, *L'Armoricain*, *L'Auxiliaire breton*, *Le Courrier de la Moselle*, *Le Courrier de Marseille*, *Le Courrier de Nantes*, *Le Courrier républicain de la Côte-d'Or*, *Le Courrier de Tarn-et-Garonne*, *Le Courrier du Cantal*, *L'Echo de Vésone*, *L'Echo du Nord*, *Le Glaneur d'Eure-et-Loire*, *L'Impartial de Besançon*, *L'Impartial de la Meurthe*, *L'Indépendant de la Moselle*, *L'Indépendant de Marseille*, *L'Industriel Alsacien*, *L'Industriel de la Champagne*, *Le Journal du Cher*, *Le Journal de Cherbourg*, *Le Journal des Pyrénées-Orientales*, *Le Mémorial d'Aix*, *La Paix* (Aube), *Le Patriote de la Meurthe et des Vosges*, *Le Sémaphore de Marseille*, *Le Spectateur du Midi*.

62 Malo, *Mémoires de Madame Dosne*, vol. I, pp. 281–2. See also Jones, *Politics and Rural Society*, pp. 235–6.

63 See *L'Evénement*, 7 December 1848; *La Gazette de Cambrai*, 9 December 1848; *L'Union*, 7 and 8 December 1848; Falloux, *Mémoires d'un royaliste*, vol. I, p. 384; Hugo, *Choses vues*, p. 1,123; Rémusat, *Mémoires de ma vie*, vol. IV, p. 379.

64 Castellane, *Journal*, vol. IV, pp. 118–19.

65 Malo, *Mémoires de Madame Dosne*, vol. I, p. 266, and pp. 271–2.

66 Ibid., vol. I, p. 256.

67 *Le Bien public*, 1 November 1848; *La Patrie*, 9 November 1848, p. 2; *L'Union*, 1 November 1848.

68 L'Union, 6 November 1848; Malo, Mémoires de Madame Dosne, vol. I, p. 268.
69 Commissaire, Mémoires et souvenirs, vol. I, p. 182; Malo, Mémoires de Madame Dosne, vol. I, p. 280.
70 Malo, Mémoires de Madame Dosne, vol. I, p. 256.
71 See the advertisement in Le Journal des Débats, 11 July 1848, p. 4: 'Avis aux Voyageurs. Hôtel du Rhin, 4 et 6, place Vendôme, spécialité de tables d'hôte à 3 fr. 50 c., le vin compris: à cinq heures et à six heures et demie. Les loyers de tous les appartements et chambres sont diminués.' See also Hugo, Choses vues, p. 757.
72 G. Bapst (ed.), Le Maréchal Canrobert: souvenirs d'un siècle, 6 vols, Paris, E. Plon, Nourrit et Cie, 1898–1913, vol. I, pp. 501–2.
73 J. Simon, Premières années, Paris, E. Flammarion, 1901, p. 400.
74 See Mérimée to Mme de Boigne, 18 June 1848, and to Francisque-Michel, 20 January 1849 (Mérimée, Correspondance générale, vol. V, pp. 332–3 and p. 434); Rémusat, Mémoires de ma vie, vol. IV, pp. 356–63; L'Union, 27 September 1848.
75 Le Bien public, 17 September, 10 June, and 9 December 1848: 'cette candidature n'est que l'éclatante promiscuité de toutes les opinions, de tous les malentendus, de tous les malaises, de tous les regrets et de toutes les espérances'.
76 Le Journal des Débats, 27 October 1848.
77 Proudhon, Carnets, vol. III, p. 111. Cf. A. Darimon, A Travers une révolution, 1847–1855, Paris, E. Dentu, 1884, pp. 70–5.
78 Malo, Mémoires de Madame Dosne, vol. I, p. 282.
79 Darimon, A Travers une révolution, p. 76.
80 Le Constitutionnel, 28 November 1848; La Patrie, 29 November 1848.
81 La Haute-Auvergne (Saint-Flour, Cantal), 7 December 1848.
82 Louis Napoleon's candidature was backed by a number of senior army officers, including Baragueys d'Hilliers, Bugeaud, Changarnier and Oudinot. See L'Evénement, 5 December 1848, p. 3.
83 See Le Père Duchêne, ancien fabricant de fourneaux, December 1848, p. 2. L'Extinction du pauperisme first appeared in a republican newspaper, Le Progrès du Pas-de-Calais.
84 A. de Tocqueville to G. de Beaumont, 4 November 1848 (Correspondance d'Alexis de Tocqueville et de Gustave de Beaumont, vol. II, p. 86).
85 George Sand complained and suggested that Louis Napoleon Bonaparte was anti-republican and should not be a presidential candidate. See Sand, Correspondance, vol. VIII, pp. 717–19; La Démocratie pacifique, 5 December 1848; Le Peuple, 6 December 1848; La Réforme, 5 December 1848, pp. 1–2.
86 Sand, Correspondance, vol. VIII, p. 717. In general, see A.-J. Tudesq, 'La Légende napoléonienne en France en 1848', Revue historique, 218 (1957), pp. 64–85.
87 Rémusat, Mémoires de ma vie, vol. IV, pp. 369–73.
88 See A. de Tocqueville to G. de Beaumont, 27 October 1848 (Correspondance d'Alexis de Tocqueville et de Gustave de Beaumont, vol. II, p. 80): 'Abbatucci serpente en tous sens, promettant ici, promettant là, se glissant à toutes les oreilles et déployant une fertilité de moyens et une activité prodigieuses'.
89 Malo, Mémoires de Madame Dosne, vol. I, p. 270, pp. 280–1, p. 283, pp. 286–300.
90 Journal de Rennes (Rennes, Ille-et-Vilaine), 23 November and 5 December 1848. Cf. E. F., vicomte de Beaumont-Vassy, Mémoires secrets du XIXe siècle, Paris, Sartorius, 1874, pp. 345; Goallou, Hamon, commissaire du gouvernement, p. 196.
91 A Paris newspaper, Le Crédit, calculated on 9 December 1848 that 190 provincial newspapers supported Cavaignac, 103 Louis Napoleon Bonaparte, and 48 Ledru-Rollin.
92 Véron, Mémoires d'un bourgeois de Paris, vol. VI, pp. 87–9.
93 Le Constitutionnel, 9 December 1848, p. 3.
94 La Liberté, 8 November 1848, p. 2, 23 November 1848, and 2 December 1848, p. 2.
95 See, for example, the emphasis on the name Napoleon in L'Evénement, 10 December

1848 ('Il est un nom qui résume tous les souvenirs du passé, toutes les espérances de l'avenir; c'est le nom de l'homme que le peuple a le plus aimé et qui a le plus aimé le peuple; c'est le nom de Napoléon') and in the *Journal de Louis-Napoléon Bonaparte*, December 1848 ('Louis-Napoléon est un nom qui est un souvenir et qui est une espérance').

96 Hautpoul, *Mémoires*, p. 319.

97 Malo, *Mémoires de Madame Dosne*, vol. I, p. 268.

98 *La République*, 31 October 1848; *L'Ariégeois* (Foix), 18 November 1848; N. W. Senior, *Journals Kept in France and Italy from 1848 to 1852, with a Sketch of the Revolution of 1848*, 2 vols, London, Henry S. King and Co., 1871, vol. II, p. 180.

99 See Bergier, *Le Journal d'un bourgeois de Lyon*, p. 171.

100 *Correspondance d'Alexis de Tocqueville et de Gustave de Beaumont*, vol. II, p. 71.

101 L. Faucher, *Biographie et correspondance*, 2 vols, Paris, Guillaumin et Cie, 1875, vol. I, p. 229, p. 230, p. 231 and p. 236.

102 See *La Haute-Auvergne*, 16 December 1848: 'Un ciel magnifique, un soleil de mai ont favorisé cette grande journée du 10 décembre'.

103 Castellane, *Journal*, vol. IV, p. 121.

104 Hautpoul, *Mémoires*, p. 320.

105 Malo, *Mémoires de Madame Dosne*, vol. II, p. 13: 'Partout le plus grand calme, et un air de fête'.

106 Ties of personal friendship at least partly accounted for some of the few votes cast for Lamartine. See Crèvecoeur de Perthes, *Sous dix rois*, p. 184 and pp. 212–13.

Bibliography

Primary sources

Manuscript sources

Archives Nationales (Paris)

67 AP 2, 4, 7, 8 Laurent-Antoine Pagnerre papers.
108 AP 2, 3 Hippolyte Carnot papers.
369 AP 2 Adolphe Crémieux papers.
C 925 Procès-verbaux des Comités de l'Assemblée Constituante.

Public Record Office (London)

FO 27, 803, 804, 805, 806 Dispatches of the Marquess of Normanby to Viscount Palmerston.

Published official documents

Bulletins de la République, émanés du Ministère de l'Intérieur du 13 mars au 6 mai 1848. G. Delmas (ed.) Paris, Bureau central, 1848.
Procès-verbaux du Gouvernement provisoire et de la Commission du pouvoir exécutif (24 février–22 juin 1848). C. H. Pouthas (ed.) Paris, Imprimerie nationale, 1950.
Rapport de la Commission d'enquête sur l'insurrection qui a éclaté dans la journée du 23 juin et sur les évènements du 15 mai. 3 vols. Paris, 1848.

Newspapers and periodicals

1 Paris

L'Accusateur public, L'Aigle républicain, L'Ami du peuple en 1848, L'Assemblée nationale, L'Atelier: organe spécial de la classe laborieuse, L'Avant-Garde: Journal des Ecoles, Le Bien public, Le Bonapartiste républicain, La Caramagnole: Journal des enfants de Paris, Le Charivari, La Commune de Paris: Moniteur des clubs, La Constitution: Journal des vrais intérêts du pays, Le Constitutionnel, Le Corsaire, Le Courrier français, Le Crédit, La Démocratie pacifique, Le Drapeau de la République: Echo des Gardes nationales de France, Le Droit, L'Ere nouvelle, L'Esprit du peuple: Courrier des rues, L'Evénement, La Famille: Organe politique, social, littéraire et scientifique des intérêts généraux, La France: Journal quotidien, La Fraternité de 1845: organe du communisme, Galignani's Messenger, La Gazette de France, Le Journal: Journal de Louis-Napoléon Bonaparte, Le Journal des Débats, Le Journal pour rire, Le Lampion, La Lanterne du Quartier-Latin, La Liberté: Journal quotidien, Le Mois, Le Monde de 1848/Le Monde républicain, Le Moniteur universel, Le Napoléonien: Journal quotidien, politique et littéraire, Le National, L'Opinion publique, L'Organisation du travail: Journal des ouvriers, La Patrie, Le Père Duchêne, Le Peuple, Le Peuple constituant: Journal quotidien, Le Populaire, La Presse, La Réforme, Le Représentant du Peuple: Journal quotidien des travailleurs, La République, La République rouge, La Révolution de 1848, La Révolution démocratique et sociale, La Revue des Deux Mondes, Revue et Gazette musicale de Paris, La Revue nationale, Le Siècle, Le Spectateur républicain: Journal du soir et du matin, Le Travail: Véritable organe des intérêts populaires, L'Union monarchique/L'Union, L'Univers, La Voix des clubs: journal quotidien des assemblées, La Vraie République.

2 Provincial

L'Abeille de la Vienne (Poitiers, Vienne), L'Ariégeois (Foix, Ariège), L'Avenir national (Limoges, Haute-Vienne), L'Aveyron républicain (Rodez, Aveyron), Le Bien public (Mâcon, Saône-et-Loire), Le Courrier de l'Ain (Bourg, Ain), Le Courrier du Bas-Rhin (Strasbourg, Bas-Rhin), Le Courrier du Cantal (Aurillac, Cantal), Le Courrier de la Drôme et de l'Ardèche (Valence, Drôme), Le Courrier de la Gironde (Bodeaux, Gironde), Le Courrier du Havre (Le Havre, Seine-Inférieure), Le Courrier de Lyon (Lyons, Rhône), Le Courrier du Pas-de-Calais (Arras, Pas-de-Calais), Le Courrier républicain de la Côte-d'Or (Dijon, Côte-d'Or), Le Courrier républicain du département de Seine-et-Oise (Versailles, Seine-et-Oise), Le Courrier de la Somme (Amiens, Somme), Le Courrier de Tarn-et-Garonne (Montauban, Tarn-et-Garonne), L'Echo de Cambrai (Cambrai, Nord), L'Echo de la République (Nantua, Ain), L'Echo de l'Aveyron (Rodez, Aveyron), L'Echo du Lot (Cahors, Lot), L'Echo du Nord (Lille, Nord), L'Emancipation (Toulouse, Haute-Garonne), L'Etoile (Pamiers, Ariège), Le Franc-Comtois (Besançon, Doubs), La Gazette de Cambrai, Echo du Nord et du Pas-de-Calais (Cambrai, Nord), La Haute-Auvergne (Saint-Flour, Cantal), L'Impartial de Rouen (Rouen, Seine-Inférieure), L'Indépendant (Toulouse, Haute-Garonne), L'Indicateur (Bordeaux, Gironde), L'Indicateur corrézien (Tulle, Corrèze), L'Indicateur de la Champagne (Reims, Marne), L'Intérêt public (Caen, Calvados), Le Journal de Cherbourg (Cherbourg, Manche), Le Journal de Loir-et-Cher (Blois, Loir-et-Cher), Le Journal de Lot-et-Garonne (Agen, Lot-et-Garonne), Le Journal de Maine-et-Loire (Angers, Maine-et-Loire), Le Journal de Rennes (Rennes, Ille-et-Vilaine), Le Journal de Rouen (Rouen, Seine-Inférieure), Le Journal de Saône-et-Loire (Mâcon, Saône-et-Loire), Le Journal d'Indre-et-Loire (Tours, Indre-et-Loire), Le Journal du Loiret (Orléans, Loiret), Le Journal du peuple (Bayonne, Basses-Pyrénées), La Liberté (Arras, Pas-de-Calais), La Liberté (Avignon, Vaucluse), La Liberté (Mont-de-Marsan, Landes), La Liberté pour tous (Nîmes, Gard), Le Mémorial d'Aix (Aix-en-Provence, Bouches-du-Rhône), Le Mercure ségusien (St Etienne, Loire), Le Messager du Midi (Montpellier, Hérault), L'Océan (Brest, Finistère), L'Opinion (Auch, Gers), L'Ordre (Limoges, Haute-Vienne), Le Patriote jurassien (Lons-le-Saunier, Jura), Le Patriote de Saône-et-Loire (Chalon-sur-Saône, Saône-et-Loire), Le Peuple électeur (Toulon, Var), Le Peuple souverain; Journal de Lyon (Lyons, Rhône), La Phare de la Rochelle (La Rochelle, Charente-Inférieure), Le Progrès de Pas-de-Calais (Arras, Pas-de-Calais), La Provence (Aix-en-Provence, Bouches-du-Rhône), Le Républicain des Ardennes (Sedan, Ardennes), Le Républicain du Jura (Lons-le-Saunier, Jura), Le Républicain de Loir-et-Cher (Blois, Loir-et-Cher), Le Républicain de Lot-et-Garonne (Agen, Lot-et-Garonne), Le Républicain de

Vaucluse (Avignon, Vaucluse), *Le Sémaphore de Marseille* (Marseilles, Bouches-du-Rhône), *Sentinelle des Pyrénées* (Bayonne, Basses-Pyrénées), *La Tribune de la Gironde* (Bordeaux, Gironde), *L'Union républicaine* (Mâcon, Saône-et-Loire).

Contemporary histories

Arago, J. E. V. *Histoire de Paris: Ses Révolutions, ses gouvernements et ses événements de 1841 à 1852*. 2 vols. Paris, Dion-Lambert, 1855.

Babaud-Laribière, F. S. L. *Histoire de l'Assemblée nationale consituante*. 2 vols. Paris, Michel Lévy frères, 1850.

Balleydier, A. *Histoire de la Garde mobile depuis les barricades de février*, Paris, Pillet fils aîné, 1848.

Barthélemy, C. *Histoire de la monarchie de juillet*. Paris, H. Gautier, 1887.

Blanc, J. J. L. *La Révolution de février au Luxembourg*. Paris, Michel Lévy frères, 1849.

—— *Pages d'histoire de la révolution de février 1848*. Paris, Bureau de Nouveau Monde, 1850.

—— *Histoire de la Révolution de 1848*. 2 vols. Paris, Lacroix, Verboeckhoven et Cie, 1870.

Castéra, N. *Le Triomphe de la liberté, ou histoire la plus complète de la révolution des 22, 23, et 24 février 1848*. Paris, Robert, 1848.

Castille, H. *Histoire de la Seconde République française*. 4 vols. Paris, V. Lecou, 1854–6.

—— *Les Massacres de juin 1848, d'après des documents historiques*. Paris, Chez les principaux libraires, 1869.

Chamier, Captain. *A Review of the French Revolution of 1848: from the 24th of February to the election of the first president*. 2 vols. London, Reeve, Benham and Reeve, 1849.

Comberousse, C. de. *Histoire de l'Ecole Centrale des Arts et Métiers*. Paris, Gauthier-Villars, 1879.

Corkran, J. F. *History of the National Constituent Assembly, from May 1848*. 2 vols. London, Richard Bentley, 1849.

Delvau, A. *Histoire de la Révolution de février*. Paris, Blosse et Garnier, 1850.

Dubail, R. *Campagne réformiste de 1847*. Paris, Paulin, 1848.

Gallois, C. A. G. L. *Histoire de la Révolution de 1848*. 4 vols. Paris, Naud et Gourju, 1849–50.

Garnier-Pagès, L. A. *Un Episode de la Révolution de 1848: l'impôt des 45 centimes*. Paris, Pagnerre, 1850.

—— *Histoire de la Révolution de 1848*. 10 vols. Paris, Pagnerre, 1861–72.

La Hodde, L. de. *La Naissance de la République en février 1848*. Paris, Chez l'éditeur, 1850.

Lamartine, A. de. *Histoire de la Révolution de 1848*. 2 vols. Paris, Perrotin, 1849.

Longepied, A. and Laugier. *Comité révolutionnaire, Club des clubs et la Commission*. Paris, Garnier frères, 1850.

Lucas, A. *Les Clubs et les clubistes, histoire complète, critique et anecdotique des clubs et des comités électoraux fondés à Paris depuis la révolution de 1848: déclarations de principes, règlements, motions et publications des sociétés populaires*. Paris, E. Dentu, 1851.

Marx, K. *Surveys from Exile*. D. Fernbach (ed.) Harmondsworth, Penguin Books, 1977.

Ménard, L. *Prologue d'une révolution, février–juin 1848*. Paris, Au bureau du Peuple, 1849.

Mitchell, D. G. *The Battle Summer*. New York, Baker and Scribner, 1850.

Montépin, X. A., comte de. *Le Gouvernement provisoire: histoire anecdotique et politique de ses membres*. Paris, A. Cadot, 1848.

Nougarède, A. *La Vérité sur la Révolution de février 1848*. Paris, Amyot, 1850.

Pagès-Duport, P. A. S. J. *Journées de juin: Récit complet des événements des 23, 24, 25, 26 et des jours suivants.* Paris, T. Pitrat et fils, 1848.

Pardigon, F. *Episodes des journées de juin 1848.* London, Jeffs, 1852.

Pelletan, E. *Histoire des trois journées de février 1848.* Paris, Louis Colas, 1848.

Pierre, V. S. *Histoire de la République de 1848.* 2 vols. Paris, E. Plon, 1873–8.

Regnault, E. *Histoire du Gouvernement provisoire.* Paris, V. Lecou, 1850.

—— *Révolution française: Histoire de huit ans, 1840–1848.* 3 vols. Paris, Pagnerre, 1851–2.

Robin, C. P. *Histoire de la Révolution française.* 2 vols. Paris, Penaud frères, 1849–50.

Sarrans, J. B. *Histoire de la Révolution de février 1848.* 2 vols. Paris, Administration de librairie, 1851.

Sauzet, P. J. P. *La Chambre des députés et la Révolution de février.* Paris, Perisse frères, 1851.

Stern D. (M. de F., comtesse d'Agoult) *Histoire de la Révolution de 1848.* 3 vols. Paris, Gustave Sandré, 1850–3.

Thomas, E. *Histoire des ateliers nationaux.* Paris, Michel Lévy frères, 1848.

Treillard, M. *La République à Lyon sous le gouvernement provisoire.* Paris, Gabriel Roux, Lyons, Charavay frères, 1849.

Tricaud, L., comte de. *Histoire du département de l'Ain du 24 février au 20 décembre 1848.* Bourg-en-Bresse, P. Comte-Milliet, 1872.

Turnbull, D. *The French Revolution of 1830: the events which produced it, and the scenes by which it was accompanied.* London, Henry Colburn and Richard Bentley, 1830.

Weill, A. *Dix mois de révolution, depuis le 24 février jusqu'au 10 décembre 1848.* Paris, Les Principaux libraires, 1869.

Memoirs, correspondence, speeches and printed sources

Aberdeen, G. H. Gordon, Earl of. *The Correspondence of Lord Aberdeen and Princess Lieven, 1832–1854.* E. Jones Parry (ed.) 2 vols. London, Royal Historical Society, 1938–9 (Camden Third Series, vols 60 and 62).

Achard, L. A. E. *Souvenirs personnels d'émeute et de révolution.* Paris, Michel Lévy frères, 1872.

Agoult, M. de Flavigny, comtesse d'. *Une Correspondance romantique: Madame d'Agoult, Liszt, Henri Lehmann.* Paris, Flammarion, 1947.

Allies, T. W. *Journal in France in 1845 and 1848, with Letters from Italy in 1847.* London, Longman, 1849.

Alton-Shée, Edmond de Lignères, comte d'. *Souvenirs de 1847 et de 1848.* Paris, Maurice Dreyfous, 1879.

Ancelot, M. L. V. *Un Salon de Paris, 1824 à 1864.* Paris, E. Dentu, 1866.

Apponyi, R., Count. *Vingt-cinq ans à Paris, 1826–1850: Journal du comte Rodolphe Apponyi, attaché de l'ambassade d'Autriche à Paris.* E. Daudet (ed.) 4 vols. Paris, Plon-Nourrit et Cie, 1913–26.

Armaillé, M. C. A. La Forest, comtesse d'. *Quand on savait vivre heureux, 1830–1850.* Paris, Plon, 1934.

Audebrand, P. *Aux électeurs du département de Saône-et-Loire.* Autun, Dejussieu, 1848.

—— *Souvenirs de la tribune des journalistes, 1848–1852.* Paris, E. Dentu, 1867.

—— *Nos Révolutionnaires: pages d'histoire contemporaine, 1830–1880.* Paris Bibliothèque des Deux Mondes, 1886.

Balzac, H. de. *Correspondance de Balzac.* R. Pierrot (ed.) 5 vols. Paris, Garnier fréres, 1960–9.

—— Lettres à Madame Hanska. R. Pierrot (ed.) 4 vols. Paris, Les Bibliophiles de l'originale, 1967–71.

Barante, A. G. P. Brugière, baron de. Souvenirs du baron de Barante, 1782–1866. 8 vols. Paris, Calmann Lévy, 1890–1901.

Barbier, H. A. Souvenirs personnels et silhouettes contemporaines. Paris, E. Dentu, 1883.

Barrot, C. H. O. Mémoires posthumes. 4 vols. Paris, Charpentier et Cie, 1875–6.

Beaumont-Vassy, E. F., vicomte de. Mémoires secrets du XIXe siècle. Paris, Sartorius, 1874.

Benoît, J. M. Souvenirs de la République de 1848. Geneva, Imprimerie Duchamp et Cie, Corraterie, 1855.

Bergier, J. Le Journal d'un bourgeois de Lyon en 1848. J. Godart (ed.) Paris, Presses universitaires de France, 1924.

Beslay, C. V. 1830–1848–1870: Mes souvenirs. Paris, Sandoz et Fischbacher, 1873.

Biré, E. Mes souvenirs, 1846–1870. Paris, J. Lamarre, 1908.

Blanc, J. J. L. Organisation du travail. Paris, Société de l'industrie fraternelle, 1847.

—— 1848 Historical Revelations: inscribed to Lord Normanby. London, Chapman and Hall, 1858.

—— Discours politiques, 1847 à 1881. Paris, Germer-Baillière et Cie, 1882.

Blosseville, B. E. Poret, marquis de. Souvenirs du marquis de Blosseville. L. Passy (ed.) Evreux, C. Hérissey, 1898.

Blount, Sir E. C. Memoirs. S. J. Reid (ed.) London, Longmans, Green and Co., 1902.

Bocher, C. Mémoires de Charles Bocher (1816–1907), précédés des souvenirs de famille (1760–1816). Paris, Ernest Flammarion, 1906.

Boissy, H. E. O. Rouillé, marquis de. Mémoires du marquis de Boissy, 1798–1866. P. Breton (ed.) 2 vols. Paris, E. Dentu, 1870.

Bonde, H. E. F., Baroness. Paris in '48: letters from a resident describing the events of the revolution by Baroness Bonde. C. E. Warr (ed.) London, John Murray, 1903.

Boucher, H. Souvenirs d'un Parisien pendant la Seconde République. 2 vols. Paris, Perrin et Cie, 1908–9.

Boutin, C. Les Murailles révolutionnaires de 1848. Paris, E. Picard, 1869.

Broglie, J. V. A., duc de. Mémoires du duc de Broglie. 2 vols. Paris, Calmann-Lévy, 1938–41.

Brun-Lavainne, E. B. J. Mes Souvenirs. Lille, Imprimerie de Lefebvre-Ducrocq, 1855.

Bugeaud, T. R., maréchal, duc d'Isly. Lettres inédites du maréchal Bugeaud, duc d'Isly. Captain E. Tattet (ed.) Paris, Emile-Paul frères, 1922.

Cabet, E. Bien et mal, danger et salut, après la révolution de février 1848. Paris, P. Martinon, 1849.

Canler, L. Mémoires de Canler, ancien chef du service de la Sûreté. Paris, J. Hetzel, 1862.

Canrobert, F. A. C., maréchal. Le Maréchal Canrobert: souvenirs d'un siècle. C. G. Bapst (ed.) 6 vols. Paris, E. Plon, Nourrit et Cie, 1898–1913.

Carnot, L. H. Le Ministère de l'Instruction publique et des cultes, depuis le 24 février jusqu'au 5 juillet 1848. Paris, Pagnerre, 1848.

Castellane, E. V. E. B., maréchal, comte de. Journal du maréchal de Castellane, 1804–1862. 5 vols. Paris, E. Plon, Nourrit et Cie, 1895–7.

Caussidière, M. Mémoires de Caussidière, ex-préfet de police et représentant du peuple. 2 vols. Paris, Michel Lévy frères, 1849.

Chambolle, M. A. Retours sur la vie: appréciations et confidences sur les hommes de mon temps. Paris, E. Plon, Nourrit et Cie, 1912.

Chenu, J. E. A. *Les Conspirateurs . . . Les sociétés secrètes: La préfecture de police sous Caussidière: Les corps-francs*. Paris, Garnier frères, 1850.

—— *Les Montagnards de 1848, encore quatre nouveaux chapitres, précédés d'une réponse à Caussidière et autres Démocs-Socs*. Paris, D. Giraud et J. Dagneau, 1850.

Chérest, A. A. *La Vie et les œuvres de A. T. Marie, avocat, membre du gouvernement provisoire*. Paris, A. Durand et Pédone-Lauriel, 1873.

Circourt, A., comte de. *Adolphe de Circourt: souvenirs d'une mission à Berlin en 1848*. 2 vols. Paris, A. Picard et fils, 1908–9.

Claudin, G. *Mes Souvenirs, les boulevards de 1840–1870*. Paris, C. Lévy, 1884.

Colman, H. *European Life and Manners: in familiar letters to friends*. Boston, C. C. Little and J. Brown. London, J. Peterham, 1849.

Comminges, M. B. E., comte de. *Souvenirs d'enfance et de régiment, 1831–1870/1*. Paris, E. Plon, Nourrit et Cie, 1910.

Commissaire, S. *Mémoires et souvenirs*. 2 vols. Lyons, Meton, Paris, Garcet et Nisius, 1888.

—— *Compte rendu du banquet de Limoges, 2 janvier 1848*. Boussac, Imprimerie de Pierre Leroux, 1848.

Condsidérant, V. *Le Socialisme devant le vieux monde ou le vivant devant les morts*. Paris, Librairie phalanstérienne, 1848.

Corbon, C. A. *Le Secret du peuple de Paris*. Paris, Pagnerre, 1863.

Corlieu, Dr A. *De Février à juin*. Château-Thierry, Marchand, 1888.

Couraye du Parc, J. *Au Secours de Paris: Campagne d'un Garde National coutançais*. Avranches, 1942.

Cournot, A. A. *Souvenirs (1760–1860)*. Paris, Hachette, 1913.

Crémieux, I. M. A. *Liberté! Plaidoyers et discours politiques de Adolphe Crémieux*. Paris, Picon-Lamy et Dewez, 1869.

—— *En 1848: discours et lettres de M. A. Crémieux*. Paris, Calmann-Lévy, 1883.

Crèvecour de Perthes, J. B. de. *Sous dix rois: souvenirs de 1791 à 1860*. 8 vols. Paris, Jung-Treuttel, 1863–8.

—— *Curiosités révolutionnaires: Les affiches rouges: Reproduction exacte et histoire critique de toutes les affiches ultra-républicaines placardées sur les murs de Paris depuis le 24 février 1848*. Paris, D. Giraud et J. Dagneau, 1851.

Cuvillier-Fleury, A. A. *Journal intime de Cuvillier-Fleury*. E. Bertin (ed.) 2 vols. Paris, E. Plon, Nourrit et Cie, 1900–3.

Darimon, A. *A Travers une révolution, 1847–1855*. Paris, E. Dentu, 1884.

Delessard, E. *Souvenirs de 1848: L'Ecole centrale aux ateliers nationaux*. Paris, E. Bernard et Cie, 1900.

Delmas, G. *Curiosités révolutionnaires: Le citoyen Proudhon devant l'Assemblée nationale, par Junius (Gaëtan Delmas): Exposé de la doctrine du citoyen Proudhon, son projet de désert, son discours à la Chambre des Représentants du peuple, rapport du citoyen Thiers: Compte rendu de la séance du 31 juillet 1848*. Paris, Bureau central, 1848.

Delvau, A. *Les Murailles révolutionnaires de 1848*. 2 vols. Paris, E. Picard, 1867–8.

Denormandie, E. *Notes et souvenirs*. Paris, Léon Chailley, 1896.

—— *Discours de M. Ledru-Rollin prononcé an banquet du Chalet le 22 septembre 1848 suivi des remerciements de F.-V. Raspail*. Paris, Georges Dairnvael, 1849.

Dosne, F. *Mémoires de Madame Dosne, l'égérie de M. Thiers*. H. Malo (ed.) 2 vols. Paris, Plon, 1928.

Doudan, X. *Mélanges et lettres*. 4 vols. Paris, Calmann-Lévy, 1876–7.

Du Camp, M. *Souvenirs de l'année 1848*. Paris, Hachette, 1876.

—— *Souvenirs littéraires, 1822–1880*. 2 vols. Paris, Hachette, 1882–3.

—— *Souvenirs d'un demi-siècle*. 2 vols. Paris, Hachette, 1949.

Dulac, Clément. *Profession de foi du Citoyen Clément Dulac, agriculteur à Chabans, département de la Dordogne*. Périgueux, Imprimerie Lavertujon, 1848.

Dumas, A. *Révélations sur l'arrestation d'Emile Thomas*. Paris, Michel Lévy frères, 1848.

Duvergier de Hauranne, P. *De la Réforme parlementaire et de la réforme électorale*. Paris, Paulin, 1847.

Estourmel, J., comte d'. *Derniers souvenirs du comte Joseph d'Estourmel*. Paris, E. Dentu, 1860.

Etex, A. *Les Souvenirs d'un artiste*. Paris, E. Dentu, 1877.

Falloux, A. F. P., comte de. *Mémoires d'un royaliste*. 2 vols. Paris, Perrin, 1888.

Faucher, L. *Biographie et correspondance*. 2 vols. Paris, Guillaumin et Cie, 1875.

Faure, P. *Journal d'un combattant de février*. Jersey, C. Le Feuvre, 1859.

Flaubert, G. *Correspondance*. vol. 2. Paris, Louis Conard, 1936.

Freycinet, C. L. de Saulces de. *Souvenirs, 1848–1878*. Paris, Ch. Delagrave, 1912.

Girardin, E. de. *Bon sens, bonne foi*. Paris, Michel Lévy frères, 1848.

—— *Journal d'un journaliste au secret*. Paris, Michel Lévy frères, 1848.

Goodrich, S. G. *Recollections of a Lifetime, or Men and Things I Have Seen: in a series of familiar letters to a friend, historical, biographical, anecdotical, and descriptive*. 2 vols. New York and Auburn, Miller, Orton and Mulligan, 1857.

Got, E. *Journal d'Edmond Got, sociétaire de la Comédie-Française, 1822–1901*. M. Got (ed.) 2 vols. Paris, Plon-Nourrit et Cie, 1910.

Gouache, J. *Lille: Dijon: Chalon. Banquets démocratiques*. Paris, Au bureau de *La Réforme*, 1848.

Gudin, T., baron. *Souvenirs du Baron Gudin, peintre de la marine (1820–1870)*. E. Béraud (ed.) Paris, Plon, Nourrit et Cie, 1921.

Guizot, F. P. G. *De la Démocratie en France*. Paris, Victor Masson, 1849.

—— *Mémoires pour servir à l'histoire de mon temps*. 8 vols. Paris, Michel Lévy, 1858–67.

Hautpoul, General A., marquis d'. *Mémoires du général Alphonse d'Hautpoul, pair de France, 1789–1865*. Paris, Perrin, 1906.

Houssaye, A. *Les Confessions: Souvenirs d'un demi-siècle, 1830–1880*. 6 vols. Paris, E. Dentu, 1885–91.

Hugo, V. M. *Choses vues*. S. Gaudon (ed.) Paris, Robert Laffont, 1987.

Imbert de Saint-Amand, A. L., baron. *La Révolution de 1848*. Paris, E. Dentu, 1894.

Jaubert, C. d'A. *Souvenirs: Lettres et correspondances*. Paris, J. Hetzel, 1881.

Jay, E. *Aux Electeurs des cantons de Vif et de Saint-Laurent-du-Pont*. Grenoble, Imprimerie de Prudhomme, 1848.

Joigneaux, P. *Souvenirs historiques*. 2 vols. Paris, Marpon et Flammarion, 1891.

Joinville, F. F. P. L. M. d'Orléans, prince de. *Vieux souvenirs, 1818–1848*. Paris, Calmann-Lévy, 1894.

Josserand. *Notice historique sur l'établissement de la république dans le département de l'Ain, par un membre de la Société d'émulation de l'Ain*. Bourg-en-Bresse, Millet-Bottier, 1850.

Lamartine, A. de. *La France parlementaire, 1834–1851: Œuvres oratoires et écrits politiques*. 6 vols. Paris, A. Lacroix, Verboeckhoven et Cie, 1864–5.

Lamennais, F. de. *Correspondance générale*. vol. 8, *1841–1854*. L.Le Guillou (ed.) Paris, Armand Colin, 1981.

Lechevalier, J. *Aux Electeurs du département de la Seine*. Paris, 1848.

Ledru-Rollin, A. A. *Discours politiques et écrits divers*. 2 vols. Paris, Germer-Baillière et Cie, 1879.

Lefrançais, G. *Souvenirs d'un révolutionnaire*. Paris, Editions de la Tête des Feuilles, 1972.

Legouvé, E. *Soixante ans de souvenirs*. 2 vols. Paris, J. Hetzel, 1886–7.

Lejean, G. *Guillaume Lejean, Charles Alexandre, correspondance (1846–1869): deux républicains bretons dans l'entourage de Lamartine et de Michelet*. J. Y. Guillou (ed.) Paris, Editions Jean Touzet, 1993.

Le Pays de Bourjolly, General J. A. *De l'armée et 40 jours de 1848 à Lyon*. Paris, J. Dumaine, 1853.

Leroux, P. H. *Compte-rendu du banquet de Limoges, 2 janvier 1848*. Boussac, P. Leroux, 1848.

—— *Projet d'une constitution démocratique et sociale*. Paris, Gustave Sandré, 1848.

Lesseps, C. *Exposé de principes de M. Charles Lesseps, président du club républicain de la fraternité*. Paris, Felix Malteste et Cie, 1848.

Lewald, F. *A Year of Revolutions: Fanny Lewald's recollections of 1848*. H. B. Lewis (ed.) Providence and Oxford, Berghahn Books, 1997.

Ligne, C. J., princesse de. *Souvenirs de la princesse de Ligne, 1815–1850*. Brussels, G. Van Oest, 1923.

Limet, C. *Un Vétéran du barreau parisien: quatre-vingts ans de souvenirs, 1827–1907*. Paris, A. Lemerre, 1908.

Maillé, B. J., duchesse de. *Mémoires, 1832–1851*. X. de La Fournière and F. d'Agay (eds) Paris, Perrin, 1989.

Marmier, X. *Journal (1848–1890)*. E. Kaye (ed.) 2 vols. Geneva, Librairie Droz, 1968.

Marrast, A. *Les Funérailles révolutionnaires*. Paris, Pagnerre, 1848.

Martin, H. *Manuel de l'instituteur pour les élections*. Paris, Pagnerre, 1848.

Massa, A. P. Regnier, marquis de. *Souvenirs et impressions*. Paris, Calmann-Lévy, 1897.

Melun, A. M. J., vicomte de. *Mémoires du vicomte Armand de Melun*. Comte Le Camus (ed.) 2 vols. Paris, J. Leday, 1891.

Mérimée, P. *Correspondance générale*. M. Parturier (ed.) vol. 5, 1847–1849. Paris, Le Divan, 1946.

Merruau, C. *Souvenirs de l'Hôtel de Ville de Paris, 1848–1852*. Paris, E. Plon et Cie, 1875.

Monnier, D. *Souvenirs d'un octogénaire de province*. Lons-le-Saunier, Imprimerie de Gauthier frères, 1871.

Montfort, H. *Biographie politique et militaire du général Cavaignac*. Paris, Victor Magen, 1848.

Nadaud, M. *Mémoires de Léonard, ancien garçon maçon*. M. Agulhon (ed.) Paris, Hachette, 1976.

Normanby, C. H. Phipps, Marquess of. *A Year of Revolution from a Journal Kept in Paris in 1848*. 2 vols. London, Longman, Bown, Green, Longmans and Roberts, 1857.

Nouguier, J. L. *Souvenirs et impressions d'un ex-journaliste pour servir à l'histoire contemporaine*. Paris, Michel Lévy frères, 1856.

Ollivier, O. E. *L'Empire libéral: Etudes, récits, souvenirs*. 18 vols. Paris, Garnier frères, 1895–1918.

Pocquet du Haut-Jussé, B. *Correspondance politique de Barthélémy Pocquet, rédacteur du 'Journal de Rennes', 1848–1878*. Paris, Librairie Klincksieck, 1976.

Poumiès de La Siboutie, F. L. *Souvenirs d'un médecin de Paris, 1789–1863*. Paris, Plon-Nourrit, 1910.

—— *Premier banquet de la République démocratique et sociale, du mardi 17 octobre 1848*. Paris, Félix Malteste et Cie, 1848.

Proudhon, P. J. *Carnets de P.-J. Proudhon*. P. Haubtmann (ed.) 3 vols. Paris, Marcel Rivière et Cie, 1960–8.

Quentin-Bauchart, A. *Etudes et souvenirs sur la deuxième république et le second empire (1848–1870): mémoires posthumes publiés par son fils*. 2 vols. Paris, Plon-Nourrit et Cie, 1901–2.

Reiset, M. A., vicomte de. *Souvenirs du lieutenant-général vicomte de Reiset (1775–1832), publiés par son petit-fils le vicomte de Reiset*. 3 vols. Paris, Calmann-Lévy, 1899–1902.

Rémusat, C. de. *Mémoires de ma vie*. C. H. Pouthas (ed.) 5 vols. Paris, Plon, 1958–67.

Renouvier, C. *Manuel républicain de l'homme et du citoyen*. Paris, Pagnerre, 1848.

Rodrigues, B. O. *Projet de Constitution populaire pour la République française*. Paris, Napoléon Chaix et Cie, 1848.

Sainte-Beuve, C. A. *Portraits contemporains*. 5 vols. Paris, Michel Lévy frères, 1869–71.

Sand, G. *Correspondance*. G. Lubin (ed.) vol. 8, *Juillet 1847 – décembre 1848*. Paris, Editions Garnier frères, 1971.

Senior, N. W. *Journals Kept in France and Italy from 1848 to 1852, with a Sketch of the Revolution of 1848*. 2 vols. London, Henry S. King and Co., 1871.

—— *Conversations with M. Thiers, M. Guizot, and Other Distinguished Persons, during the Second Empire*. 2 vols. London, Hurst and Blackett, 1878.

Simon, J. *Premières années*. Paris, E. Flammarion, 1901.

Simpson, J. P. *Pictures from Revolutionary Paris, Sketched during the First Phases of the Revolution of 1848*. 2 vols. Edinburgh and London, W. Blackwood and Sons, 1849.

Thiers, M. J. L. A. *Notes et souvenirs de M. Thiers, 1848*. Paris, 1902.

Tocqueville, A. de. *Souvenirs*. L. Monnier (ed.) Paris, Gallimard, 1964.

—— *Correspondance d'Alexis de Tocqueville et de Gustave de Beaumont*. A. Jardin (ed.) 3 vols. Paris, Gallimard, 1967.

—— *Correspondance d'Alexis de Tocqueville et de Francisque de Corcelle*. P. Gibert (ed.) 2 vols. Paris, Gallimard, 1983.

Truquin, N. *Mémoires et aventures d'un prolétaire à travers la révolution*. P. Lejeune (ed.) Paris, François Maspero, 1977.

Véron, L. D. *Mémoires d'un bourgeois de Paris*. 6 vols. Paris, Gabriel de Gonet, 1853–5.

Vigny, A. de. *Mémoires inédits, fragments et projets*. J. Sangnier (ed.) Paris, Gallimard, 1958.

Villeneuve-Bargemont, J. R., comte de. *Souvenirs de 60 ans*. Paris, Simon Racon et Cie, 1870.

Secondary sources

Books

Aboucaya, C. *Les Structures sociales et économiques de l'agglomération lyonnaise à la veille de la Révolution de 1848*. Paris, Librairie du Recueil Sirey, 1963.

—— *Actes du congrès historique du centenaire de la révolution de 1848*. Paris, Presses universitaires de France, 1948.

Aguet, J.-P. *Les Grèves sous la Monarchie de Juillet (1830–1847): contribution à l'étude du mouvement ouvrier français*. Geneva, Droz, 1954.

Agulhon, M. *Une Ville ouvrière au temps du socialisme utopique: Toulon de 1815 à 1851*. Paris, Mouton, 1970.

—— *The Republican Experiment, 1848–1852*. Cambridge, Cambridge University Press, 1973.

—— *Marianne into Battle: republican imagery and symbolism in France, 1789–1880*. Cambridge, Cambridge University Press, 1981.

—— *The Republic in the Village: the people of the Var from the French Revolution to the Second Republic.* Cambridge, Cambridge University Press, 1982.

—— *Histoire vagabonde: idéologies et politique dans la France du XIXe siècle.* Paris, Gallimard, 1988.

—— *Les Quarante-huitards.* Paris, Gallimard, 1992.

Alexander, R. S. *Bonapartism and Revolutionary Tradition in France: the fédérés of 1815.* Cambridge, Cambridge University Press, 1991. (ed.)

—— *French History since Napoleon.* London, Arnold, 1999.

—— *Re-writing the French Revolutionary Tradition: liberal opposition and the fall of the Bourbon monarchy.* Cambridge, Cambridge University Press, 2003.

Alméras, H. d'. *La Vie parisienne sous la République de 1848.* Paris, Albin Michel, 1921.

Amann, P. H. *Revolution and Mass Democracy: the Paris club movement in 1848.* Princeton, New Jersey, Princeton University Press, 1975.

Aminzade, R. *Class, Politics, and Early Industrial Capitalism: a study of mid-nineteenth-century Toulouse, France.* Albany, State University of New York, 1981.

—— *Ballots and Barricades: class formation and republican politics in France, 1830–1871.* Princeton, New Jersey, Princeton University Press, 1993.

Amson, D. *Adolphe Crémieux: L'oublié de la gloire.* Paris, Le Seuil, 1988.

Antony, A. *La Politique financière du Gouvernement provisoire, février–mai 1848.* Paris, Arthur Rousseau, 1909.

Armengaud, A. *Les Populations de l'Est-Aquitain au début de l'époque contemporaine: recherches sur une région moins développée (vers 1845 – vers 1871).* Paris, Mouton, 1961.

Barry, D. *Women and Political Insurgency: France in the mid-nineteenth century.* London, Macmillan, 1996.

Bartier, J., et al. *1848. Les Utopismes sociaux: utopie et action à la veille des journées de février.* Paris, Sédès, 1981.

Bastid, P. *Doctrines et institutions politiques de la Seconde République.* 2 vols. Paris, Hachette, 1945.

—— *Un Juriste pamphlétaire: Cormenin, précurseur et consituant de 1848.* Paris, Hachette, 1948.

—— *Les Institutions politiques de la monarchie parlementaire française, 1814–1848.* Paris, Recueil Sirey, 1954.

Bazin, R. *Le Duc de Nemours.* Paris, Emile-Paul frères, 1907.

Beach, V. W. *Charles X of France: his life and times.* Boulder, Colorado, Pruett, 1971.

Becherer, R. *Science plus Sentiment: César Daly's formula for modern architecture.* Ann Arbor, 1984.

Beck, T. D. *French Legislators, 1830–1834: a study in quantitative history.* Berkeley, University of California Press, 1974.

Bellanger, C., et al. *Histoire générale de la presse française.* vol. 2, *1815–1871.* Paris, Presses universitaires de France, 1969.

Berenson, E. G. *Populist Religion and Left-wing Politics in France, 1830–1852.* Princeton, New Jersey, Princeton University Press, 1984.

Bernstein, S. *Auguste Blanqui and the Art of Insurrection.* London, Lawrence and Wishart, 1971.

Berthier de Sauvigny, G. de. *La Restauration.* Paris, Flammarion, 1955.

—— *La Révolution parisienne de 1848 vue par les américains.* Paris, Service des Travaux Historiques de la Ville de Paris, 1984.

Bezucha, R. J. *The Lyon Uprising of 1834: social and political conflict in the early July monarchy.* Cambridge, Mass., Harvard University Press, 1974.

Bluche, F. *Le Bonapartisme.* Paris, Presses universitaires de France, 1981.

Bonet, G. *L'Indépendant des Pyrénées-Orientales: l'histoire d'un journal, un journal dans l'histoire, 1846–1848.* Perpignan, 1987.

Bowman, F. P. *Le Christ des barricades, 1789–1848.* Paris, Les Editions du cerf, 1987.

Bullen, R. *Palmerston, Guizot and the Collapse of the Entente Cordiale.* London, Athlone Press, 1974.

Burton, R. D. E. *Baudelaire and the Second Republic: writing and revolution.* Oxford, Clarendon Press, 1991.

Bury, J. P. T. and R. P. Tombs. *Thiers, 1797–1877: a political life.* London, Allen and Unwin, 1986.

Cabane, H. *Histoire du clergé de France pendant la Révolution de 1848.* Paris, Bloud et Cie, 1908.

Calman, A. *Ledru-Rollin and the Second French Republic.* New York, Columbia University Press, 1922.

Caucanas, S. and R. Cazals. *Armand Barbès et les hommes de 1848.* Carcassone, Les Audois, 1999.

Charles, A. *La Révolution de 1848 et la seconde république à Bordeaux et dans le département de la Gironde.* Bordeaux, Editions Delmas, 1934.

Chevalier, L. *Labouring Classes and Dangerous Classes in Paris during the First Half of the Nineteenth Century.* London, Routledge and Kegan Paul, 1973.

Collingham, H. A. C. *The July Monarchy: a political history of France, 1830–1848.* London, Longman, 1988.

Collins, I. *The Government and the Newspaper Press in France, 1848–1881.* Oxford, Oxford University Press, 1959.

Collins, R. W. *Catholicism and the Second French Republic, 1848–1852.* New York, Columbia University, 1923.

Corbin, A. *Archaïsme et modernité en Limousin au XIXe siècle, 1845–1880.* 2 vols. Paris, Marcel Rivière, 1975.

Crémieux, A. *La Révolution de février: étude critique sur les journées des 21, 22, 23 et 24 février 1848.* Paris, Edouard Cornéby, 1912.

Dallas, G. *The Imperfect Peasant Economy: the Loire country, 1800–1914.* Cambridge, Cambridge University Press, 1982.

Daumard, A. *La Bourgeoisie parisienne de 1815 à 1848.* Paris, SEVPEN, 1963. (ed.)

—— *Les Fortunes françaises au XIXe siècle.* Paris, Mouton, 1973.

De Luna, F. A. *The French Republic under Cavaignac, 1848.* Princeton, New Jersey, Princeton University Press, 1969.

Dessal, M. *La Révolution de 1848 et la Seconde République dans le département d'Eure-et-Loir.* Chartres, Imprimerie Lainé et Tantet, 1948.

Dommanget, M. *Auguste Blanqui et la révolution de 1848.* Paris, Mouton, 1972.

—— *Histoire du drapeau rouge.* Paris, Editions de l'Etoile, n.d.

Duhart, J. and J. *La Révolution de 1848 à Givors (26 février – 15 juillet).* Paris, Editions Sociales, 1973.

Dupâquier, J., et al. *Histoire de la population française.* 4 vols. Paris, Presses universitaires de France, 1988–91.

Duveau, G. *1848: the making of a revolution.* London, Routledge and Kegan Paul, 1967.

Farwell, B. (ed.) *The Changed Image: French lithographic caricature, 1816–1848.* Santa Barbara, California, Santa Barbara Museum of Art, 1989.

Fitzpatrick, B. *Catholic Royalism in the Department of the Gard, 1814–1852.* Cambridge, Cambridge University Press, 1983.

Fortescue, W. *Alphonse de Lamartine: a political biography.* London and Canberra, Croom Helm, New York, St Martin's Press, 1983.

Furet, F. *Revolutionary France, 1770–1880.* Oxford, Blackwell, 1988.

Gallaher, J. G. *The Students of Paris and the Revolution of 1848.* London and Amsterdam, Southern Illinois University Press, 1980.

Gildea, R. *The Past in French History.* New Haven and London, Yale University Press, 1994.

Girard, L. *La Garde nationale, 1814–1871.* Paris, Plon, 1964.

—— *Nouvelle histoire de Paris: la Deuxième République et le Second Empire, 1848–1870.* Paris, Hachette, 1981.

Goallou, H. *Hamon, commissaire du gouvernement, puis préfet d'Ille-et-Vilaine (3 mars 1848 – 25 janvier 1849).* Rennes, Librairie C. Klincksieck, 1974.

Godechot, J. (ed.) *La Révolution de 1848 à Toulouse et dans la Haute-Garonne.* Toulouse, Préfecture de la Haute-Garonne, 1948.

Goldstein, R. J. *Censorship of Political Caricature in Nineteenth-Century France.* Kent, Ohio, and London, Kent State University Press, 1989.

Gordon, D. M. *Merchants and Capitalists: industrialization and provincial politics in mid-nineteeth-century France.* Alabama, University of Alabama Press, 1985.

Gosselin, R. *Les Almanacs républicains: traditions révolutionnaires et culture politique des masses populaires de Paris, 1840–1851.* Paris, L'Harmattan, 1992.

Gossez, R. *Les Ouvriers de Paris: l'organisation, 1848–1851.* La Roche-sur-Yon, Imprimerie centrale de l'Ouest, 1968.

Gould, R. G. *Insurgent Identities: class, community, and protest in Paris from 1848 to the Commune.* Chicago and London, University of Chicago Press, 1995.

Griffiths, D. A. *Jean Reynaud, encyclopédiste de l'époque romantique, d'après sa correspondance inédite.* Paris, Marcel Rivière et Cie, 1965.

Guichonnet, P. *William de La Rive: un témoin genevois de la Révolution de 1848.* Paris, Société de la Révolution de 1848, 1953.

Guillemin, H. *La Première résurrection de la République.* Paris, Gallimard, 1967.

Harsin, J. *Barricades: the war of the streets in revolutionary Paris, 1830–1848.* New York and Houndmills, Palgrave, 2002.

Higgs, D. *Ultraroyalism in Toulouse from its Origins to the Revolution of 1830.* Baltimore and London, Johns Hopkins University Press, 1973.

Howarth, T. E. B. *Citizen-King: the life of Louis-Philippe, King of the French.* London, Eyre and Spottiswoode, 1961.

Huard, R. *La Préhistoire des partis: le mouvement républicain en Basse-Languedoc, 1848–1881.* Paris, Presses de la Fondation nationale des sciences politiques, 1982.

Hunt, H. J. *Le Socialism et le Romantisme en France: étude de la presse socialiste de 1830 à 1848.* Oxford, Clarendon Press, 1935.

Ibarrola, J. *Structure sociale et fortune dans la campagne proche de Grenoble en 1847.* Paris, Mouton et Cie, 1966.

Isser, N. *Antisemitism during the Second French Empire.* New York, Peter Lang, 1991.

Jardin, A., and A. J. Tudesq. *Restoration and Reaction, 1815–1848.* Cambridge, Cambridge University Press, 1983.

Jeannet, A. *La Seconde République en Saône-et-Loire*. Mâcon, 1984.

Johnson, C. H. *Utopian Communism in France: Cabet and the Icarians*. Ithaca and London, Cornell University Press, 1974.

Johnson, D. *Guizot: aspects of French history, 1787–1874*. London, Routledge and Kegan Paul, 1963.

Jones, P. M. *Politics and Rural Society: the southern Massif Central, c. 1750–1880*. Cambridge, Cambridge University Press, 1985.

Judt, T. *Marxism and the French left: studies in labour and politics in France, 1830–1981*. Oxford, Clarendon Press, 1986.

Julien-Laferrière, F. *Les Députés fonctionnaires sous la Monarchie de Juillet*. Paris, Presses universitaires de France, 1970.

Kenney, E. K., and J. M. Merriman. *The Pear: French graphic arts in the golden age of caricature*. South Hadley, Mass., 1991.

Kent, S. *The Election of 1827 in France*. Cambridge, Mass., Harvard University Press, 1975.

Kerr, D. S. *Caricature and French Political Culture, 1830–1848*. Oxford, Oxford University Press, 2000.

Labrousse, E. *Le Mouvement ouvrier et les idées sociales en France de 1815 à la fin du XIXe siècle*. Paris, Centre de documentation universitaire, 1949. (ed.)

—— *Aspects de la crise et de la dépression de l'économie française au milieu du XIXe siècle, 1846–1851*. La Roche-sur-Yon, Société d'Histoire de la Révolution de 1848, 1956.

La Gorce, P. de. *Histoire de la Seconde République*. 2 vols. Paris, E. Plon, Nourrit et Cie, 1904.

Laven, D., and L. Riall (eds). *Napoleon's Legacy: problems of government in Restoration Europe*. Oxford and New York, Berg, 2000.

Ledré, C. *La Presse à l'assaut de la monarchie, 1815–1848*. Paris, Armand Colin, 1960.

Legouvé, E. *Jean Reynaud*. Paris, Charpentier, 1864.

Lehning, J. R. *The Peasants of Marlhes: economic development and family organization in nineteenth-century France*. London, Macmillan, 1980.

Léon, P. *Géographie de la fortune et structures sociales à Lyon au XIXe siècle, 1815–1914*. Lyons, Centre d'histoire économique et sociale de la région lyonnaise, 1974.

—— *Histoire économique et sociale de la France*. vol. 3, *L'Avènement de l'ère industrielle (1789 – années 1880)*. Paris, Presses universitaires de France, 1976.

Lévêque, P. *Une Société en crise: la Bourgogne au milieu du XIXe siècle (1846–1852)*. Paris, Jean Touzot, 1983.

—— *Une Société provinciale: la Bourgogne sous la monarchie de juillet*. Paris, Editions Jean Touzot, 1983.

Lex, L. and P. M. Siraud. *Le Conseil général et les conseillers généraux de Saône-et-Loire (1789–1889)*. Mâcon, Belhomme, 1888.

Lhomme, J. *La Grande bourgeoisie au pouvoir, 1830–1880: essai sur l'histoire sociale de la France*. Paris, Presses universitaires de France, 1960.

Loubère, L. A. *Louis Blanc and his Contribution to the Rise of French Jacobin-Socialism*. Evanston, Illinois, Northwestern University Press, 1961.

—— *Radicalism in Mediterranean France: its rise and decline, 1848–1914*. Albany, State University of New York Press, 1974.

Magraw, R. *France, 1815–1914: the bourgeois century*. Oxford, Fontana, 1983.

Mansel, P. *Louis XVIII*. London, Blond and Briggs, 1981.

—— *Paris between Empires, 1814–1852: monarchy and revolution*. London, Phoenix, 2003.

McKay, D. C. *The National Workshops: a study in the French Revolution of 1848*. Cambridge, Mass., Harvard University Press, 1965.

McPhee, P. *The Politics of Rural Life: political mobilization in the French countryside, 1846–1852*. Oxford, Clarendon Press, 1992.

Ménager, B. *Les Napoléon du peuple*. Paris, Aubier, 1988.

Merley, J. *La Haute-Loire de la fin de l'Ancien Régime aux débuts de la troisième République, 1776–1886*. 2 vols. Le Puy, Cahiers de la Haute-Loire, 1974.

Merriman, J. M. (ed.) *1830 in France*. New York, New Viewpoints, 1975.

—— *The Agony of the Republic: the repression of the Left in revolutionary France, 1848–1851*. New Haven and London, Yale University Press, 1978.

—— *The Red City: Limoges and the French nineteenth century*. Oxford, Oxford University Press, 1985.

Moss, B. H. *The Origins of the French Labour Movement, 1830–1914: the socialism of skilled workers*. Berkeley, University of California Press, 1976.

Neely, S. *Lafayette and the Liberal Ideal, 1814–1824: politics and conspiracy in an age of reaction*. Carbondale and Edwardsville, Southern Illinois University Press, 1991.

Perrod, P. A. *Jules Favre, avocat de la liberté*. Lyons, La Manufacture, 1988.

Pierrard, P. *1848 . . . les pauvres, l'évangile et la révolution*. Paris, Desclée, 1977.

Pilbeam, P. M. *The 1830 Revolution in France*. London, Macmillan, 1991.

—— *Republicanism in Early Nineteenth-century France, 1814–1871*. London, Macmillan, 1995.

Pimienta, R. *La Propagande bonapartiste en 1848*. Paris, Bibliothèque de la Révolution de 1848, 1911.

Pinkney, D. H. *The French Revolution of 1830*. Princeton, New Jersey, Princeton University Press, 1972.

—— *Napoleon III and the Rebuilding of Paris*. Princeton, New Jersey, Princeton University Press, 1972.

—— *Decisive Years in France, 1840–1847*. Princeton, New Jersey, Princeton University Press, 1986.

Popkin, J. D. *Press, Revolution, and Social Identities in France, 1830–1835*. University Park, Pennsylvania, Pennsylvania State University Press, 2002.

Porch, D. *Army and Revolution: France, 1815–1848*. London, Routledge and Kegan Paul, 1974.

Posener, S. *Adolphe Crémieux, 1796–1880*, 2 vols. Paris, Félix Alcan, 1933–4.

Pouthas, C. H. *La Population française pendant la première moitié du XIXe siècle*. Paris, Presses universitaires de France, 1956.

Price, R. *The French Second Republic: a social history*. London, B. T. Batsford, 1972.

—— (ed.) *1848 in France*. London, Thames and Hudson, 1975.

—— (ed.) *Revolution and Reaction: 1848 and the Second French Republic*. London, Croom Helm, 1975.

—— *The Economic Modernisation of France, 1730–1880*. London, Croom Helm, 1975.

—— *The Modernization of Rural France: communications networks and agricultural market structures in nineteenth-century France*. London, Hutchinson, 1983.

—— *A Social History of Nineteenth-century France*. London, Hutchinson, 1988.

—— (ed.) *Documents on the French Revolution of 1848*. London, Macmillan, 1996.

Rader, D. L. *The Journalists and the July Revolution in France: the role of the political press in the overthrow of the Bourbon Restoration, 1827–30*. The Hague, Martinus Nijhoff, 1973.

Reddy, W. M. *The Rise of Market Culture: the textile trade and French society, 1750–1900.* Cambridge, Cambridge University Press, 1984.

Renauld, G. *Adolphe Crémieux, homme d'Etat français et franc-macon: le combat pour la République.* Paris, Detrad, 2002.

Richardson, N. *The French Prefectoral Corps, 1814–1830.* Cambridge, Cambridge University Press, 1966.

Rocal, G. *1848 en Dordogne.* 2 vols. Paris, E. H. Guitard, 1934.

Rosanvallon, P. *Le Moment Guizot.* Paris, Gallimard, 1985.

—— *Le Sacre du citoyen: histoire du suffrage universel en France.* Paris, Gallimard, 1992.

—— *La Monarchie impossible: les chartes de 1814 et de 1830.* Paris, Picard, Fayard, 1994.

Saboya, M. *Presse et architecture au XIXe siècle: César Daly et la 'Revue générale de l'architecture et des travaux publics'.* Paris, Picard, 1991.

Schmidt, C. *Les Journées de juin 1848.* Paris, Hachette, 1926.

—— *Des Ateliers nationaux aux barricades de juin.* Paris, Presses universitaires de France, 1948.

Schmidt, N. *Victor Schoelcher et l'abolition de l'esclavage.* Paris, Fayard, 1994.

Sée, H. *La Vie économique de la France sous la monarchie censitaire, 1815–1848.* Paris, Félix Alcan, 1927.

Seignobos, C. *La Révolution de 1848 – Le Second Empire.* Paris, A. Colin, 1921.

Serman, W. and J. P. Bertaud. *Nouvelle histoire militaire de la France, 1789–1919.* Paris, Fayard, 1998.

Sewell, W. H. *Work and Revolution in France: the language of labour from the old regime to 1848.* Cambridge, Cambridge University Press, 1980.

—— *Structure and Mobility: the men and women of Marseille, 1820–1870.* Cambridge, Cambridge University Press, 1985.

Simpson, F. A. *The Rise of Louis Napoleon.* London, Longmans, Green and Co., 1950.

Skuy, D. *Asassination, Politics, and Miracles: France and the royalist reaction of 1820.* Montreal, McGill-Queen's University Press, 2003.

Spitzer, A. B. *Old Hatreds and Young Hopes: the French Carbonari against the Bourbon Restoration.* Cambridge, Mass., Harvard University Press, 1971.

—— *The French Generation of 1820.* Princeton, New Jersey, Princeton University Press, 1987.

Stewart-McDougall, M. L. *The Artisan Republic: revolution, reaction, and resistance in Lyon, 1848–1851.* Kingston and Montreal, McGill-Queen's University Press, 1984.

Ten-Doesschate, P. and G. P. Weisberg (eds). *The Popularization of Images: visual culture under the July monarchy.* Princeton, New Jersey, Princeton University Press, 1994.

Tersen, E. *Quarante-huit.* Paris, Club français du livre, 1957.

Thureau-Dangin, P. *Histoire de la monarchie de juillet.* 7 vols. Paris, E. Plon, Nourrit et Cie, 1897–1904.

Tollu, P. *Montalembert: les libertés sous le Second Empire.* Paris, Editions Albatros, 1987.

Tombs, R. *France, 1814–1914.* London and New York, Longman, 1996.

Traugott, M. *Armies of the Poor: determinants of working-class participation in the Parisian insurrection of June 1848.* Princeton, New Jersey, Princeton University Press, 1985.

Tudesq, A.-J. *Les Grands notables en France, 1840–1849: étude historique d'une psychologie sociale.* 2 vols. Paris, Presses universitaires de France, 1964.

—— *L'Election présidentielle de Louis-Napoléon Bonaparte.* Paris, Armand Colin, 1965.

Van Davidson, R. *Did We Think Victory Great?: the life and ideas of Victor Considérant.* Lanham, University Press of America, 1988.

Vidalenc, J. *Le Peuple des campagnes: la société française de 1815 à 1848.* Paris, Marcel Rivière et Cie, 1969.

Vigier, P. *La Seconde République dans la région alpine.* 2 vols. Paris, Presses universitaires de France, 1963.

Vincent, K. S. *Pierre-Joseph Proudhon and the Rise of French Republican Socialism.* Oxford and New York, Oxford University Press, 1984.

Wassermann, S. *Les Clubs de Barbès et de Blanqui en 1848.* Paris, Edouard Cornély et Cie, 1913.

Weill, G. *Histoire du parti républicain en France de 1814 à 1870.* Paris, Félix Alcan, 1900.

Articles

Aguet, J. P. 'Le Tirage des quotidiens de Paris sous la Monarchie de Juillet', *Revue suisse d'histoire*, 10 (1960), pp. 216–86.

Agulhon, M. 'Le Problème de la culture populaire en France autour de 1848', *Romantisme*, 9 (1975), pp. 50–64.

Alexander, R. S. 'Restoration Republicanism Reconsidered', *French History*, 8 (1994), pp. 442–69.

Amann, P. 'Prelude to Insurrection: the "Banquet of the People"', *French Historical Studies*, 1 (1960), pp. 436–44.

—— 'Writings on the Second French Republic', *Journal of Modern History*, 34 (1962), pp. 409–29.

—— 'The Changing Outlines of 1848', *American Historical Review*, 68 (1963), pp. 938–53.

—— 'The Huber Enigma: revolutionary or police spy?', *International Review of Social History*, 12 (1967), pp. 190–203.

—— 'Du neuf on the "Banquet of the People"', *French Historical Studies*, 5 (1968), pp. 344–50.

—— 'A *Journée* in the Making: May 15, 1848', *Journal of Modern History*, 42 (1970), pp. 42–69.

Barthélemy Saint-Hilaire, J. 'La Commission exécutive de mai 1848', *Revue politique et parlementaire*, 51 (1907), pp. 318–24.

Baughman, J. J. 'The French Banquet Campaign of 1847–48', *Journal of Modern History*, 31 (1959), pp. 1–15.

—— 'Financial Resources of Louis-Philippe', *French Historical Studies*, 4 (1965), pp. 63–83.

Beck, T. D. 'Occupation, Taxes, and a Distinct Nobility under Louis-Philippe', *European Studies Review*, 13 (1983), pp. 403–22.

Bezucha, R. J. 'The French Revolution of 1848 and the Social History of Work', *Theory and Society*, 12 (1983), pp. 469–84.

Blaisdell, L. L. 'Aloysius Huber and May 15, 1848: new insights into an old mystery', *International Review of Social History*, 29 (1984), pp. 34–61.

Bouderd, P. 'La Proclamation de la IIe République dans le département de la Creuse', *Mémoires de la société des sciences naturelles et archéologiques de la Creuse*, 30 (1948), pp. 277–95.

Bullen, R. 'Guizot and the *Sonderbund* Crisis, 1846–1848', *English Historical Review*, 86 (1971), pp. 497–526.

Caspard, P. 'Aspects de la lutte des classes en 1848: le recrutement de la garde nationale mobile', *Revue historique*, 252 (1974), pp. 81–106.

Chalmin, P. 'Une Institution militaire de la Seconde République: la Garde nationale mobile', *Etudes d'histoire moderne et contemporaine*, 2 (1948), pp. 36–82.

Childs, E. C. 'Big Trouble: Daumier, *Gargantua*, and the censorship of political caricature', *Art Journal*, 51 (1992), pp. 26–37.

Christofferson, T. R. 'The French National Workshops of 1848: the view from the provinces', *French Historical Studies*, 11 (1980), pp. 505–20.

Cobban, A. 'The Influence of the Clergy and the "instituteurs primaires" in the Election of the French Constituent Assembly, April 1848', *English Historical Review*, 57 (1942), pp. 334–44.

—— 'Administrative Pressure in the Election of the French Constituent Assembly, April 1848', *Bulletin of the Institute of Historical Research*, 25 (1952), pp. 133–59.

Cox, M. R. 'The Liberal Legitimists and the Party of Order under the Second French Republic', *French Historical Studies*, 5 (1968), pp. 446–64.

Crouzet, F. 'Essai de construction d'un indice annuel de la production industrielle française au XIXe siècle', *Annales, E. S. C.*, 25 (1970), pp. 56–99.

Cuno, J. 'The Business and Politics of Caricature: Charles Philipon and La Maison Aubert', *Gazette des Beaux-Arts*, 106 (1985), pp. 95–112.

Dubuc, A. 'Les Emeutes de Rouen et d'Elbeuf (27, 28 et 29 avril 1848)', *Etudes d'histoire moderne et contemporaine*, 2 (1948), pp. 243–75.

Fasel, G. W. 'The French Election of April 23, 1848: suggestions for a revision', *French Historical Studies*, 5 (1968), pp. 285–98.

—— 'Urban Workers in Provincial France, February–June 1848', *International Review of Social History*, 17 (1972), pp. 661–74.

—— 'The Wrong Revolution: French republicanism in 1848', *French Historical Studies*, 8 (1974), pp. 654–77.

Forbes, A. W. '"Let's Add the Stomach": satire, absurdity and July monarchy politics in Proudhon's *What is Property?*', *French Historical Studies*, 24 (2001), pp. 679–705.

Forestier, H. 'Dans l'Yonne, au lendemain de la Révolution de février 1848:Les commissaires du Gouvernement provisoire d'après les journaux auxerrois contemporains', *Annales de Bourgogne*, 19 (1947), pp. 275–83.

—— 'Le Mouvement bonapartiste dans l'Yonne en 1848: la presse et l'opinion', *Annales de Bourgogne*, 21 (1949), pp. 114–34.

Fortescue, W. 'Poetry, Politics and Publicity, and the Writing of History: Lamartine's *Histoire des Girondins* (1847)', *European History Quarterly*, 17 (1987), pp. 259–84.

—— 'Lamartine, lettres politiques 1847–1848', in C. Croisille and M. R. Morin (eds), *Autour de la correspondance de Lamartine*, Clermont-Ferrand, Université Blaise Pascal, 1991, pp. 31–110.

—— 'Lamartine et l'élection présidentielle du 10 décembre 1848', in S. Bernard-Griffiths and C. Croisille (eds), *Relire Lamartine aujourd'hui*, Librairie Nizet, 1993, pp. 133–41.

—— 'Divorce Debated and Deferred: the French debate on divorce and the failure of the Crémieux divorce bill in 1848', *French History*, 7 (1993), pp. 137–62.

—— 'Lettres retrouvées de Lamartine, 1815–1868', in C. Croisille and M. R. Morin (eds), *Autour de Lamartine: journal de voyage, correspondances, témognages, iconographie*, Clermont-Ferrand, Presses universitaires Blaise Pascal, 2002, pp. 61–107.

—— 'Morality and Monarchy: corruption and the fall of the regime of Louis-Philippe in 1848', *French History*, 16 (2002), pp. 83–100.

Frazer, I. 'La Vie secrète de César Daly: naissance illégitime, parti légitimiste, *cause*

Fouriériste', in H. Lipstadt (ed.), *Architecte et ingénieur dans la presse: polémique, débat, conflit*, Paris, 1980, pp. 233–91.

Gemie, S. 'Balzac and the Moral Crisis of the July Monarchy', *European History Quarterly*, 19 (1989), pp. 469–94.

Gonnet, P. 'Esquisse de la crise économique en France de 1827 à 1832', *Revue d'histoire économique et sociale*, 33 (1955), pp. 249–92.

Gossez, R. 'La Résistance à l'impôt: les quarante-cinq centimes', *Société d'histoire de la Révolution de 1848*, 15 (1953), pp. 89–132.

Haury, P. 'Les Commissaires de Ledru-Rollin en 1848', *La Révolution française*, 57 (1909), pp. 438–74.

Higgs, D. 'Politics and Landownership among the French Nobility', *European Studies Review*, 1 (1971), pp. 105–21.

Higonnet, P. B. 'La Composition de la Chambre des Députés de 1827 à 1831', *Revue historique*, 239 (1968), pp. 351–78.

Higonnet, P. L.-R. and T. B. Higonnet. 'Class, Corruption, and Politics in the French Chamber of Deputies, 1846–1848', *French Historical Studies*, 5 (1967), pp. 204–24.

Holroyd, R. 'The Bourbon Army, 1815–1830', *Historical Journal*, 14 (1971), pp. 529–52.

Isser, N. 'The Revolution of 1848 and Human Rights: the Jews', in J. Sweet (ed.), *Proceedings of the Western Society for French History*, 12 (1986), pp. 343–56.

Jones, P. M. 'An Improbable Democracy: nineteenth-century elections in the Massif Central', *English Historical Review*, 97 (1982), pp. 530–57.

Katan, Y. 'Les Colons de 1848 en Algérie: mythes et réalités', *Revue d'histoire moderne et contemporaine*, 31 (1984), pp. 177–202.

Kent, S. 'Electoral Lists of France's July monarchy, 1830–1848', *French Historical Studies*, 7 (1971), pp. 117–27.

Koepke, R. L. 'The Failure of Parliamentary Government in France, 1840–1848', *European Studies Review*, 9 (1979), pp. 433–55.

—— 'The *Loi des patentes* of 1844', *French Historical Studies*, 11 (1980), pp. 398–430.

—— 'The Short, Unhappy History of Progressive Conservatism in France, 1846–1848', *Canadian Journal of History*, 18 (1983), pp. 187–216.

Lévy, C. 'Les Paysans de l'Yonne vers 1848', *Annales de Bourgogne*, 23 (1951), pp. 180–90.

—— 'Un Journal "rouge" sous la Seconde République, *L'Union républicaine* d'Auxerre', *Annales de Bourgogne*, 33 (1961), pp. 145–59.

Livesey, J. 'Speaking the Nation: radical republicans and the failure of political communication in 1848', *French Historical Studies*, 20 (1997), pp. 459–80.

Loubère, L. A. 'The Emergence of the Extreme Left in Lower Languedoc, 1848–1851: social and economic factors in politics', *American Historical Review*, 7 (1968), pp. 1,019–51.

Louvel, A. 'L'Ecole d'Administration de 1848', *Etudes d'histoire moderne et contemporaine*, 2 (1948), pp. 19–36.

Machu, L. 'L'Importance du banquet de Lille dans la campagne de réforme (7 novembre 1847)', *Revue du Nord*, 31 (1949), pp. 5–12.

Marcilhacy, C. 'Les Caractères de la crise sociale et politique de 1846 à 1852 dans le département du Loiret', *Revue d'histoire moderne et contemporaine*, 6 (1959), pp. 5–59.

Margadant, J. B. 'Gender, Vice, and the Political Imaginary in Postrevolutionary France: reinterpreting the failure of the July monarchy, 1830–1848', *American Historical Review*, 104 (1999), pp. 1461–96.

Matagrin, A. 'Le Rachat des chemins de fer en 1848', *Revue socialiste*, 15 October 1904, pp. 417–46, 15 November 1904, pp. 529–71.

McPhee, P. B. 'The Crisis of Radical Republicanism in the French Revolution of 1848', *Historical Studies* (Melbourne), 16 (1974), pp. 71–88.

—— 'A Reconsideration of the "Peasantry" of Nineteenth-century France', *Peasant Studies*, 9 (1981), pp. 5–25.

Merriman, J. M. 'The Norman Fires of 1830: incendiaries and fear in rural France', *French Historical Studies*, 9 (1976), pp. 451–66.

Meyers, P. V. 'Teachers in Revolutionary France: the *instituteurs* in 1848', *Consortium on Revolutionary Europe Proceedings, 1977*, Athens, Georgia, 1978, pp. 151–61.

Newman, E. L. 'The Blouse and the Frock Coat: the alliance of the common people of Paris with the liberal leadership and the middle class during the last years of the Bourbon Restoration', *Journal of Modern History*, 46 (1974), pp. 26–59.

Pilbeam, P. M. 'The Emergence of Opposition to the Orleanist Monarchy, August 1830–1 April 1831', *English Historical Review*, 85 (1970), pp. 12–28.

—— 'Popular Violence in Provincial France after the 1830 Revolution', *English Historical Review*, 91 (1976), pp. 278–97.

—— 'The Growth of Liberalism and the Crisis of the Bourbon Restoration', *Historical Journal*, 25 (1982), pp. 351–66.

—— 'The Economic Crisis of 1827–32 and the 1830 Revolution in Provincial France', *Historical Journal*, 32 (1989), pp. 319–38.

—— 'The 'Liberal' Revolution of 1830', *Historical Research*, 63 (1990), pp. 162–77.

—— 'Republicanism in Early Nineteenth-century France, 1814–1835', *French History*, 5 (1991), pp. 30–47.

—— 'Dream Worlds?: religion and the early socialists in France', *Historical Journal*, 43 (2000), pp. 499–515.

Pochon, J. 'Edgar Quinet et les luttes du Collège de France, 1843–1847', *Revue d'histoire littéraire de la France*, 70 (1970), pp. 619–27.

Pouthas, C. H. 'Les Ministres de Louis-Philippe', *Revue d'histoire moderne et contemporaine*, 1 (1954), pp. 102–30.

—— 'La Réorganisation du ministère de l'Intérieur et la réconstitution de l'administration préfectorale par Guizot en 1830', *Revue d'histoire moderne et contemporaine*, 9 (1962), pp. 241–63.

Price, R. D. 'Popular Disturbances in the French Provinces after the July Revolution', *European Studies Review*, 1 (1971), pp. 323–50.

—— 'The French Army and the Revolution of 1830', *European Studies Review*, 3 (1973), pp. 243–67.

—— 'Legitimist Opposition to the Revolution of 1830 in the French Provinces', *Historical Journal*, 17 (1974), pp. 755–78.

—— 'Techniques of Repression: the control of popular protest in mid-nineteenth-century France', *Historical Journal*, 25 (1982), pp. 859–87.

—— 'Poor Relief and Social Crisis in Mid-nineteenth-century France', *European Studies Review*, 13 (1983), pp. 423–54.

Rader, D. L. 'The Breton Association and the Press: propaganda for 'legal resistance' before the July Revolution', *French Historical Studies*, 2 (1961), pp. 64–82.

Riou, M. 'L'Election présidentielle de décembre 1848 en Ardèche', *Revue du Vivarais*, 2 (1974), pp. 82–96.

Saurin, M. 'L'Ecole d'Administration de 1848', *Politique d'aujourd'hui*, 7–8 (1964–5), pp. 105–95.

Savigear, P. 'Carbonarism and the French Army, 1815–24', *History*, 54 (1969), pp. 198–211.

Smith, R. J. 'The Students of the Ecole d'Administration, 1848–9', *History of Education*, 16 (1987), pp. 245–58.

Soboul, A. 'Les Troubles agraires de 1848, documents', *1848 et les Révolutions du XIXe siècle*, 39 (1948), pp. 1–20 and 39–61.

Spang, R. '"La Fronde des nappes": fat and lean rhetoric in the political banquets of 1847', in C. F. Coates (ed.), *Repression and Expression: literary and social coding in nineteenth-century France*, New York, Peter Lang, 1996, pp. 167–78.

Spitzer, A. B. 'The Elections of 1824 and 1827 in the Department of the Doubs', *French History*, 3 (1989), pp. 153–76.

Stearns, P. N. 'Patterns of Industrial Strike Activity in France During the July Monarchy', *American Historical Review*, 70 (1965), pp. 371–94.

Tilly, C. and L. Lees. 'Le Peuple de juin 1848', *Annales ESC*, 29 (1974), pp. 1061–91.

Traugott, M. 'The Mobile Guard in the French Revolution of 1848', *Theory and Society*, 9 (1980), pp. 683–720.

—— 'Determinants of Political Orientation: class and organization in the Parisian insurrection of 1848', *American Journal of Sociology*, 86 (1980), pp. 32–49.

—— 'The Crowd in the French Revolution of February, 1848', *American Historical Review*, 93 (1988), pp. 638–52.

Tudesq, A.-J. 'La Légende napoléonienne en France en 1848', *Revue historique*, 218 (1957), pp. 64–85.

Vidalenc, J. 'La Province et les journées de juin', *Etudes d'histoire moderne et contemporaine*, 2 (1948), pp. 83–144.

Weber, E. 'The Second Republic, Politics, and the Peasant', *French Historical Studies*, 11 (1980), pp. 521–50.

Wright, V. 'L'Ecole nationale d'administration de 1848–1849: un échec révélateur', *Revue historique*, 255 (1976), pp. 21–42.

Unpublished theses

Applebaum, D. R. 'The *Juges de Paix* and the Provisional Government of 1848 in France'. PhD thesis, University of Wisconsin, 1973.

Baughman, J. J. 'The Political Banquet Campaign in France, 1847–1848'. PhD thesis, University of Michigan, 1953.

Cox, M. R. 'The Legitimists under the Second Republic'. PhD thesis, Yale University, 1966.

Fasel, G. W. 'The French Moderate Republicans, 1837–1848'. PhD thesis, Stanford University, 1965.

Liu, M. 'Education and Revolution: the impact of 1848 on France'. MA thesis, University of East Anglia, 1990.

Luzkow, J. L. 'The Press and the Making of Class Politics: the debates of *Le Constitutionnel* and *Le Représentant du Peuple* under the French Second Republic'. PhD thesis, Saint Louis University, 1981.

Mallory, H. J. 'Public Force in Paris, February 22 to June 26, 1848'. PhD thesis, University of Michigan, 1975.

McPhee, P. 'The Seed-Time of the Republic: society and politics in the Pyrénées-Orientales, 1846–1852'. PhD thesis, University of Melbourne, 1977.

Remy, E. 'La Vie politique dans le département des Vosges, 1848–1860'. Thèse de doctorat, University of Nancy, 1982.

Index